mob one

mob one

Delicious meals
in one pot, pan or tray

EBURY PRESS

INTRODUCTION 6
GET THE MOST OUT OF THIS BOOK 8

MORNING ONES 12
EASY ONES 40
SPEEDY ONES 86
FEASTING ONES 128
FANCY ONES 158
FRESH ONES 190
SLOW ONES 220
SWEET ONES 246

CONVERSION TABLES 274
INDEX 276
ACKNOWLEDGEMENTS 284
ABOUT MOB 287

One Pan?
No Problem.

Simplicity is the key when it comes to cooking. The best recipes are often built on a few simple principles and a handful of ingredients. They work because they don't needlessly over-complicate anything with unnecessary flourishes or overblown techniques. Because the truth is no one (and we mean no one) needs to be using a blowtorch in the kitchen. That clean, uncomplicated approach to cooking is one we've embraced in *Mob One*. Which is, just in case you didn't realise it, the book you're holding in your hands right now.

This is a back-to-basics cookbook rammed with one-pan, one-pot, one-tray and one-bowl recipes that'll save you on more than just the washing up. The dishes you'll find in here are easy, affordable and – above all else – undeniably delicious to eat.

Whether you're an impatient cook in need of quick weeknight solutions, a wannabe chef looking to get more confident on the hob or simply someone who appreciates the joys of minimal clean-up, you're in the right place. Don't believe us? Why not take a moment to leaf through the pages ahead and get a little sneak peek of what we've got to offer? We'll wait right here until you're done doing that. Seriously. Go and have a look. Like, now.

Finished leafing? Great! What did you think? All looks fairly sound, doesn't it?

The eagle-eyed among you will have noticed that we've split the cookbook up into chapters to suit every occasion, and each and every 'One' is packed to the rafters with dishes you'll want to get on the table, stat. All the recipes are injected with high-energy flavours and we've worked hard to keep them as accessible and approachable as possible. From a triple 'ch' traybake with chicken, chickpeas and chorizo (see page 66), to a one-pan spaghetti dish that somehow tastes exactly like the buffalo wings you'd order when you're three beers deep at your favourite dive bar (see page 116), all of the recipes in *Mob One* have been made with your satisfaction in mind. We've taken price and time into consideration but the most important factor of all – aside from, y'know, the one-pan gimmick – is that they taste damn good. It's as simple as that. This is a cookbook for eaters.

Although the main part of each recipe is made in just one pan, you'll find that some of the dishes have delicious salsas, salads and slaws served alongside them, with an occasional piece of toast for mopping up the juices (so not technically in one pot here, but there's no more washing up so we beg for your forgiveness!).

WHAT TO EXPECT?

Well, there's a Gochujang Chilli con Carne on page 136 that'll turn more than a few heads at your next dinner party, Coffee-Roasted Pork Belly you can whip out on special occasions (see page 165), and even an easy-as-it-gets Sweet Potato Laksa-Spiced Soup topped with plenty of lovely fresh gubbins and ingredients to cook up on page 52. And that's literally just three of the recipes in this book – there's over a hundred more for you to check out, enjoy and make for your loved ones. Whatever the assignment is, rest assured there's a one-vessel dish in this cookbook ready to step up to the challenge. Want to cook something impressive for your crush? Take a look at what's filed under Fancy Ones on page 176 and knock 'em up a beautifully cooked Salmon, Crushed Potatoes + Olive Salsa. Craving something sweet? Get a load of the Malted Chocolate Mousse hanging about on page 257 in Sweet Ones. Feel like taking your time with a rewarding weekend project? Try your hand at literally anything in the Slow Ones section. One pan? No problem.

Get the Most Out of This Book

Now, we don't know where you are right now – maybe you're standing in a bookshop, frantically trying to decide which cookbook best says 'happy birthday, mate' or maybe you're sitting at your kitchen table cracking open the spine of the thoughtful present that your incredibly tasteful friend bought you the other week – but you might have noticed that there are QR codes strewn throughout this book, and there's good reason for it.

Follow the QR codes that we've kindly included on every chapter opener and you'll be sent to a bespoke collection on our website packed with dozens of dishes that fit the same brief. Scan the code at the start of Speedy Ones, for instance (page 86), and you'll have access to a treasure trove of quick and delicious recipes you can make in under half an hour. We've done the same for the rest of the chapters as well. And that's not all we've done.

It's our mission at Mob to make you love cooking and that's why you'll find QR codes nuzzled up next to every single recipe in this cookbook. Yes, doing that required a lot of additional black ink, but we like to think it was worth it. These individual codes will take you through to a specific recipe or matching collection on our website that we're convinced you'll get a kick out of. Think of it like us offering you a bite of our pizza even though you ordered the carbonara – a little taste of what you can get when you join the Mob.

Let's Get Started

A poor craftsman blames his tools but, c'mon, we all know that having the right equipment in the kitchen can make a big difference. There's a reason that every chef is obsessed with sharpening their knife and would sooner part with one of their kidneys than their favourite copper frying pan.

　　Follow this little QR code here and you'll be directed to a short, sweet and extremely useful guide we've written about all of the pots and pans that will make your life a hell of a lot easier, and make cooking these recipes an absolute breeze. Don't worry, you don't need these pans to make the recipes in this book, but we promise you they're worth the investment.

If you like the dishes here, there's plenty more on our website where we have thousands of recipes, articles and meal plans – find them here.

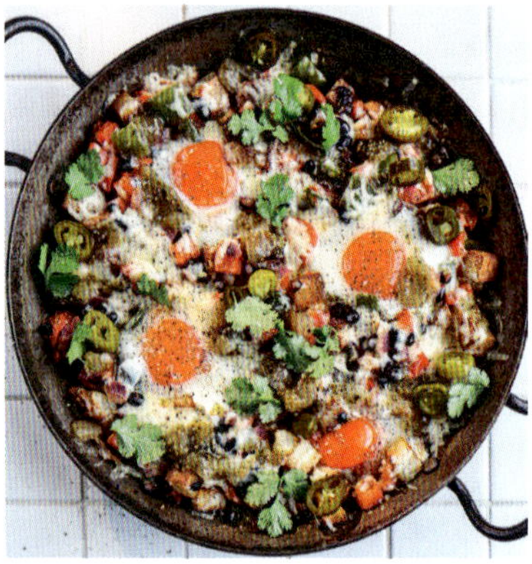
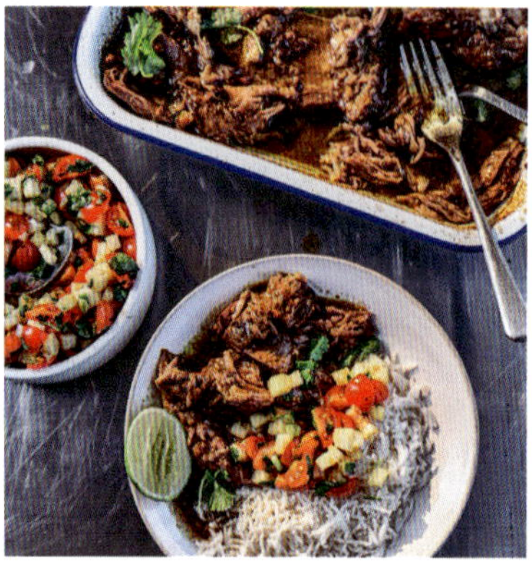
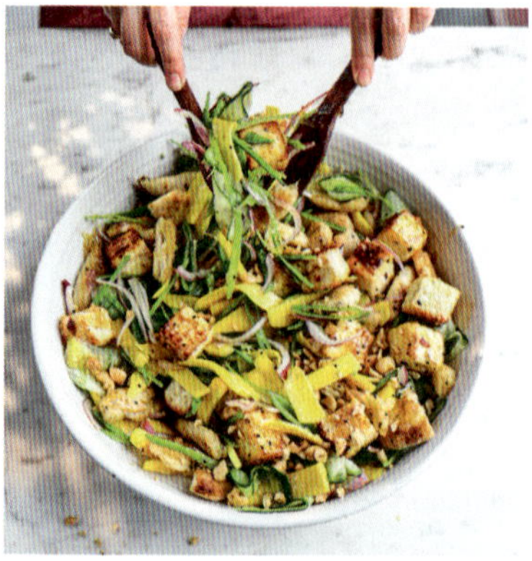
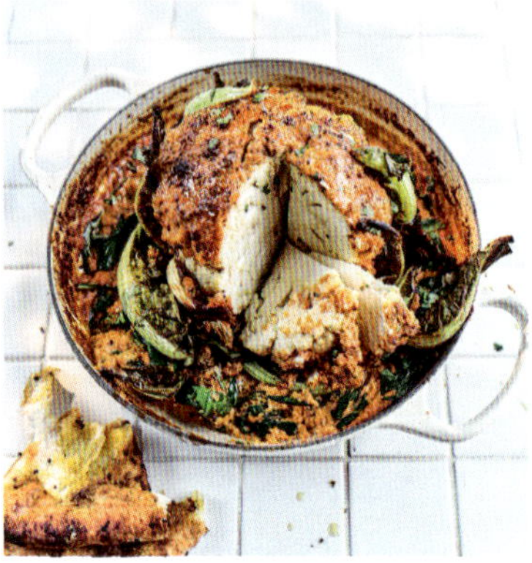
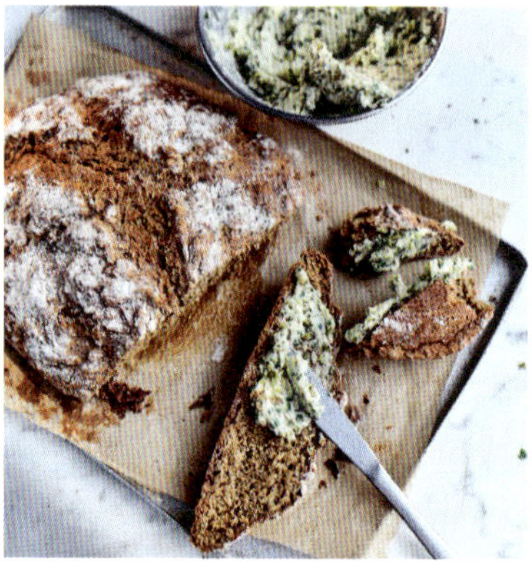
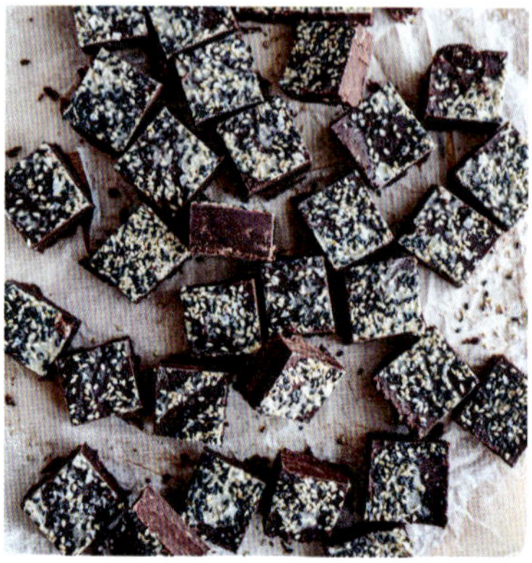
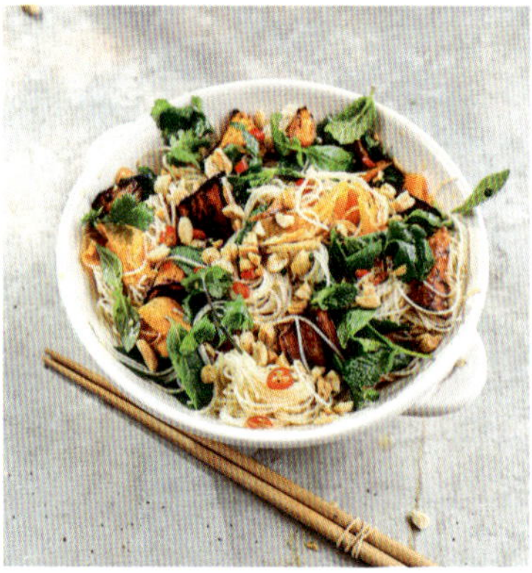
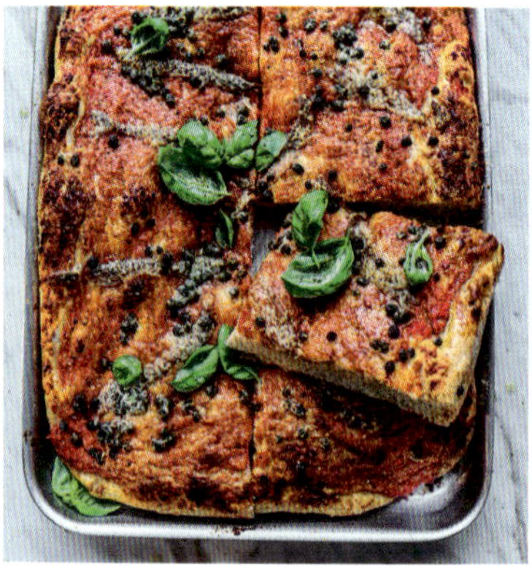
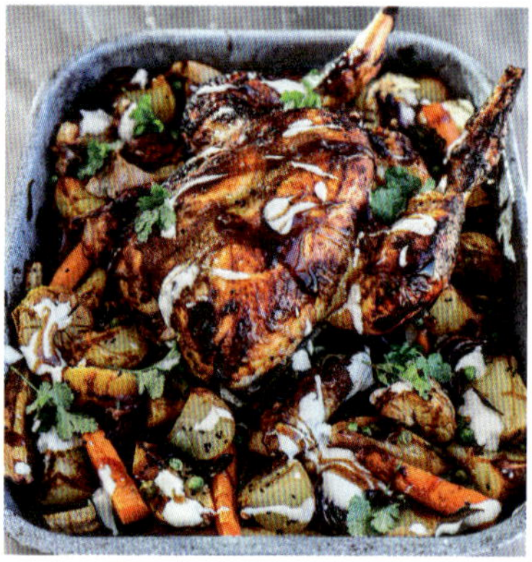
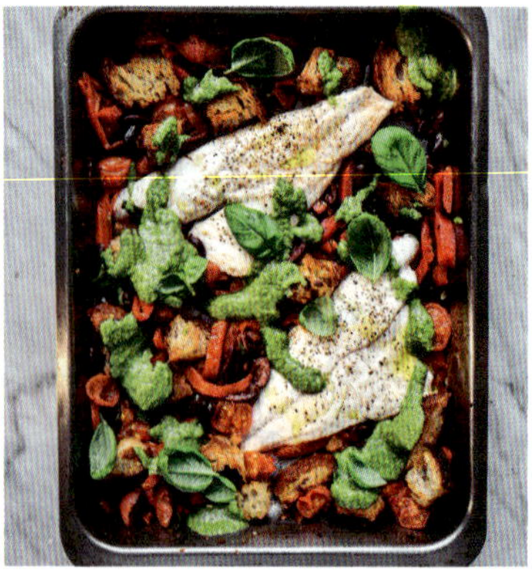
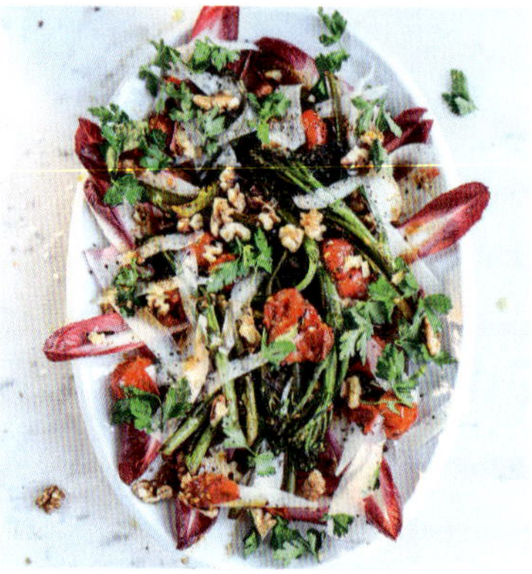
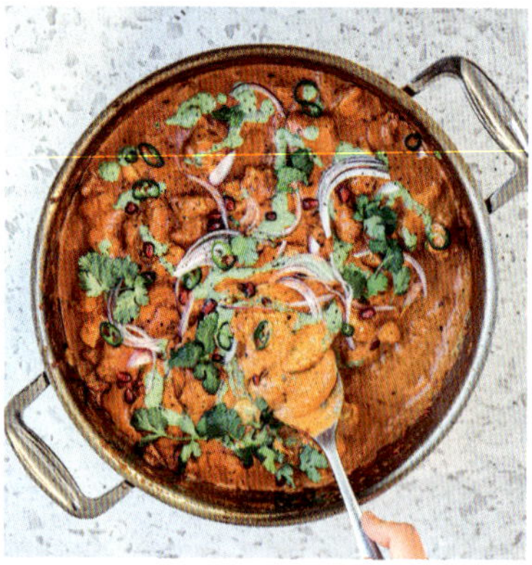

11

ONE MORNING ONE MORNING ONE MORNING ONE MORNING

MORNING ONES
MORNING ONES
MORNING ONES
MORNING

Kimchi Omelette Bagel

Serves 1
Takes 15 minutes

Use a medium non-stick frying pan

Veggie

2 eggs
1 bagel
a few knobs of butter
75g kimchi, drained well
55g mature Cheddar cheese
hot sauce, to serve
salt and black pepper

Scan for more tasty recipes like this one

Now, we don't want to go and encourage heavy drinking here, but we were reliably informed by one of our recipe testers that this one is an absolute godsend on a hangover. Make of that what you will.

01. Crack the eggs into a bowl, add a little salt and pepper and whisk until fully combined. Cut the bagel in half horizontally.

02. Set the frying pan over a medium-high heat and add a tiny knob of butter, then swirl the pan to coat. Toast the bagel halves in the pan, pressing cut-side down, for 1 minute, then flip them over. Load one half of the bagel with the kimchi, then grate over the Cheddar. Remove both halves from the pan.

03. Heat another big knob of the butter in the pan, reducing the heat slightly. Pour in the eggs. Cook gently, lifting up the edges to let the egg run underneath. When just cooked, fold each side of the egg in on itself tightly to create a neat square.

04. Lift the omelette onto the cheesy bagel and top with the lid, then carefully transfer the whole thing back to the pan and cook over a medium heat for 1 minute. Carefully flip it over and cook until the cheese is super melted, around 1–2 minutes.

05. Remove from the pan, splash over hot sauce and enjoy.

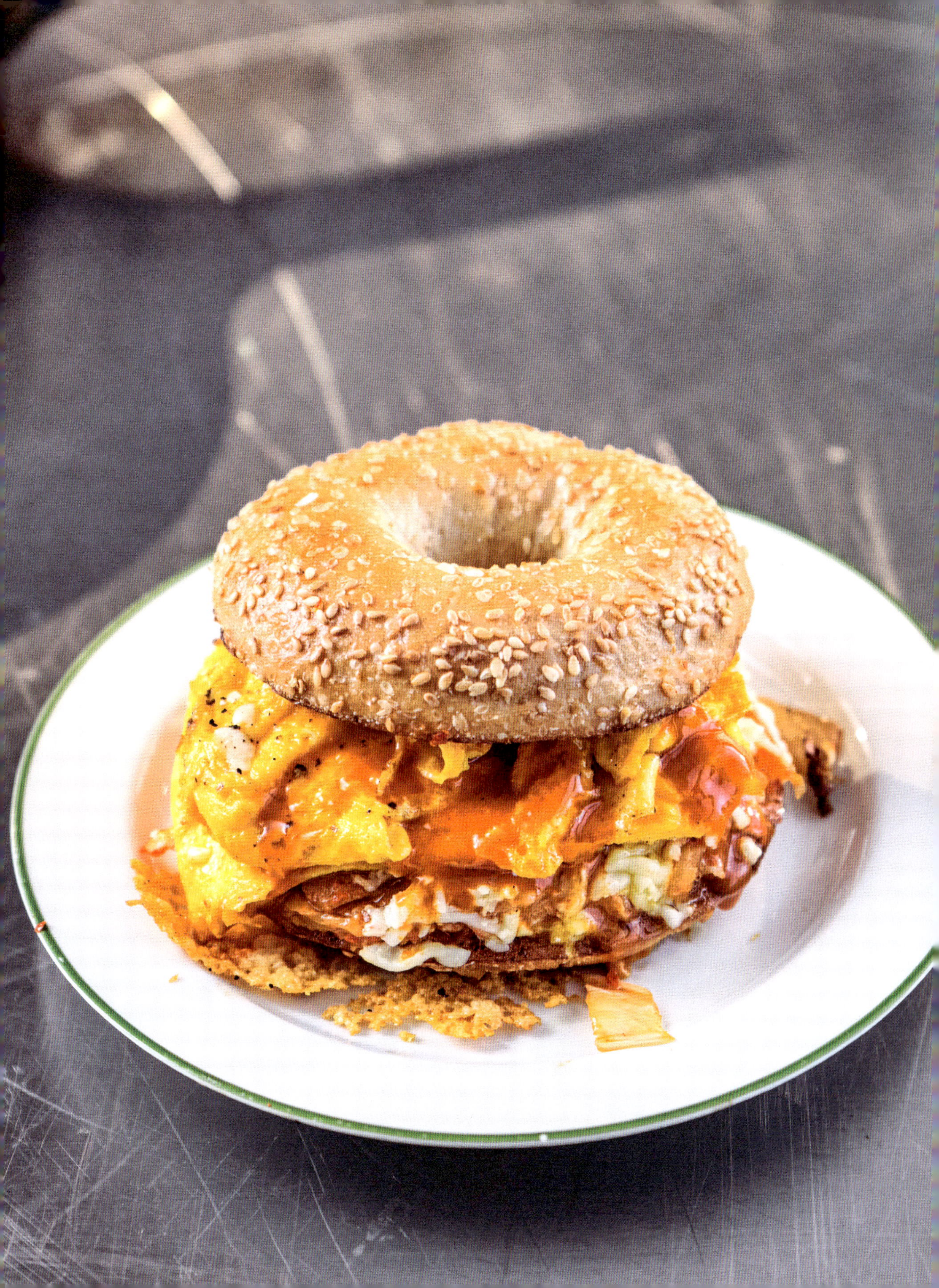

Salsa Roja Eggs

Scan for more tasty recipes like this one

Serves 2
Takes 30 minutes

Use a large non-stick frying pan with a lid

Veggie, Gluten-free

1 small onion
3 garlic cloves
1 red chilli
4 vine tomatoes (about 200g)
2 tsp vegetable oil
1 tbsp chipotle paste
a handful of coriander, plus extra leaves to garnish
1 lime
4 eggs
75g feta
50ml soured cream
salt and black pepper

TO SERVE
100g salted tortilla chips
hot sauce (optional; check the label if making this gluten-free)

This is our totally inauthentic (but totally delicious) spin on Mexican chilaquiles. Instead of soaking the tortillas in salsa and topping them off with a fried egg, we flipped the dish on its head by baking the eggs in the salsa and serving them with tortillas on the side for essential dunking.

01. Roughly chop the onion, garlic and chilli, then tip into the frying pan with the whole tomatoes. Pour over the oil, season and toss together really well. Set the frying pan over a high heat. Once smoking hot, cook for 2–3 minutes, tossing occasionally, until really charred and blackened in spots.

02. Tip everything from the pan into a high-powered blender or food processor, then add the chipotle paste and coriander, stalks and all. Cut the lime and squeeze in half of the juice, then whizz until you have a smooth salsa. Taste and adjust the seasoning with salt, pepper and lime juice.

03. Pour the sauce back into the frying pan and bring to a gentle simmer. Bubble gently for 5 minutes until thickened slightly, then crack the eggs into the sauce, one at a time. Cover with the lid and cook very gently for 4–6 minutes until the whites are just set.

04. Remove from the heat and crumble over the feta, spoon over the soured cream and sprinkle with extra coriander leaves.

05. To serve, cut the remaining lime half into wedges to squeeze over and have ready a big pile of tortilla chips for dunking and some hot sauce, if you like it spicy.

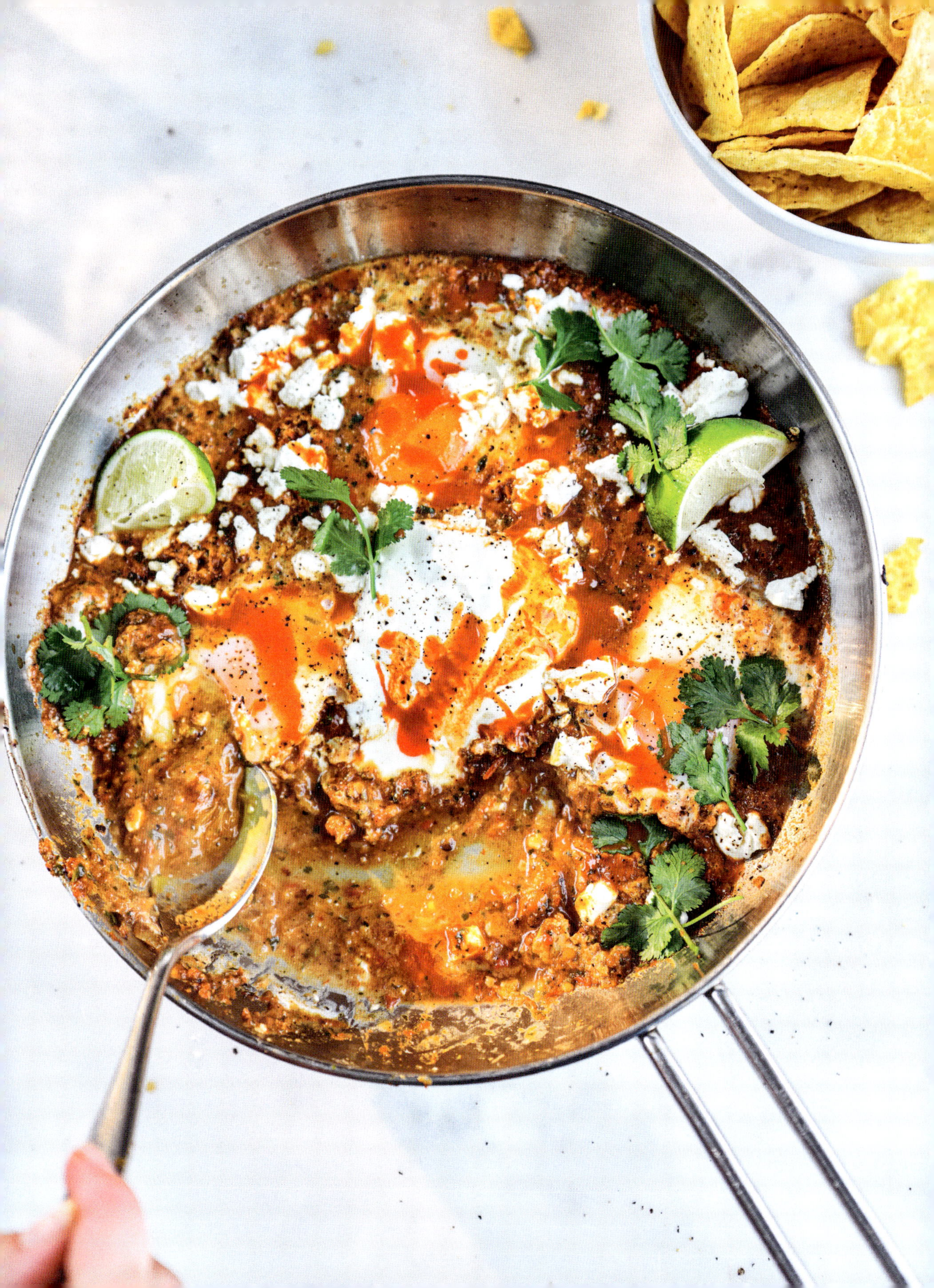

Hash Brown Tortilla + Herby Salad

Serves 4
Takes 25 minutes

Use a medium non-stick frying pan

Veggie, Gluten-free

10 eggs
1 tsp mild paprika
1 brown onion
4 tbsp olive oil
7 hash browns, defrosted (check the label if making this gluten-free)
salt and black pepper

FOR THE SALAD
1 x 450g jar of roasted red peppers, drained
1 sweet white onion
25g flat leaf parsley
1 lemon
2 tbsp olive oil

We've smashed together two of our favourite breakfast items to make something that's extremely tasty. And a little chaotic. The best thing about this hash brown-Spanish tortilla hybrid is you don't have to go through the rigmarole of frying loads and loads of sliced potatoes. It's quick, it's easy, and it's topped with a herby roasted pepper salad. That's brunch sorted, then.

01. Crack the eggs into a bowl and whisk together with the paprika and ½ teaspoon of salt. Set aside.

02. Thinly slice the brown onion. Heat 3 tablespoons of the oil in the frying pan over a medium-high heat, add the sliced onion and cook for 4–5 minutes until softened and translucent. Add the hash browns and break them up into small chunks with a spatula. Cook for 3–4 minutes until softened.

03. Meanwhile, make the salad. Thinly slice the peppers and white onion, then pick the parsley leaves, discarding the stalks. Put all the ingredients into a bowl. Zest half of the lemon into the bowl, then squeeze in the juice. Drizzle in the oil, season and mix together.

04. Pour the egg mixture into the frying pan and cook for 2–3 minutes, stirring and shaking the pan often, until the mixture thickens slightly. Continue to cook, without shaking, for 2–3 minutes until the sides and bottom are set – the mixture should still be wet in the middle.

05. Using a spatula, loosen the edges of the egg. Place a plate on top of the frying pan and invert the tortilla onto it. Add the remaining oil to the pan, then slide the tortilla back into it, wet-side down, tucking in the sides. Cook for a further 1–2 minutes until just set.

06. Serve with the salad.

Scan for more tasty recipes like this one

MORNING ONES

Herby, Cheesy Breakfast Flatbread

Serves 4
Takes 45 minutes

Use a large baking tray

Veggie

plain flour, for dusting (optional)
400g ready-to-roll pizza dough
20g chives
25g tarragon, leaves only
3 green chillies
100g Cheddar cheese
300g garlic and herb soft cheese (we use Boursin)
100g ready-grated mozzarella
5 eggs
1 tablespoon nigella seeds or sesame seeds (optional)
salt and black pepper

Scan for more tasty recipes like this one

This big, ooey gooey cheese boat is inspired by Georgian khachapuri. We've recreated the cosy heft of those cheese-stuffed flatbreads using pre-made pizza dough, a combination of soft cheeses spiked with spicy chillies and heaps of fresh herbs. Tear off the edges and dunk them in the runny egg for the perfect bite.

01. Preheat the oven to 200°C/180°C fan. Line the baking tray with baking paper.

02. Lightly dust the work surface with flour if the pizza dough is sticky. Roll it into a large rectangle, the same size as your baking tray. Transfer to the tray, then roll the edges of the dough inwards, tucking them in on themselves, so you have a thick border.

03. Finely chop the chives, tarragon leaves and 2 of the chillies. Thinly slice the remaining chilli and reserve for the garnish. Add the herbs and chopped chillies to a bowl, then grate in the Cheddar, crumble in the soft cheese and add the mozzarella. Mix well to combine, then season.

04. Load the cheese mixture into the centre of the rectangle, then spread it evenly within the border. Whisk 1 of the eggs in a bowl, then brush it over the edges of the dough. Sprinkle with nigella seeds, if using.

05. Bake for 15 minutes at the bottom of the oven until the dough is lightly golden and the cheese is melty. Remove from the oven and make 4 wells with the back of a spoon, then crack an egg into each well. Return to the oven for 6–8 minutes until most of the whites are set. (It's OK if they still look a bit wobbly, they will keep cooking in the hot cheese.)

06. Sprinkle with the reserved sliced chilli, then tear off an edge of the boat and use to mix the runny eggs into the cheese. Enjoy!

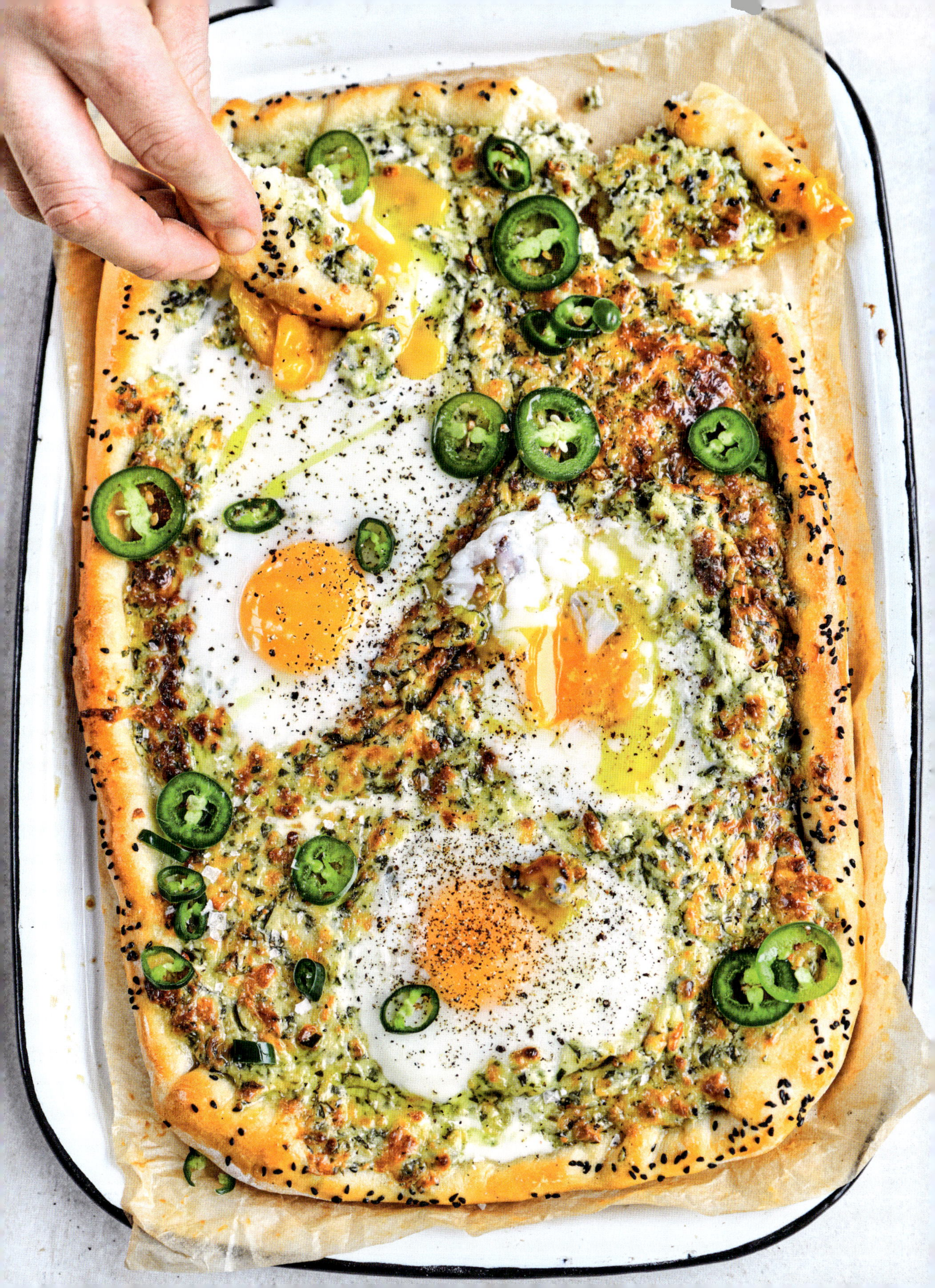

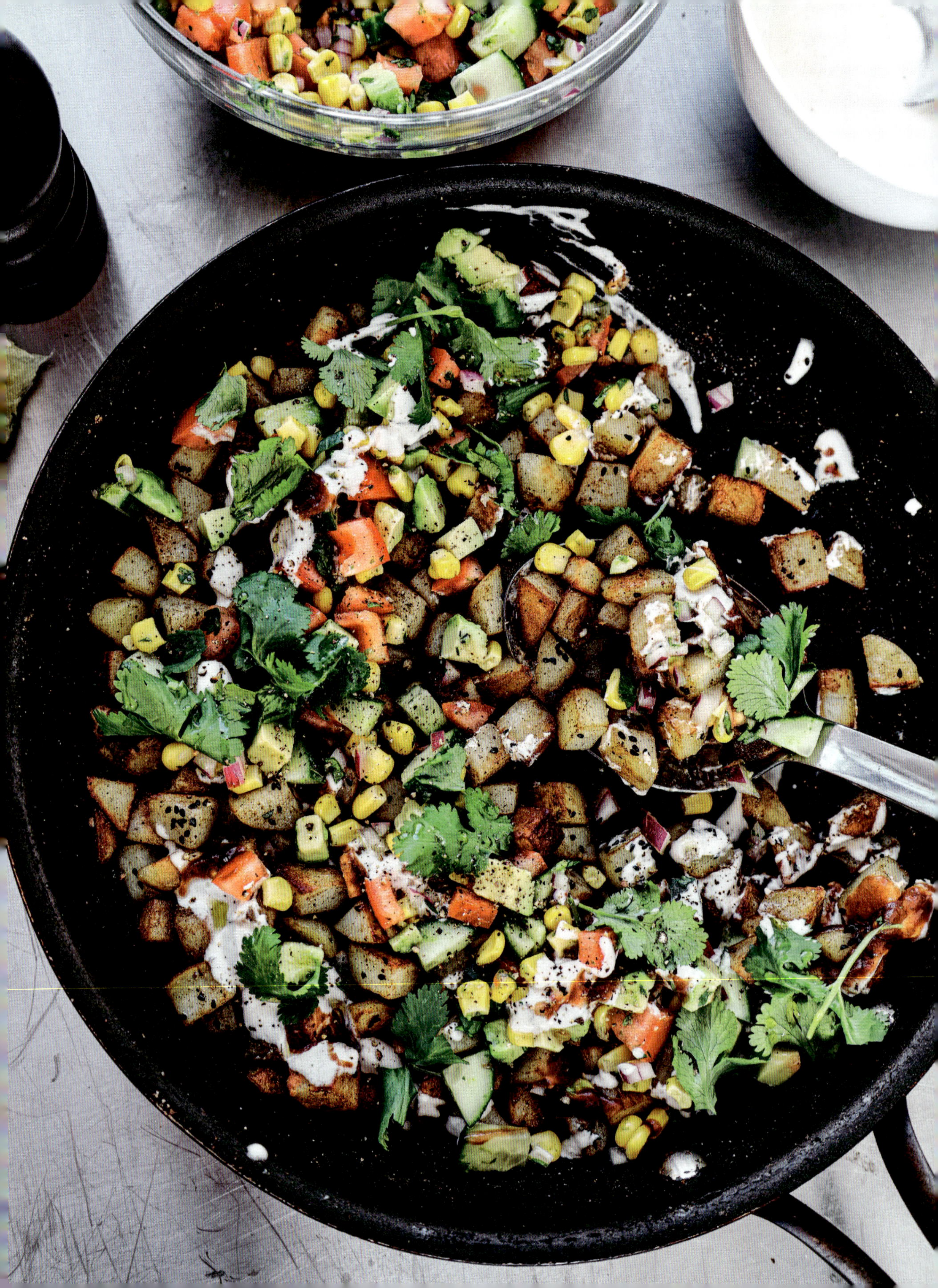

Masala Hash Breakfast Skillet

Scan for more tasty recipes like this one

Serves 2–3
Takes 30 minutes

Use a large, heavy non-stick frying pan

Vegan, Gluten-free

750g Maris Piper potatoes, unpeeled
3 tbsp sunflower oil
1 tbsp garam masala
1 tbsp nigella seeds
2 tbsp tamarind chutney, to serve
salt and black pepper

FOR THE SALSA
1 x 200g tin of sweetcorn, drained
1 large tomato (about 150g)
¼ cucumber
½ red onion
1 avocado
a small handful of coriander
2 limes

A giant spiced hash, laced with garam masala and nigella seeds, topped with a fresh sweetcorn salsa, loaded with tamarind chutney? Don't mind if we do. This is a perfect vegan breakfast, but would also be amazing fried in ghee with a fried egg on top.

01. Cut the potatoes into to 1.5cm cubes.

02. Heat the oil in the frying pan over a medium-high heat, then add the potatoes and cook for 15 minutes, stirring often, until they're almost tender. Stir through a big pinch of salt and the garam masala and nigella seeds and fry for a final 5 minutes until fragrant and the potatoes are crisp and tender.

03. Meanwhile, make the salsa. Put the sweetcorn into a bowl. Dice the tomato, cucumber, red onion and avocado so everything is pretty much the same size as the sweetcorn and add to the bowl. Finely chop the coriander and stir most of it through (save some for the garnish). Zest both limes into the bowl and season generously, then squeeze in the juice of 1½ limes, slicing the remaining half into wedges for garnish.

04. When the hash is cooked through, load it up with the sweetcorn salsa and drizzle the tamarind chutney over the whole thing. Scatter with the reserved coriander and serve with the lime wedges.

Bacon + Hot Honey Sheet Pancakes

Serves 4
Takes 35 minutes

Use a large lipped baking tray

12 smoked streaky bacon rashers
70g unsalted butter
500ml buttermilk
2 tsp vanilla extract
2 eggs
40g icing sugar
75g cornflour
250g plain flour
5 tsp baking powder
hot honey (or honey warmed with chilli flakes), to serve
salt

Scan for more tasty recipes like this one

Next time you've got a crowd over for breakfast, whip out a baking tray and make them a batch of the fluffiest-ever, lowest-effort pancakes. Hot honey trumps maple syrup in every way imaginable.

01. Preheat the oven to 220°C/200°C fan.

02. Line your lipped baking tray with baking paper, then arrange the bacon on the tray in an even layer. Pop in the oven for 12–14 minutes, turning after 10 minutes, until golden and nice and crisp, then remove from the tray and keep warm.

03. Meanwhile, make the batter. Put the butter into a large microwave-safe bowl and microwave in 15-second bursts, stirring after each interval, until melted (this should take about 30 seconds). Pour in the buttermilk and vanilla, then whisk in the eggs. Add the icing sugar, cornflour, flour and baking powder with a big pinch of salt. Mix well with a hand whisk to combine.

04. Pour the batter straight into the tray (the bacon fat will grease it) and smooth out to the edges. Bake for 15 minutes until puffy and golden on top.

05. Cut the sheet pancake into 8 slices, then serve with the bacon rashers and a big drizzle of hot honey.

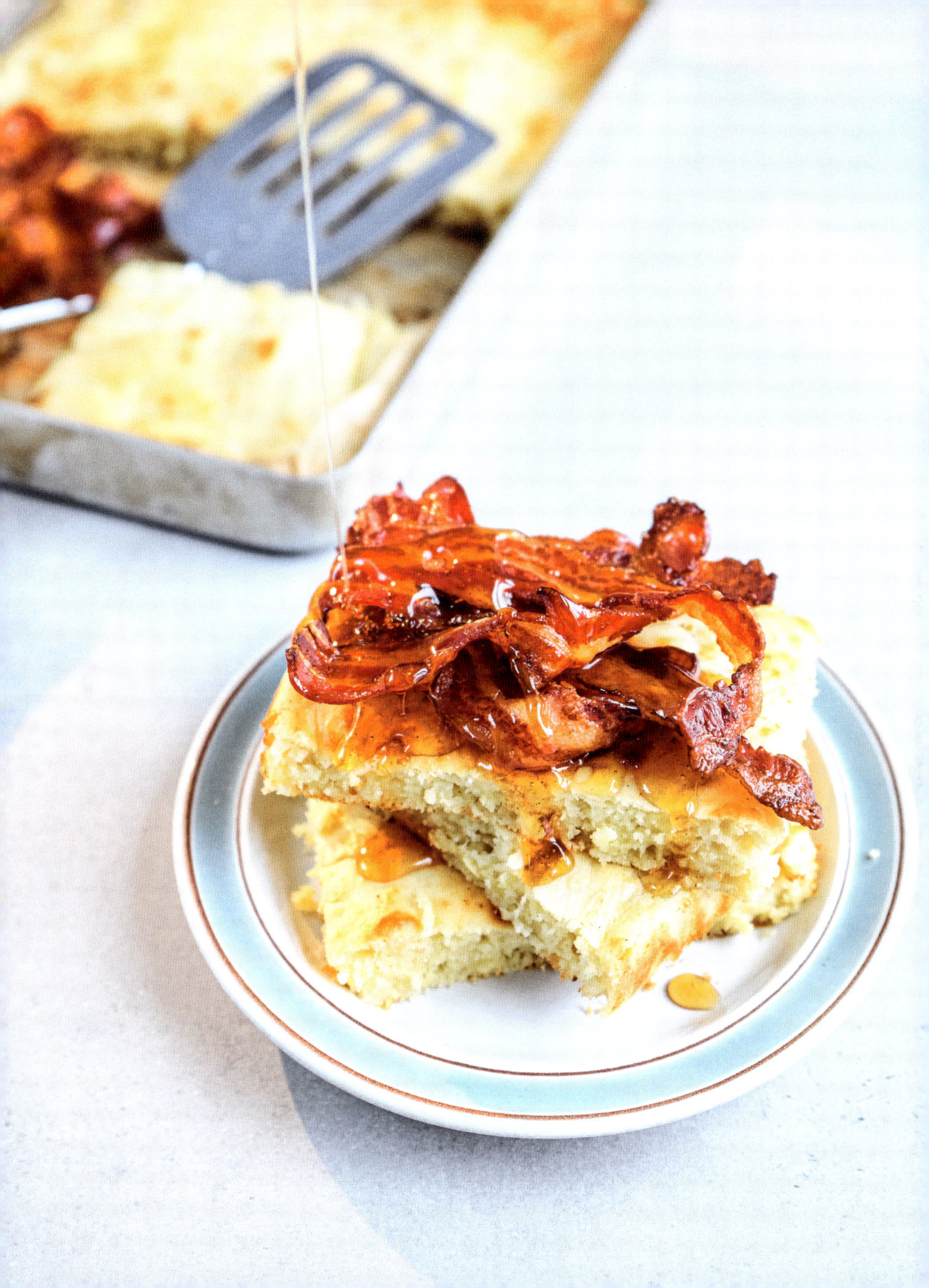

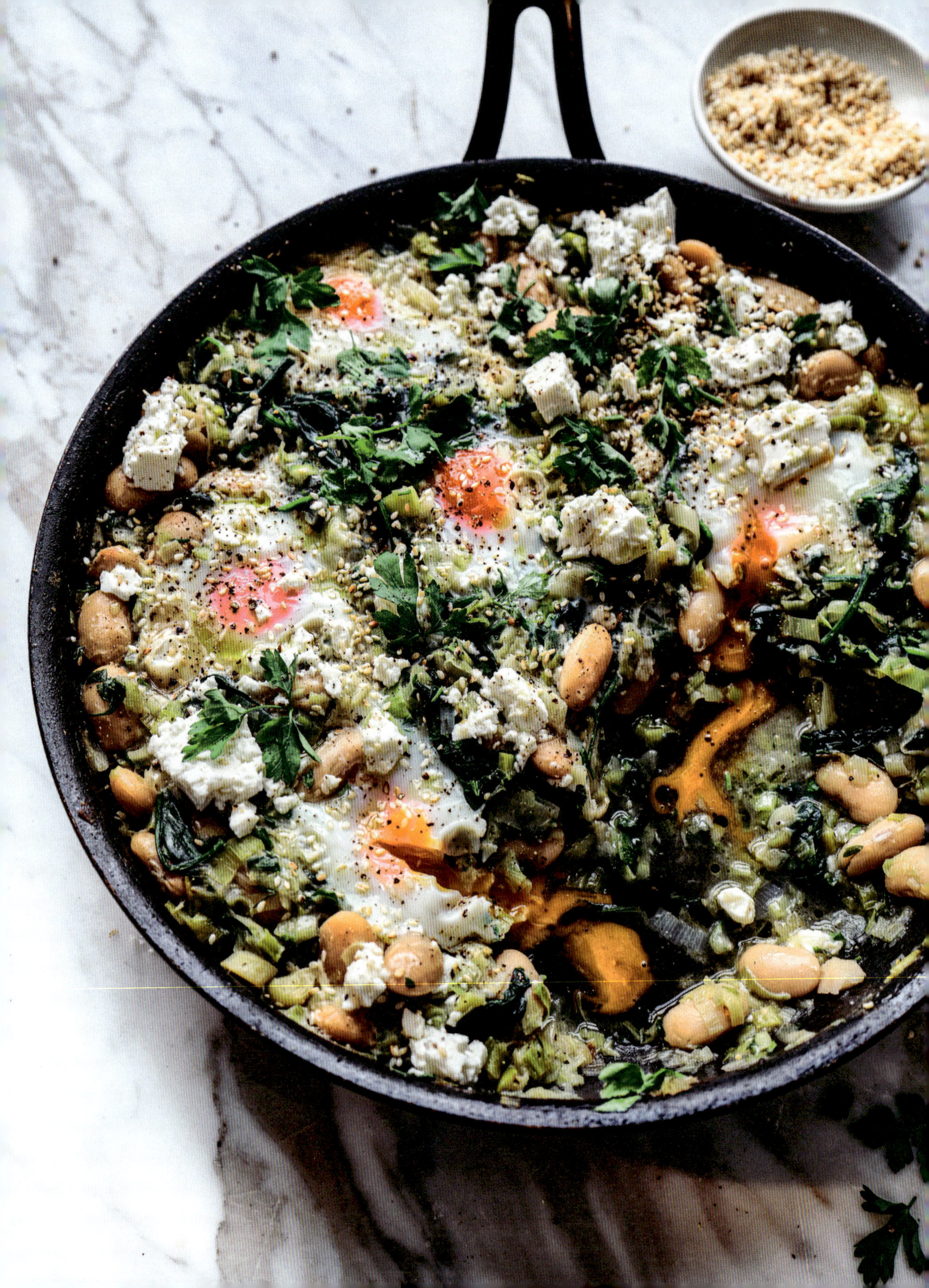

Leeky Butter Bean Baked Eggs

Serves 4
Takes 45 minutes

Use a large non-stick frying pan with a lid

Veggie

750g leeks
3 garlic cloves
25g flat leaf parsley
1½ tsp fennel seeds
3 x 400g tins of butter beans
1½ tbsp Dijon mustard
1½ lemons
6 eggs
salt, black pepper and olive oil

TO SERVE
75g feta
toasted sesame seeds
bread or toast

Scan for more tasty recipes like this one

We shared a leek-y bean dish on the website that everyone absolutely loved, so we thought, why not try this as a wintery breakfast or brunch option? We've topped it with feta, but you can easily drizzle it with tahini or yoghurt if you want to change it up.

01. Finely slice the leeks, then tip into a large bowl and rinse well with cold water.

02. Add a glug of olive oil to the frying pan over a medium-high heat and add the leeks, along with a big pinch of salt. Cook for around 10–15 minutes, stirring often, until softened.

03. Meanwhile, finely slice the garlic and roughly chop most of the parsley, saving some leaves to serve.

04. Add the sliced garlic and fennel seeds to the leeks and cook for a minute. Drain 2 tins of butter beans, then add to the pan along with the Dijon mustard and the final tin of beans, including the water from the tin. Bubble for 5 minutes, until thickened, then use a spoon to crush the beans a little to thicken it further.

05. Add the juice of the lemons and the chopped parsley, then season with salt and pepper. Use a spoon to make a divot in the mixture, then crack an egg into the hole you've made. Repeat with the remaining eggs, then cover the pan with the lid and cook for 10–15 minutes, until the whites of the eggs are set but the yolks are still runny.

06. Crumble the feta over the top, top with the sesame seeds and the reserved parsley leaves, then serve with big chunks of bread or toast alongside.

Harissa Soufflé Omelette

Scan for more tasty recipes like this one

Serves 2
Takes 25 minutes

Use a small ovenproof non-stick frying pan with a lid

Veggie, Gluten-free

200g cherry tomatoes
2 tbsp rose harissa
75g Red Leicester cheese
a bunch of chives
   (about 10g)
6 eggs
2 tbsp double cream
a large knob of butter
salt and black pepper

TIP: If the folding feels a bit intimidating, cook the whole mixture in the pan for 2–3 minutes, then slide under the grill for 3–4 minutes until risen and serve whole.

This will be the lightest, fluffiest omelette you'll ever make. Packed full of harissa and often-neglected Red Leicester, it's exactly the sort of dish you'd expect to see at a fancy brunch spot for £15.

---

01. Set the dry frying pan over a high heat. Once hot, add the tomatoes, and cook for 4–6 minutes until blistered and softening. Remove the tomatoes to a plate and stir in ½ tablespoon of the harissa and season. Rinse the pan clean.

02. Meanwhile, finely grate the cheese and chop the chives.

03. Carefully separate the eggs into 2 large bowls, making sure not to get any yolk in the whites. Whisk the egg whites until they are white, fluffy and holding their shape – you want as much air in them as possible.

04. Add a big pinch of salt to the yolks and whisk for a couple of minutes until lightened. Whisk in the cream, 1 tablespoon of the harissa, the chives and three-quarters of the cheese and plenty of black pepper. Fold the whites into the yolk mixture, being careful to keep as much air in as possible.

05. Set the pan back over a medium-high heat and add half of the butter. Once the butter is foaming, pour in half of the egg mixture. Cook for 2 minutes until set on the bottom but still wobbly on top, sprinkle with half the remaining cheese and cover with the lid. Cook for 1–2 minutes further, then tip onto a plate and fold over. Repeat with the other half of the mixture.

06. Top with the charred tomatoes and drizzle over the remaining harissa to serve.

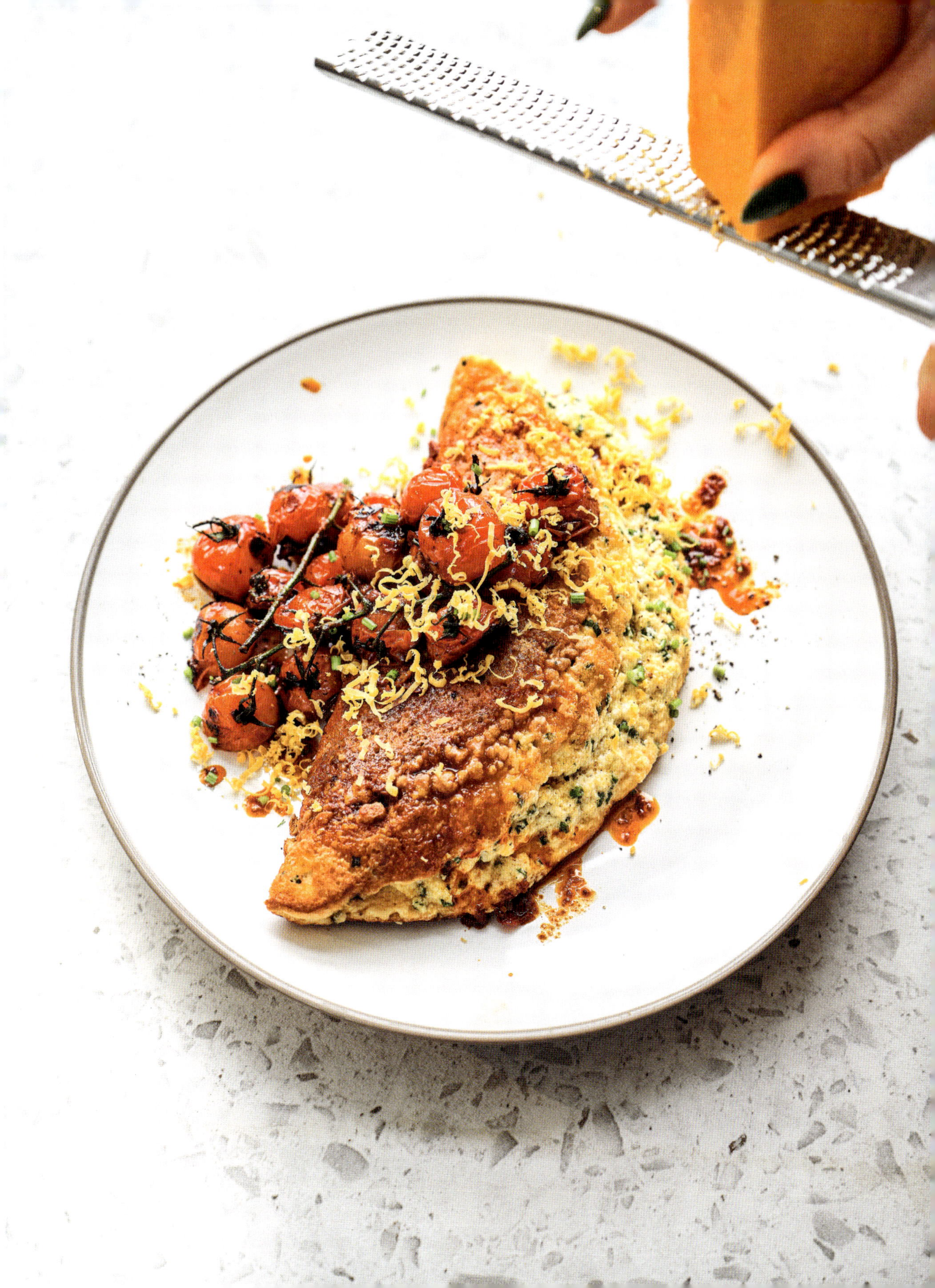

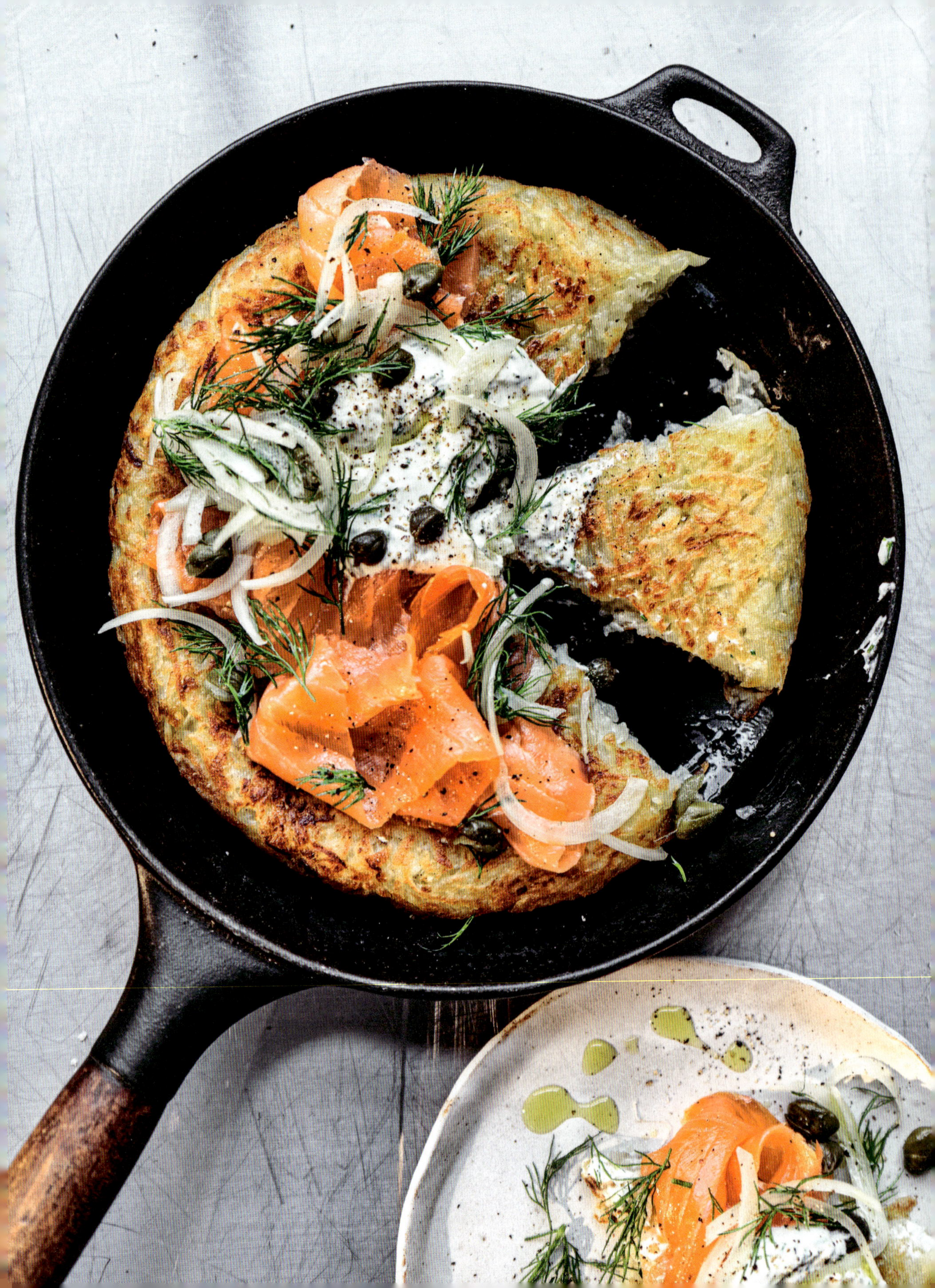

Crispy Rösti + Smoked Salmon

Serves 4
Takes 40 minutes

Use a 20–23cm non-stick frying pan

Gluten-free

1kg Maris Piper potatoes
1 white onion
6 tbsp olive oil
200g smoked salmon
salt and black pepper

FOR THE ONION SALAD
1 white onion
15g dill
3 tbsp capers
1 tbsp olive oil

FOR THE GARLIC + HERB SOURED CREAM
20g chives
200g soured cream
2 tsp garlic granules

Scan for more tasty recipes like this one

A crispy, sharing-sized rösti served with smoked salmon, garlicky soured cream and an insanely fresh dill, caper and onion salad. We've basically taken all the best bits of a salmon bagel and thrown them onto a plate with some lacy, fried potatoes. Perfect for a crowd.

01. Peel the potatoes, then coarsely grate with the onion onto a clean tea towel. Season generously with salt and toss together, then gather the ends of the towel and twist over a sink to wring out as much liquid as possible.

02. Heat the oil in the frying pan over a medium-high heat, then evenly scatter the potato and onion mixture into the pan. Using the back of a spoon, press down on the mixture to compact it. Reduce the heat to medium and cook for 12–15 minutes until golden – reduce the heat if it's browning too quickly. Once the underside has turned golden, give the pan a small shake to loosen and then use a large spatula to flip the rösti over, or invert onto a plate and slide back into the pan if you're struggling. Cook on the other side until golden, around 5–7 minutes.

03. Meanwhile, start the salad. Very thinly slice the onion. Rinse under cold water, then put into a bowl. Pick the dill leaves, discarding the stalks, then add to the onion and cover with ice-cold water.

04. To make the garlic and herb soured cream, finely chop the chives. Put the soured cream into a bowl and stir in the chives and garlic granules, then season with salt and plenty of black pepper. Set aside.

05. Drain the onion and dill mixture, tip back into the bowl and stir through the capers and oil.

06. Serve the rösti with dollops of the garlic and herb soured cream, the smoked salmon and the onion salad.

MORNING ONES

Tomatillo + Chilli Hash

Scan for more tasty recipes like this one

Serves 4
Takes 40 minutes

Use a large non-stick frying pan with a lid

Veggie, Gluten-free

400g baby potatoes
2 tbsp extra virgin olive oil
2 peppers (red, green or orange)
1 red onion
3 garlic cloves
1 green chilli
200g cherry tomatoes
150g Cheddar cheese
1 x 400g tin of black beans, drained
1 tbsp ground cumin
4 eggs
salt and black pepper

TO SERVE
4 tbsp shop-bought tomatillo or tomato salsa
10 pickled jalapeño slices
a handful of coriander leaves
1 lime

This glorious dish, which tastes like the inside of a breakfast burrito, is a real use-up-what-you've-got situation. Any limp veg you've got lingering at the bottom of your fridge will taste infinitely better covered in tomatillo salsa and pickled jalapeños. That's a fact.

01. Don't bother peeling the potatoes, just cut them into 1.5cm chunks. Heat the olive oil in the frying pan, then pop in the potatoes and cook over a medium-high heat for 20 minutes until soft and golden.

02. While the potatoes are cooking, deseed and dice the peppers and dice the red onion into a similar size as the potatoes. Finely chop the garlic and chilli, then halve the cherry tomatoes. Grate the Cheddar and set aside.

03. Once the potatoes are golden, add the peppers, onion, garlic and chilli and sauté for 5 minutes until softened. Add the tomatoes, black beans and cumin and stir well to combine. Season to taste.

04. Sprinkle the Cheddar over the top, then make 4 wells in the mixture and crack an egg into each well. Cook for 4–6 minutes with the lid on until the whites are set.

05. Remove from the heat and drizzle with the salsa, dot over the pickled jalapeños and scatter with the coriander leaves. Serve with the lime, cut into wedges, for a pop of acidity.

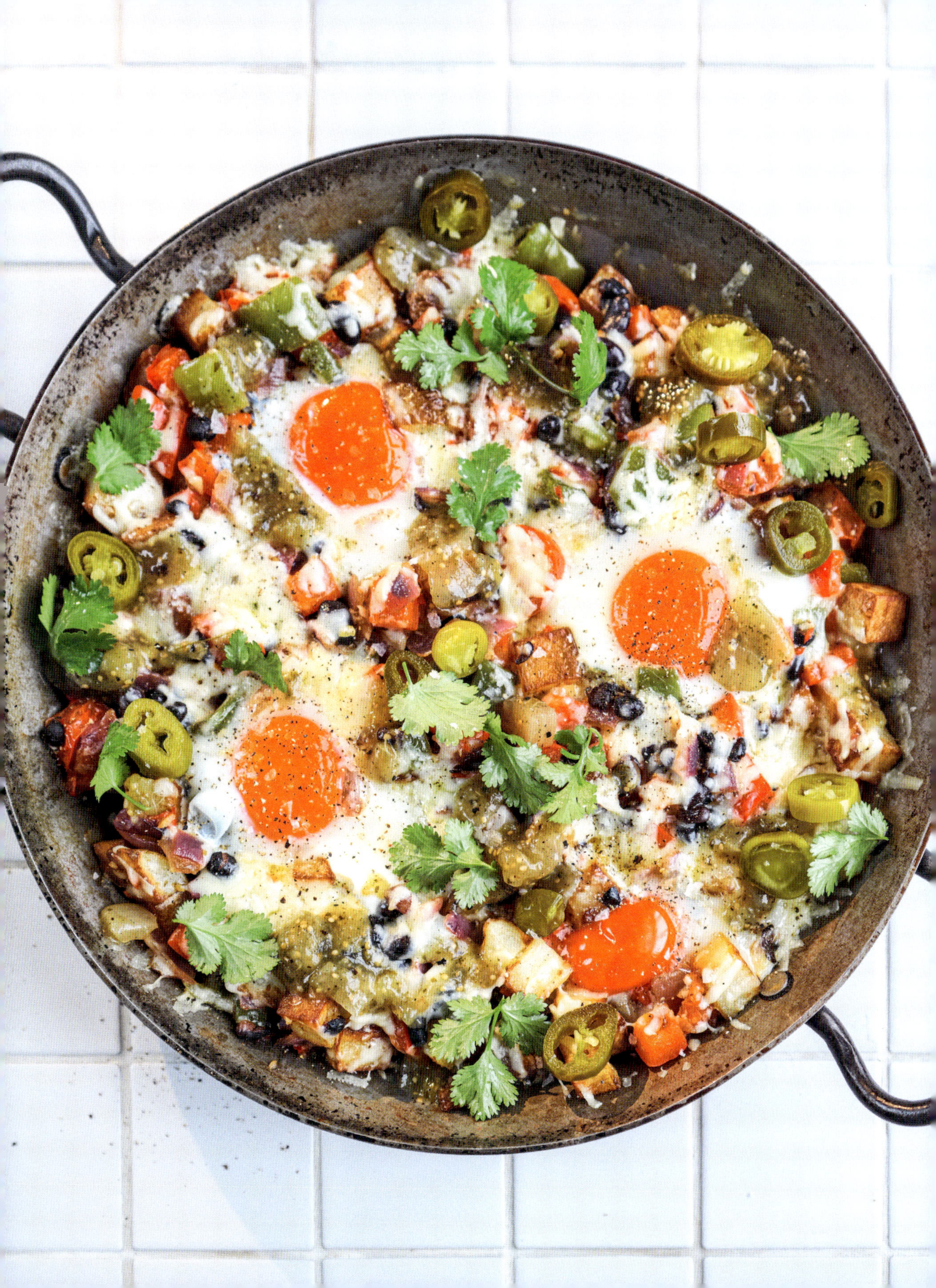

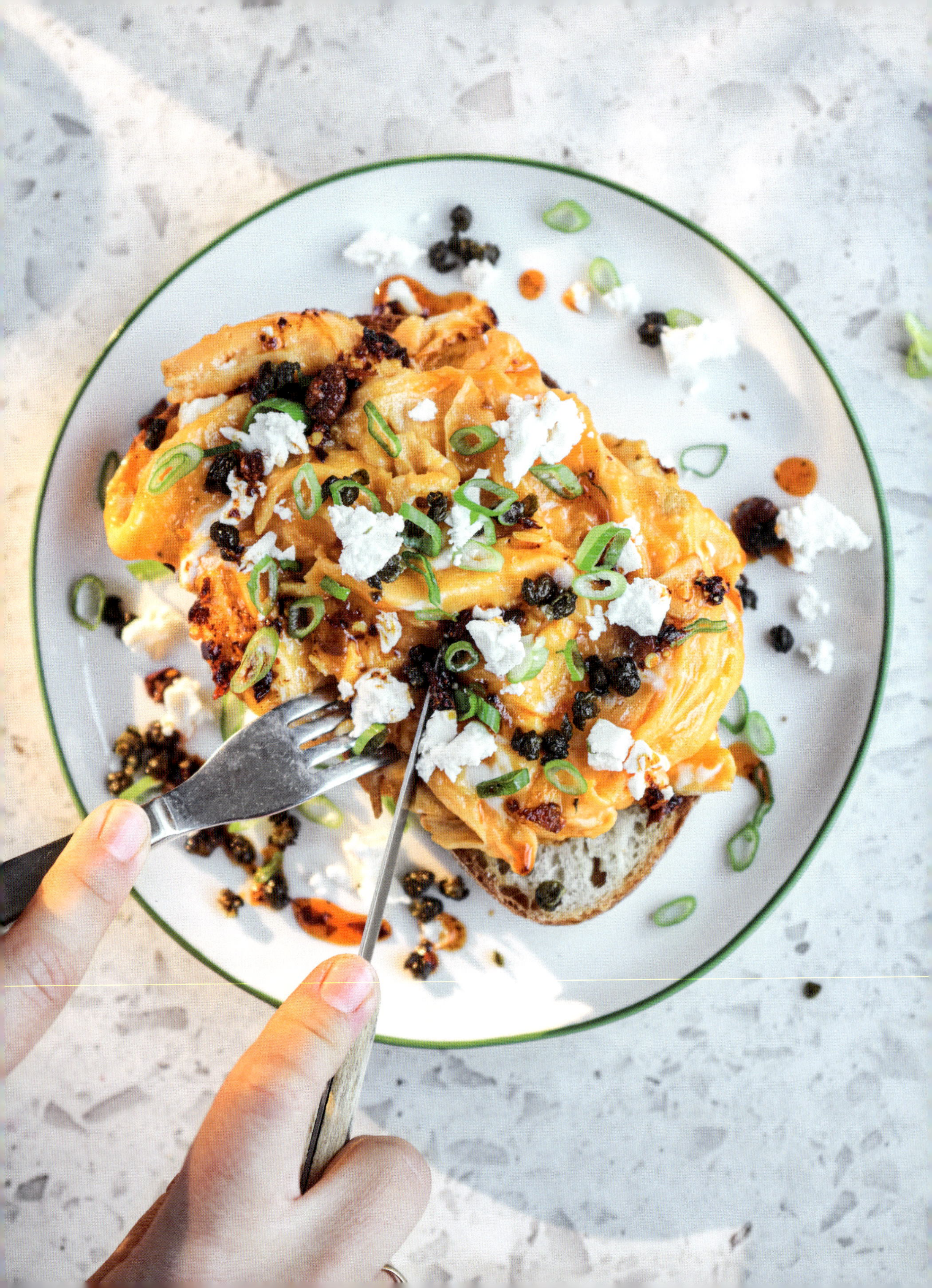

Silky Scramble with Popped Capers + Feta

Serves 1
Takes 15 minutes

Use a small non-stick frying pan with a lid

Veggie

1 tsp cornflour
3 eggs
1 thick slice of sourdough
2 tbsp olive oil, plus extra to drizzle
1 garlic clove
1 spring onion
1 tbsp capers
30g feta
1 tbsp chilli oil
salt

Scan for more tasty recipes like this one

Try this Hong Kong-style riff on a classic breakfast staple. Traditionally served in Hong Kong diners known as cha chaan teng, these eggs have a custard-like texture that sets them apart from fluffier, French-style scrambles. The capers, feta and chilli oil are far from authentic additions, but we've thrown them in because they're cupboard staples that go great with eggs.

01. In a small bowl, whisk together the cornflour and 1 tablespoon of water with a fork until combined. Crack in the eggs with a pinch of salt and whisk well until smooth. Set aside.

02. Toast the sourdough, then drizzle with olive oil. Halve the garlic clove and rub it all over the toast. Set aside. Finely slice the same garlic clove and the spring onion. Set aside.

03. Heat the olive oil in the frying pan over a high heat, add the capers and fry for 1–2 minutes, or until popped and crisp, then remove with a slotted spoon onto a plate.

04. Add the garlic to the hot oil and fry for 30 seconds, or until aromatic (you don't want too much colour here).

05. Pour in the eggs, reduce the heat to low and immediately take the pan off the heat. Use a spatula to drag the edges of the egg into the centre of the pan to create big beautiful curtain folds, tilting the pan to fill any empty gaps with runny egg. Repeat until the egg won't slide around the pan anymore. If the egg is too runny, occasionally place it back over the heat to help create these folds.

06. When all the folds have been made, set the pan back over a low heat, cover with the lid and steam for 15–30 seconds. Divide the egg into 4 pieces and fold on top of each other on the sourdough toast. Crumble the feta on top, swirl over the chilli oil and top with the popped capers and spring onion.

Sausage, Baked Beans + Runny Eggs

Scan for more tasty recipes like this one

Serves 4
Takes 35 minutes

Use a large, deep ovenproof frying pan

1 tbsp olive oil
8 pork sausages (get the best you can)
2 x 400g tins of baked beans
2 tsp Worcestershire sauce
2 tsp hot sauce, plus extra to serve (optional)
4 eggs
50g mature Cheddar cheese
4 thick slices of toasted, buttered bread, to serve
salt and black pepper

Eggs in purgatory? Great. Sausage, baked beans and eggs in purgatory? Even greater. This is a one-pan fry-up where there's none of the washing up and all of the flavour gets dialled into the beans.

01. Preheat the oven to 190°C/170°C fan.

02. Heat the frying pan over a medium-high heat. Once hot, drizzle in the oil, then add the sausages. Fry for 4–6 minutes until golden on each side, then add both tins of beans. Season lightly, add the Worcestershire sauce and hot sauce and mix well, then transfer to the oven and bake for 10 minutes.

03. Remove the pan from the oven and make 4 wells in the beans. Crack an egg into each well, then return the pan to the oven for 8–10 minutes until the whites are just set and the sausages are cooked through.

04. Meanwhile, finely grate the cheese.

05. Scatter the cheese over the beans and serve with hot, buttered toast for yolk dunking, sauce mopping and sausage munching, plus extra hot sauce, if you like.

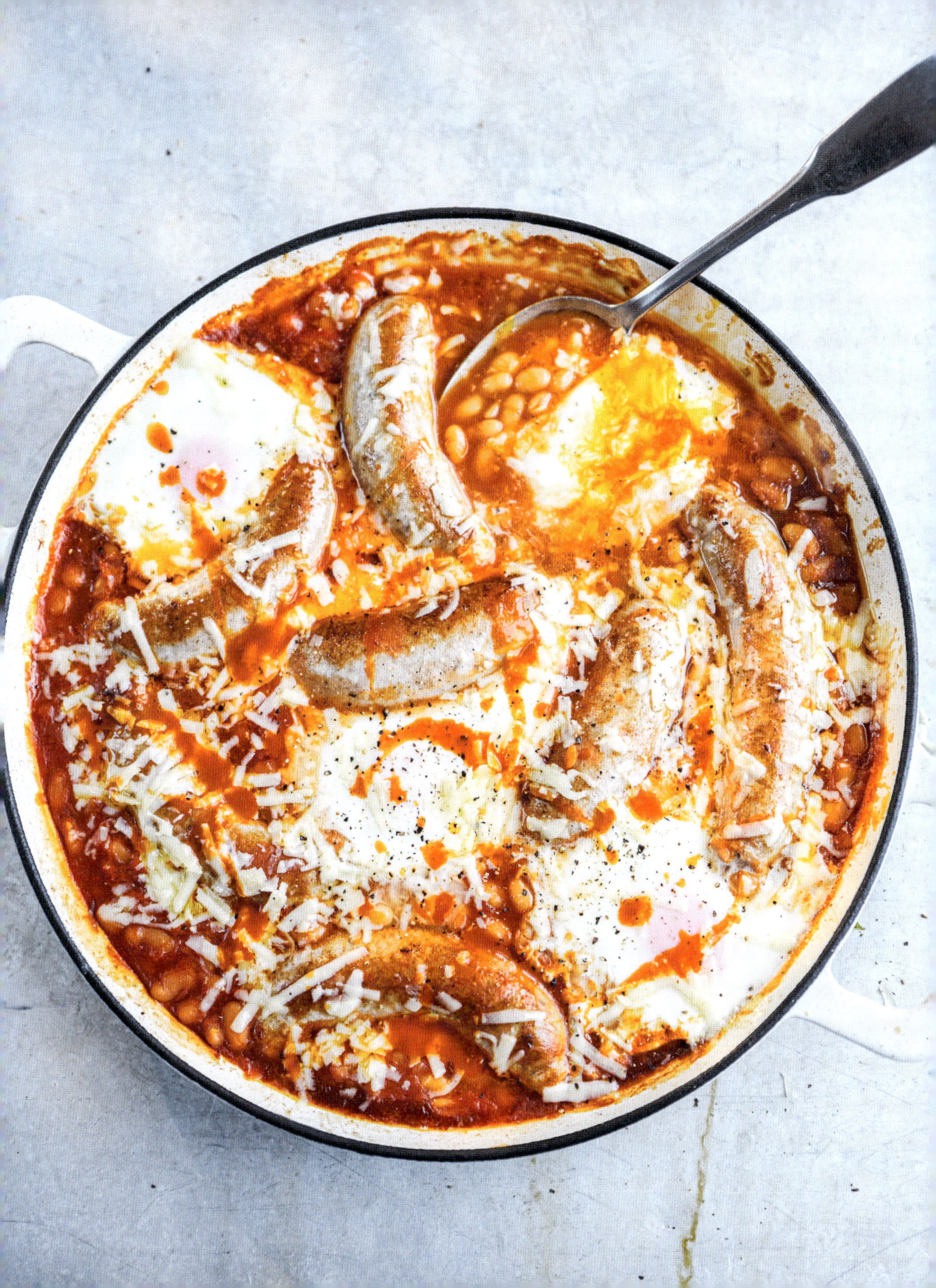

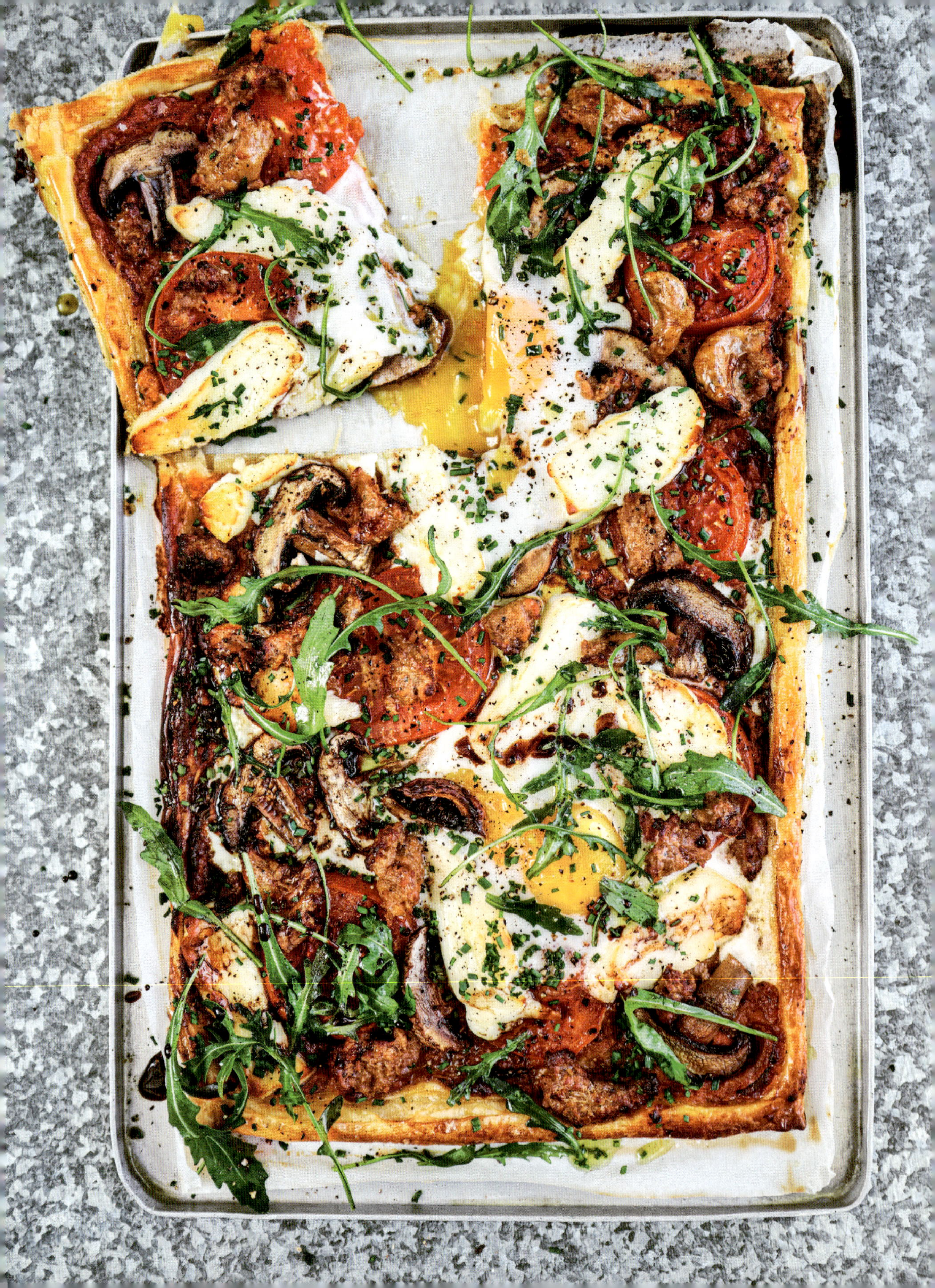

Full English Tart

Serves 4
Takes 50 minutes

Use a large baking tray

Veggie

3 medium tomatoes (about 150g)
150g chestnut mushrooms
1 x 225g pack of halloumi
2 large garlic cloves
1 x 280g jar of sun-dried tomatoes in oil, drained
1 x 320g sheet of ready-rolled puff pastry
3 plant-based sausages (optional)
3 eggs
a small handful of chives
a handful of rocket
1 tbsp balsamic glaze
salt and black pepper

Scan for more tasty recipes like this one

All the best bits of a vegetarian full English whacked onto the perfect vehicle: a slab of buttery, flaky puff pastry. Forget toast – this is the only way we're eating breakfast from here on in.

01. Preheat the oven to 200°C/180°C fan.

02. Cut the tomato into 1cm-thick slices, slice the mushrooms 0.5cm thick and cut the halloumi into 8 slices. Set aside.

03. Pop the garlic into a food processor with the sun-dried tomatoes and whizz until you have a smooth paste. Season.

04. Unroll the puff pastry onto the baking tray, keeping it on the baking paper it comes with. Using a sharp knife, lightly score a 2cm border around the edge, taking care not to pierce all the way through, then use a fork to prick inside the border.

05. Spread the sun-dried tomato paste over the puff pastry within the border, then arrange the sliced tomatoes, mushrooms and halloumi on top. Tear the sausages into small pieces and scatter over, if using.

06. In a small bowl, whisk 1 of the eggs, then brush over the pastry border.

07. Bake for 20 minutes, then remove the tart from the oven and carefully crack the remaining eggs on top. Return to the oven for 6–8 minutes until the whites are set and the pastry is golden brown.

08. Finely chop the chives, then scatter over the tart with the rocket and drizzle over the balsamic glaze.

EASY

ONES

Baked White Fish + Garlic Croutons

Serves 2
Takes 20 minutes

Use a baking tray

20g basil, plus extra leaves to garnish
3 garlic cloves
½ shallot
2 tbsp red wine vinegar
7 tbsp extra virgin olive oil
100g pitted Kalamata olives
150g cherry tomatoes
150g jarred roasted red peppers, drained
4 sprigs of oregano
2 slices of sourdough
2 sea bass or sea bream fillets
salt and black pepper

Scan for more tasty recipes like this one

The vibrant basil dressing is what makes this an ideal summer evening dinner for when you want to spend zero time slaving over the hob. Mopping up every last drop of sauce with the garlicky croutons is the best bit of all. Go ahead and swap out the sea bass for any other fish you like.

01. Preheat the oven to 220°C/200°C fan.

02. Put the basil, stalks and all, 1 of the garlic cloves, the shallot, vinegar and 5 tablespoons of the olive oil into a food processor and blitz until smooth. Set the dressing aside.

03. Halve the olives and cherry tomatoes, then cut the red peppers into thin strips. Strip the leaves from the oregano sprigs. Mix everything together on the chopping board.

04. Tear the sourdough into chunky croutons and place on the baking tray. Finely grate the remaining garlic onto the bread, then drizzle over the remaining olive oil and use your hands to coat evenly.

05. Make space for the sea bass fillets in the middle of the tray and scatter the olive, tomato and pepper mixture on top of the fish. Season generously.

06. Roast for 10 minutes, or until the fish is just cooked through and the bread is crisp and golden. Drizzle the basil dressing over the fish, sprinkle with extra basil leaves and enjoy.

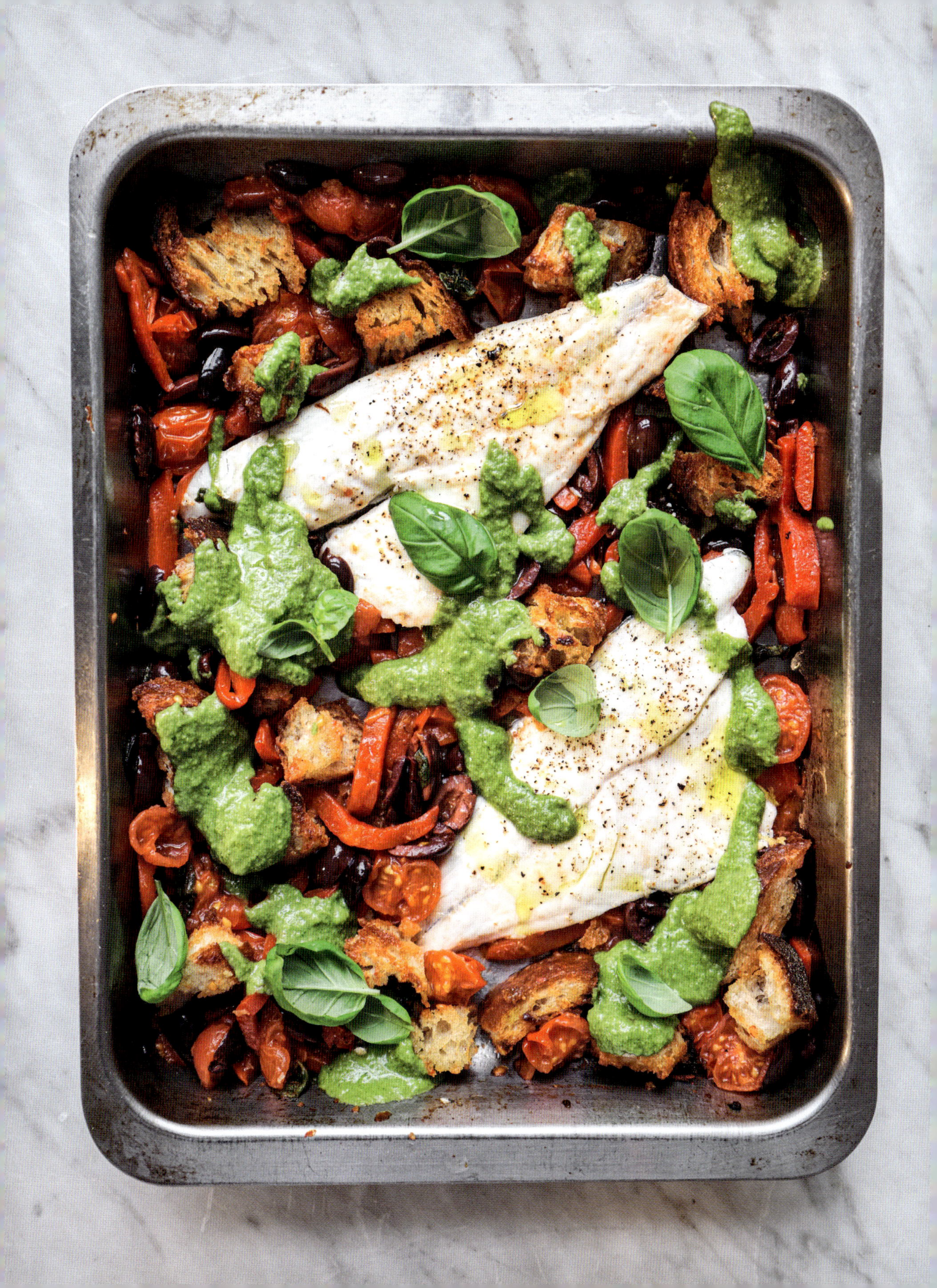

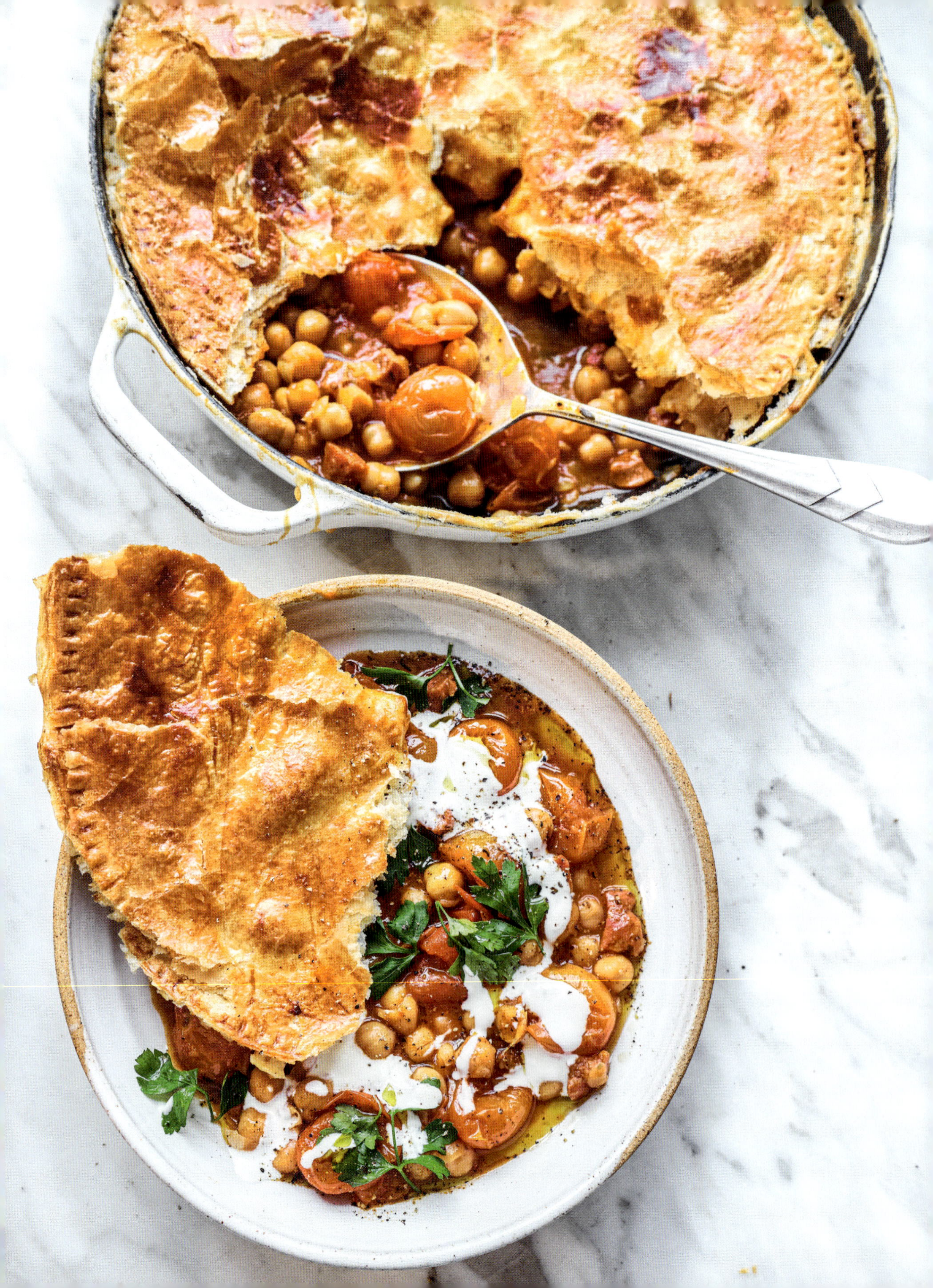

Spicy Chickpea Pie

Serves 4
Takes 1 hour

Use a large ovenproof frying pan

Veggie

2 garlic cloves
800g cherry tomatoes
1 tbsp olive oil
3 tbsp harissa
1 x 400g tin of cherry tomatoes
3 x 400g tins of chickpeas
1 vegetable stock cube
1 lemon
25g flat leaf parsley
1 egg
1 x 500g block of puff pasty
yoghurt, to serve
salt

Scan for more tasty recipes like this one

A one-pan veggie pie, perfect for a midweek meal or for serving to friends or family if you want to show off without having to work too hard! You can swap the chickpeas for any kind of white bean if you want to change it up.

01. Preheat the oven to 220°C/200°C fan.

02. Finely slice the garlic. Poke the cherry tomatoes with the tip of a knife, this will encourage them to pop! Place the frying pan over a medium-high heat and add the olive oil. Add the garlic and cherry tomatoes to the pan and stir for 2–3 minutes, until they start to burst. Add the harissa and the tinned tomatoes. Bubble over a medium heat for 15–20 minutes.

03. Add the chickpeas to the pan with their water and the stock cube. Use a potato masher or fork to crush the mix a little – this will thicken the sauce.

04. Add the juice of half the lemon and remove the pan from the heat. Finely chop half of the parsley and stir through.

05. Whisk the egg in a small bowl. Use a brush or spoon to dab some egg around the edge of the pan. Roll out the pastry so it is large enough to fit the top of your pan, then drape it over the top, using a fork to press against the edges and seal the pastry to the pan. Brush the pastry with beaten egg, add a pinch of salt on top and bake for 25–30 minutes.

06. Serve the pie in bowls (the filling should be loose) with a dollop of yoghurt and the reserved parsley on top.

EASY ONES

Spiced Sweetcorn Fritters

Scan for more tasty recipes like this one

Serves 4
Takes 25 minutes + resting

Use a large, deep roasting tin

Veggie

4 tbsp vegetable oil
4 eggs
200g plain flour
200ml whole milk
2 tbsp Thai red curry paste
15g Thai basil, plus extra leaves to garnish
2 fresh lime leaves
a thumb-sized chunk of fresh ginger
2 red chillies
1 tbsp vegan fish sauce
1 x 200g tin of sweetcorn, drained
a few sprigs of coriander, to garnish
salt

FOR THE DIPPING SAUCE
2 garlic cloves
1 red chilli
3 tbsp vegan fish sauce
3 tbsp lime juice
2 tbsp caster sugar

TIP: Use a muffin tin to make 12 individual fritters.

We were desperate to include some crunchy little Thai-style fritters in this book, and we found a way to get them an insanely crispy base by pouring the batter straight into hot oil. We've spiced them with red curry paste, fragrant lime leaves, Thai basil and ginger. Unbelievably moreish and so, so impressive – perfect for starter-y nibble at a dinner party.

01. Preheat the oven to 240°C/220°C fan.

02. Pour the oil into the roasting tin and place in the oven to heat.

03. Whisk the eggs, flour, milk and curry paste in a bowl or jug until smooth and lump free. Leave to rest for 20 minutes while the oil gets hot in the oven. Alternatively, make the batter well in advance and leave to rest for up to 6 hours in the fridge.

04. Meanwhile, finely chop the basil and finely shred the lime leaves. Peel and grate the fresh ginger, then thinly slice the chillies. Stir in the basil, lime leaves, ginger, half the chillies, the fish sauce and sweetcorn with a big pinch of salt.

05. When the oil is hot, working carefully with oven gloves on, remove the tin from the oven and pour in the batter quickly, spreading it with a spoon to the corners if necessary – it may splatter as the oil will be very hot. Return to the oven for 20 minutes until golden, burnished and puffed.

06. Meanwhile, make the dipping sauce. Grate or mince the garlic and finely chop the chilli, then put both into a bowl. Add the remaining ingredients with 100ml of water and mix together.

07. Slice the sweetcorn fritter into squares, scatter with the coriander sprigs, some Thai basil leaves and the remaining chilli and serve immediately with the dipping sauce alongside.

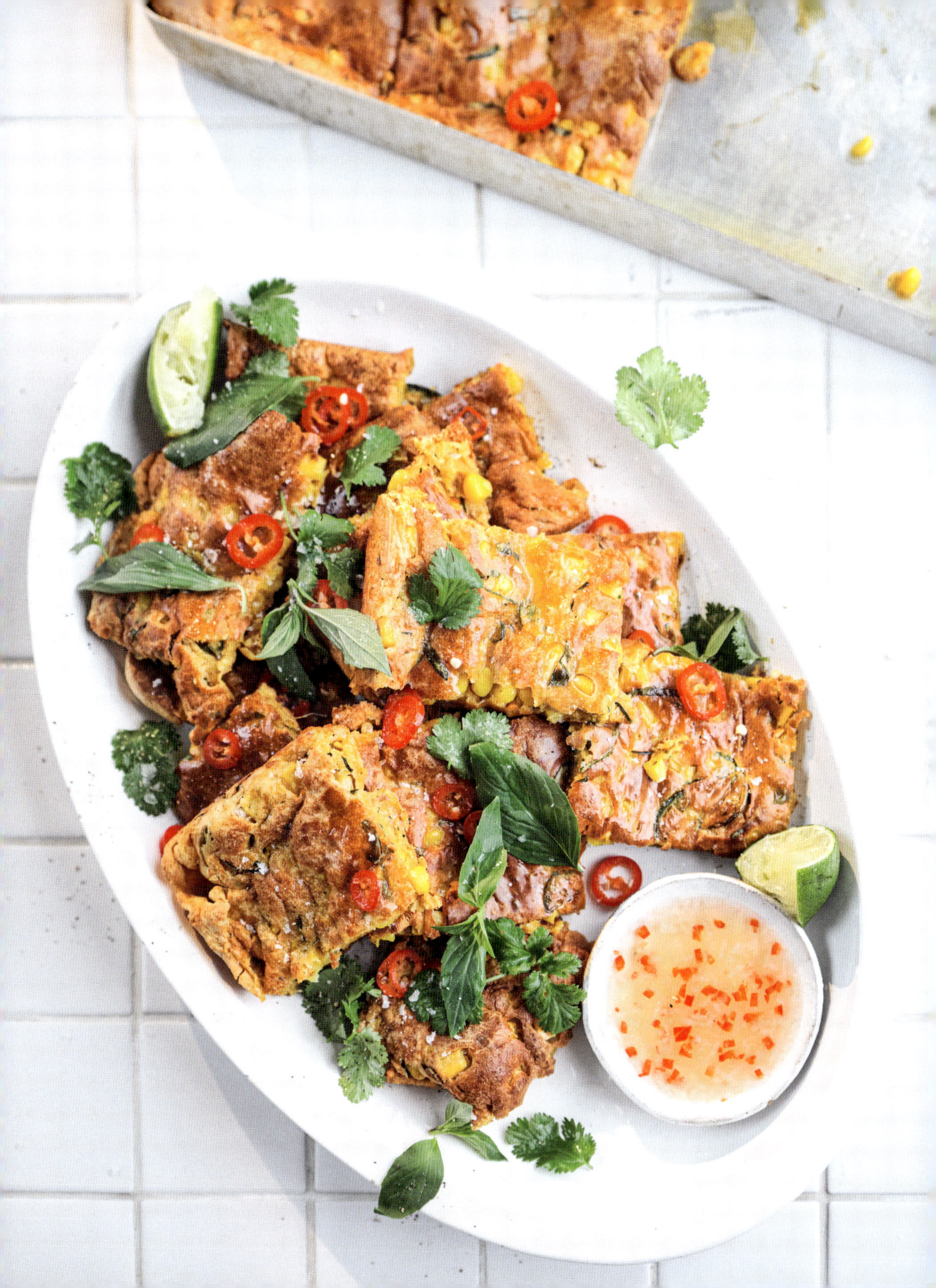

Fish Curry with Onion Bhaji Topper

Scan for more tasty recipes like this one

Serves 4
Takes 35 minutes

Use a deep ovenproof frying pan

This is a super-simple fish curry that's packed with flavour. The bhajis go all crispy on the top but stay squidgy on the bottom thanks to soaking in a bit of that lush curry sauce. Banging.

450g skinless hake fillets
4 fat garlic cloves
a thumb-sized chunk of fresh ginger
200g Tenderstem broccoli
8 shop-bought onion bhajis
2 tbsp lime pickle
1 tbsp vegetable oil
1 tbsp black mustard seeds
1 tbsp cumin seeds
2 tbsp madras curry powder
2 tbsp mango chutney
1 x 400ml tin of full fat coconut milk
200g sugar snap peas
a handful of coriander leaves, to garnish
1 lime, to serve
salt and black pepper

TIP: If there are any leftover bhajis, stick them on a baking tray and bake in the oven with the curry.

01. Preheat the oven to 190°C/170°C fan.

02. Cut the hake into chunky pieces, then put onto a plate and place in the fridge while you make the curry.

03. Start with the prep. Finely grate the garlic, then peel and finely grate the ginger. Cut the broccoli into bite-sized pieces. Tear the onion bhajis into pieces. Chop the lime pickle.

04. Heat the oil in the frying pan over a medium-high heat, add the black mustard and cumin seeds and fry for 1 minute until they start to pop, then add the garlic and ginger and cook for 30 seconds. Stir in the curry powder and cook for another minute before adding the lime pickle and mango chutney. Pour in the coconut milk.

05. Bring to a simmer, then season lightly. Stir in the sugar snaps and broccoli, then nestle in the chunky hake pieces and top with the onion bhaji pieces.

06. Transfer to the oven and bake for 20 minutes until the bhaji pieces have crisped and the fish is cooked through.

07. Tear and scatter the coriander leaves over the curry. Serve with the lime, cut into wedges, for squeezing over.

EASY ONES

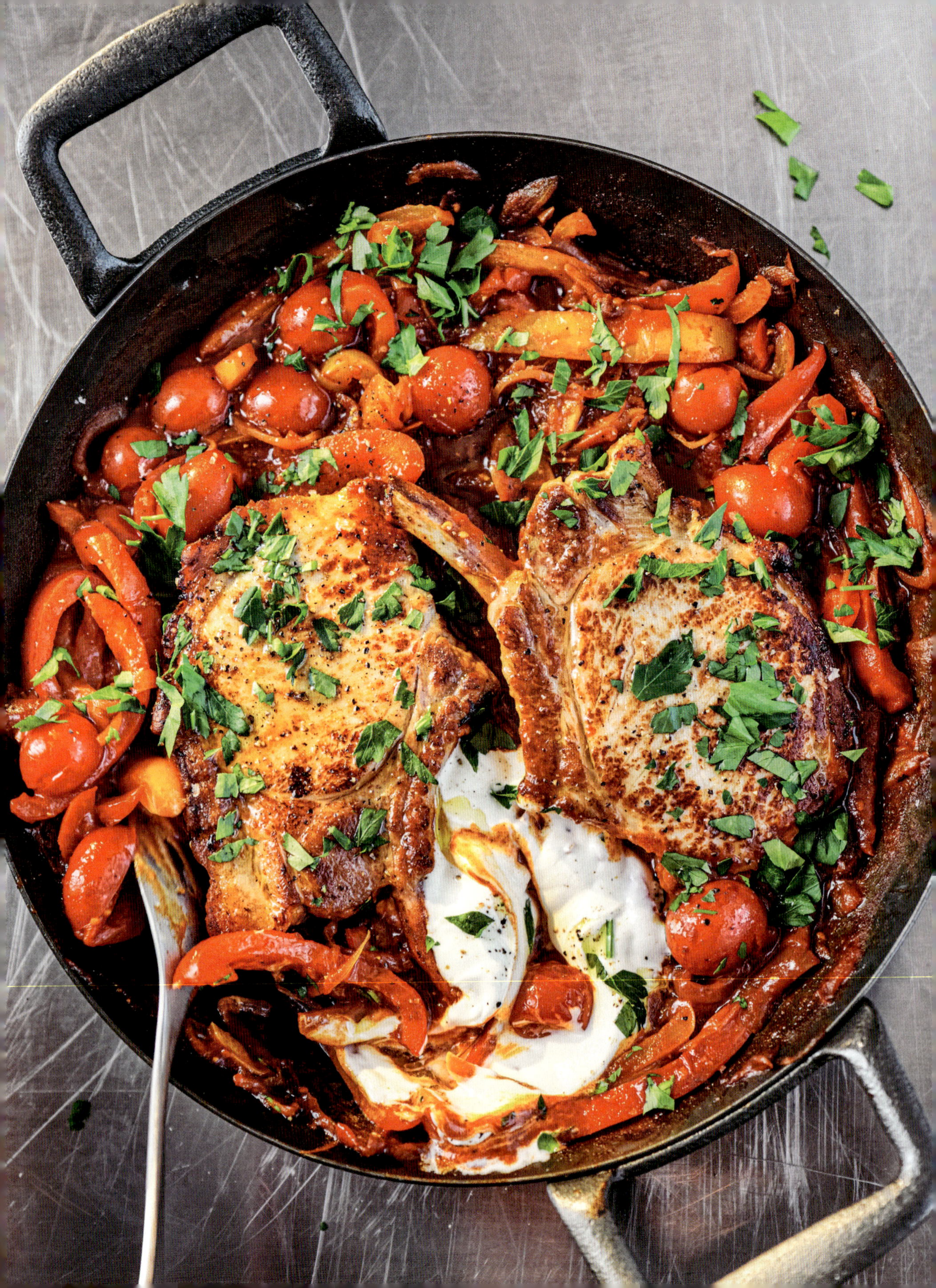

Pork Chops in Smoked Paprika Sauce

Serves 2
Takes 40 minutes

Use a large frying pan

Gluten-free

1 onion
2 garlic cloves
1 red pepper
1 yellow or orange pepper
2 x bone-in pork chops (about 250g each)
½ tbsp olive oil
1 tbsp sweet smoked paprika, plus extra (optional) to serve
100ml dry white wine
1 x 400g tin of cherry tomatoes
salt and black pepper

TO SERVE
1 x 250g microwaveable pouch of rice
a handful of flat leaf parsley leaves
75ml soured cream

Scan for more tasty recipes like this one

Nothing beats a big, chunky pork chop. Be sure to get the fat nice and crispy at the start of your cook – no one likes a flabby bit of pork, even if it's dredged in a banging, goulash-inspired tomato sauce.

01. First, prepare the veg. Thinly slice the onion and garlic, then deseed and slice the peppers. Set the vegetables aside.

02. Remove the rind from the pork chops and lightly score the fat, making cuts about 1cm deep. Rub the chops all over with the oil, then season generously.

03. Set the frying pan over a high heat until hot. Using tongs, put the chops, fat-side down, into the pan. Carefully hold them there for 2–3 minutes to crisp and render the fat, before laying them on their side. Cook for 3 minutes, then flip over and repeat on the other side. Remove to a plate and cover with foil.

04. Add the onion and peppers to the pan with a pinch of salt (you won't need oil as the chops will have rendered plenty of fat). Cook for 5–6 minutes until everything is getting a little charred and softened, then reduce the heat to low-medium and add the garlic and smoked paprika. Cook for 1 minute, then pour in the wine and bubble away for a few minutes.

05. Add the tomatoes along with a splash of water and simmer for 5 minutes, then season. Return the chops to the pan, nestling them in the sauce, and simmer for a further 7–10 minutes, depending on how chunky your pork chops are, until they are cooked through.

06. Just before serving, ping your rice in the microwave according to the packet instructions.

07. Divide the chops and sauce between 2 serving plates, tear over the parsley and spoon over the soured cream. Sprinkle over some more paprika, if you're feeling fancy, and serve with the rice.

Sweet Potato Laksa-Spiced Soup

Serves 4
Takes 45 minutes

Use a large saucepan with a lid

Vegan

---

6 shallots
6 large garlic cloves
5cm piece of fresh ginger
1 lemongrass stalk
750g sweet potatoes
1 tbsp neutral-flavoured oil
100g laksa paste
1 x 400ml tin of coconut milk
2 limes
salt

FOR THE BEANSPROUT GARNISH
2 fresh lime leaves
10cm piece of fresh ginger
a handful of coriander
1 red chilli
2 handfuls of beansprouts
2–3 tbsp crispy onions
olive oil, to drizzle

Scan for more tasty recipes like this one

Laksa paste is one of our favourite store-cupboard ingredients – its fragrant and heady mix of galangal, lemongrass and ginger makes it a superb shortcut for adding an extra whack of flavour into your food. Topped with a crunchy beansprout garnish, this warming soup is as easy as it is impressive.

01. First, the veg prep! Roughly chop the shallots and garlic, then peel and roughly chop the ginger. Bash the lemongrass stalk. Peel the sweet potatoes, then cut into 2cm chunks.

02. Heat the oil in the saucepan over a medium heat, add the shallots and cook for 5–7 minutes until they begin to colour. Add the garlic, ginger and lemongrass and cook for a further 2 minutes. Stir in the laksa paste and cook for 1 minute, then add the sweet potatoes.

03. Pour in the coconut milk, then fill the tin with water, swill it around and pour in, ensuring the sweet potatoes are covered with liquid. Bring to the boil, then reduce to a simmer, cover with the lid and cook for 20 minutes, or until the sweet potatoes are very soft.

04. Meanwhile, prepare the garnish. Thinly slice the lime leaves, then peel the ginger and cut into matchsticks. Roughly chop the coriander and slice the red chilli. Mix on the chopping board together with the beansprouts and crispy onions.

05. Remove the soup from the heat and, using a stick blender, blitz until smooth. Juice the limes, then add the juice and season to taste with salt. If it's a little thick, loosen with 100–200ml of hot water.

06. Ladle the soup into 4 bowls, then top each with a handful of the beansprout garnish and a drizzle of olive oil.

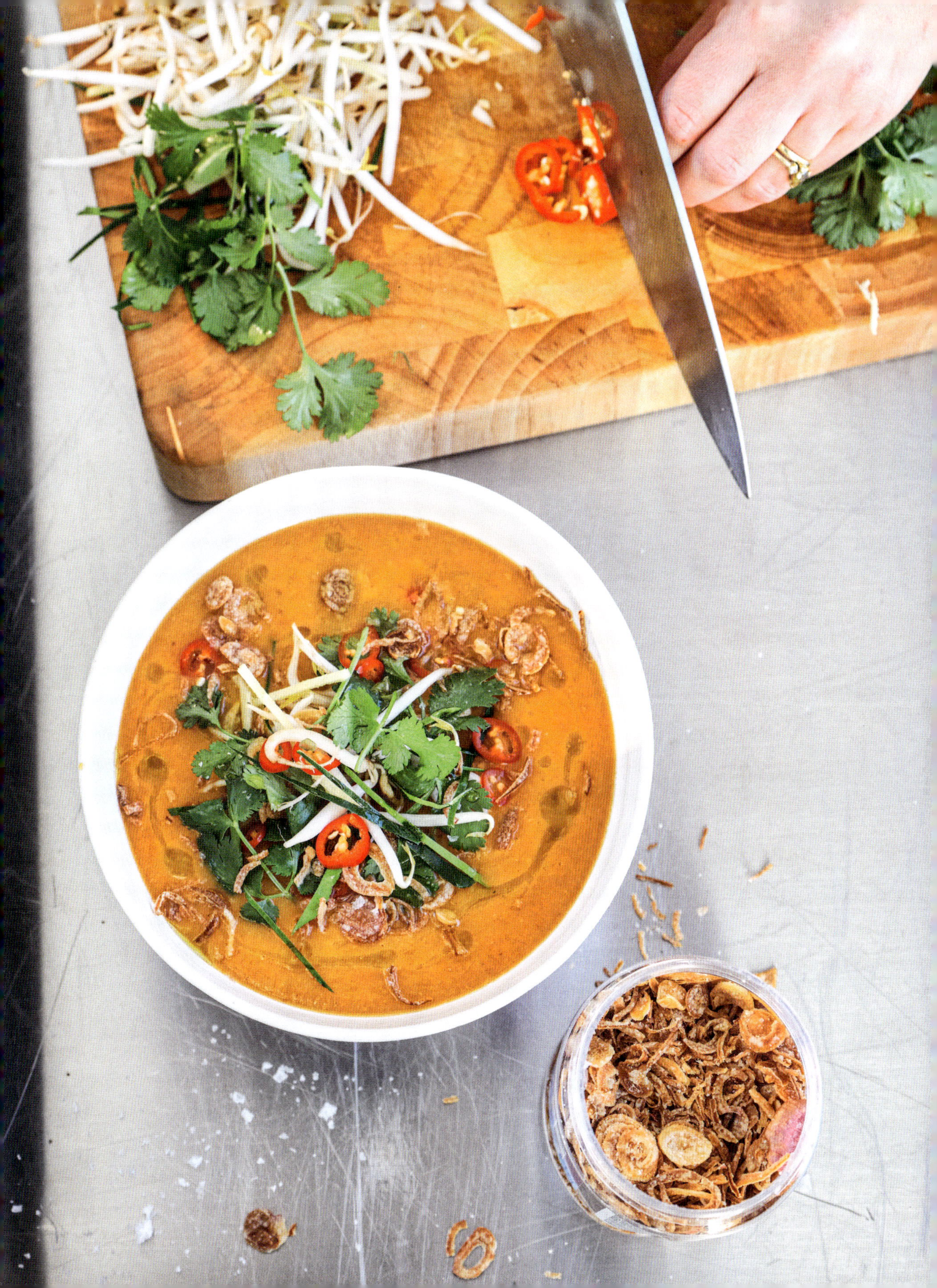

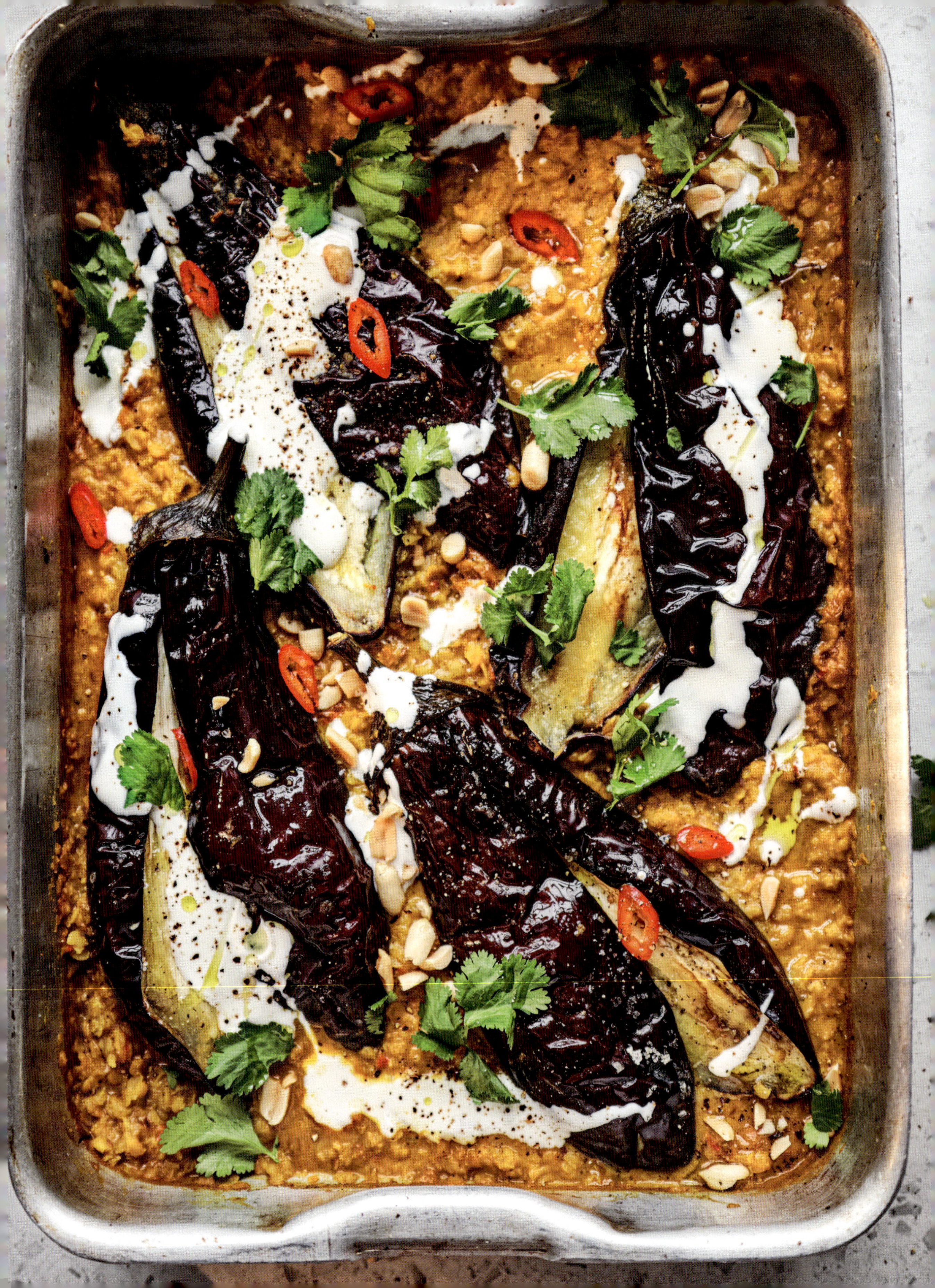

Aubergine Dal Traybake

Scan for more tasty recipes like this one

Serves 4
Takes 1 hour

Use a roasting tin

Vegan

4 aubergines
2 garlic cloves
a thumb-sized chunk of fresh ginger
2 red chillies
1 tsp ground turmeric
1 tsp garam masala
1 tsp cumin seeds
1 tbsp tomato purée
1 x 400ml tin of coconut milk + 400ml water
200g red lentils
salt and black pepper

TO SERVE
coconut yoghurt
10g coriander
50g peanuts
1 lime

Creamy coconutty spiced lentils topped with melting aubergines. This dish is perfect for throwing together when you want to make something vegan friendly and impressive with minimal effort.

01. Preheat the oven to 220°C/200°C fan. Prick the aubergines with a fork, lay them in the tin, then bake for 30 minutes.

02. Meanwhile, grate the garlic and ginger into a small bowl. Finely chop 1 of the chillies and add to the bowl along with the spices, then stir in the tomato purée. Whisk in the coconut milk and water and season well with salt and pepper.

03. Remove the aubergines from the oven, lift out of the tray and slice lengthways, keeping the top in tact. Turn down the oven to 200°C/180°C fan. Scatter the lentils around the base of the dish, pour over the coconut mix, then top with the aubergines, spreading a little in the pan. Return to the oven for 30 minutes.

04. To serve, finely slice the remaining chilli. Top the dal with the chilli, yoghurt, coriander leaves and peanuts and serve with the lime, cut into wedges.

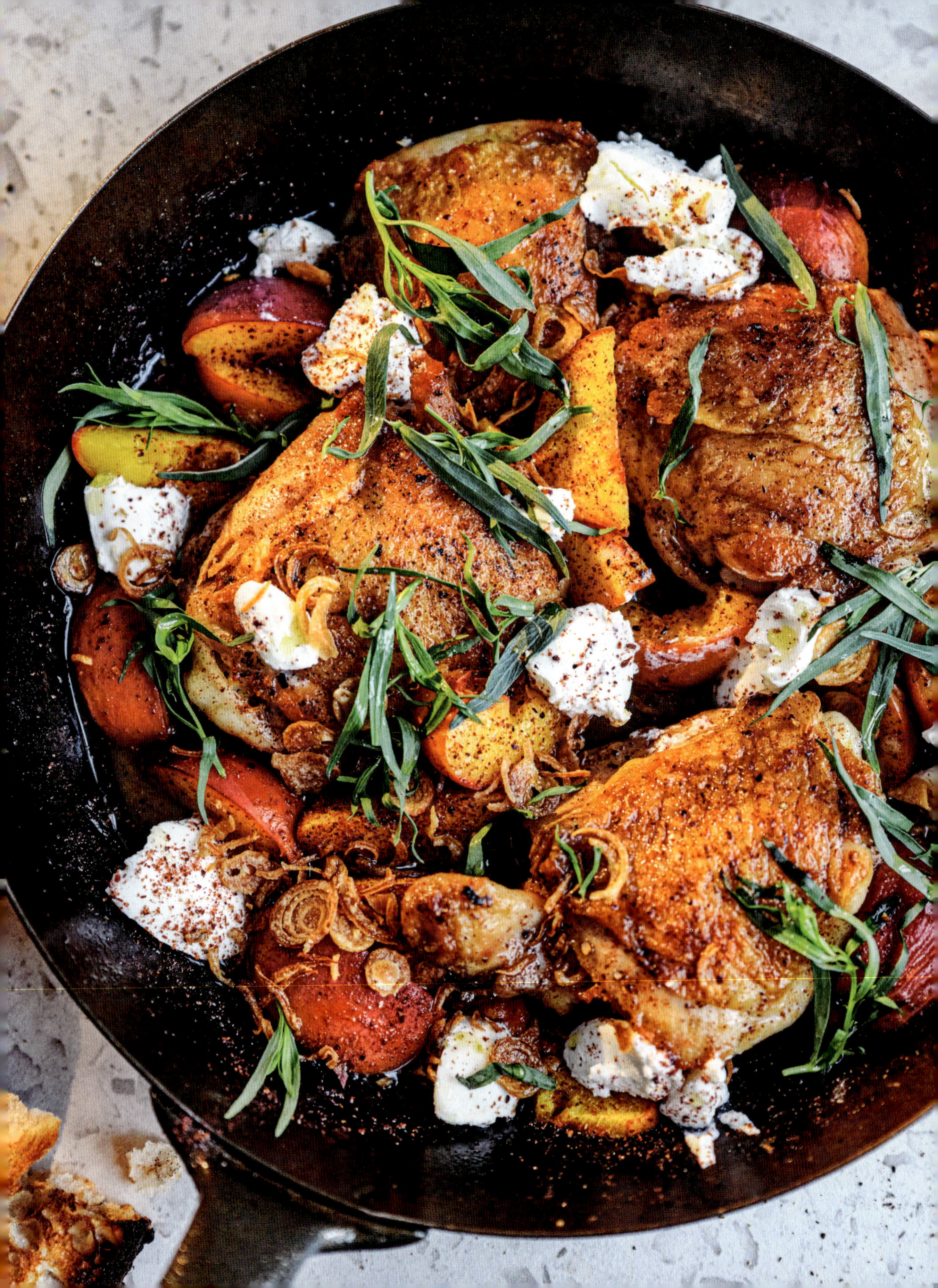

Chicken, Peaches + Goat's Cheese

Serves 2
Takes 20 minutes

Use an ovenproof frying pan

4 bone-in, skin-on chicken thighs
2 peaches
1 tbsp sumac
2 tbsp sherry vinegar
100g soft goat's cheese
a large handful of tarragon leaves
3 tbsp crispy onions
2 slices of toasted sourdough, to serve
salt and black pepper

Scan for more tasty recipes like this one

Oh, boy – this is a stunner of a main. Crispy, juicy chicken thighs with sweet, bursting peaches, heady tarragon and tangy goat's cheese. It's got all the flavours you want. And need. Pop a couple of slices of sourdough in the toaster to mop up the juices and thank us later.

01. Preheat the oven to 200°C/180°C fan.

02. Season the chicken thighs generously with salt and pepper. Pop them, skin-side down, into the frying pan and cook over a low heat until the fat has rendered out and the skin is crisp, about 6–7 minutes. (It helps if you can pop something heavy on top, like the base of another pan or a chef's press, to help as much skin as possible to be in contact with the pan.)

03. Meanwhile, cut the peaches into wedges. Discard the stones.

04. Flip the chicken thighs over in the pan, nestle the peaches around them and sprinkle it all with the sumac. Whack in the oven for 10 minutes, or until the chicken is cooked through and the peaches have softened.

05. Sprinkle the vinegar over the chicken and shake the pan to spread it evenly. Dollop over the goat's cheese, tear over the tarragon leaves and scatter with the crispy onions. Mop everything up with the sourdough toast and enjoy.

EASY ONES

Triple Lemon Risotto

Scan for more tasty recipes like this one

Serves 4
Takes 50 minutes

Use a large, deep non-stick frying pan

Gluten-free, Veggie

---

1 onion
2 garlic cloves
1 preserved lemon
2 lemons
2 tbsp olive oil
1 tsp fennel seeds
250g risotto rice
100ml dry white wine
1.2 litres hot stock (check the label if making this gluten-free)
50g vegetarian Italian hard cheese or Parmesan
30g butter
salt and black pepper

TO SERVE
a large handful of flat leaf parsley leaves
2 tbsp dukkah

SWAP: If you can't find dukkah, sprinkle za'atar on top for a lovely zesty twist.

This dish really makes the most out of the humble lemon: it's got sweet charred lemons, it's got lip-puckering fresh lemons *and* it's got some preserved lemons thrown in there too. If you're looking for the lemoniest risotto in town, this is the ticket.

---

01. Finely dice the onion, then finely chop the garlic. Scoop out the flesh from the preserved lemon and discard, then chop the skin. Set aside.

02. Start by charring one of the lemons. Set the dry frying pan over a high heat. Once hot, slice a lemon in half and place the halves, cut-side down, in the pan. Cook for 2–3 minutes until blackened, then remove to a plate.

03. Reduce the heat to low and add the oil and onion to the pan with a big pinch of salt. Cook for 5–7 minutes until softened but not coloured. Add the garlic and preserved lemon with the fennel seeds and cook for a further 2 minutes, then in tip the rice. Continue to cook for 2 minutes, stirring, until the rice starts to make a popping sound, then add the wine and cook, stirring, until it's totally absorbed.

04. Add the stock, a big splash at a time, waiting until each splash has been absorbed before adding more and stirring often. Once all the stock has been added, the rice should be cooked through, about 10–15 minutes.

05. Finely grate the cheese into the pan, then add the butter and stir through. Juice the remaining lemon and add to the risotto. Season to taste and add a little water if it needs loosening. Cut the charred lemon into wedges.

06. Spoon the risotto into 4 bowls and serve scattered with the parsley and dukkah, with the charred lemon wedges alongside to squeeze over.

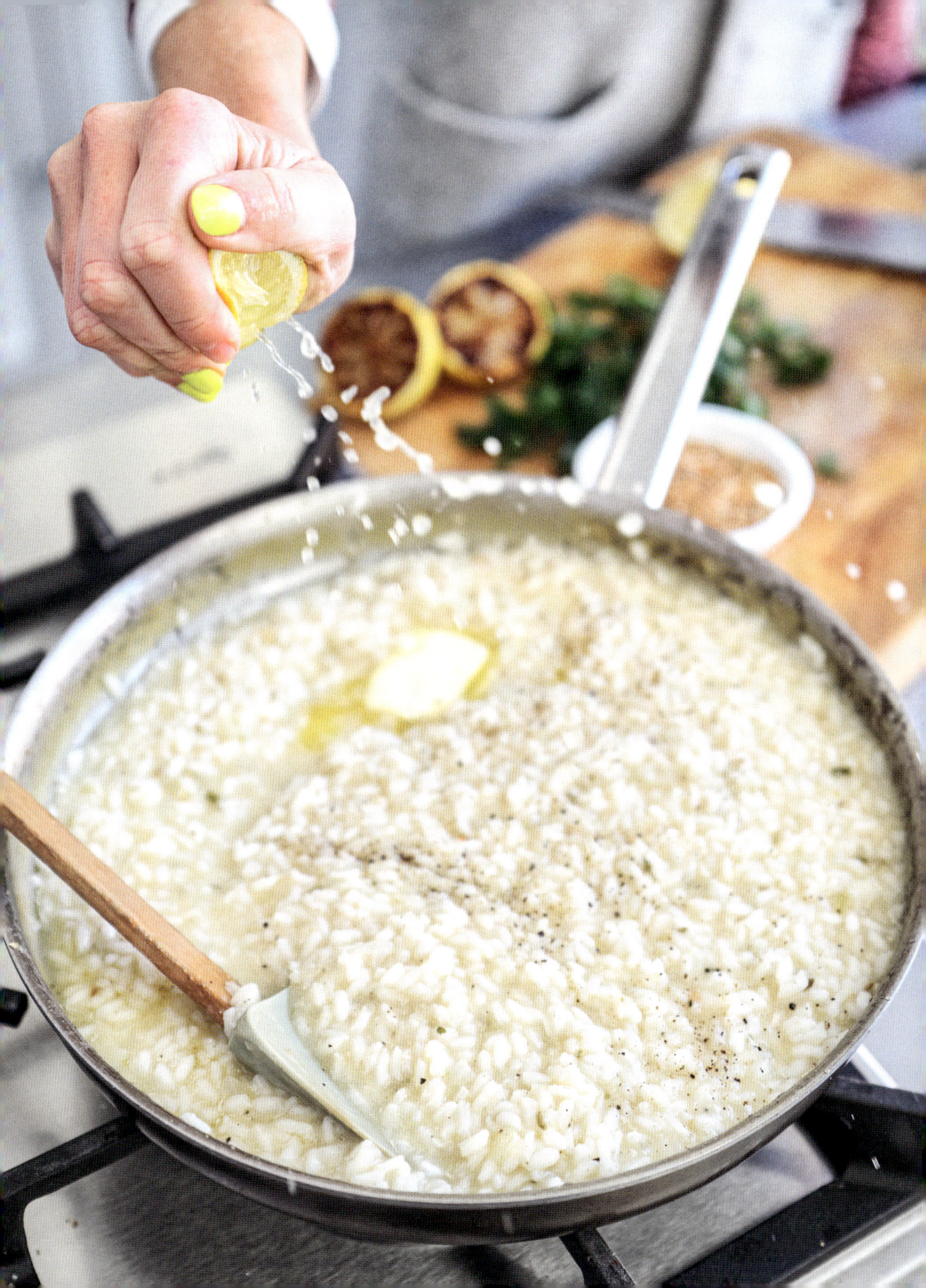

Mint + Peanut Pesto Noodles

Serves 2
Takes 30 minutes

Use a large, deep frying pan

Veggie

50g plain flour
1 x 280g block of tofu, drained
3 tbsp olive oil
2 tbsp honey
50g toasted sesame seeds, plus extra to serve
200g Tenderstem broccoli
2 x 90g packs of instant noodles
chilli flakes, to serve
salt and black pepper

FOR THE PESTO
25g mint
25g coriander
2 tbsp smooth peanut butter
2 limes
1 tbsp soy sauce
olive oil

Scan for more tasty recipes like this one

This pesto is up there with one of the most addictive sauces we've ever made – it's packed with mint and peanut butter and it's a painfully simple way of dressing up instant noodles. The sauce is dreamy and all, but this dish is really taken to another level by the crispy sesame-crusted tofu.

01. Start with the tofu. Mix together the flour and some salt and pepper. Cut the tofu into 2cm chunks, then toss in the seasoned flour. Heat 2 tablespoons of the oil in the frying pan over a medium-high heat, add the tofu and fry for 5 minutes, turning regularly, until browned all over. Tip away any residue flour from the bowl.

02. Drizzle over the honey and toss well, then tip back into the bowl along with the toasted sesame seeds and toss until the chunks are coated in the seeds. Set aside.

03. Make the pesto. Put most of the mint and coriander (reserve a little of each for the garnish) and the peanut butter into a food processor and blitz until smooth. Halve the limes, squeeze in the lime juice, then add the soy sauce and enough olive oil to make a drizzle-able consistency. Season well. You can do this by hand if you finely chop the herbs!

04. Roughly chop the Tenderstem. Heat the remaining oil in the pan, add the broccoli and cook over a high heat for 5 minutes until cooked through, then use tongs to transfer the noodles into the pan along with about 500ml of boiling water. If your noodles come with a sachet of flavour, add that here too. Add the pesto and toss well.

05. Remove from the heat and toss until the water has been absorbed and you have a glossy sauce. Scatter with the sesame tofu, reserved herbs and any leftover toasted sesame seeds. Finish with a big pinch of chilli flakes.

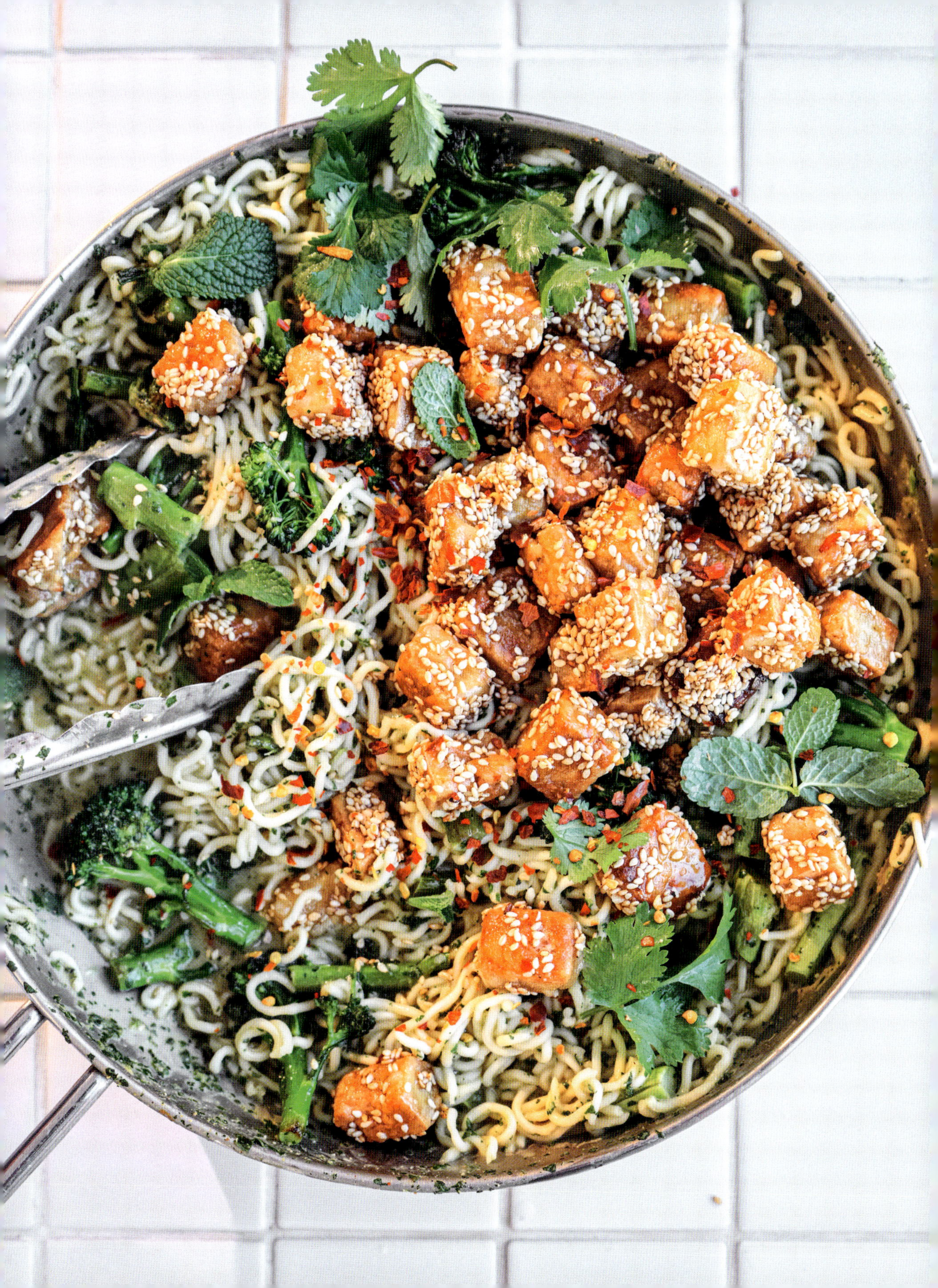

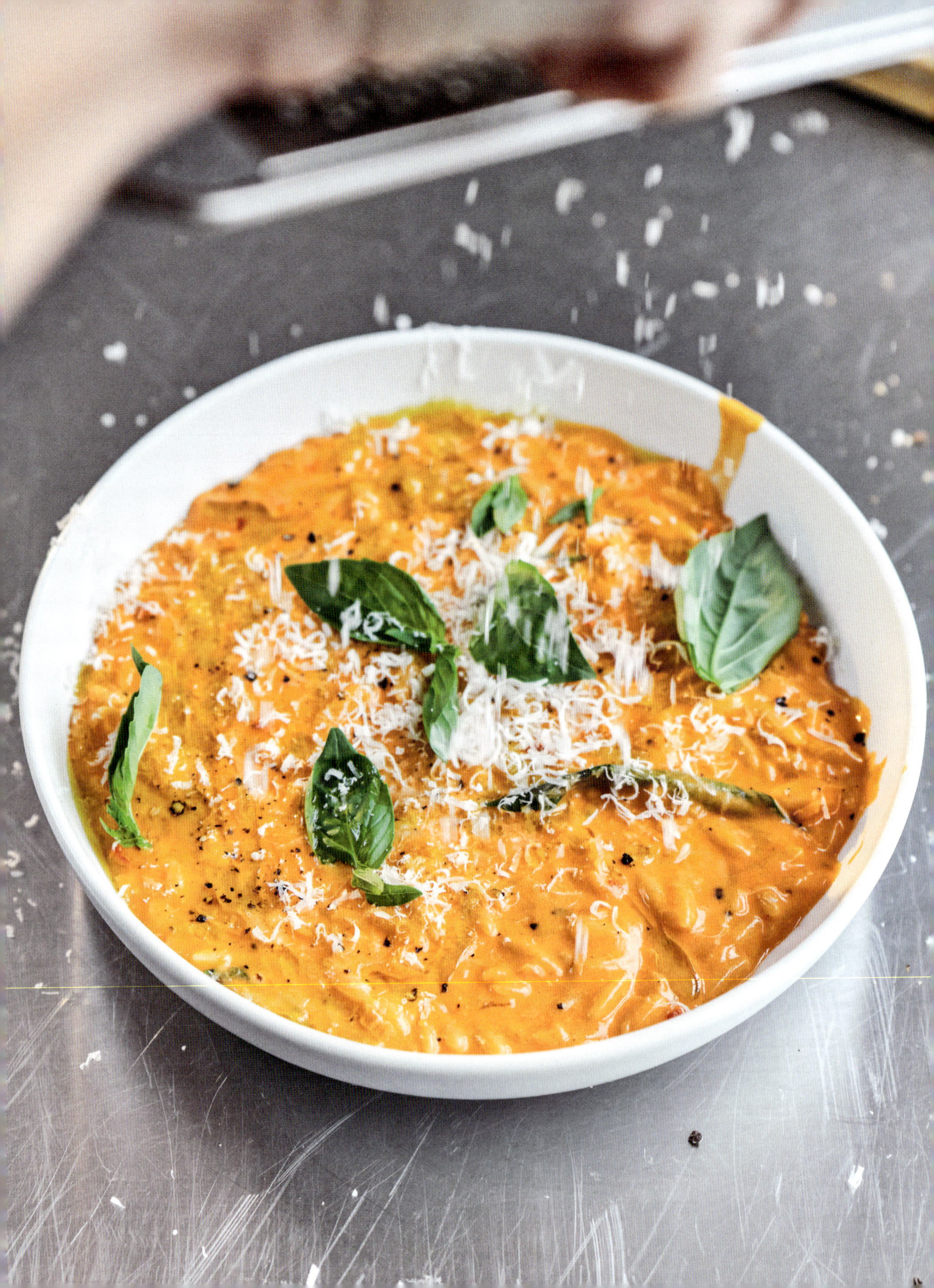

Vodka Orzotto

Serves 4
Takes 40 minutes

Use a deep frying pan

Veggie

1 onion
2 red chillies
3 garlic cloves
2 tbsp olive oil
150g tomato purée
500g orzo
50ml vodka
150g vegetarian Italian hard cheese or Parmesan, plus extra to serve
200ml double cream
25g basil leaves
salt and black pepper

Scan for more tasty recipes like this one

Our vodka rigatoni has always been a firm favourite, so naturally we wanted to team it up with one of our all-time favourite ingredients: orzo. We've used the orzo in the same way that you'd use rice for risotto, though it cooks much faster, which means you get to eat it much sooner. We'll be chalking that up as a win.

01. Finely chop the onion, chillies and garlic.

02. Heat the oil in the frying pan over a medium heat, add the onion with a big pinch of salt and gently fry for 5–10 minutes until softened. Add the chillies and garlic and fry for 2 minutes, then stir in the tomato purée and cook for another minute.

03. Tip in the orzo and, once coated, add the vodka, allowing it to cook off for 1–2 minutes.

04. Add 1 litre of boiling water, a little at a time, allowing each big splash to be fully absorbed before adding the next. When all the water is fully absorbed, the orzo should be plump and tender, with a slight bite, about 15 minutes. You may need to add more water and continue to cook if it feels too al dente.

05. Meanwhile, finely grate the cheese.

06. Stir the cream and cheese into the orzotto and season well with salt and black pepper. Stir in half of the basil leaves and loosen with more water, if needed.

07. Spoon into 4 bowls, then serve topped with extra grated cheese and the remaining basil leaves.

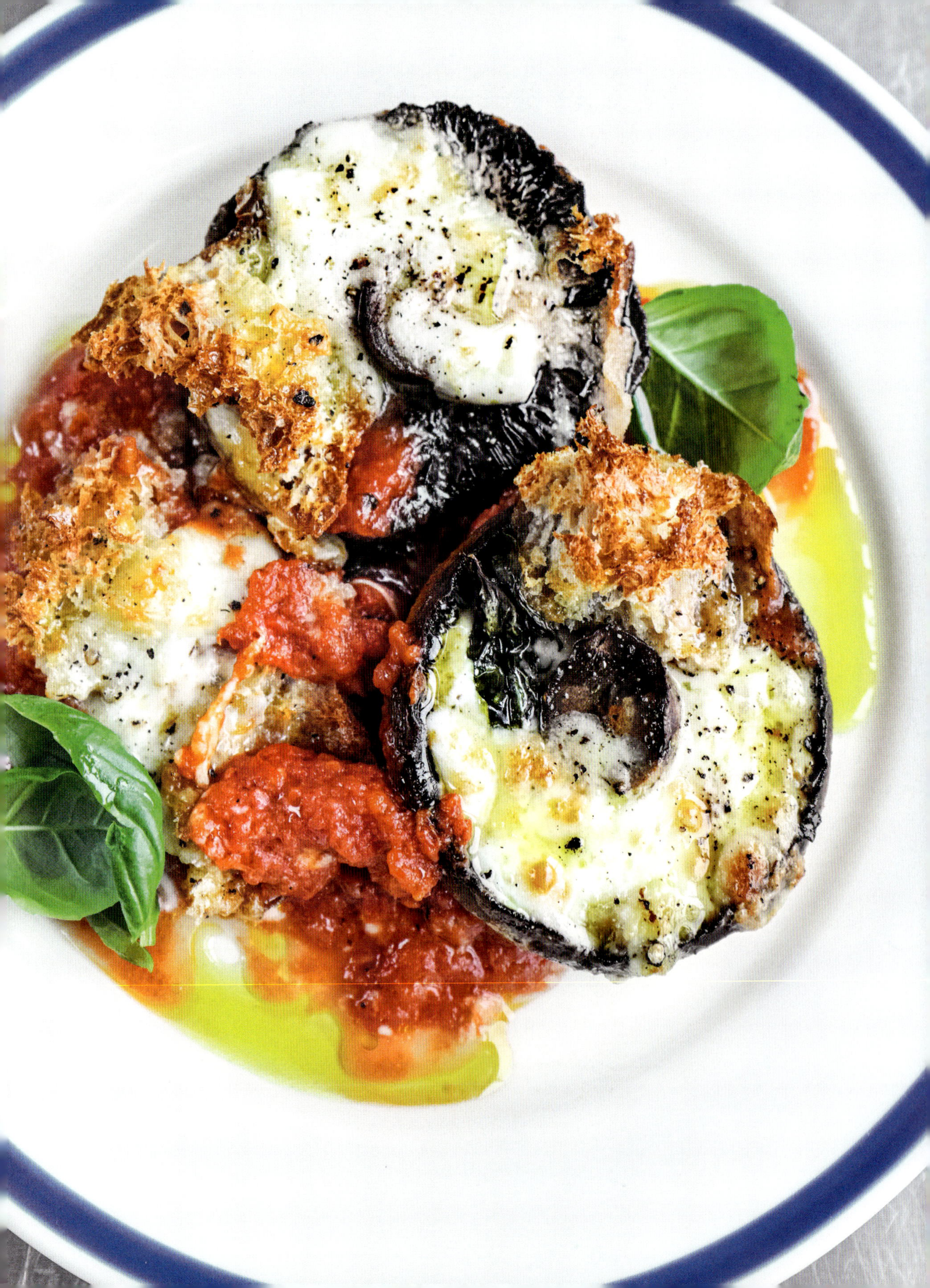

Roasted Portobello Caprese

Scan for more tasty recipes like this one

Serves 4
Takes 40 minutes

Use a roasting tin (not porcelain, as it has to be hob-safe)

Veggie

8 portobello mushrooms
4 garlic cloves
half a ciabatta
200g Taleggio (swap for a vegetarian Brie if making this for veggies)
200g buffalo mozzarella
olive oil
2 x 400g tins of chopped tomatoes (finely chopped if you can find them)
25g basil
salt and black pepper

FOR THE ROCKET SALAD
15g vegetarian Italian hard cheese or Parmesan
80g rocket
2 tbsp balsamic vinegar
3 tbsp olive oil

We've injected some serious tricolore salad vibes into these cheesy portobello mushrooms. Mixing together Taleggio and mozzarella is what gives it a real tangy, funky pop.

01. Preheat the oven to 220°C/200°C fan.

02. Peel the mushrooms and thinly slice the garlic. Tear the ciabatta into chunky croutons and cut the Taleggio and mozzarella into chunks.

03. Set the roasting tin over a high heat and add plenty of olive oil. Tip in the garlic and cook for 2–3 minutes until starting to colour. Tip in the tomatoes, season with salt and lots of black pepper and cook for a further 5–6 minutes. Add the mushrooms, cup-side up, then scatter over the cheeses, croutons and half of the basil. Slide into the oven and bake for 20 minutes until golden and bubbling.

04. Meanwhile, make the salad. Using a peeler, shave the cheese into a bowl, then toss together with the rocket. Add the vinegar, oil and a little salt and pepper and toss again.

05. Serve the mushrooms from the tin with the reserved basil and rocket salad on the side.

EASY ONES

Chicken, Chorizo + Chickpeas

Scan for more tasty recipes like this one

Serves 4
Takes 30 minutes

Use a roasting tin

Gluten-free

---

6 skin-on chicken thighs
2 small red onions
3 garlic cloves
1 pack of cooking chorizo (check the label if making this gluten-free)
120g pitted green olives (we used Gordal)
1 x 570g jar of chickpeas, or 2 x 400g tins of chickpeas (we used queen chickpeas)
2 tbsp sherry vinegar
2 tbsp extra virgin olive oil
30g Manchego
a small handful of flat leaf parsley leaves
salt and black pepper

TIP: To bulk this meal out further (and if not making gluten-free), tear in a half loaf of ciabatta when you return the tray to the oven.

We've got all of the 'ch' sounds in this guy. Chicken, chorizo, chickpeas and sherry vinegar are tossed in a roasting tin with lots of red onions and olives for a Spanish-style supper. With a gorgeous Manchego parsley flurry on top, this tastes like all of your favourite tapas plates rolled into one. It's a combo we think you'll be pretty ch-uffed with.

---

01. Preheat the oven to 240°C/220°C fan.

02. Lay the chicken thighs, skin-side down, in the roasting tin and season generously. Roast for 10 minutes.

03. Meanwhile, cut the red onions into wedges, bash the unpeeled garlic cloves, slice the chorizo and halve the olives.

04. Remove the tin from the oven, flip the chicken over and nestle in the onions, smashed garlic, chorizo, olives and chickpeas. Drizzle over the vinegar and olive oil and season well.

05. Return to the oven for 10–15 minutes until the chicken thighs are golden and cooked through.

06. Finely grate the Manchego. Serve the chicken sprinkled with the grated Manchego and scatter the parsley leaves on top.

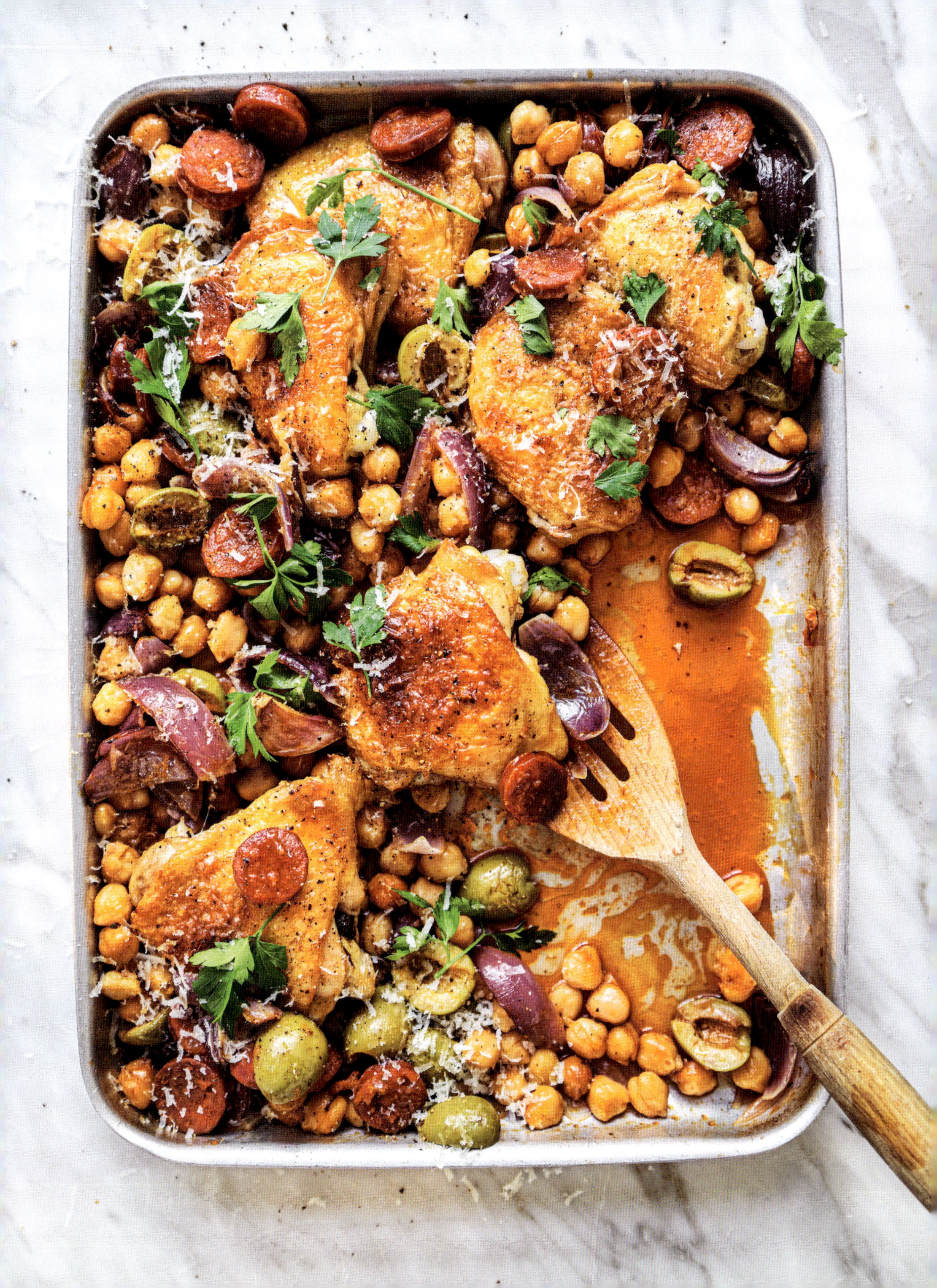

Aubergine + Tomato Stew with Tahini Swirl

Scan for more tasty recipes like this one

Serves 2
Takes 40 minutes

Use a large frying pan

Veggie

---

2 medium aubergines
1 onion
4 garlic cloves
15g flat leaf parsley
5 tbsp ghee
2 tsp Lebanese 7-spice
200ml passata
150ml hot vegetable stock
2 tsp sugar
2 tsp pomegranate molasses
salt and black pepper

TO SERVE
4 tbsp tahini
70g natural yoghurt
2 pitta breads

TIP: Keep any leftover passata in the fridge for a few days (or freeze in a small Tupperware) ready to use in your next batch of pasta sauce, soup or breakfast shakshuka.

Aubergines cooked in ghee with onion, garlic and Lebanese 7-spice – a dish inspired by fattet makdous. Served in a pomegranate molasses-spiked tomato sauce that's cooked until it's sticky and reduced, these aubergines are best enjoyed with a drizzle of tahini, some ready-made pitta chips and lots of fresh herbs.

---

01. Cut the aubergines into 2cm chunks. Finely dice the onion and finely slice the garlic. Pick the parsley leaves and thinly slice the stalks.

02. Heat 4 tablespoons of the ghee in the frying pan over a medium-high heat. Once hot, add the aubergines and fry for 15–20 minutes until golden and softened, then scoop into a bowl. Add the remaining ghee, followed by the onion, garlic, parsley stalks and Lebanese 7-spice and stir-fry for 2–3 minutes until the onion is translucent.

03. Add the passata and stock and simmer gently for 3–5 minutes until slightly reduced, stirring occasionally. Taste and season with salt, pepper, sugar and pomegranate molasses. Return the aubergines to the pan, stir and bubble for 2–3 minutes until piping hot.

04. Serve the aubergine stew with drizzles of the tahini and dollops of the yoghurt. Scatter with parsley leaves. Serve with the pitta breads, toasted, for dunking in.

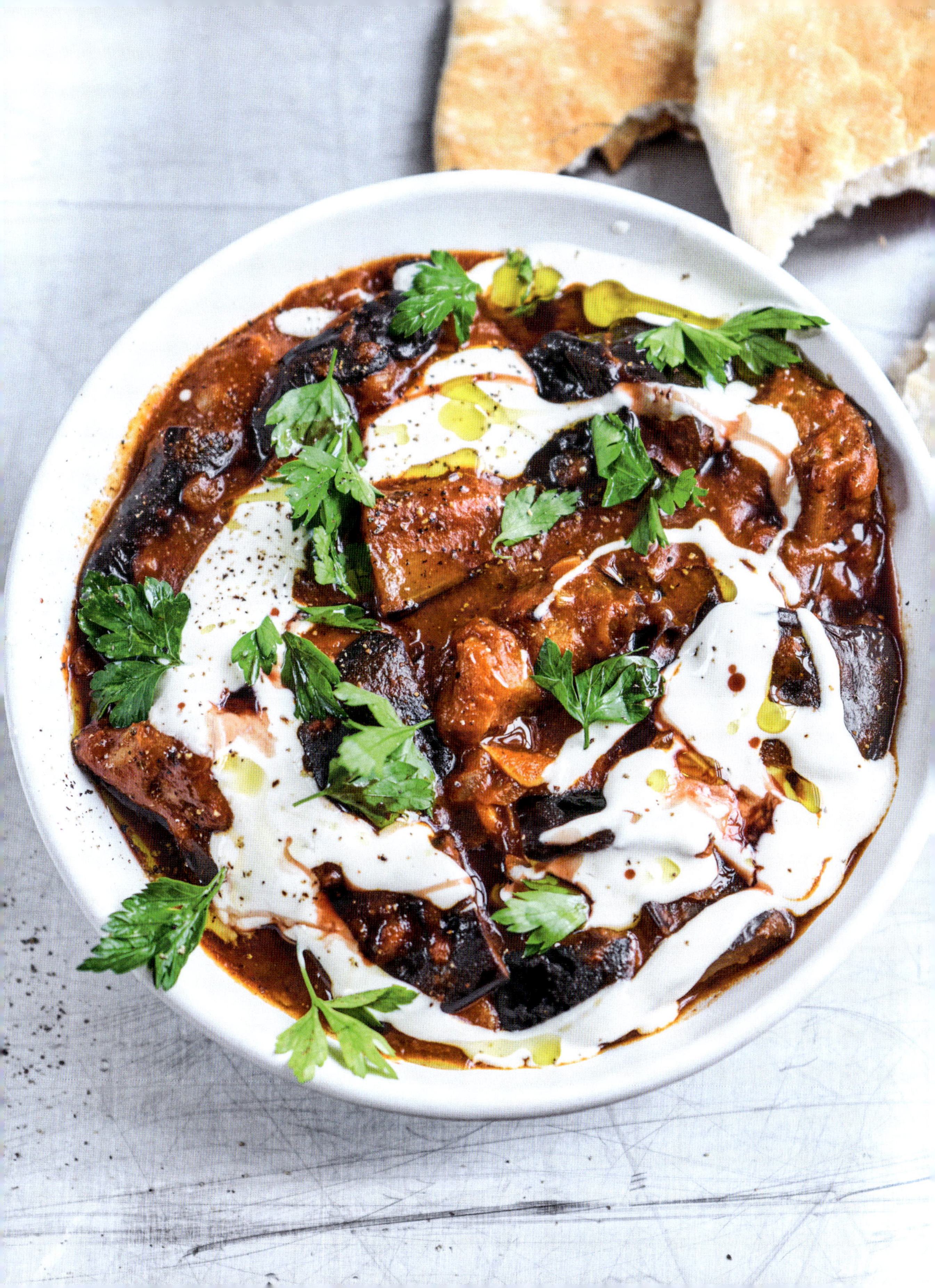

Spinach Orecchiette + Green Pangritata

Serves 4
Takes 25 minutes

Use a large, deep frying pan or large saucepan with a lid

Veggie

2 tbsp olive oil
3 garlic cloves
200g spinach
20g basil leaves
20g flat leaf parsley leaves
250g mascarpone
500g orecchiette
100g pitted green olives
1 lemon
100g vegetarian Italian hard cheese or Parmesan, plus extra to serve
salt and black pepper

FOR THE GREEN PANGRITATA
200g shop-bought croutons
5g basil leaves
5g flat leaf parsley leaves
1 green chilli

Scan for more tasty recipes like this one

Speedy, cheesy, and very, very green – this pasta is a perfect midweek meal when you want something that's packed with veg but still feels like it's on the right side of indulgent.

01. Heat the oil in the pan over a medium heat and grate or crush in the garlic. Add the spinach, basil and parsley leaves and cook for 2 minutes until wilted.

02. Spoon in the mascarpone with a big pinch of salt. Pour in 700ml of water, then use a stick blender to blitz to a smooth sauce. Season to taste and bring to the boil.

03. Stir in the orecchiette, cover with the lid and bubble for 10–12 minutes, or until the pasta is cooked through – you may need to add a splash more water if the pasta absorbs it all.

04. Meanwhile, to make the green pangritata, blitz the croutons, basil and parsley leaves and chilli in a mini food chopper or processor. Season and set aside.

05. Roughly chop the olives and stir them through the pasta. Juice the lemon and add this to the pan, then finely grate in the cheese.

06. Spoon into 4 bowls and serve topped with extra grated cheese and the pangritata.

EASY ONES

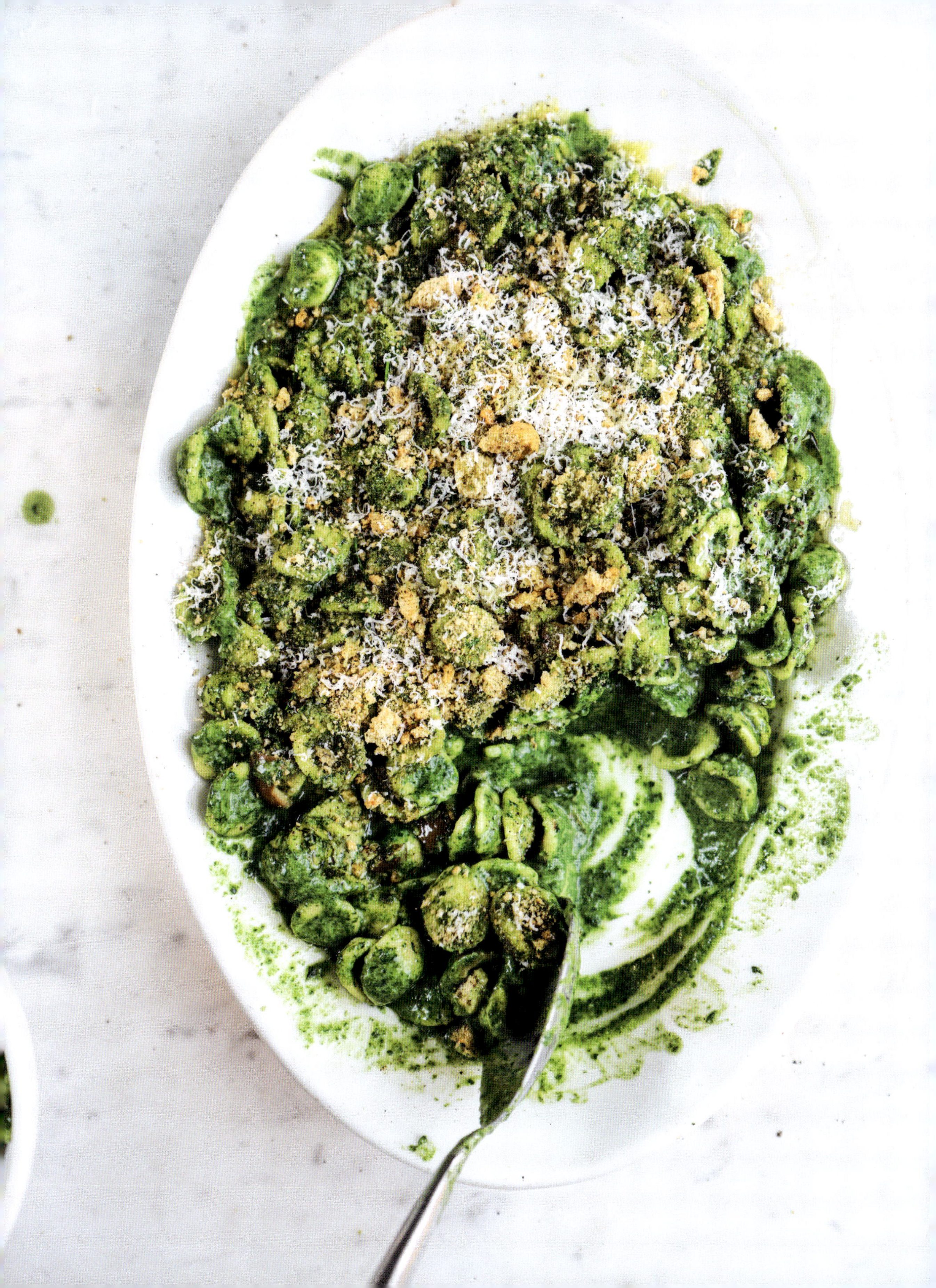

Smoky Cod Traybake Tacos

Serves 4
Takes 35 minutes

Use a baking tray

½ orange
3 garlic cloves
1½ tbsp chipotle paste
3 tbsp olive oil
4 x 150–160g skinless cod fillets
3 ripe avocados
15g coriander
8 mini corn tortillas
salt

FOR THE RADISH SALSA
1 small red onion
2 limes
100g radishes

Scan for more tasty recipes like this one

Take all of the faff out of taco night with these insanely quick fish tacos. They're smoky and zesty, and we like them with a peppery pickled onion and radish salsa on the side. A stunning, speedy dinner.

01. Preheat the grill to high.

02. To make your salsa, thinly slice the red onion, then pop into a bowl. Juice 1½ limes over the onion. Slice the radishes into thin matchsticks, then toss through the onion. Season with salt and set aside.

03. Juice the orange into a separate dish. Grate in the garlic, then stir in the chipotle paste and oil and season generously with salt. Add the cod fillets and mix to evenly coat.

04. Transfer the coated fish and any excess marinade to the baking tray and cook under the grill until starting to char and the fish is opaque and cooked through, about 10–13 minutes.

05. Meanwhile, halve the avocados, remove the stones and thinly slice the flesh. Pick the coriander leaves and set aside for garnish and finely slice the stalks and add to the salsa. Heat the corn tortillas.

06. When the fish is cooked, top with the salsa and flake the flesh.

07. Divide the avocado and fish between the tortillas. Serve topped with the coriander leaves and with the remaining lime half cut into wedges for squeezing over.

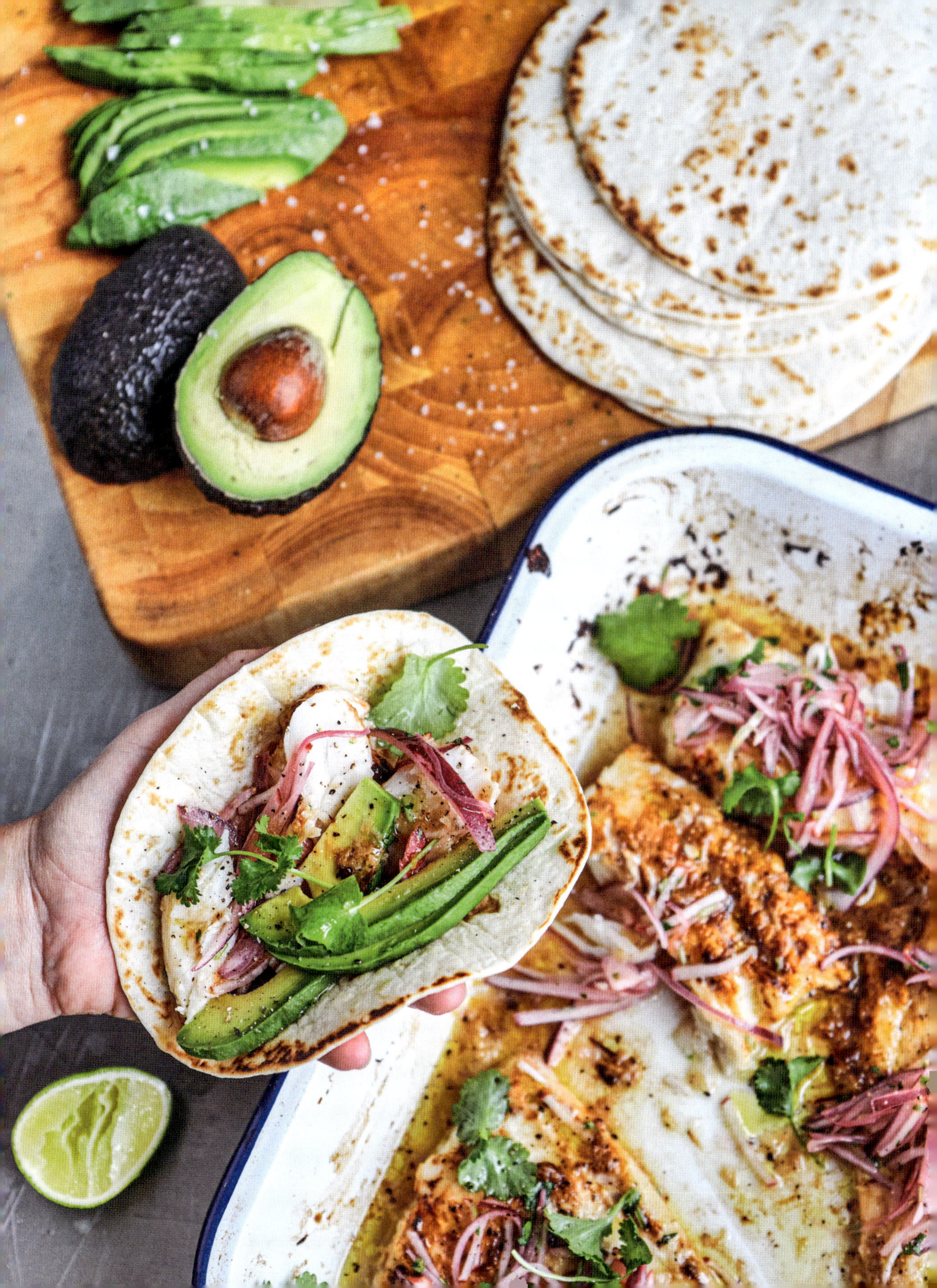

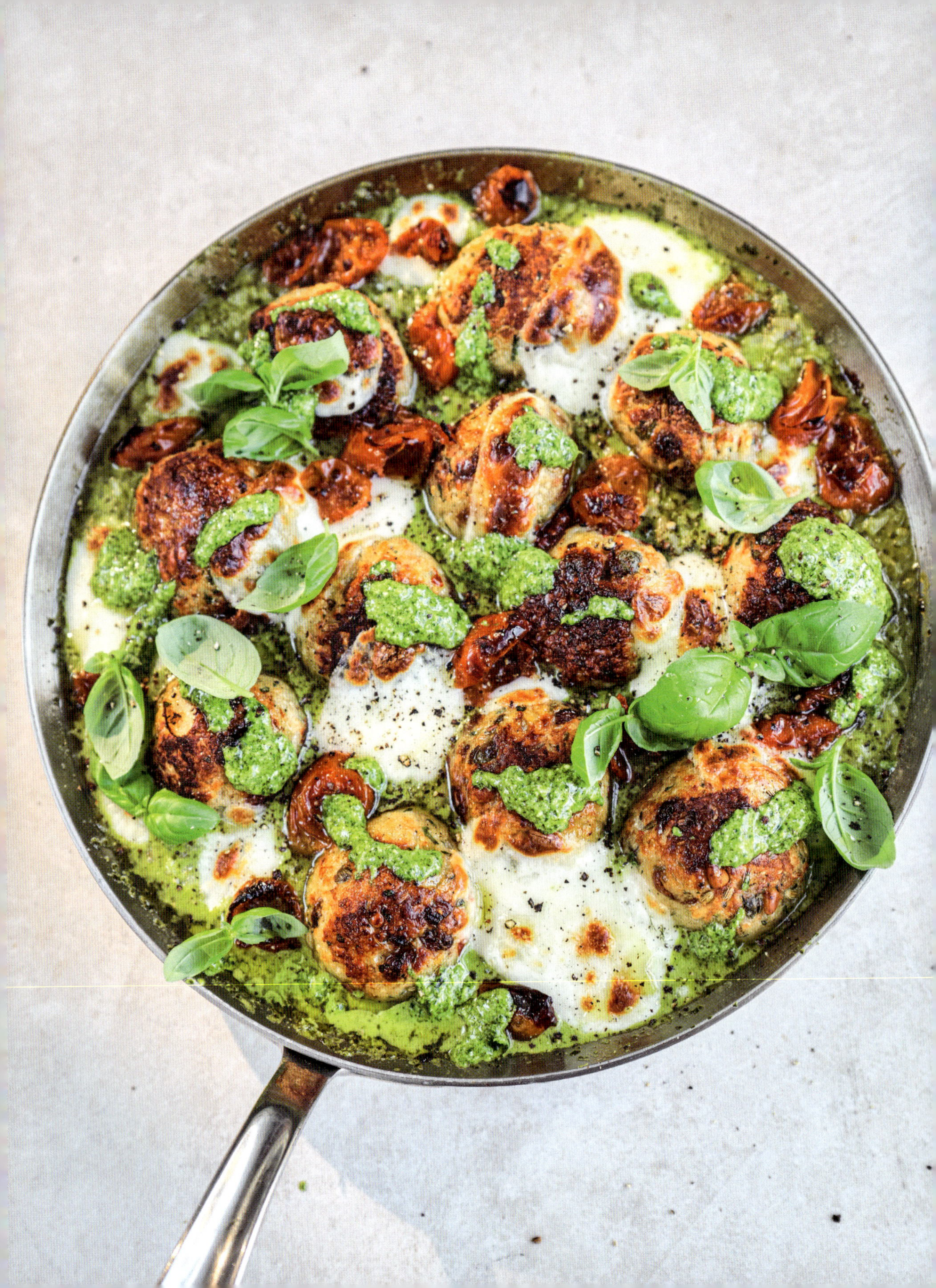

Chicken Pesto Meatballs

Serves 4
Takes 50 minutes

Use a large ovenproof non-stick frying pan

50g pine nuts
2 lemons
30g Parmesan
100g spinach
30g basil, plus extra leaves to serve
50ml extra virgin olive oil, plus extra to drizzle
2 slices of stale white bread
80ml whole milk
a large handful of flat leaf parsley
500g chicken mince
50g sultanas
2 tbsp capers
1 tbsp fennel seeds
2 tsp chilli flakes
1 tbsp Dijon mustard
2 x 250g microwaveable pouches of brown rice
½ x 280g jar of sun-dried tomatoes
1 ball of buffalo mozzarella or 200g low moisture mozzarella
salt and black pepper

Scan for more tasty recipes like this one

This vibrant green dish is a fresh take on meatballs, with milky soaked bread helping the chicken stay nice and moist. You can use shop-bought pesto here, but we love the colour that comes from the homemade pesto. To make sure your seasoning is bang on, fry off a bit of the meatball mixture before you shape them, so you can adjust to taste.

01. Toast the pine nuts in the dry frying pan over a medium heat until golden – this will only take 1–2 minutes so do watch them carefully to ensure they don't burn.

02. Tip a quarter of the nuts into a food processor (or you could use a large pestle and mortar), and the rest into a mixing bowl.

03. Zest 1 of the lemons into the food processor, and the other into the mixing bowl, then squeeze the juice of both lemons into the food processor.

04. Grate the Parmesan into the food processor. Add the spinach, basil and olive oil and blitz to combine. Season and set aside.

05. Back to the mixing bowl – add the stale bread and the milk. While the bread softens, finely chop the parsley, then add to the bowl with the chicken mince, sultanas, capers, fennel seeds, chilli flakes and mustard. Season heavily and mix with your hands until combined. Shape into 8 large meatballs.

06. Preheat the grill to its highest setting.

07. Heat a little drizzle of oil in the pan over a medium-high heat, add the meatballs and fry for 8–10 minutes until browned on all sides. Remove to a plate.

08. Empty the rice into the pan, breaking up any clumps, then stir through half of your pesto and 2 tablespoons of water (more if it's looking dry). Nestle in the chicken meatballs and scatter the sun-dried tomatoes and mozzarella on top.

09. Stick the pan under the grill and cook for 5 minutes until the meatballs are cooked through and the mozzarella is golden. Top with the remaining pesto and basil leaves and enjoy.

EASY ONES

Chicken, Lemon + Olive Stew

Serves 4
Takes 55 minutes

Use a large ovenproof casserole dish with a lid

8 skin-on chicken thighs or drumsticks
2 large onions
6 garlic cloves
1 tbsp ras el hanout
2 tsp ground cumin
1 tsp ground cinnamon
½ tsp ground turmeric
a pinch of saffron
½ tsp caster sugar
1 chicken stock cube
2 preserved lemons
160g pitted green olives
175g couscous
a large handful of coriander
1 lemon
salt

Scan for more tasty recipes like this one

Inspired by a classic Moroccan banger, with minimal washing up. Cooking the couscous in all the gorgeous tagine juices gives this a real depth of flavour. If you can't find preserved lemons, load it up with fresh lemon zest instead.

01. Set the casserole dish over a low heat. Once hot, add the chicken thighs, skin-side down, and season generously with salt. Cook for 3–4 minutes until the skin is brown and crisp.

02. Meanwhile, slice the onions and finely chop the garlic.

03. When browned, remove the chicken from the dish to a plate. Throw the onions and garlic into the chicken fat and cook for 5 minutes until starting to soften. Add the spices and sugar and fry for another minute until fragrant.

04. Crumble in the stock cube, then stir in 500ml of boiling water. Pop the chicken thighs back in and simmer over a very low heat for 30–35 minutes until the chicken is cooked through. Remove the chicken and keep warm.

05. Halve the preserved lemons and scoop out the flesh, discarding it. Finely slice the peel, then add the peel and olives to the dish. Stir to combine, then add the couscous and another 550ml of boiling water. Cover with the lid and cook for 6 minutes until the couscous is fluffy, but there is a liquid gravy remaining.

06. Meanwhile, finely chop the coriander. Halve the fresh lemon.

07. When the couscous is ready, pop the chicken thighs back on top and garnish with the chopped coriander and a squeeze of lemon juice.

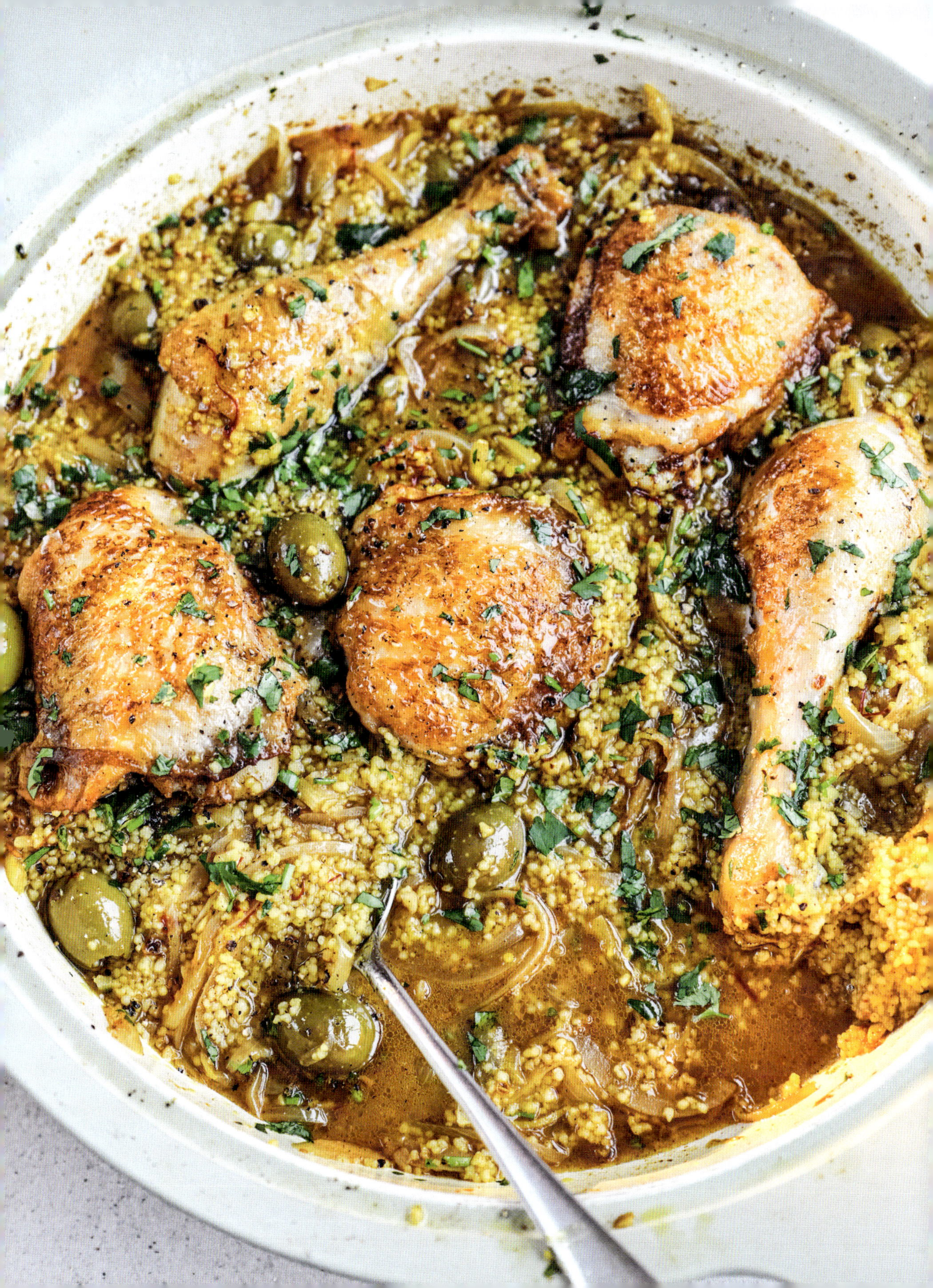

Burnt Lime Steak Fajitas

Serves 2
Takes 25 minutes

Use a non-stick frying pan

1 large ribeye or sirloin steak
3 tsp lime chipotle paste
4 tortilla wraps
4 limes
1 red onion
2 peppers (1 red and 1 green)
1 avocado
1 tbsp ground cumin
salt and black pepper

TO SERVE
40g feta
4 tbsp soured cream
pickled jalapeño slices
a handful of coriander leaves

SWAP: We've used a lime chipotle paste, but you can swap it for a regular chipotle paste mixed with the zest of 2 limes.

Scan for more tasty recipes like this one

Some sort of magic happens when you burn citrus – you get this incredible smoky flavour yet the juice of the fruit itself actually becomes sweeter and milder. That incredible juice is going to help you make the best fajitas of your life.

01. Take the steak out of the fridge, season generously and rub the lime chipotle paste all over. Set aside.

02. Heat the frying pan until hot, then, one at a time, toast the tortilla wraps for 30 seconds on each side to warm through. Wrap in a clean tea towel to keep warm.

03. Halve the limes, then place in the pan, cut-sides down, and cook for 3–4 minutes until deeply charred. Remove from the pan and set aside.

04. While the limes are charring, thinly slice the red onion, then deseed and thinly slice the peppers. Halve the avocado, remove the stone and thinly slice the flesh.

05. Pop the steak straight into the pan over a medium heat and cook for 3 minutes on each side until it is deeply golden and slightly charred (this will give you a medium steak). Remove the steak to a chopping board and leave to rest.

06. Increase the heat to high, then add the onion, peppers and cumin. Season generously. Sauté for 4–6 minutes until softened, using a wooden spoon to really scrape up all the burnt bits of flavour from the bottom of the pan (this will infuse instant smokiness to the dish). Turn off the heat and squeeze 2 halves of the burnt limes over the vegetables.

07. Slice the steak against the grain, then assemble your fajitas with the sliced avocado, crumbled feta, soured cream, pickled jalapeños and coriander leaves. Squeeze over the remaining burnt limes and enjoy!

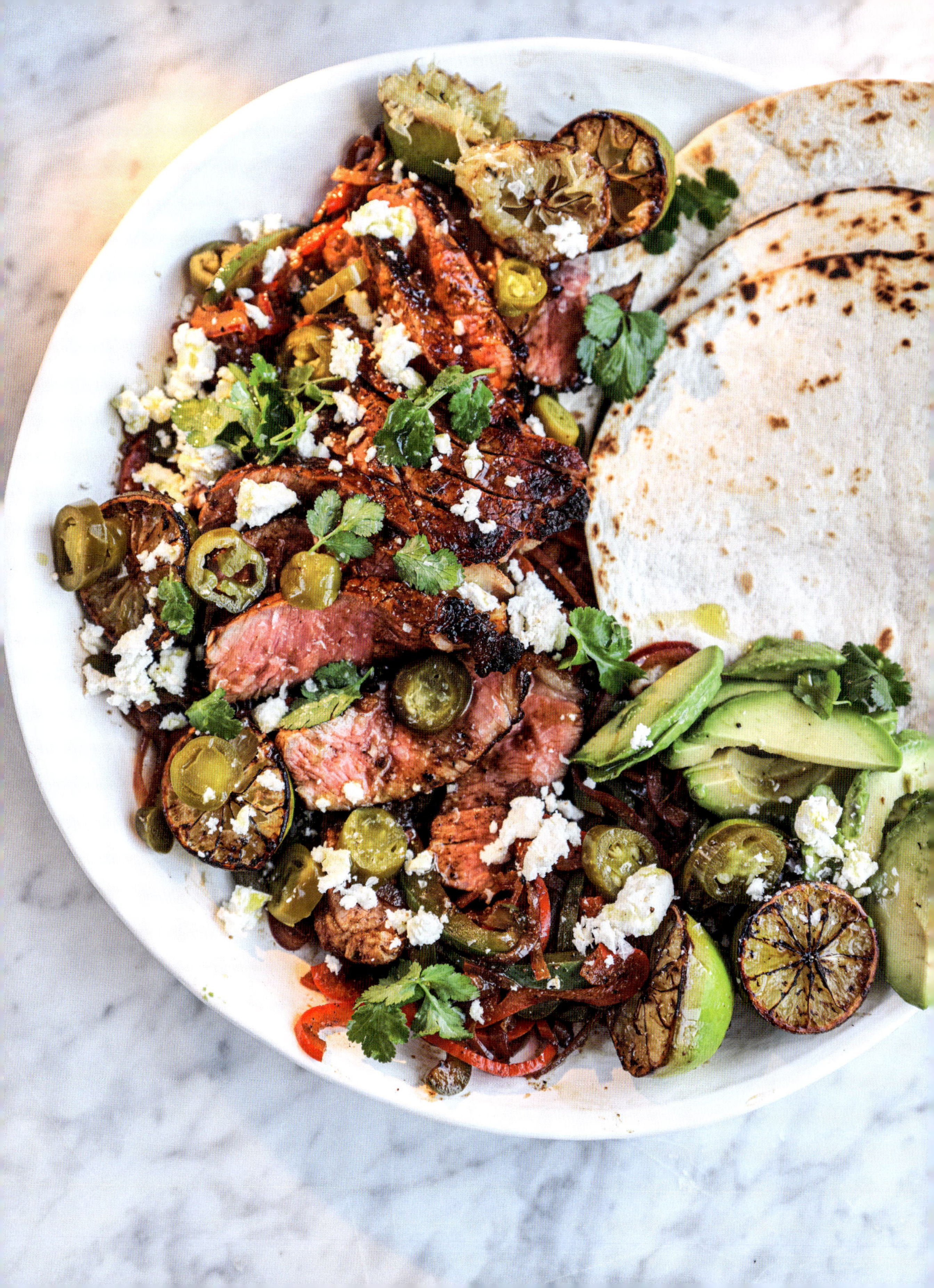

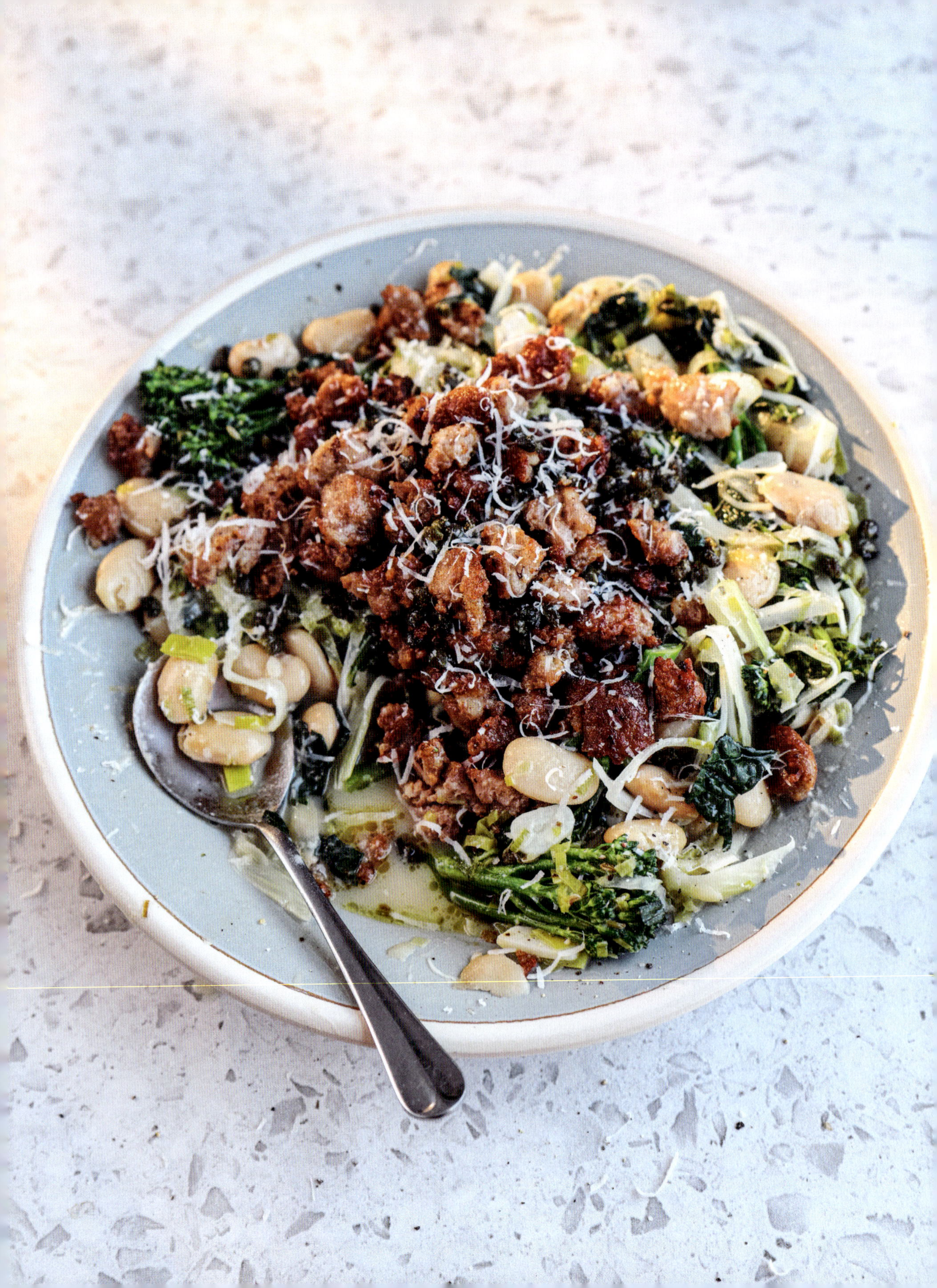

Sausage, Beans + Greens

Serves 4
Takes 35 minutes

Use a large frying pan

Gluten-free

4 tbsp extra virgin olive oil
500g pork sausages (check the label if making gluten-free)
80g capers
1 leek
1 fennel bulb
6 garlic cloves
100g cavolo nero
200g Tenderstem broccoli
1 tsp fennel seeds
1 x 570g jar of butter beans, or 2 x 400g tins of butter beans
60g Parmesan, plus extra to serve
2 tbsp sherry vinegar
salt and black pepper

Scan for more tasty recipes like this one

You know we love squishing sausages out of their skins and getting them all crispety-crunchety, and this time we've added capers into the mix for a briny kick. Once the sausage is looking golden and brown, you're going to make a speedy bean stew with leek, fennel, butter beans, kale and broccoli. That's what we call a good time.

01. Heat the olive oil in the frying pan over a medium heat. Remove the sausages from their skins and crumble into the pan, then add the capers and cook for 7–10 minutes until the sausage meat is golden and crisp.

02. Meanwhile, thinly slice the leek and fennel and finely grate the garlic. Strip the cavolo nero leaves from the woody stems and shred. Cut the broccoli into 5cm chunks.

03. When golden, remove the sausage meat and capers from the pan with a slotted spoon and set aside on a plate lined with kitchen paper.

04. Add the leek and fennel to the pan and cook for 5 minutes until softened. Add the garlic and fennel seeds and cook for a further 1–2 minutes until fragrant. Stir in the broccoli and butter beans along with the liquid from the jar and 200ml water. Simmer for 5–7 minutes until the broccoli starts to soften, then stir in the cavolo nero and cook for 2 minutes until wilted.

05. Grate the Parmesan into the pan. Add the vinegar and mix really well, then season to taste.

06. Serve the beans and greens topped with the crumbled sausage and capers, plus some extra grated Parmesan.

Tuna Kewpie Sando

Scan for more tasty recipes like this one

Serves 4
Time 30 minutes

Use a large non-stick frying pan

---

8 slices of thick white bread
150g grated Cheddar cheese
salt and black pepper

FOR THE TUNA MAYO SALAD
2 celery sticks
½ red onion
5 tbsp Kewpie mayo
1 tbsp English mustard
1 tbsp soy sauce
1 tbsp sesame oil, plus extra to fry
1 tbsp hot sauce
160g tinned tuna in olive oil, drained

SWAP: Kewpie mayo is a Japanese mayo that has become more popular and accessible. It's similar to regular mayo but much creamier, and more savoury. It is worth seeking out, but you could swap it here for regular mayo.

A Japanese-inspired take on a tuna mayo sandwich. With a little heat, a little crunch and a creamy layer of cheese, this sandwich is perfectly simple yet unmistakably comforting and nostalgic. This makes quite a lot of tuna salad, mind – so feel free to keep some in the fridge for round two the next day.

01. First, make the tuna mayo salad. Finely chop the celery and red onion, then tip into a bowl. Add all the remaining ingredients with some good cracks of black pepper, then whip everything together, creating fine flakes of tuna.

02. To assemble, divide the tuna mayo salad between 4 slices of bread, top with the cheese and the other slices of bread.

03. Heat a drizzle of sesame oil in the frying pan over a medium heat and add 2 sandos, cheese-side down to help it melt faster (keep an eye on it as it toasts quickly and can burn), cooking for 2–3 minutes, pressing down occasionally, until the bread is golden.

04. Carefully flip the sandos over and toast on the other side for a further 2–3 minutes until the crispy, golden and the cheese has melted. Repeat with the remaining sandwiches. Slice in half and enjoy.

EASY ONES

Sweet Potato + Black Bean Traybake

Scan for more tasty recipes like this one

Serves 4
Takes 1 hour 50 minutes

Use a roasting tin

Gluten-free

The ultimate midweek meal and, IMO, proof that minimal effort can still mean maximum flavour. It's got a couple of cheat codes in there – chipotle paste, chorizo and pickled jalapeños – ingredients that always take a dish from nice to seriously delicious.

4 large sweet potatoes
1 x 400g tin of black beans
2 tbsp chipotle paste
100g chorizo (check the label if making gluten-free)
2 tbsp butter
1 tsp smoked paprika
salt, black pepper and olive oil

TO SERVE
spring onions
100ml soured cream
coriander
2 tbsp pickled jalapeño slices
1 lime

01. Preheat the oven to 220°C/200°C fan. Prick the sweet potatoes with a fork and rub with olive oil, then sprinkle with a little salt. Place in the roasting tin and bake for 1–1½ hours, depending on the size of your potatoes, until the potatoes are cooked and soft.

02. Meanwhile, drain the black beans, mix with the chipotle paste and 2 tablespoons of water and season with salt and pepper. Slice the chorizo.

03. Remove the sweet potatoes from the oven and slice open. Spoon ½ tablespoon of butter, a pinch of paprika and salt into the middle of each. Use a fork to mash into the flesh a little.

04. Spoon the beans into the potatoes, and top with the slices of chorizo, then return to the oven for a final 10 minutes.

05. Slice the spring onions. Top the sweet potatoes with soured cream, coriander, pickled jalapeño slices and spring onion slices. Serve with the lime, sliced into wedges.

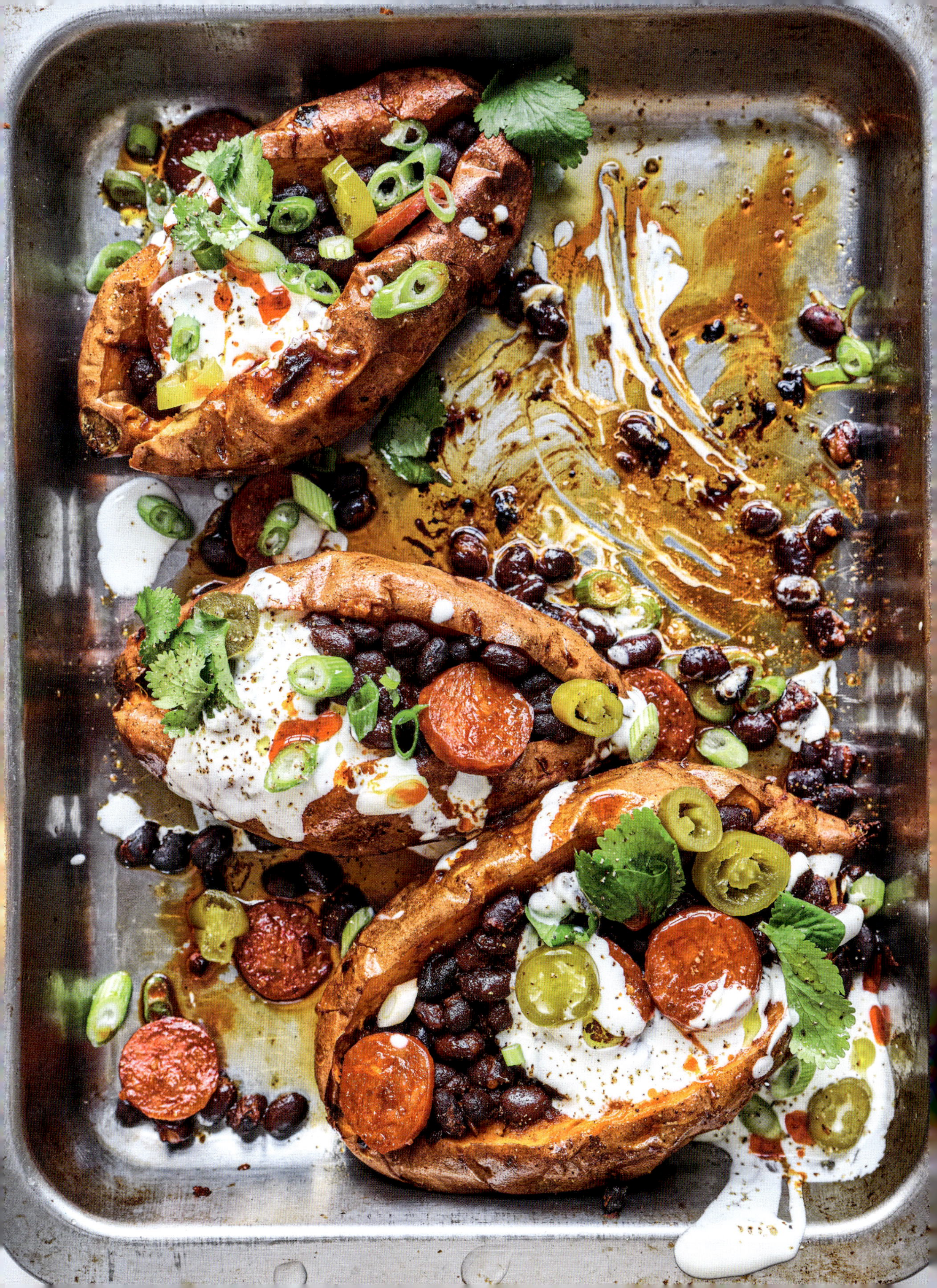

SPEED
ON
SP

Y ES
'EEDY
ONES

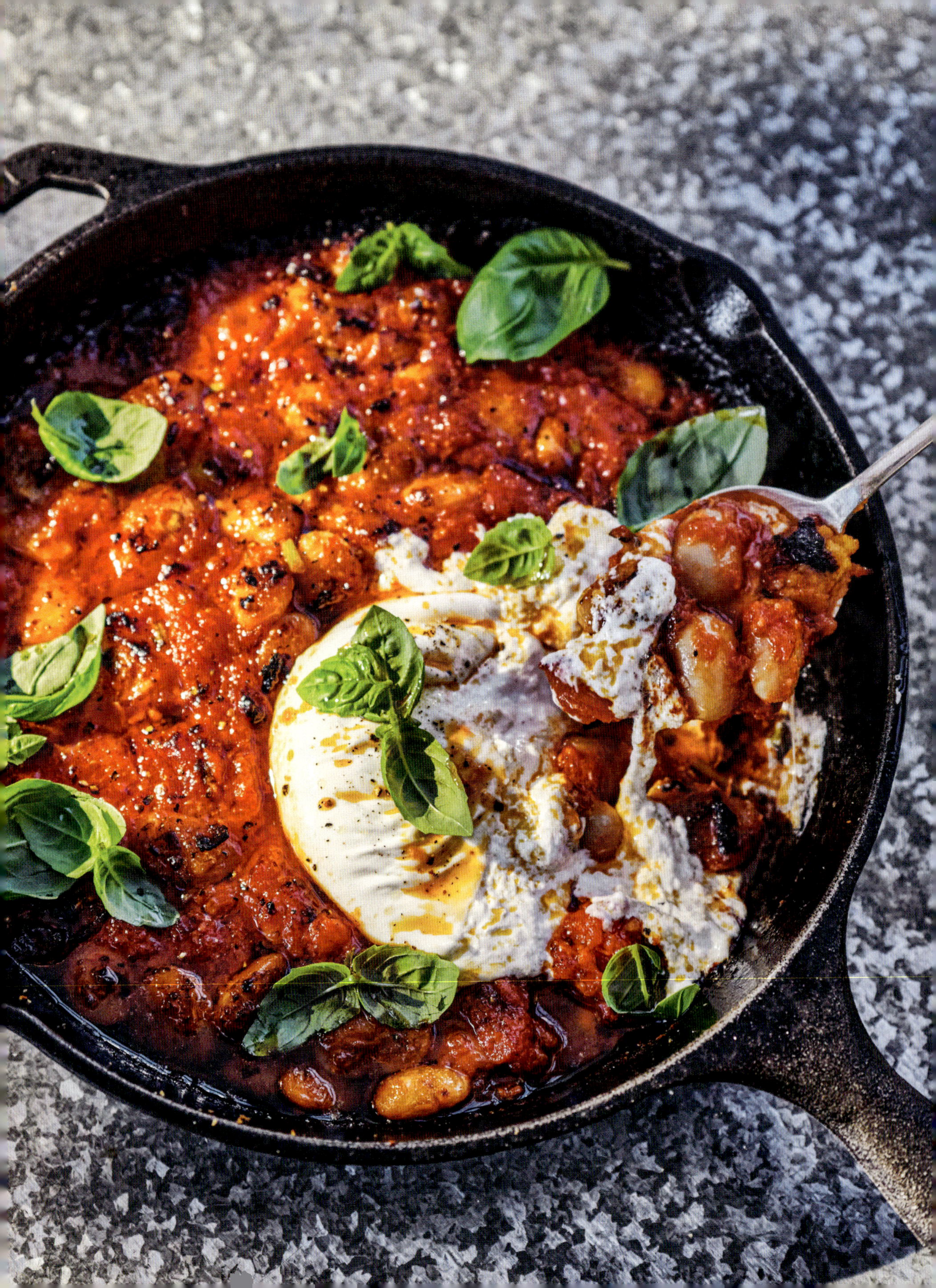

Beans Marinara

Serves 4
Takes 30 minutes

Use a deep ovenproof frying pan

Gluten-free, Veggie

20g basil
6 garlic cloves
5 tbsp extra virgin olive oil
2 x 400g tins of plum tomatoes
1 tsp sugar
1 tbsp red wine vinegar
1 x 700g jar (or 2 x 400g tins) of butter beans, drained
1 x 150g burrata (you can use vegan burrata to make this vegan)
salt and black pepper

Scan for more tasty recipes like this one

Some of the tastiest marinara sauces in the world take hours to come together. Not this one. Sticking the tomatoey beans under the grill for 10 minutes gives you a nice crispy, smoky flavour with none of the effort. A great dish to lean on when you're feeling a bit fatigued at the thought of having spaghetti for dinner again.

01. Separate the basil stalks, finely chop the stalks and tear the leaves. Set both aside.

02. Finely grate or chop the garlic and add to the frying pan with the olive oil. Bring up to a medium heat, then fry for 1 minute until fragrant and the garlic is wiggling in the pan. Throw in the basil stalks and fry for 30 seconds, then add the plum tomatoes, a big pinch of salt and the sugar. Break up the plum tomatoes with the back of a wooden spoon, increase the heat to high and cook for 10 minutes.

03. Meanwhile, preheat your grill to its highest setting.

04. Season the tomatoes with the vinegar, add the butter beans and stir. Season with salt and pepper. Stick the pan under the grill for 10–15 minutes until charred and bubbling.

05. Remove from the grill, tear over the burrata, scatter the basil leaves over the top and enjoy.

'Nduja + Pickled Pepper Pasta

Serves 4
Takes 20 minutes

Use a large pan with a lid

150g chorizo
5 garlic cloves
300g cherry tomatoes
6 pickled guindilla chilli peppers
a few sprigs of oregano
4 tbsp extra virgin olive oil
350g short pasta
700ml hot chicken stock
4 tbsp 'nduja paste
250g mascarpone
60g Parmesan
salt and black pepper

Scan for more tasty recipes like this one

A super-spicy one-pot pasta loaded with 'nduja, chorizo, cherry tomatoes and heaps of guindilla chillies – it's tingly, it's oozy and it's oh-so-satisfying. A short, spirally pasta, such as radiatori or mafalda corta, works well for this.

01. Start with the prep. Chop the chorizo into 0.5cm rounds, then finely chop the garlic. Halve the cherry tomatoes and finely slice the chillies. Strip the leaves from the oregano sprigs.

02. Heat the olive oil in the pan over a medium heat, add the garlic and chorizo and fry for 3–5 minutes until fragrant and the chorizo has released its red oil.

03. Add the tomatoes and most of the chillies and oregano (reserving some of both for garnish), the pasta, stock and 'nduja paste to the pan. Season generously, cover with the lid and bubble away, stirring occasionally, for 10–12 minutes until the pasta is al dente.

04. Remove the lid, add the mascarpone and toss vigorously to make sure most of the liquid is absorbed. Grate in most of the Parmesan and toss again until you have a nice glossy sauce.

05. Sprinkle with the reserved chillies and oregano, then grate over the remaining Parmesan and to serve.

SPEEDY ONES

91

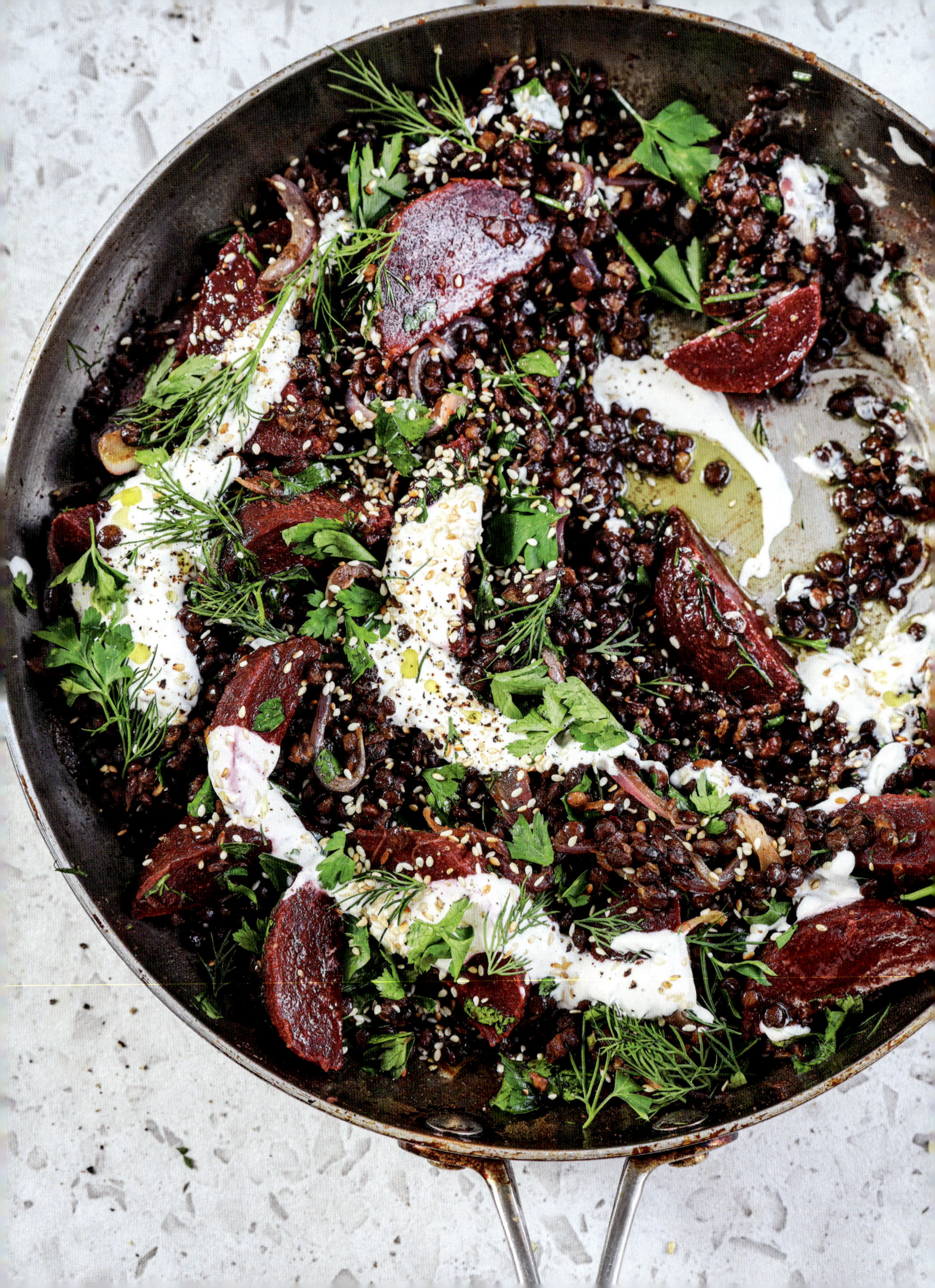

Beetroot + Lentils with Tahini Yoghurt

Scan for more tasty recipes like this one

Serves 4
Takes 30 minutes

Use a large non-stick frying pan

Gluten-free, Vegan

1 red onion
2 garlic cloves
olive oil
15g flat leaf parsley
15g dill
2 x 250g packs of cooked beetroot
1 tsp cumin seeds
1 tsp ground coriander
3 x 200g pouches of cooked Puy lentils
1 lemon
2 tbsp tahini
100g vegan yoghurt
toasted sesame seeds
chilli flakes, to serve
salt and black pepper

This dish ticks all the boxes of a speedy one-pan dish. Super easy, delicious and ready in less than 30 minutes. It happens to be vegan, but you can use dairy yoghurt if you like.

01. Peel and finely chop the red onion and garlic. Add a big glug of olive oil into the frying pan over a medium-high heat. Add the chopped onion along with a big pinch of salt and fry for 10 minutes, until totally softened.

02. Meanwhile, finely chop most of the herbs, reserving a few for the top. Slice each beetroot into 6 wedges.

03. Add the garlic, along with the spices, and cook for 2 minutes further, then add the beetroot wedges and toss well. Cook for another 2 minutes, then tip in the pouches of Puy lentils along with juice of $\frac{1}{2}$ the lemon and 2 tablespoons of water. Cook for 2–3 minutes, stirring well until everything is hot. Stir through the herbs and season well with salt and pepper. Taste and add more lemon juice to taste.

04. Whisk the tahini into the yoghurt and season well, adding a splash of water to loosen it to drizzle-able consistency.

05. Drizzle the tahini yoghurt over the lentils, then finish with toasted sesame seeds and chilli flakes before serving.

Rabokki

Scan for more tasty recipes like this one

Serves 2
Takes 10 minutes

Use a deep saucepan

Vegan

2 spring onions
150g shiitake mushrooms
2 x 100g–120g packets of instant ramen noodles (check for vegan and veggie verisions)
150g Korean rice cakes
2 tbsp gochujang or ssamjang
100g kimchi
1 tbsp sesame seeds

Rabokki is a Korean mash-up dish – even the name is a mash-up, a cross between ramyun (ramen) and tteokbokki (spicy rice cakes). Super spicy, super chewy and comforting – this makes a great work-from-home lunch.

01. Separate the spring onions into the white and green parts. Cut the white parts into 2cm lengths, then thinly slice the greens. Halve the shiitake mushrooms, or quarter if large.

02. Pour 800ml of freshly boiled water into the saucepan and set over a high heat. Add the noodles and pour in their flavour sachets. Add the rice cakes, gochujang, mushrooms and white parts of the spring onions. Simmer for 4–6 minutes, stirring occasionally, until the noodles are cooked. Add 100–200ml water if you want to loosen it a little.

03. Divide between 2 bowls and spoon in the kimchi, then scatter with the spring onion greens and sesame seeds.

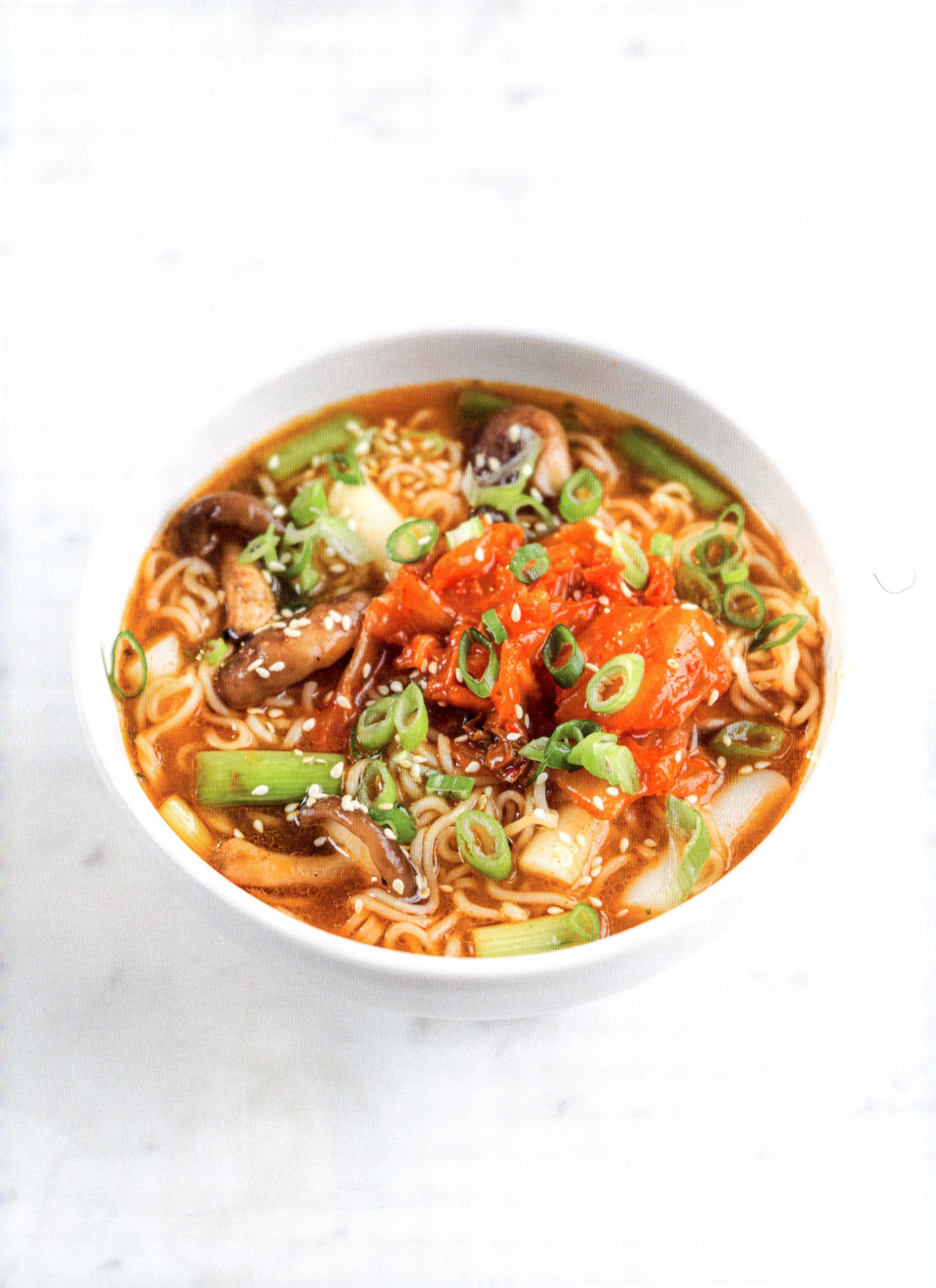

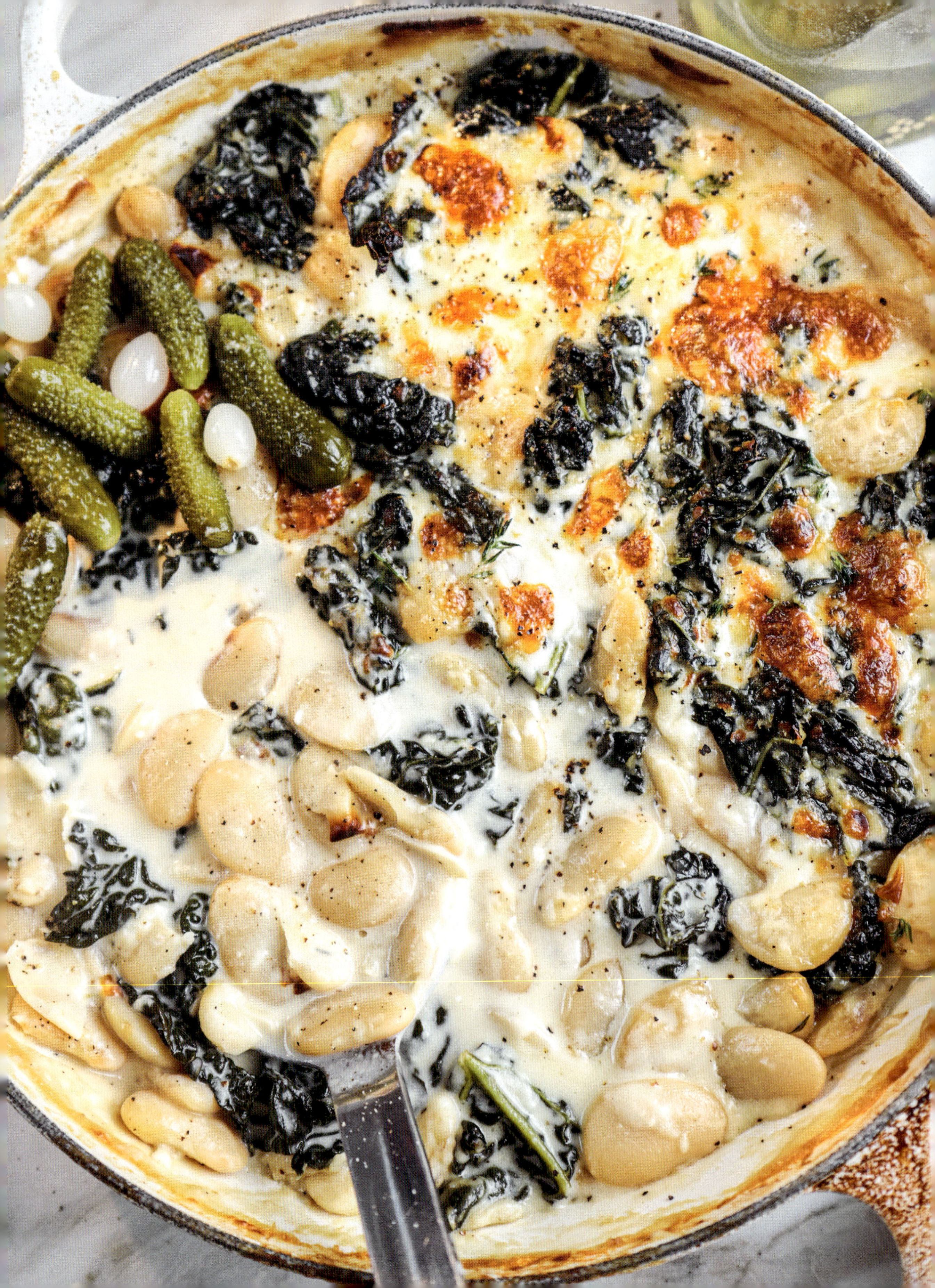

Fondue-ish Butter Beans + Cornichons

Serves 4
Takes 30 minutes

Use an ovenproof casserole dish with a lid

Veggie

3 x 400g tins of butter beans
4 garlic cloves
200g cavolo nero, kale or spinach
2 tbsp olive oil
75ml dry white wine
35g vegetarian Italian hard cheese or Parmesan
100g Taleggio (swap for a vegetarian Brie if making this for veggies)
4 sprigs of thyme
100g mascarpone
1 lemon
salt and black pepper
small jar of cornichons, to serve
crusty bread, to serve

Scan for more tasty recipes like this one

Consider this the essence of fondue, bulked out with beans and finished off with plenty of cornichons. Best served up with a vinegary salad to cut through all the richness because, boy, is she cheesy.

01. Drain 2 of the tins of butter beans. Finely slice the garlic, then strip the cavolo nero or kale leaves from the woody stems and roughly chop, finely chopping the stalks (no need to bother if using spinach).

02. Heat the oil in the casserole dish over a medium-high heat, add the garlic and cook for 3 minutes until golden. Pour in the wine and cook until the liquid has reduced by half, around 3–4 minutes.

03. Preheat the grill to its highest setting.

04. Pour in the undrained tin of butter beans with the liquid and then add the drained butter beans and the cavolo nero. Cover with the lid and cook for 5 minutes, stirring occasionally.

05. Meanwhile, grate the hard cheese and dice the Taleggio. Strip the leaves from the thyme sprigs.

06. Turn off the heat under the casserole, remove the lid and stir through the mascarpone and hard cheese until melted, then add the lemon juice and season well. Dot with the Taleggio and chuck under the grill for 5 minutes until bubbling and golden. Top with the thyme leaves, and a crack of black pepper. Serve with cornichons and bread for dunking.

SPEEDY ONES

Walnut + Za'atar Spaghetti

Scan for more tasty recipes like this one

Serves 4
Takes 20 minutes

Use a deep, wide non-stick frying pan with a lid (you'll need a pan that can fit the whole pasta lengthways)

Veggie

100g walnuts
60g vegetarian Italian hard cheese, Parmesan or Pecorino Romano, plus extra to serve
5 garlic cloves
a few sprigs of thyme
2 tbsp extra virgin olive oil
350g spaghetti
1 lemon
1 tbsp za'atar, plus extra to garnish
30g salted butter
salt and black pepper

This zesty little number is toasty, lemony, rich and incredibly easy to whip up in a flash. Don't skimp on the cheese – it cuts through the acidity and makes this a quick big fat bowl of comfort you'll turn to again and again.

01. Toast the walnuts in the dry frying pan over a medium-high heat for about 2 minutes until fragrant and releasing some of their oils. Tip out onto a chopping board and finely chop. Finely grate the cheese. Set both aside.

02. Finely chop the garlic, then strip the leaves from the thyme sprigs. Heat the olive oil in the pan, add the garlic and thyme leaves and fry for 1–2 minutes until fragrant, but not golden.

03. Pour in 1 litre of boiling water and add the spaghetti, ensuring the pasta is submerged. Cover with the lid and boil for 8–10 minutes, stirring occasionally, then remove the lid and continue to cook for 1–2 minutes until most of the liquid has been absorbed and the pasta is al dente.

04. Zest the lemon into the pan, then squeeze in the juice. Add the toasted walnuts, za'atar, butter and grated cheese and toss vigorously to combine; season if needed.

05. Serve with a sprinkle of extra za'atar and extra grated cheese.

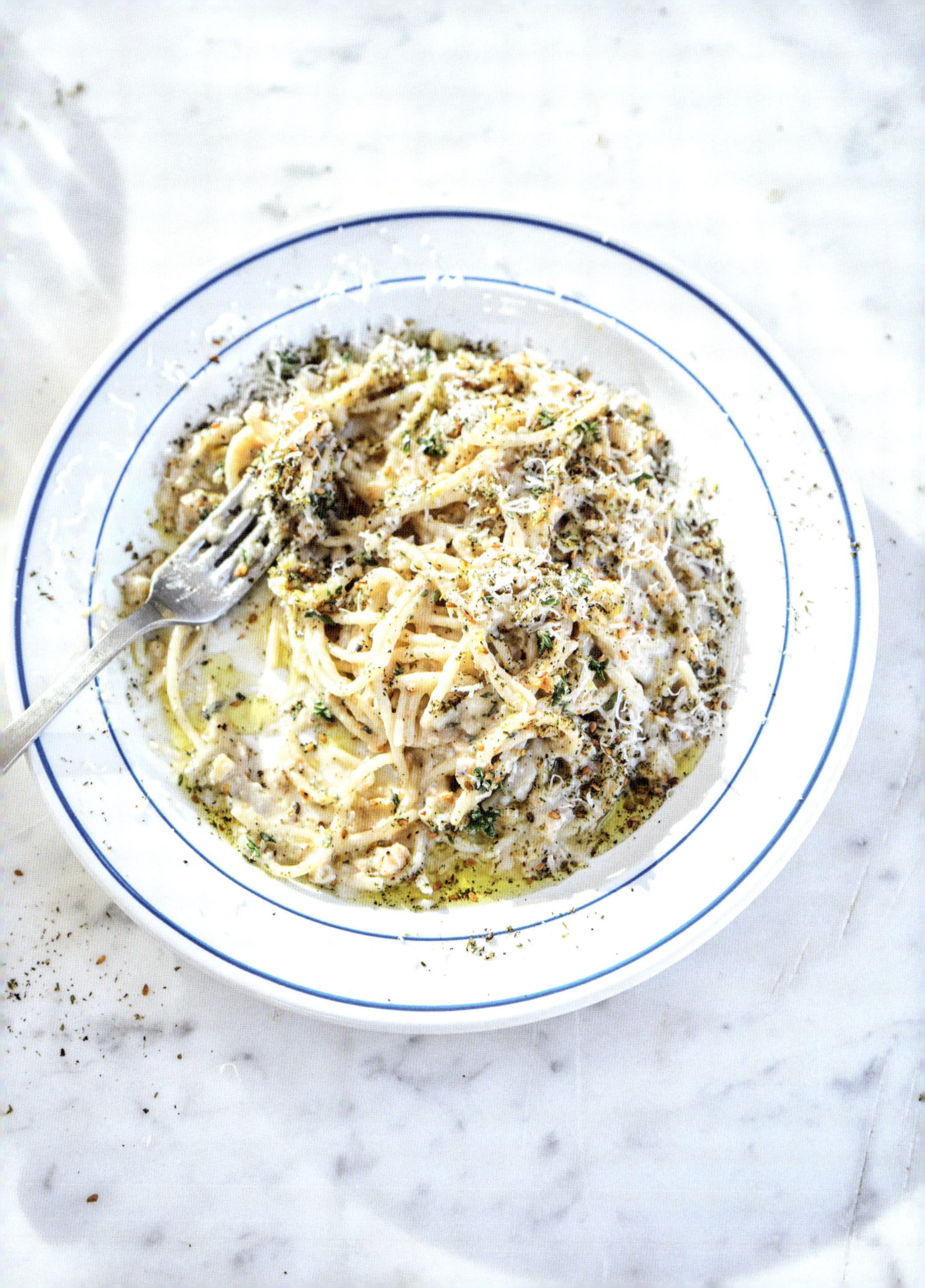

Green Curry Noodles

Scan for more tasty recipes like this one

Serves 4
Takes 20 minutes

Use a large wok

Gluten-free

a handful of salted roasted peanuts
4 spring onions
200g green beans
1 tbsp vegetable oil
2 tbsp tamari
1 tbsp fish sauce (check the label if making this gluten-free)
2 tbsp tamarind paste
2 tbsp Thai green curry paste
2 x 160ml tins coconut cream
1 tbsp caster sugar
500g raw king prawns
300g beansprouts
600g flat rice noodles
2 limes
15g Thai basil leaves, to garnish

We all know that chasing a forkful of pad Thai with a little bite of green curry is one of the best things about eating a Thai takeaway. So, we thought: why not fuse those two dishes together? This spicy, creamy dish delivers a nice and fiery kick. Feel free to swap the prawns for chicken or more veggies if that's what you fancy.

01. Start with your chopping prep. Roughly chop the peanuts and set aside for the garnish. Cut the spring onions into 3–4cm lengths and halve the green beans.

02. Set the wok over a high heat. Once hot, add the oil and green beans and stir-fry for 2 minutes until beginning to char.

03. Add the tamari, fish sauce, tamarind paste, curry paste, coconut cream and sugar and mix well until combined.

04. Throw in the prawns and cook for 1 minute, coating well. Add the beansprouts, spring onions and noodles and toss vigorously for 2 minutes until the prawns are pink, the sauce is combined and piping hot.

05. Juice the limes and use to season the noodles.

06. Garnish with the chopped peanuts and Thai basil leaves and serve immediately.

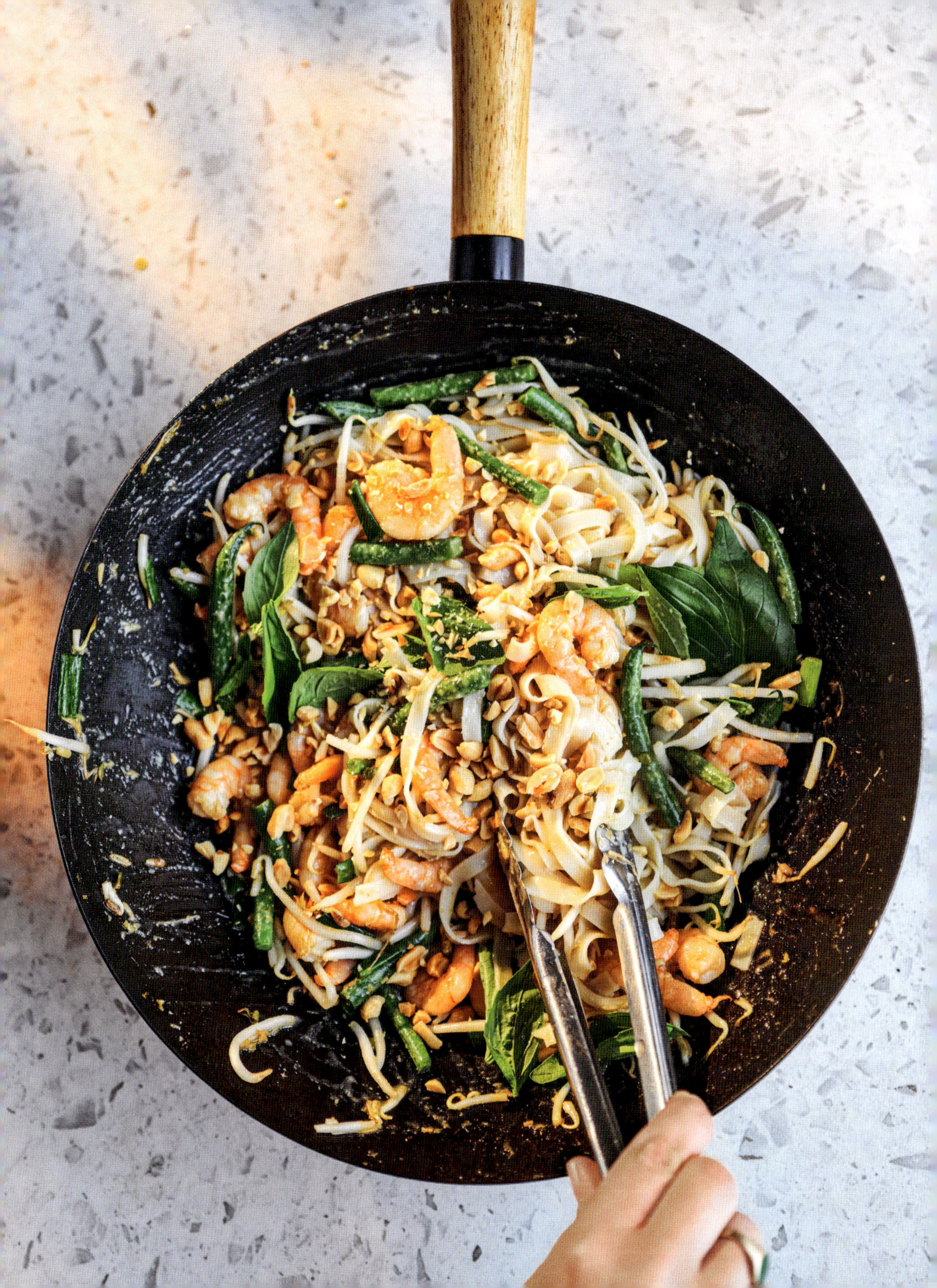

Herby Fried Rice

Serves 2
Takes 20 minutes

Use a large non-stick frying pan

Veggie, Gluten-free

200g Tenderstem broccoli
2 garlic cloves
1 green chilli
4 eggs
25g mint
25g flat leaf parsley
50g smoked almonds, to serve
2 tbsp olive oil
1 tsp fennel seeds
2 x 250g microwaveable pouches of brown rice
1 lemon
salt and black pepper

Scan for more tasty recipes like this one

This is a mash-up between a lot of different dishes – it's essentially egg-fried rice meets a herby rice salad. It's so simple, perfect for when you need something quick but super satisfying and delicious in the middle of the week.

01. Slice the broccoli into 3cm lengths. Finely slice the garlic cloves. Finely slice the green chilli. Whisk the eggs together in a bowl and season well with salt and pepper. Roughly chop the herbs. Roughly chop or crush the almonds and set aside.

02. Add the olive oil to the frying pan over a medium-high heat. Add the broccoli to the pan along with a big pinch of salt and fry for 2–3 minutes, tossing regularly, until bright green. Add the garlic, fennel seeds and most of the green chilli, saving a little to serve. Toss well, then add the brown rice, along with 2 tablespoons of water. Toss for 2–3 minutes further, using your spoon or spatula to break up the rice. Push the mix to the side of the pan.

03. Tip the eggs into the cleared side of the pan, allow to sit for a minute, then pull your spoon or spatula through the eggs to create chunky scrambled eggs. Toss through the rice.

04. Remove from the heat, add the herbs and lemon juice and stir everything together. Taste and season with plenty of salt and black pepper. Scatter with the remaining green chilli and the smoked almonds.

SPEEDY ONES

103

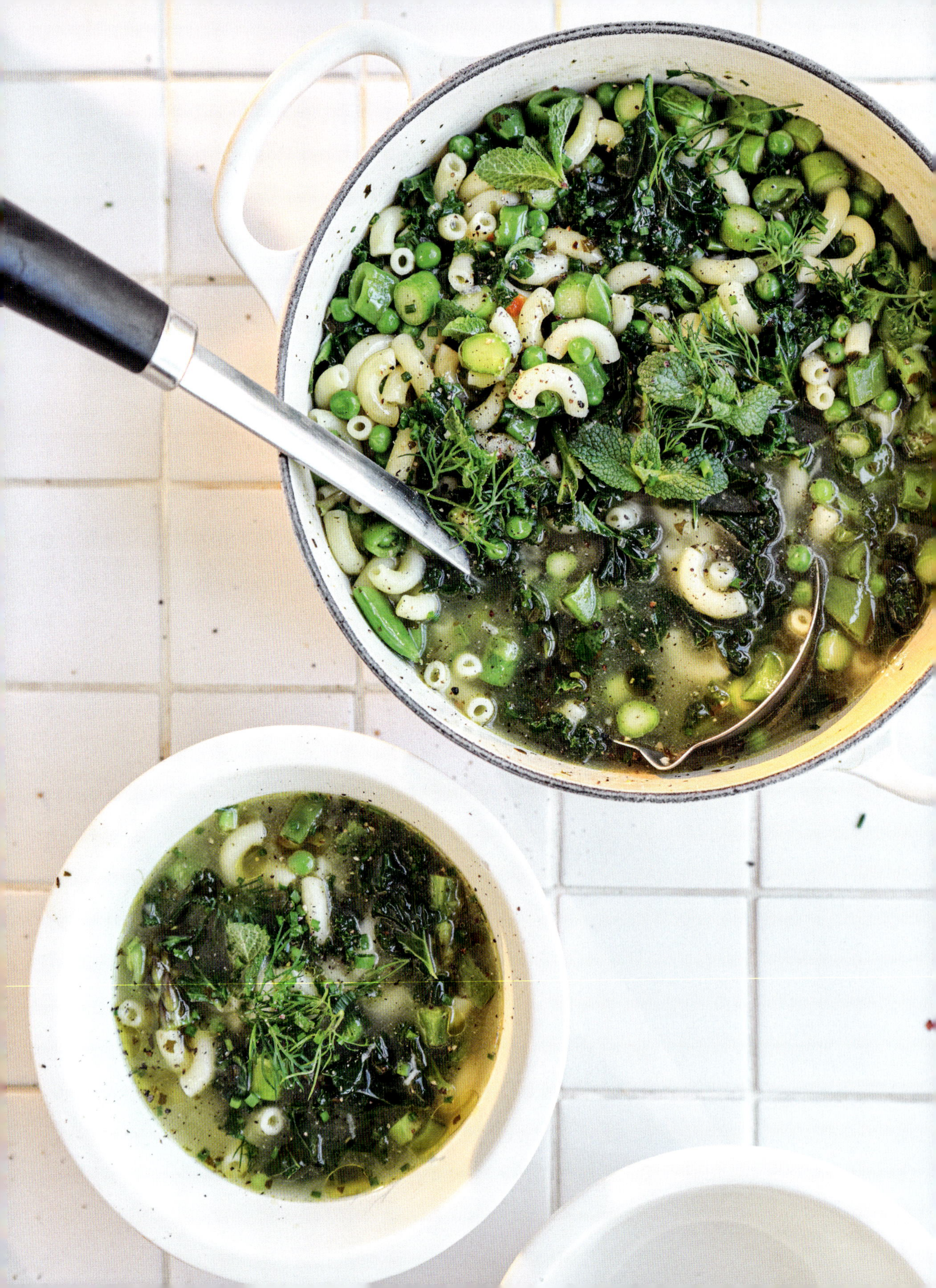

Mint-estrone

Scan for more tasty recipes like this one

Serves 4
Takes 15 minutes

Use a deep saucepan

Vegan

1 tbsp extra virgin olive oil, plus extra to drizzle
2 garlic cloves
3 tbsp mint sauce
2 litres hot vegetable stock
300g small pasta (like ditalini)
200g sugar snap peas
a bunch of asparagus (about 250g)
100g kale
a small handful of chives
100g frozen peas
1 lemon
a small handful of dill leaves
a small handful of mint leaves
salt and black pepper

TIP: You can add a splash more hot water or stock to make this more brothy, especially if reheating it.

We had to make this recipe for two reasons. Firstly, the pun was too good to pass over. Secondly, we had to find a way of using up that rogue jar of mint sauce which only comes out of the fridge once a year for your Easter roast. That sauce is the base of this spring minestrone, packed with crisp and tender vegetables and loaded with herbs.

01. Heat the olive oil in the saucepan over a medium heat, then grate in the garlic and fry for 1 minute until fragrant. Add the mint sauce and cook for 30 seconds. Pour in the stock and bring to the boil.

02. Add the pasta and boil for 6–8 minutes, or until the paste is just al dente.

03. While the pasta is cooking, cut the sugar snaps and asparagus (snap off the woody ends first) into small pieces, roughly the same size as a pea. Strip the kale leaves from the woody stems and roughly chop, finely chopping the stems. Finely chop the chives and set aside.

04. Once the pasta is ready, add all the prepared vegetables and the peas to the pan and cook for 1–2 minutes until just tender. Juice the lemon and add half to the pan, then season to taste, adding the rest of the lemon juice if you like.

05. Ladle into 4 bowls and scatter over all of the herbs. Serve with an extra drizzle of olive oil.

Chipotle Chicken + Bean Tacos

Scan for more tasty recipes like this one

Serves 2
Takes 15 minutes

Use a large non-stick frying pan

300g cooked chicken
2 garlic cloves
2 tbsp chipotle paste
1 x 200g microwaveable pouch of refried beans, or 1 x 400g tin
2 large flour tortillas
1 tbsp olive oil
150g ready-grated mixed Cheddar cheese and mozzarella
salt and black pepper

TO SERVE
a small bunch of coriander sprigs
hot sauce (optional)
1 pack of Tex-Mex dips

SWAP: You can swap the cooked chicken for the same weight of roasted veggies or a pack of raw king prawns.

This recipe is inspired by the gringa taco – a Mexican dish made by grilling a flour tortilla that's stuffed with pork, pineapple and cheese – and it's an absolute winner. Once you've tried it for yourself, and seen how easy it is, you'll be making this every week.

01. Shred the cooked chicken, then put it into a bowl. Finely slice the garlic, then add to the bowl. Spoon in the chipotle paste, season well and give it a good mix. Set aside.

02. Heat the refried beans according to the packet instructions.

03. Meanwhile, set the frying pan over a medium-high heat. Once hot, add the tortillas, one at a time, and toast for 15–30 seconds on each side. Transfer to a plate.

04. Pour half of the oil into the pan, then scatter in half of the chicken mixture in an even layer. Fry for 3 minutes, tossing every now and again, until it is starting to crisp. Arrange the chicken in a single layer in the middle-ish of the pan (about the size of your tortillas). Spoon over half of the refried beans, then scatter with half of the cheese. Put a tortilla on top and press to stick. Cook for 30 seconds to melt the cheese, then carefully flip onto a plate. Repeat with the remaining ingredients.

05. Put the tacos onto plates, tear over the coriander and add hot sauce, if you like. Serve with the Tex-Mex dips. Winner!

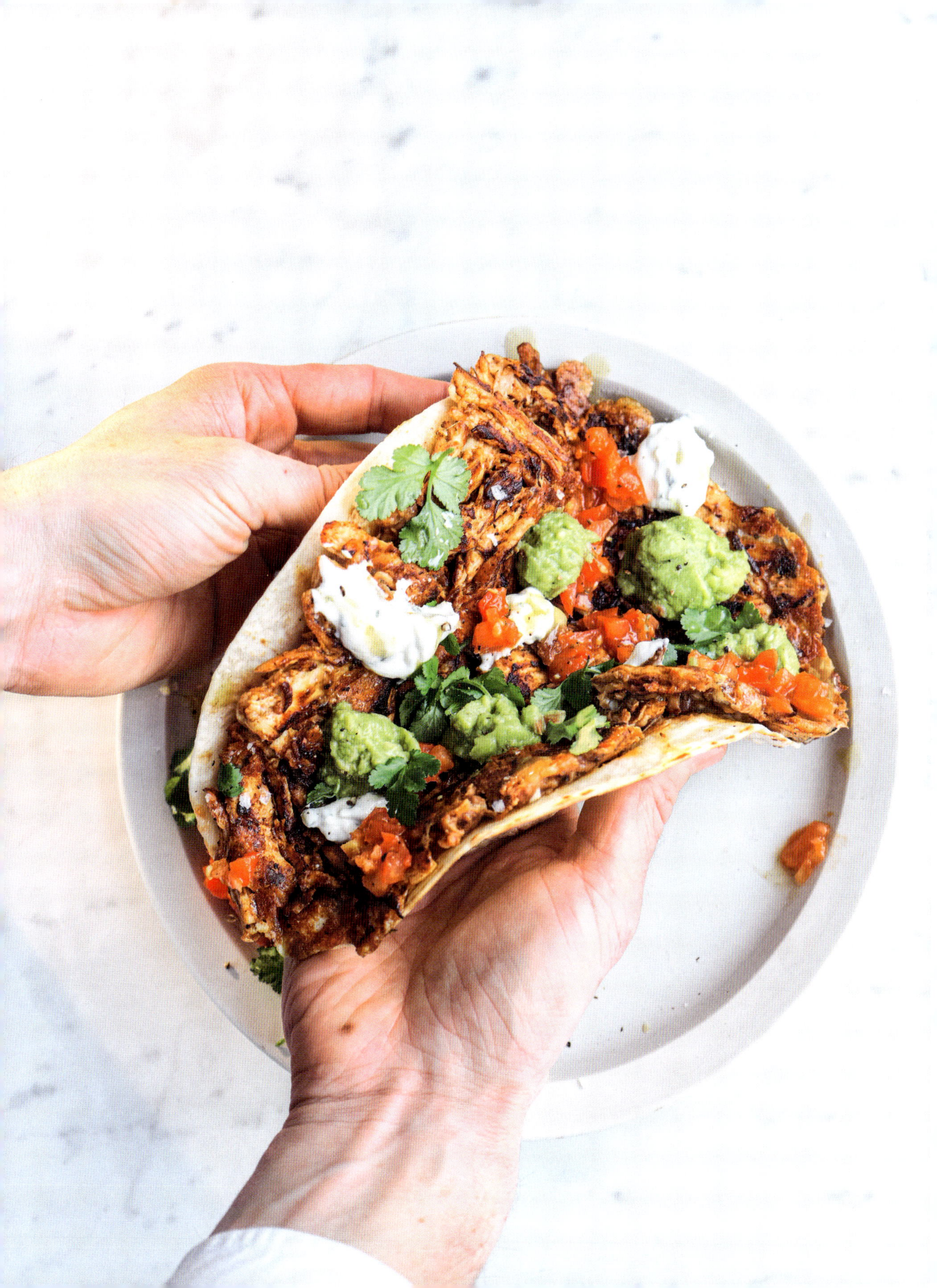

SPEEDY ONES

Bacon + Egg Yaki Udon

Serves 2
Takes 30 minutes

Use a large wok or frying pan

6 smoked streaky bacon rashers
1 onion
1 small carrot
50g shiitake mushrooms
3 spring onions
¼ large cabbage, Chinese leaf or hispi works best here
3 eggs
2 tbsp neutral-flavoured oil
300g straight-to-wok udon noodles
toasted sesame oil, to drizzle
salt

FOR THE YAKISOBA SAUCE
2 tbsp oyster sauce
2 tbsp Worcestershire sauce
1 tbsp ketchup
2 tbsp soy sauce
1 tsp sugar, or more to taste

Yaki udon is a Japanese stir-fried noodle dish, and one of our favourite weeknight meals. We've combined our favourite elements of an easy, speedy yaki udon with the kind of sauce you'd more typically find in a yakisoba. The result is a delicious noodle mash-up and the epitome of a fridge raid dinner. We've always got a few pieces of streaky bacon hanging around, but throw in any vegetables or protein you like.

01. First, whisk together all the ingredients for the yakisoba sauce. Set aside.

02. Next, prep all the remaining ingredients. Roughly slice the bacon into strips. Keeping the veg separate, peel and thinly slice the onion, then cut the carrot and the shiitake mushrooms into thin strips. Chop 2 of the spring onions into 5cm lengths and the cabbage leaves into bite-sized pieces. Peel the remaining spring onion into ribbons and set aside.

03. Crack the eggs into a bowl, add a pinch of salt and whisk well.

04. Heat the wok or frying pan over a medium-high heat, add the bacon and a splash of water and cook for 4–6 minutes until lightly golden.

Continued overleaf

Continued from previous page

05. Increase the heat to high and drizzle in 1 tablespoon of the neutral oil, add the onion and carrot and cook for 2 minutes, or until charred. Don't toss the veggies, leave them to char nicely, occasionally flipping them over to char the other side. Add the cabbage and cook for a further 1–2 minutes, or until lightly charred. Add the spring onions and shiitake mushrooms and continue to cook for 1–2 minutes, or until lightly charred.

06. Push the veg and bacon to the side and pour the remaining tablespoon of oil into the centre of the pan. Pour the eggs directly onto the oil and allow to bubble into a puffy omelette. When it has mostly set, break it up into big fluffy pieces of egg and toss with the veggie mix.

07. Pour in the yakisoba sauce around the edge of the wok and toss everything to coat, then add the noodles and immediately toss through. Add a spoon of water to create some steam and cook for 2–3 minutes.

08. Serve garnished with the spring onion ribbons and drizzled with a little toasted sesame oil.

Scan for more tasty recipes like this one

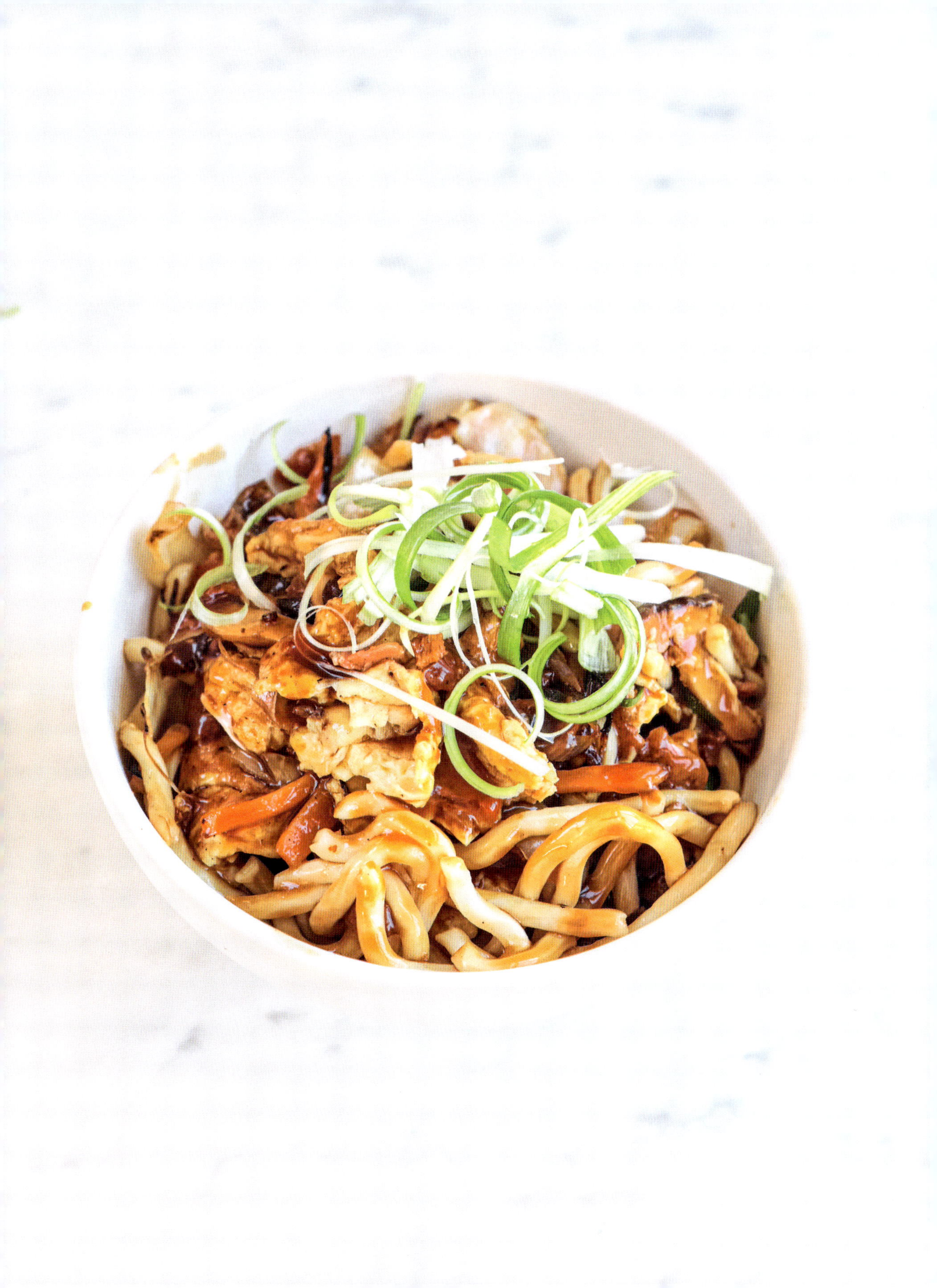

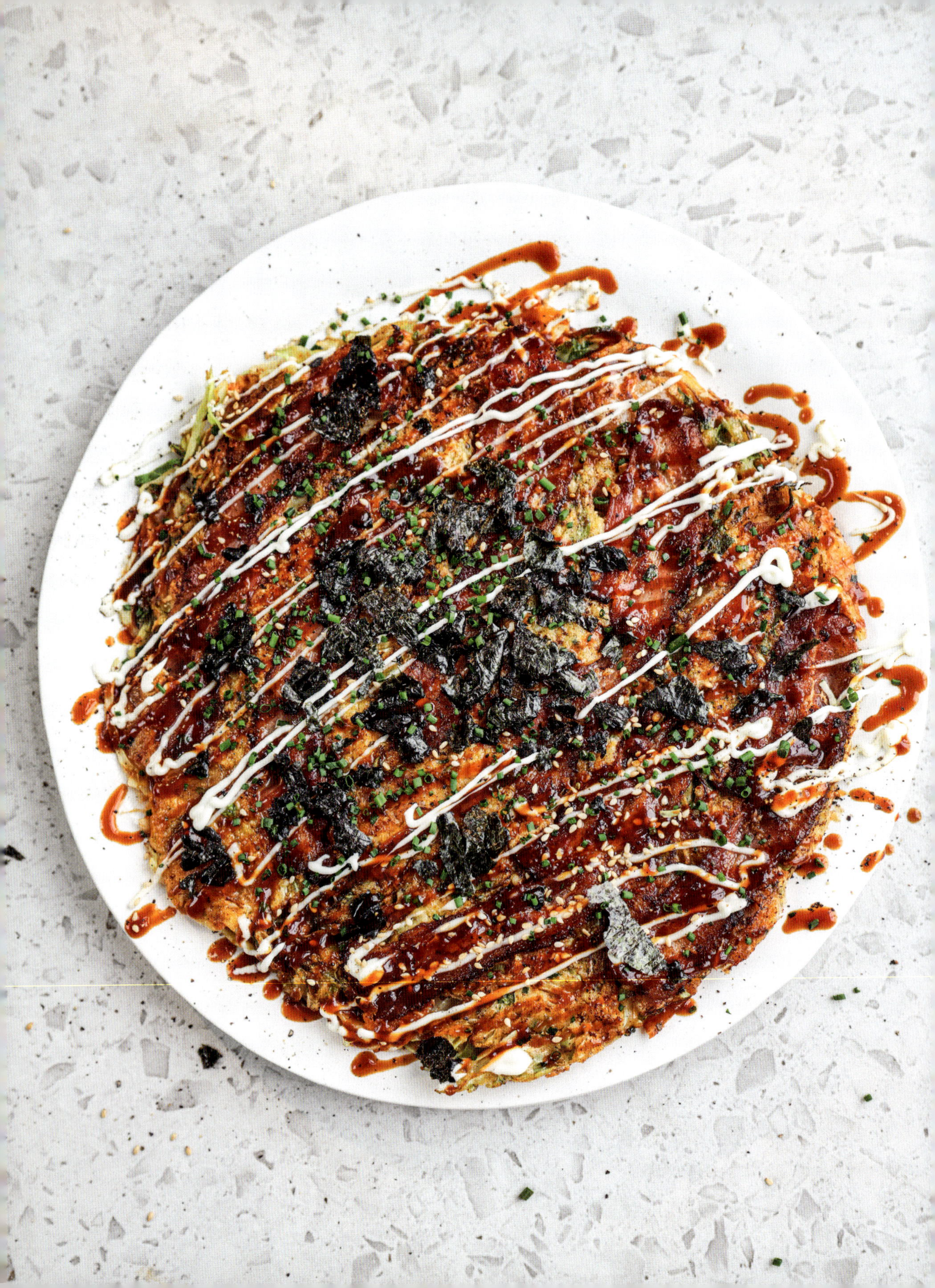

Kimchi Okonomiyaki

Serves 2
Takes 25 minutes

Use a large non-stick frying pan

½ hispi cabbage (also known as sweetheart or pointed cabbage)
10g chives
100g plain flour
1 egg
150g kimchi
1 tsp vegetable oil
6 streaky bacon rashers
3 tbsp ketchup
1½ tbsp Worcestershire sauce
1½ tbsp dark soy sauce
2 tbsp Kewpie mayonnaise (or regular mayonnaise)
1 nori sheet or 5g pack nori seaweed snack thins
salt and black pepper

Scan for more tasty recipes like this one

Okonomiyaki is a savoury Japanese pancake where everything from fresh veggies and pickles to meat or seafood get stirred into an eggy batter and cooked on a hot plate. Our version has crispy bacon on the bottom and tangy kimchi mixed through for a subtle funk. It's a mood.

01. To make the batter, first finely shred the cabbage and finely chop the chives. Tip the flour into a bowl, then crack in the egg, pour in 125ml of water and whisk until smooth. Stir through the kimchi, shredded cabbage and three-quarters of the chives (save the rest for garnish) until evenly combined, then season generously.

02. Heat the oil in the frying pan over a medium-high heat, then add the bacon rashers and cook for 4–6 minutes until beginning to crisp, then flip over.

03. Give the batter a good stir, then spoon into the pan on top of the bacon, gently spreading it so it is about 2cm thick. Cook for 3–4 minutes until it's nice and brown on the bottom; shake the pan a little and use a spatula to loosen and have a peek and to free it from the bottom of the pan.

04. Carefully slide the okonomiyaki onto a plate, then turn the pan upside-down, put over the plate and, in one movement, flip the okonomiyaki into it, so the crispy bacon bottom is now facing up. Put back over the heat and cook for 3–4 minutes until the second side is browned.

05. Meanwhile, to make the sauce, mix together the ketchup, Worcestershire sauce and soy sauce in a bowl, then brush some all over the crispy surface (or just spoon it over instead).

06. Squeeze over the mayo in a nice pattern. Scrunch up the nori and scatter over the surface.

07. Slide onto a plate, sprinkle over the reserved chives and serve with the rest of the sauce on the side.

Veggie Pasta e Ceci

Scan for more tasty recipes like this one

Serves 4
Takes 30 minutes

Use a large saucepan

Veggie

1 onion
1 carrot
2 celery sticks
3 garlic cloves
200g cavolo nero
3 tbsp extra virgin olive oil, plus extra to drizzle
1 tbsp fennel seeds
2 tbsp tomato purée
1 litre hot vegetable stock
1 x 400g tin of chickpeas, drained
100g small pasta (like orzo, tortiglioni or ditalini)
salt and black pepper

TO SERVE
50g vegetarian Italian hard cheese or Parmesan
a handful of flat leaf parsley leaves
1 lemon

This is a remix of pasta e ceci (literally 'pasta with chickpeas') where you can happily swap in any vegetable you like or use up that last bit of chorizo or bacon sitting in your fridge. Filling, comforting and satisfying, this ticks all the autumnal boxes.

01. Start by getting all your veg prepped. Finely chop the onion, carrot and celery and tip into a bowl. Thinly slice the garlic. Strip the cavolo nero leaves from the woody stems and roughly chop, finely chopping the stems.

02. Heat the olive oil in the saucepan over a medium-high heat, then tip in the onion, carrot and celery mix with the cavolo nero stems and a big pinch of salt. Cook for 2–3 minutes until softening, then add the fennel seeds, tomato purée and sliced garlic and cook for another minute.

03. Pour in the stock and bring to the boil. Add the chickpeas and pasta and bubble away, partially covered, for 6 minutes. Stir through the cavolo nero leaves and cook for a further 6–9 minutes until the pasta is just cooked. Season with salt and pepper. You can add a splash more hot water if you want the dish to be brothier.

04. Just before serving, grate the cheese and finely chop the parsley. Zest the lemon, then halve it.

05. Divide the pasta between 4 bowls, then sprinkle over each the cheese, parsley and a little of the lemon zest. Squeeze in a little of the lemon juice and finish with a drizzle of olive oil and a grind of black pepper.

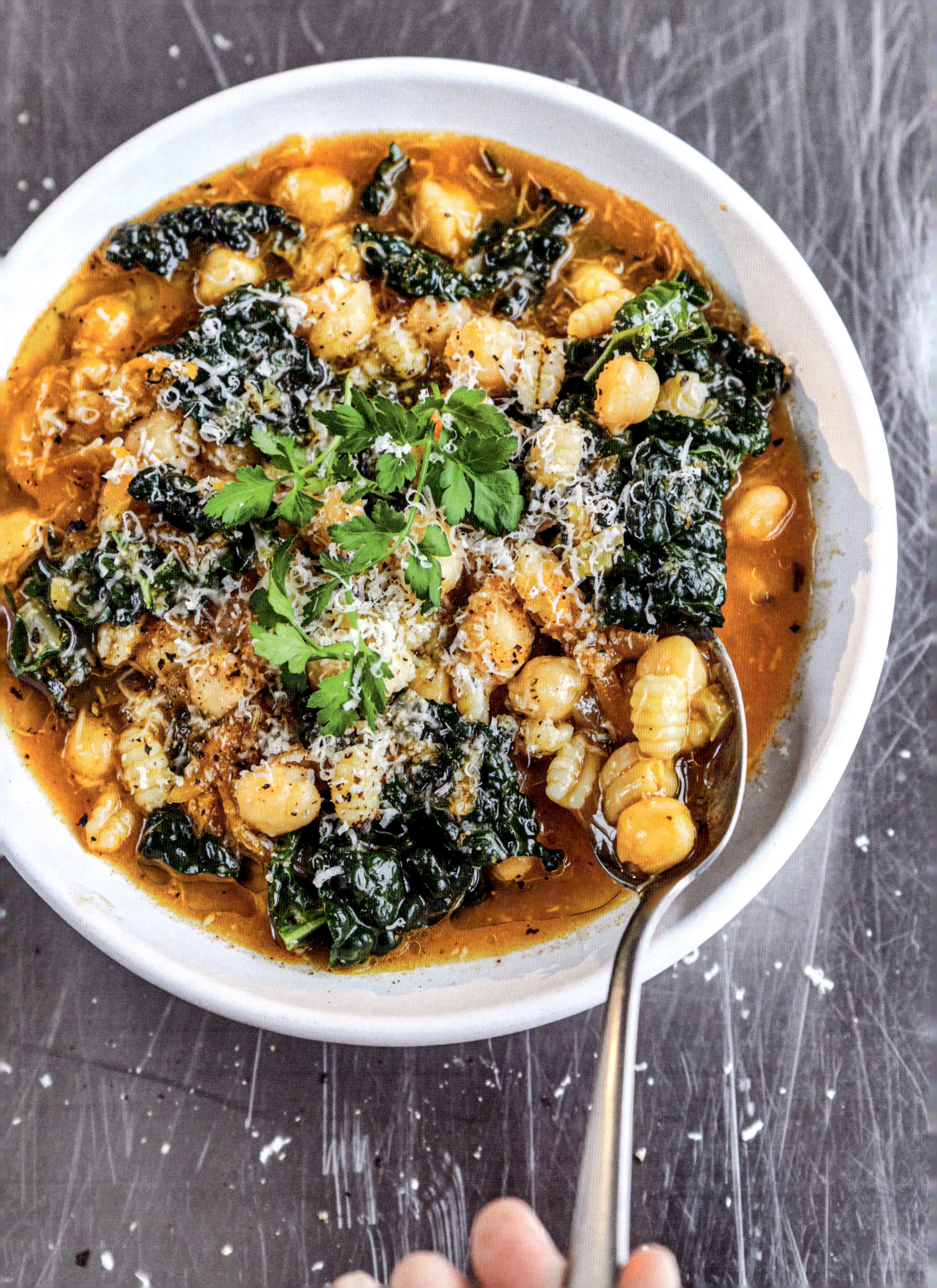

Buffalo Sauce Spaghetti

Serves 4
Takes 20 minutes

Use a wide, deep frying pan (you'll need a pan that can fit the whole pasta lengthways)

Veggie

400g spaghetti
75g butter
100g vegetarian Italian hard cheese or Parmesan, plus extra to serve
1 x 148ml bottle of hot sauce (we use Frank's)
2 tsp garlic granules
salt and black pepper

Scan for more tasty recipes like this one

If you're anything like us, then you'd eat literally anything if it was coated in buffalo sauce – a neon spicy and sharp American hot sauce. It's tangy, it's buttery and it's a damn shame you only ever really see it on dive bar chicken wings. In this recipe, we've ladled that bright orange sauce onto super silky spaghetti with a big handful of cheese. It's as good as it sounds.

01. Pour 1.25 litres of freshly boiled water into the frying pan over a high heat, then lightly season. Add the spaghetti and cook for 12–15 minutes, tossing occasionally, until the spaghetti is just al dente and has absorbed most of the water.

02. Meanwhile, cut the butter into cubes, then put into a bowl. Very finely grate in the cheese, then stir in the hot sauce and garlic granules.

03. Once the pasta is al dente, spoon the butter sauce into the pan, turn off the heat and cook and toss for a few minutes until the sauce is really glossy and nicely coating the pasta; season a little if needed.

04. Divide between 4 bowls and serve with extra grated cheese over the top.

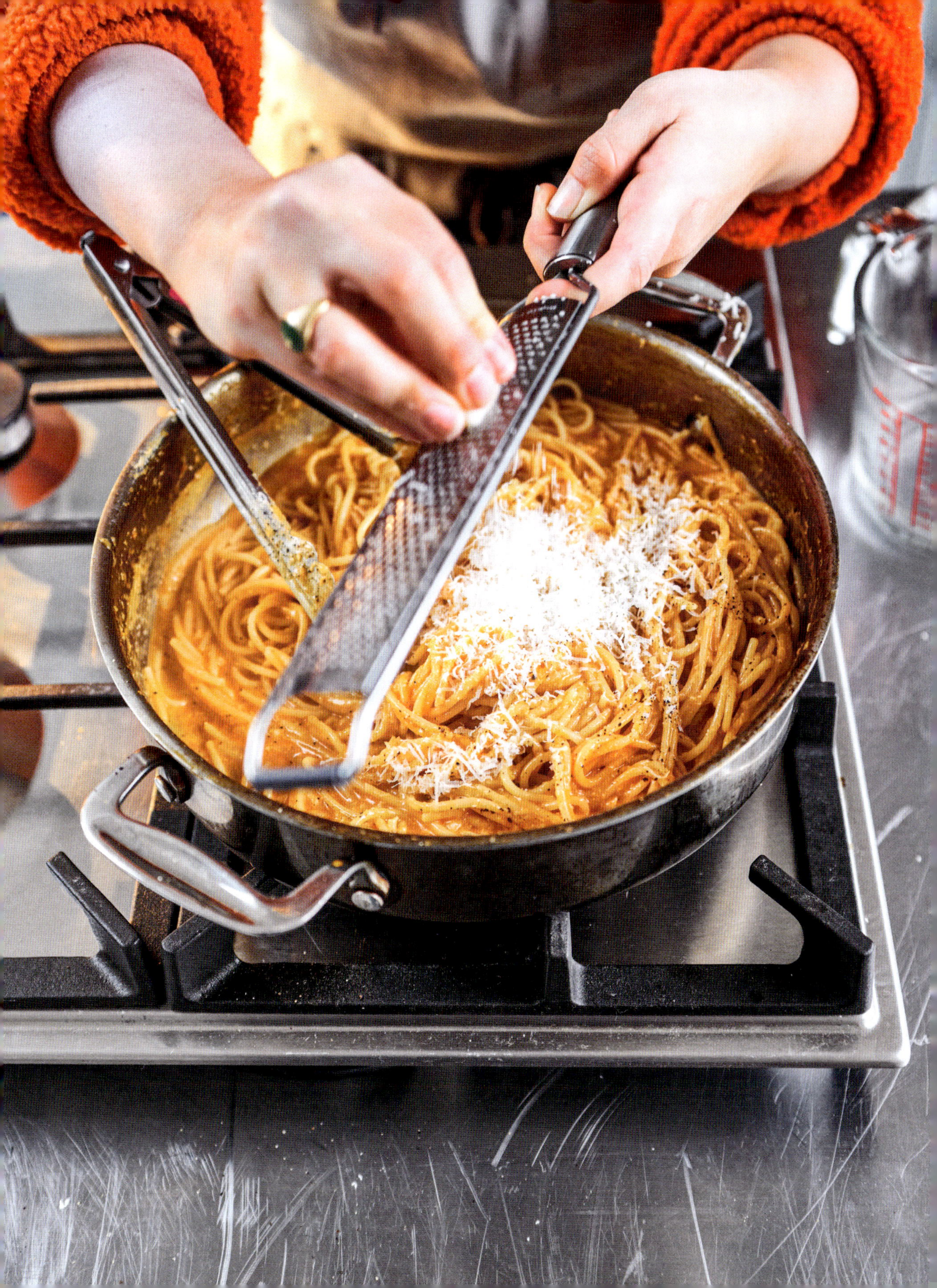

Herby Sizzled Feta

Scan for more tasty recipes like this one

Serves 2 (or 4 as a starter)
Takes 10 minutes

Use a small saucepan

Veggie, Gluten-free

200g feta
10g dill
15g flat leaf parsley
15g coriander
3 spring onions
20g dried sour cherries
5 tablespoons (75ml) olive oil
100g fresh cherries
1 large baguette, to serve (use gluten-free if needed)

TIP: If you can't find sour cherries, substitute with dried cranberries.

We've taken a simple block of feta and seriously jazzed it up with a sizzling herb oil inspired by the flavours of kuku sabzi – a hugely popular herby Persian frittata. Ideal for a fancy appetiser or an indulgent cheesy lunch.

01. Roughly break the feta into a serving dish and set aside.

02. Finely chop all the herbs, stalks and leaves. Finely slice the spring onions, then mince the sour cherries.

03. Heat the oil in the saucepan over a medium heat, add the herbs and spring onions and cook until dark green, about 3–4 minutes. Stir in the sour cherries.

04. Drizzle the herb oil over the feta.

05. Using your hands, break the fresh cherries apart, discarding the pits and making sure the juices drop onto the feta.

06. Serve with the crusty baguette.

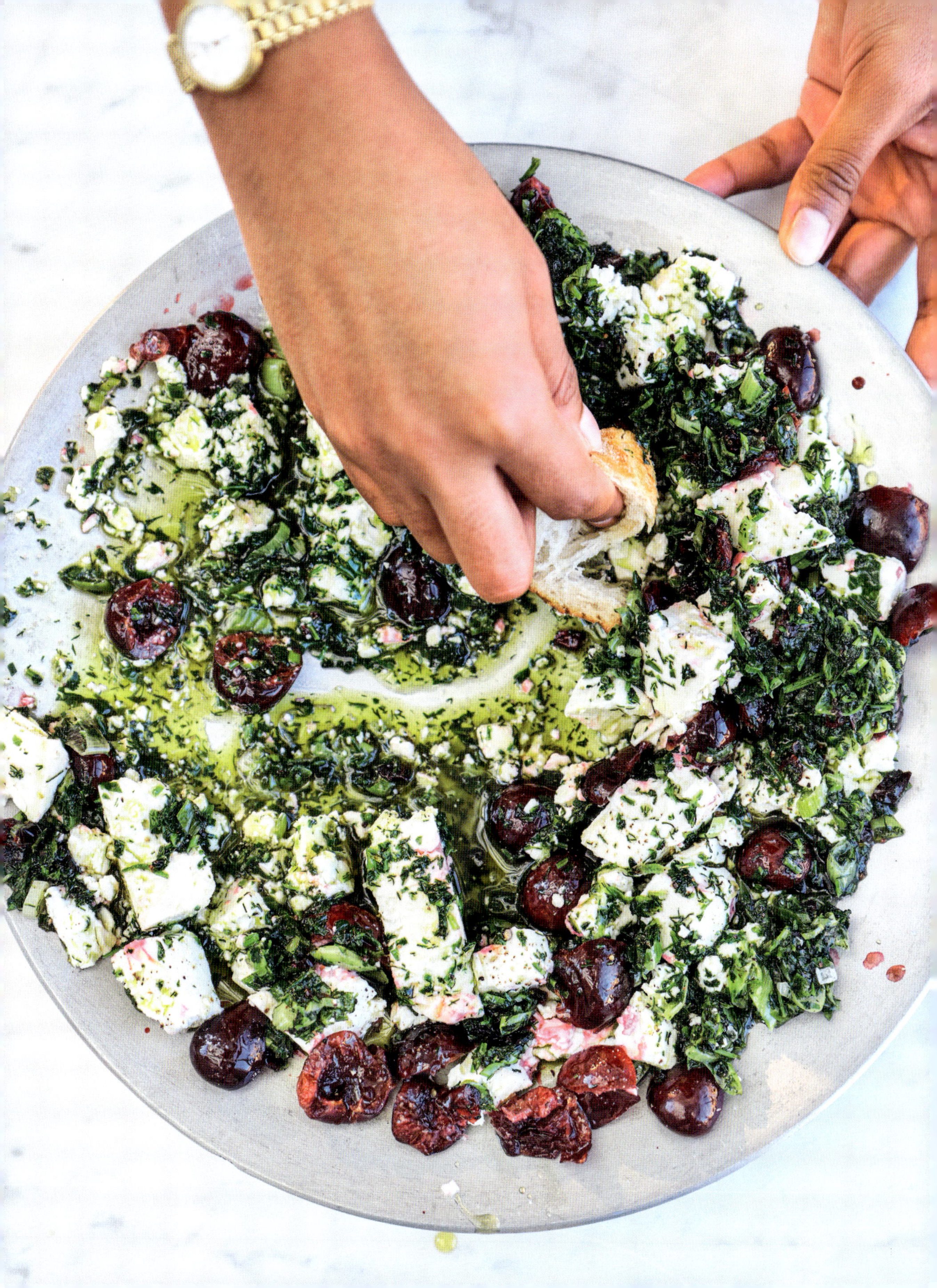

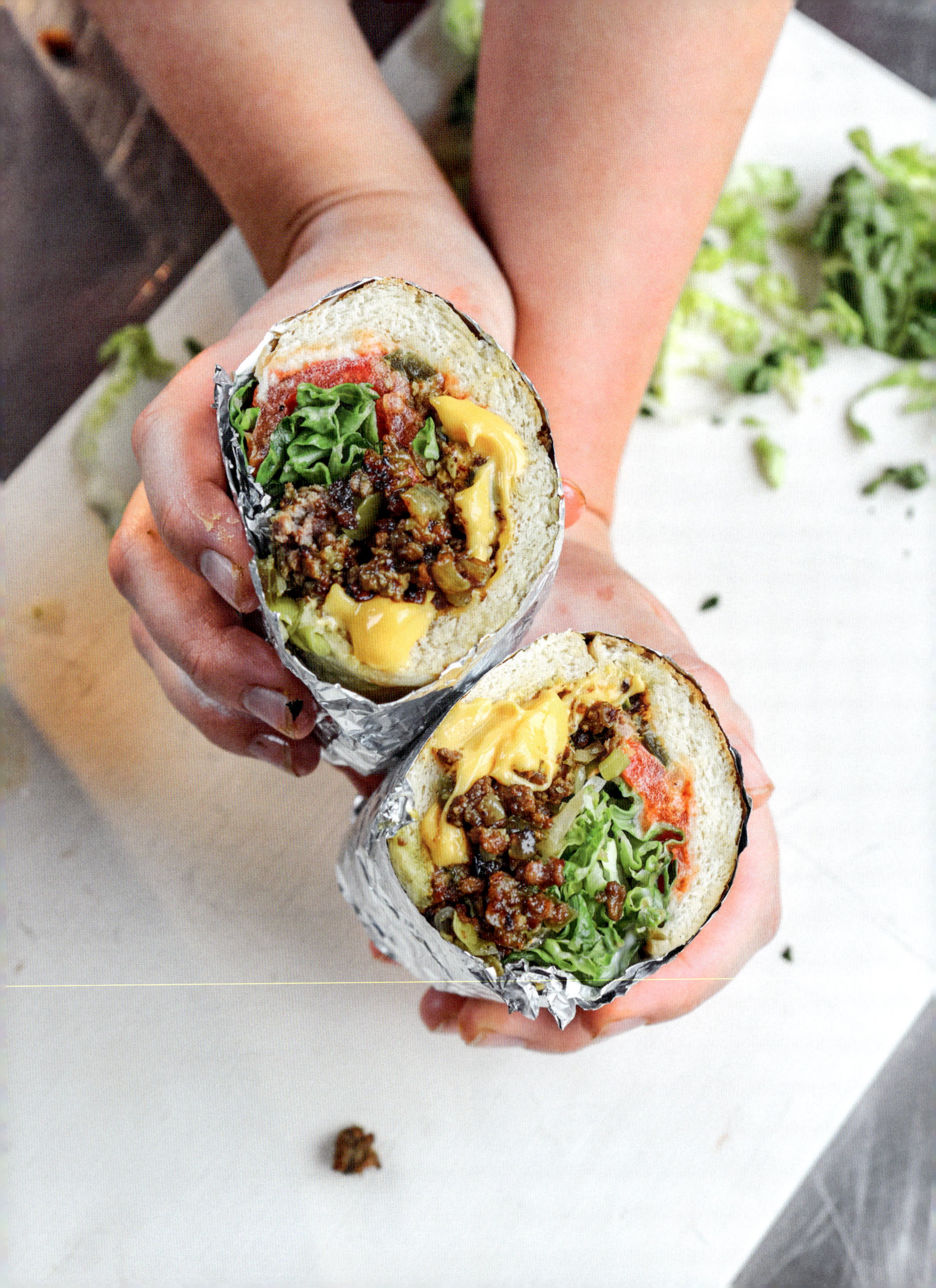

Pickle-y Chopped Cheese

Serves 2
Takes 25 minutes

Use a large non-stick frying pan

1 small onion
1 small green pepper
2 sub rolls (or large hot dog buns)
a large knob of butter
300g beef mince, 20% fat
½ tsp garlic granules
½ tsp dried oregano
½ tsp ground turmeric
4 slices of pre-sliced cheese
2 tbsp ketchup
2 tbsp mayonnaise
salt

FOR THE TOPPINGS
3 tbsp pickled jalapeño slices
5 baby pickled onions
4 pickled guindilla chilli peppers
1 Little Gem lettuce
1 tomato

You might not have heard of a chopped cheese before, but you won't stop thinking about them once you've made one for yourself. An NYC institution, the chopped cheese is a sandwich you can find in pretty much every corner shop or bodega in the city. It's essentially a mashed-up cheeseburger inside a sandwich roll. We've loaded ours with our favourite pickle-y bits: pickled jalapeños, pickled chillies and pickled onions. A stellar speedy lunch.

01. First, prepare your toppings. Finely chop the pickled jalapeños, onions and chillies and mix together on your chopping board. Very thinly shred the lettuce and slice the tomato into rounds. Set aside.

02. Dice the onion, then deseed and dice the green pepper.

03. Halve the sub rolls, keeping them attached at one corner. Set the frying pan over a high heat. Once hot, add the butter and sub rolls, cut-side down, and toast until golden (about 40–60 seconds). Set aside on 2 large pieces of baking paper or foil (you will use these to wrap the subs later).

Continued overleaf

Continued from previous page

04. Add the mince, spices, onion and green pepper to the pan with a big pinch of salt. Fry over a high heat, breaking up the mince with a spatula or wooden spoon and blending everything together, then leave undisturbed for 1–2 minutes to get a nice crisp bottom.

05. Divide the mixture in half, pushing each half to opposite sides of the pan. Lay 2 cheese slices over each half and let the cheese melt into the meat, about 1–2 minutes.

06. Using a spatula, scoop each half of the mixture onto the base of a sub roll (the cheese will bind the mince together and stop it being so crumbly). Sprinkle over the chopped pickle mixture, then top with the shredded lettuce and tomato slices.

07. Spread the ketchup and mayo over the lids.

08. Bring up the foil at the sides of the rolls to help you contain all of the filling and wrap up the rolls. Use a serrated knife to slice through the middle of each sub and enjoy.

Scan for more tasty recipes like this one

SPEEDY ONES

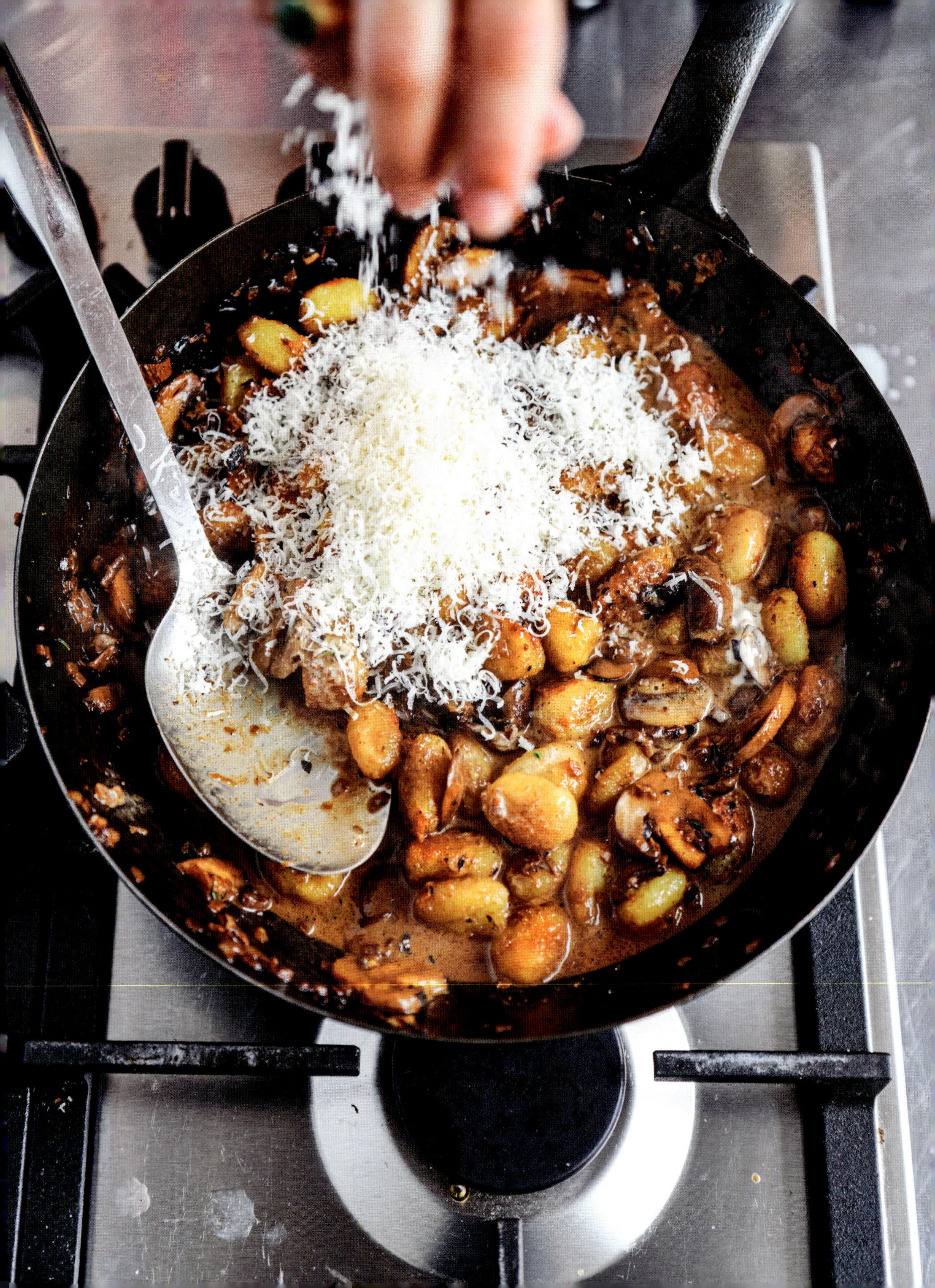

Crispy Mushroom Gnocchi

Serves 2
Takes 25 minutes

Use a medium non-stick frying pan

Veggie

15g dried porcini mushrooms
250g chestnut mushrooms
2 shallots
4 garlic cloves
4 sprigs of thyme, plus extra leaves to garnish
4 tbsp extra virgin olive oil
500g gnocchi
30g vegetarian Italian hard cheese or Parmesan
3 tbsp crème fraîche (about 50g)
50g butter
1 tablespoon sherry vinegar or red wine vinegar

Scan for more tasty recipes like this one

This mushroom and crispy gnocchi number is bright, zesty and full of umami. The sharp crème fraîche and thyme sauce tastes like a ray of sunshine on a crisp spring day. By which we mean: lovely.

01. Roughly chop the porcini mushrooms, then tip into a mug or heatproof glass and cover with 300ml of boiling water. Set aside.

02. Next, prepare the rest of the veg. Slice the chestnut mushrooms. Finely chop the shallots and mince the garlic. Strip the leaves from the thyme sprigs.

03. Add 2 tablespoons of the olive oil to the frying pan over a high heat, add the gnocchi and sauté until golden and crisp, about 3–4 minutes. Remove from the pan and set aside.

04. Add the remaining olive oil to the pan, add the sliced mushrooms and fry for 3–5 minutes until deeply browned, then add the shallots, garlic and thyme leaves and fry for 2 minutes until fragrant and nearly soft. Add the porcini pieces with their soaking liquid and bubble away for 2–3 minutes until slightly reduced.

05. Meanwhile, grate the cheese.

06. Add the crème fraîche, butter and vinegar to the pan, reintroduce the gnocchi and toss vigorously to combine. Bubble for a final 1–2 minutes if needed, to thicken. Sprinkle over the cheese, garnish with thyme leaves and enjoy.

Yoghurt Chicken Curry

Scan for more tasty recipes like this one

Serves 4
Takes 30 minutes

Use a large wok or frying pan with a lid

Gluten-free

1kg skinless, boneless chicken thighs
1 tbsp olive oil
a large piece of fresh ginger
10 garlic cloves
2 tsp ground cumin
½ tsp ground coriander
1 tbsp garam masala
1 tsp hot chilli powder
2 tsp caster sugar
150g Greek yoghurt
500ml passata
1 small red onion, to garnish
1 green chilli, to garnish
200ml double cream
50g butter
1 tsp dried fenugreek leaves
1–2 limes
pomegranate seeds, to garnish
basmati rice and naan (optional), to serve
salt and black pepper

FOR THE CORIANDER YOGHURT
100g Greek yoghurt
15g coriander, plus extra leaves to serve
1 lime

The key to getting that signature butter chicken (aka chicken makhani) flavour in this dish is dried fenugreek leaves. They make all the difference to the depth of the dish and you'll be extremely grateful once you've added them in.

01. Heat the wok or frying pan over a medium-high heat until hot. Meanwhile, chop the chicken into 3cm chunks, then add both the oil and chicken to the hot wok or pan. Cook for 10 minutes until golden with no visible pink bits.

02. Peel the ginger, then finely grate it and the garlic directly into the wok or pan and fry for 1 minute until fragrant. Add the dried spices and sugar, then add the yoghurt and stir vigorously to combine and stop it from splitting.

03. Reduce the heat to medium, add the passata and stir well, then cover with the lid and bubble gently for 5 minutes.

04. Meanwhile, make the coriander yoghurt. Put the yoghurt and finely chopped coriander into a bowl, zest in the lime and mix together, then season to taste.

05. For the garnish, very thinly slice the red onion and green chilli. Set aside.

06. Remove the lid from the wok or pan, increase the heat to high and continue to cook until the oil separates, about 5 minutes. Once you see some oil on the surface, stir through the cream, butter and fenugreek leaves.

07. Juice 1 lime and use to season the curry, adding more to taste. Season to taste with salt and pepper.

08. Ladle into 4 bowls and spoon over the coriander yoghurt. Garnish with the red onion, chilli and pomegranate seeds. Serve with rice and naan, if you like.

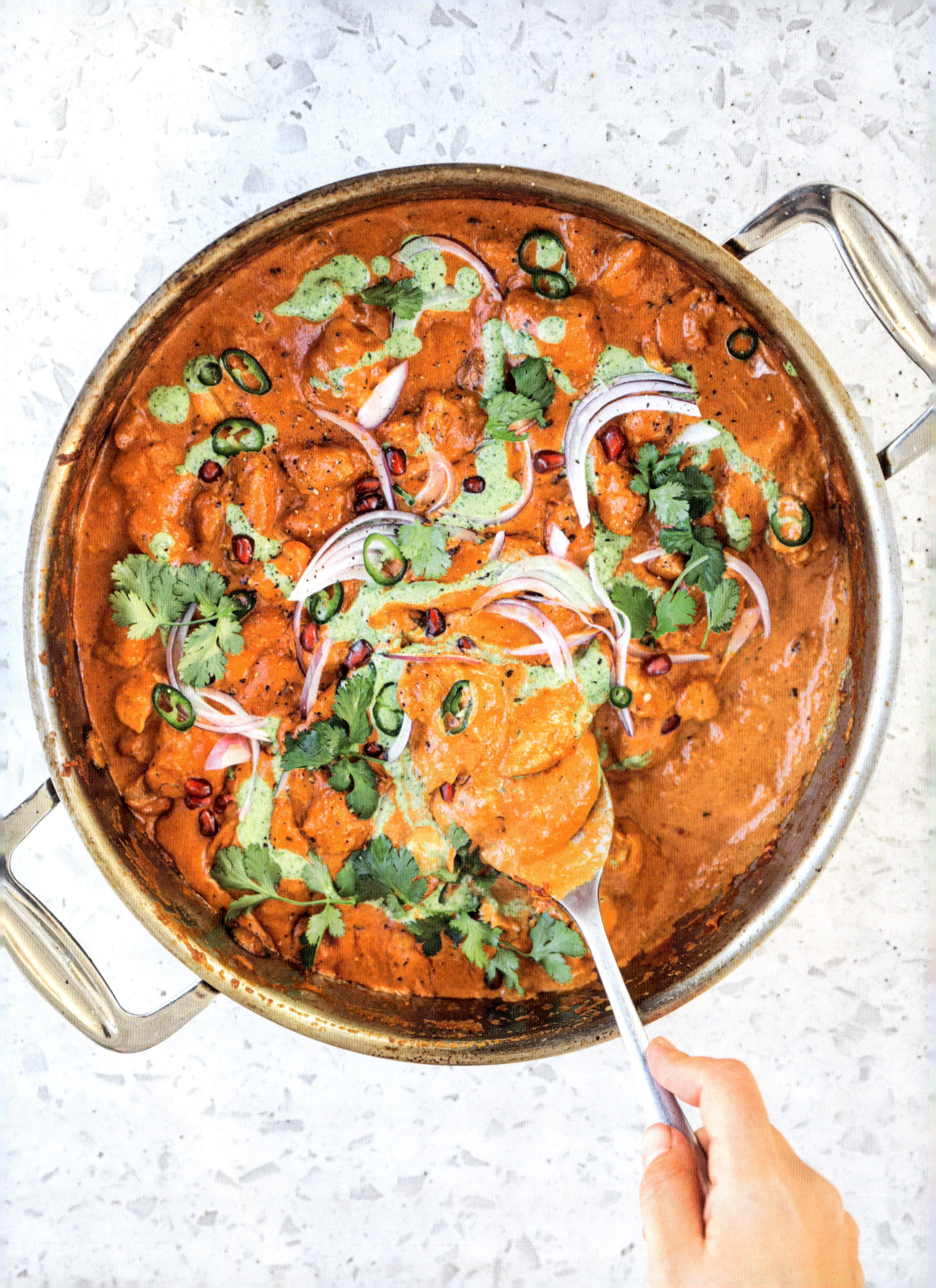

FEASTING ONES

FEASTING ONES

Tikka Roast Chicken

Serves 4
Takes 1 hour 30 minutes
+ marinating

Use a large roasting tin

Gluten-free

1 large chicken (about 1.7kg)
200g natural yoghurt
125g tikka masala paste (check the label if making this gluten-free)
300g parsnips
300g carrots
1 large red onion
1 garlic bulb
1 lemon
700g Maris Piper potatoes
5g fresh curry leaves
1 tbsp curry powder
3 tbsp olive oil
100g frozen peas
1 tbsp nigella seeds
salt and black pepper

TO SERVE
100g natural yoghurt
100ml tamarind chutney
a large handful of coriander leaves

Scan for more tasty recipes like this one

We know we always say: 'you really have to make this'. But, honestly, you *really* have to make this. It's a killer Indian-inspired roast you can make in a single tray. Chuck it all in, forget about it for an hour, and then prepare to have your mind blown at the first bite. Don't skimp on the yoghurt and tamarind chutney drizzle at the end – they really make it pop.

01. Pop the chicken into the roasting tin. Season generously with salt. In a small bowl, mix together the yoghurt and tikka masala paste, then massage this all over the chicken. Leave to marinate for 30–60 minutes.

02. Preheat the oven to 220°C/200°C fan.

03. Cut the parsnips and carrots into batons, then slice the onion into wedges (discard the skin). Halve the garlic bulb around its equator. Cut the lemon into 4 wedges. Cut the potatoes into 2–3cm chunks.

04. Scatter all the vegetables, curry leaves and the lemon wedges around and under the chicken, sprinkle with the curry powder. Drizzle with the oil and season. Roast for 1 hour–1 hour 10 minutes (check often after 30 minutes and cover with foil if it's starting to catch) or until the skin of the chicken is deeply burnished, the juices run clear when the thickest part of the leg is pierced with a sharp knife and the vegetables are tender and golden.

05. Add the frozen peas and nigella seeds to the tin and stir to combine, then return to the oven for 5 minutes until the peas are warmed through.

06. Serve with a generous drizzle of yoghurt, tamarind chutney and a scattering of coriander leaves.

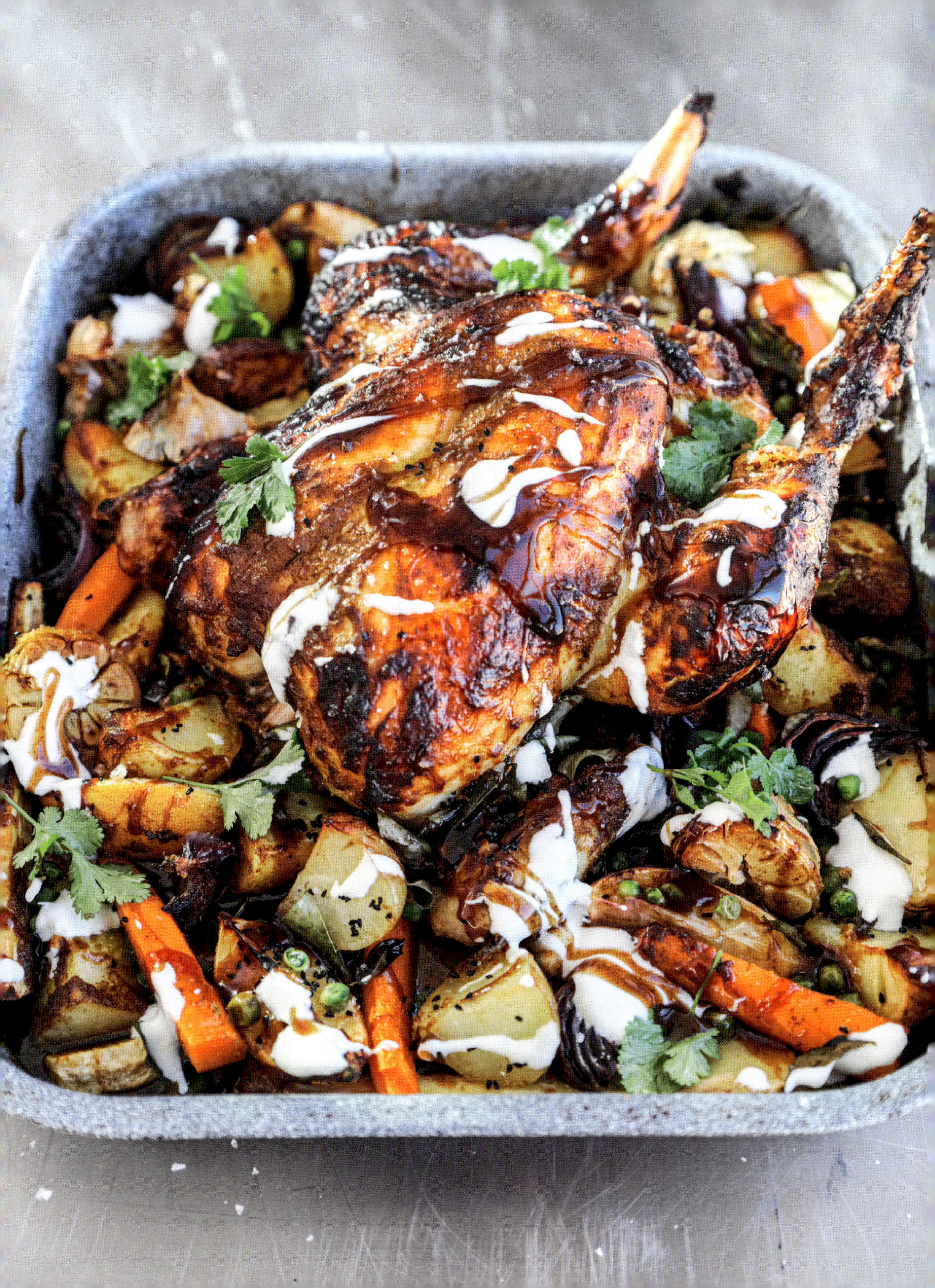

Aubergine + Halloumi Spiced Rice

Serves 4
Takes 1 hour 15 minutes

Use a large ovenproof non-stick frying pan with a lid

Veggie, Gluten-free

1 large aubergine
1 x 225g pack of halloumi
1 onion
50g butter
olive oil
3 tbsp curry paste (we like madras) (check the label if making this gluten-free)
350g basmati and wild rice
250g cherry tomatoes
600ml hot vegetable stock (check the label if making this gluten-free)

FOR THE CHUTNEY + GARNISH
3 chillies (we like a mix)
50g coriander, plus extra leaves to serve
90g salted cashews
1 tsp cumin seeds
4 tbsp olive oil
1 lemon
salt

Scan for more tasty recipes like this one

A big, comforting pan of spiced rice, inspired by the flavours of pilau rice. We've used halloumi here because it's easy to find and we love the salty tang it brings to the party. What really makes this pop is the herby cashew chutney that's drizzled on top at the end. Gorge.

01. Preheat the oven to 220°C/200°C fan. Cut the aubergine and halloumi into 2cm pieces, then slice the onion.

02. Set the dry frying pan over a medium heat. Once hot, add the halloumi and cook for about 1–2 minutes on all sides until golden. Remove from the pan and set aside. Turn up the heat and add the aubergine – no need for oil yet! – and keep cooking until nice and golden, around 8–10 minutes. Remove from the pan and set aside with the halloumi.

03. Add the butter and a splash of oil to the pan followed by the onion, then reduce the heat to medium and cook for about 10 minutes until softened. Stir in the curry paste and cook for 30 seconds, then return the halloumi and aubergine to the pan.

04. Rinse the rice in a sieve until the water runs clear, then add to the pan with the cherry tomatoes and stock. Cover with the lid, transfer to the oven and cook for 25 minutes. Remove the lid, then cook for a further 15 minutes until golden.

05. Meanwhile, make the cashew chutney. Finely slice 1 of the chillies, then set aside. Put the remaining chillies, the coriander and 50g of the cashews into a food processor with the cumin seeds, olive oil and 2 tablespoons of cold water. Juice the lemon and add to the processor, then season with salt and blitz until smooth.

06. Serve the spiced rice topped with the chutney, the reserved sliced chilli, the remaining cashews and some whole coriander leaves.

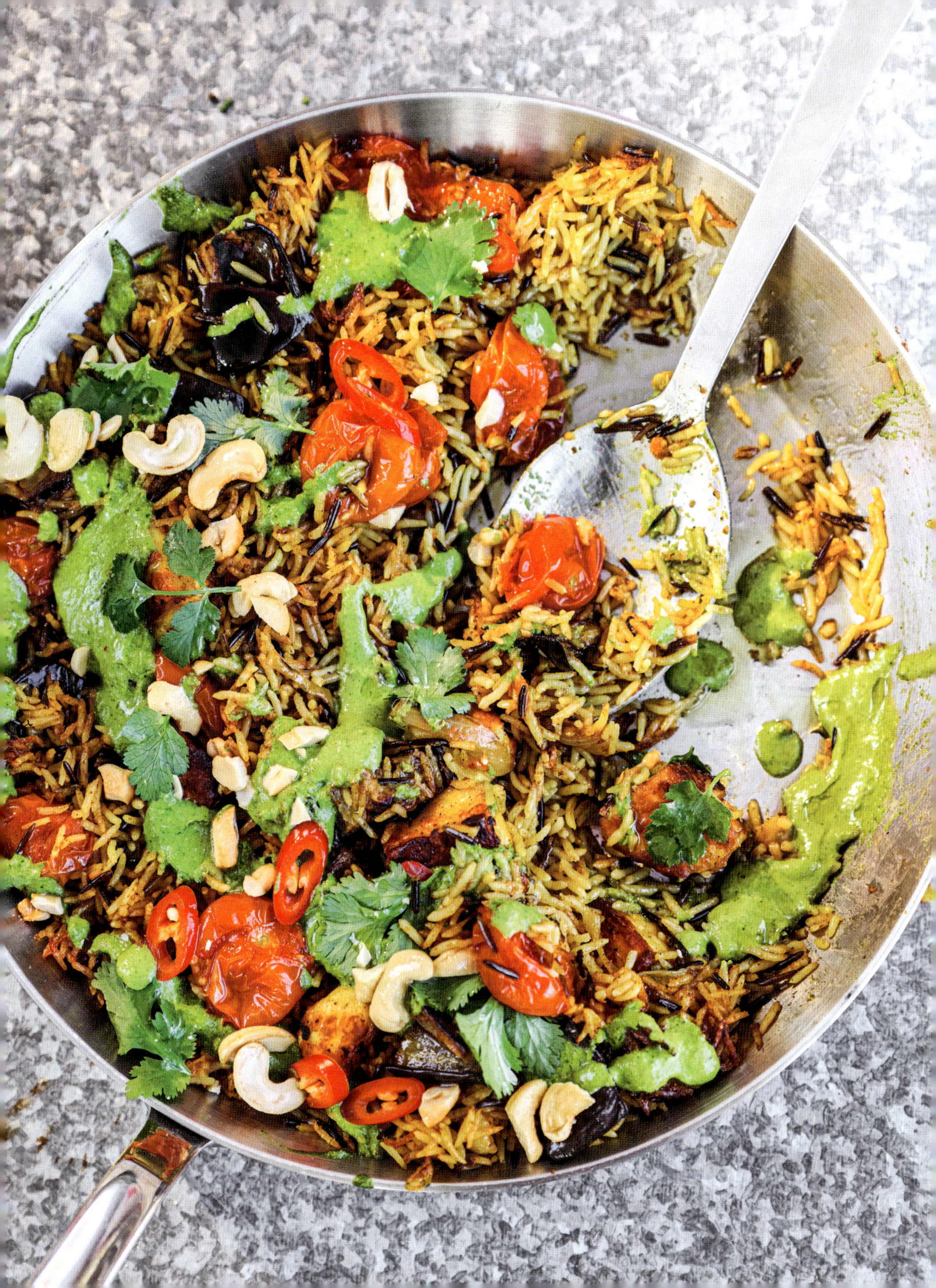

French Onion Orzo

Serves 4–6
Takes 1 hour

Use a large, deep frying pan

---

5 tbsp olive oil
45g breadcrumbs
6 onions (about 1kg)
150ml dry white wine
500g orzo
1 litre hot beef stock
2 bay leaves
6 sprigs of thyme
15g chives
35g Gruyère
8 tbsp Worcestershire sauce
salt and black pepper

Scan for more tasty recipes like this one

Name a more iconic duo. This is like a French onion soup that's been turned into a sticky orzo. Topped with melted Gruyère, golden breadcrumbs and chives, it's a super comforting winter warmer.

---

01. Add 2 tablespoons of olive oil and the breadcrumbs to the frying pan set over a medium-high heat and toast for 3–5 minutes, until golden. Transfer to a plate and set aside.

02. Finely slice the onions. Add to the pan along with the remaining 3 tablespoons of olive oil and a big pinch of salt. Cook for 30 minutes or so, until the onions are soft and well caramelised, reducing the heat a little if they start to catch. Add the white wine and cook for 2–3 minutes, until reduced by half. Stir in the orzo, along with the beef stock, bay leaves and thyme. Bubble for 10 minutes, stirring often, until the orzo has sucked up all the juices.

03. Finely slice the chives and set aside. Grate the Gruyère.

04. Stir in the Worcestershire sauce and most of the grated Gruyère. Season with salt and pepper.

05. Serve garnished with the chives, the remaining cheese and the golden breadcrumbs.

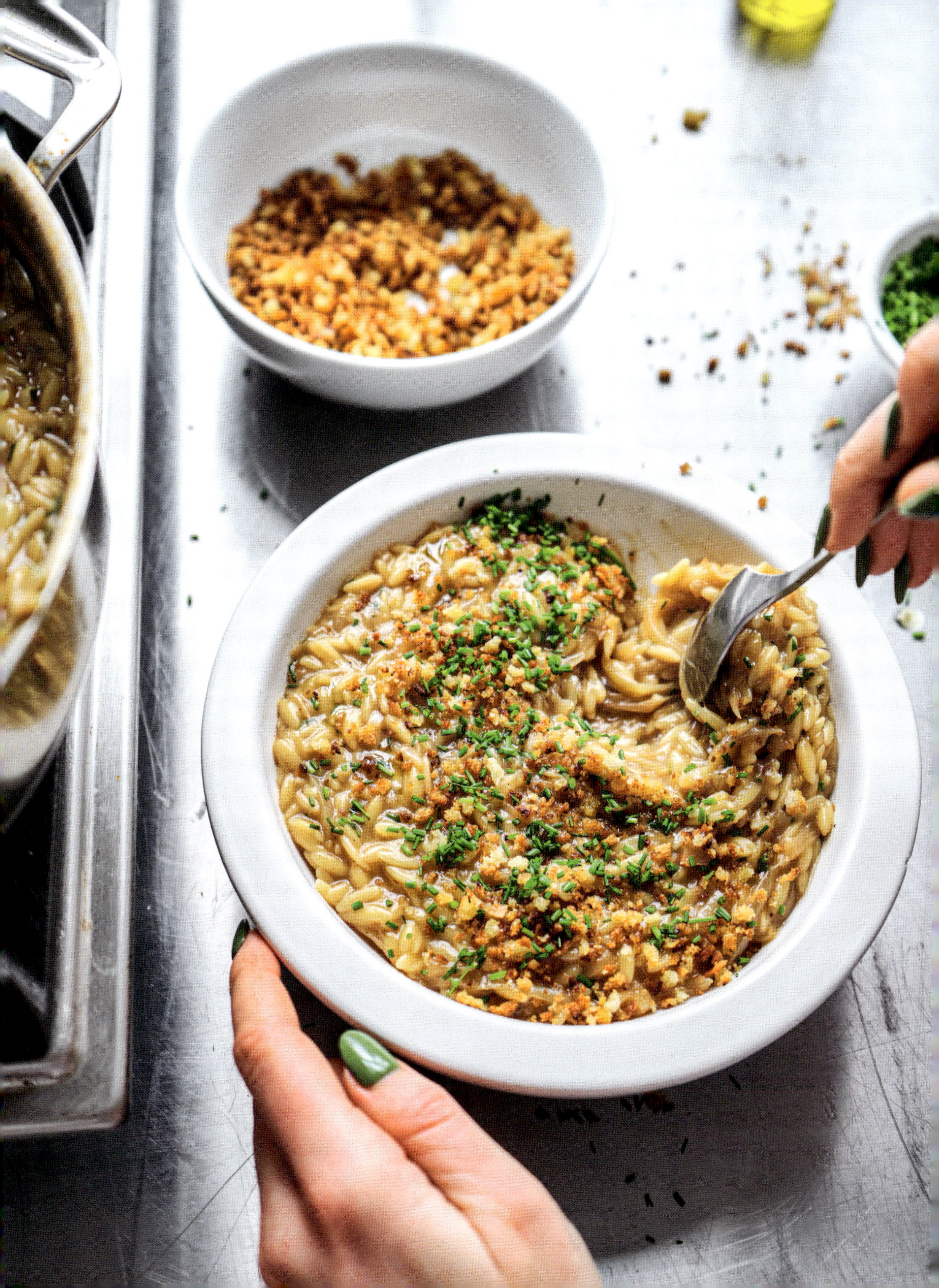

Gochujang Chilli con Carne

Serves 6
Takes 2 hours

Use an ovenproof casserole dish

2 tbsp extra virgin olive oil
200g smoked bacon lardons
3 celery sticks
2 red onions
2 peppers (1 red and 1 green)
8 garlic cloves
a large handful of coriander
1kg beef mince
4 tbsp gochujang
3 tbsp soy sauce
800ml passata
1 litre hot beef stock
2 x 400g tins of mixed beans
2 limes
salt and black pepper

TO SERVE
Cheddar cheese
a few spring onions
2 limes
2–3 x 250g microwaveable pouches of rice
soured cream

Scan for more tasty recipes like this one

We've swapped chillies and chilli powder for gochujang, a sweet and spicy Korean spice paste with funk and depth, which infuses this chilli con carne with an insanely rich flavour. Serve with the usual suspects – rice, Cheddar, soured cream – and wait for everyone to ask about your secret ingredient.

01. Set the casserole dish over a low heat, add the oil and bacon lardons and bring up to a sizzle. Cook for 5–8 minutes until the fat has rendered out and the lardons are golden and crisp.

02. Meanwhile, finely chop the celery and red onions, then deseed and finely chop the peppers (or chuck all the veg in a food processor to speed things up).

03. Add the celery, onions and peppers to the dish and cook for 8 minutes until soft and reduced in volume.

04. Finely chop the garlic, then pick the coriander leaves and finely chop the stalks.

05. Add the garlic and coriander stalks to the dish and fry for 1 minute until fragrant.

06. Increase the heat to medium, then add the mince and cook until browned, stirring regularly and breaking up the meat with a wooden spoon.

07. Add the gochujang, soy sauce, passata and stock, reduce the heat to low and simmer for 1½ hours until the meat is tender and the sauce has thickened and is nice and glossy. Pour in the drained and rinsed beans, juice the limes, then season the chilli generously with the lime juice, salt and pepper.

08. Just before serving, grate the Cheddar, slice the spring onions and cut the limes into wedges. Heat the rice in the microwave according to the packet instructions.

09. Serve the chilli with the rice, cheese, spring onions, lime wedges and soured cream.

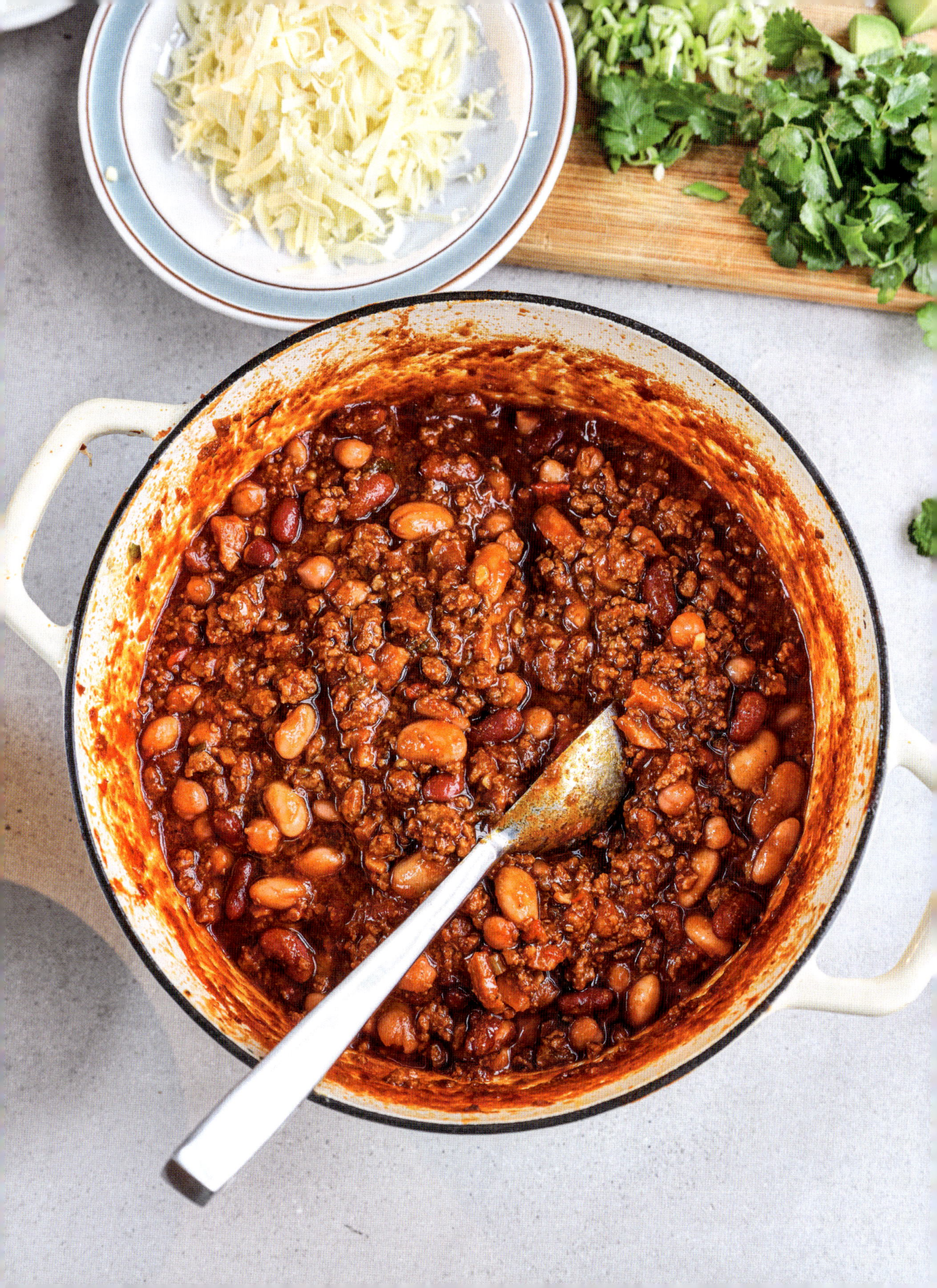

Whole Miso-Roasted Butternut Squash

Serves 4
Takes 1 hour 40 minutes

Use a large roasting tin

Vegan

1 large butternut squash
1 tbsp olive oil, to drizzle
1 bunch of spring onions
2 x 250g microwaveable pouches of jasmine rice
1 lime
2 tbsp tahini
1 cucumber

FOR THE MISO GLAZE
3 tbsp olive oil
3 tbsp miso
2 tbsp maple syrup
2 tbsp soy sauce
a thumb-sized chunk of fresh ginger
3 garlic cloves
salt and black pepper

TO SERVE
½ small bunch of coriander leaves
toasted sesame seeds
chilli oil (optional)
1 lime

Cooking squash like this is (a) really impressive, and (b) painfully easy. Placing the squash cut-side down allows it to steam until soft and tender, and the seeds can be scooped out. Doused in a flashy lime and tahini dressing, squash doesn't get much tastier.

01. Preheat the oven to 200°C/180°C fan.

02. Cut the butternut squash in half lengthways, drizzle with a little oil, then lie the halves, cut-side down, in the roasting tin. Roast for 1 hour.

03. Meanwhile, to make the glaze, whisk the oil, miso, maple syrup and soy sauce together in a bowl. Peel the ginger, then grate it and the garlic into the bowl. Add 1 tablespoon of water and whisk well. Season well.

04. Finely slice the spring onions. When the squash is cooked, remove the tin from the oven and carefully flip the halves over, then scoop out the seeds and discard. Tip the rice around the squash, along with most of the spring onions (save some for the garnish). Drizzle the miso glaze all over. Slide back into the oven and cook for a further 20–30 minutes until sticky and caramelised.

05. To make a dressing, juice the lime into a bowl and whisk in the tahini, then gradually add 3–4 tablespoons of water, whisking after each addition (don't worry when it seizes, just keep adding the water), until it turns into a cream dressing. Season with salt.

06. Slice the cucumber in half lengthways, then remove the seedy centres and slice on an angle into 1 cm-thick half-moons.

07. Remove the squash from the oven and leave to cool for a few minutes, then scatter the cucumber slices around it and drizzle with the tahini dressing. Top with the reserved spring onions, the coriander leaves and a scattering of toasted sesame seeds. Drizzle with chilli oil, if you like. Serve with the lime, cut into wedges, for squeezing over.

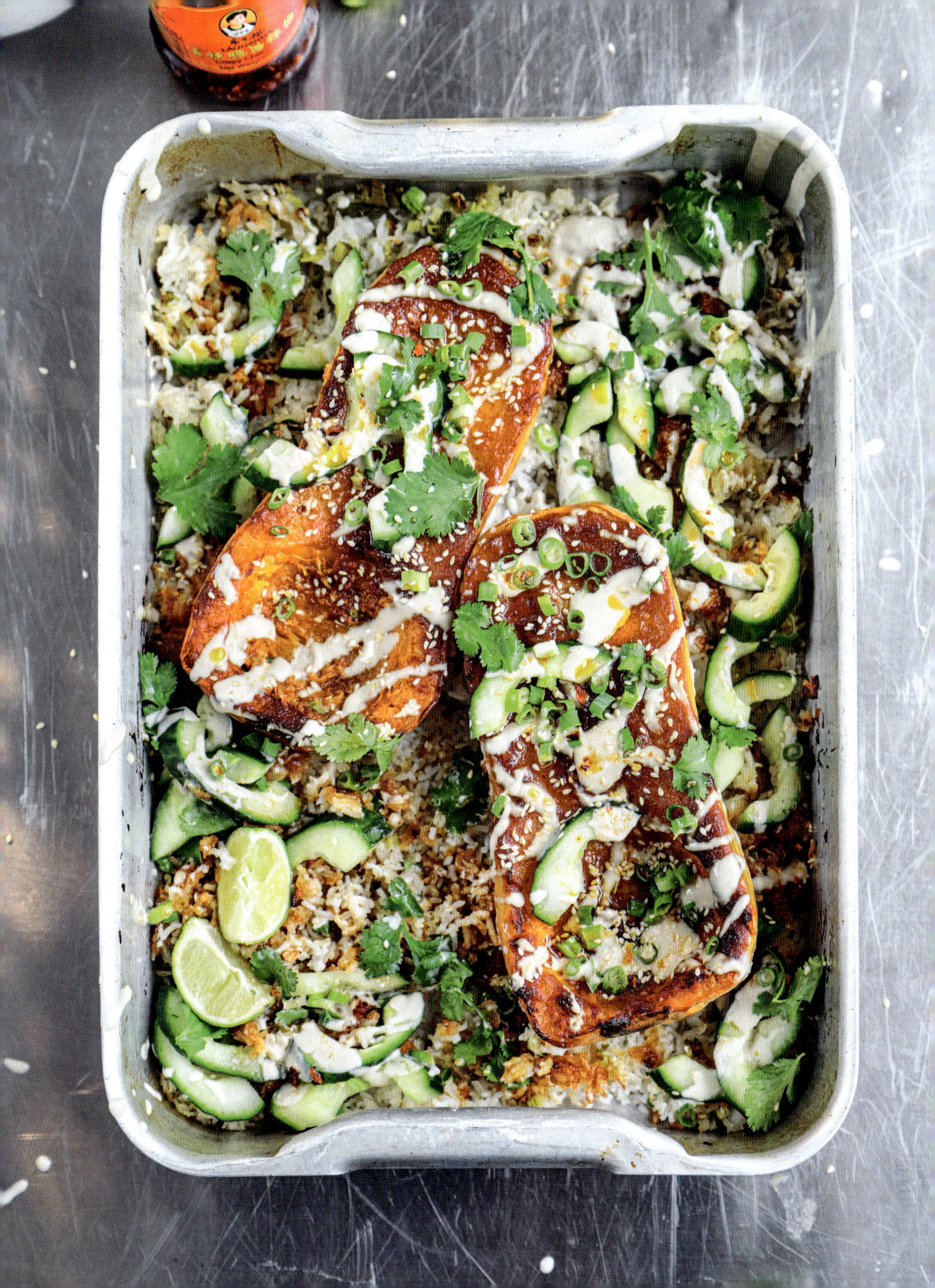

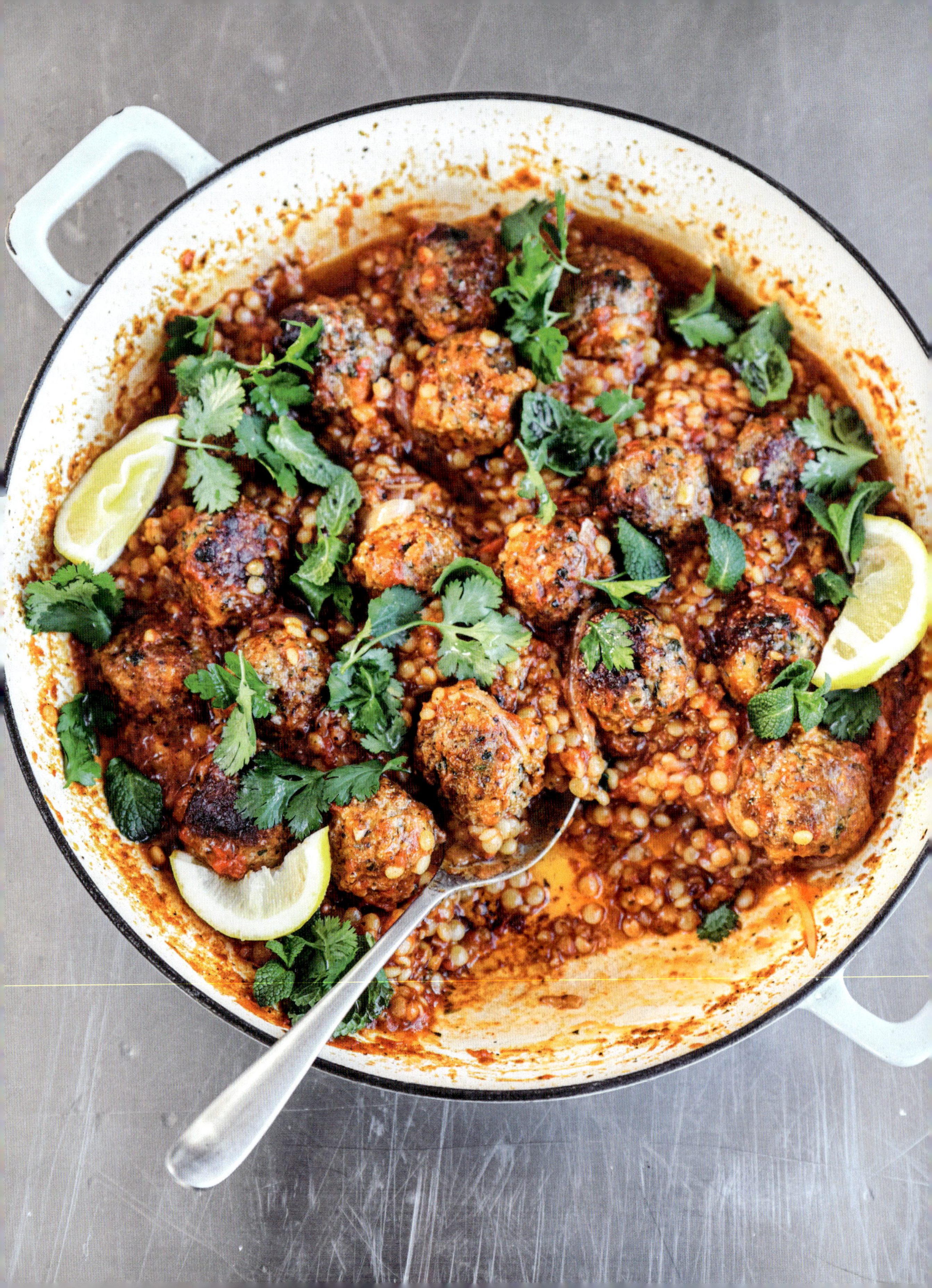

Moroccan-Spiced Lamb Meatballs

Scan for more tasty recipes like this one

Serves 4
Takes 50 minutes

Use a large non-stick frying pan or shallow casserole pan with a lid

2 slices of stale white bread (about 75g)
100ml whole milk
500g lamb mince
1 lemon
2 garlic cloves
1 tbsp ras el hanout
1 red chilli
a small handful of flat leaf parsley leaves, plus extra to garnish
a small handful of mint leaves, plus extra to garnish
a small handful of coriander leaves, plus extra to garnish
2 tbsp olive oil
2 preserved lemons
2 shallots
2 tbsp tagine paste or harissa
1 x 400g tin of finely chopped tomatoes
500ml hot chicken stock
200g giant couscous
salt and black pepper

Punchy ras el hanout lamb meatballs bobbing in a gorgeous tomato sauce that we've spiked with preserved lemon and tagine paste. This is some serious tucker, all right.

01. First, make your meatballs. Tear up the bread into chunks and place in a large bowl, then pour over the milk. Add the lamb mince, then finely grate in the lemon zest and garlic. Add the ras el hanout. Finely chop the chilli, parsley, mint and coriander, then add to the bowl and mix well with your hands to combine. Season generously, then roll into golf-ball-sized meatballs.

02. Heat the oil in the frying pan over a medium-high heat, add the meatballs and fry on all sides for 1–2 minutes until deeply golden. Remove from the pan and set aside.

03. Halve the preserved lemons and scoop out and discard the flesh, then thinly slice the peel. Thinly slice the shallots.

04. Add the preserved lemon peel and shallots to the pan and fry over a medium heat for 5 minutes until the shallots are soft. Add the tagine paste and fry for 1 minute until fragrant. Add the chopped tomatoes, stock and couscous and cook over a medium heat, uncovered for 5 minutes, stirring regularly.

05. Reduce the heat to low, nestle the meatballs back in the pan and cover with the lid. Cook for 10–15 minutes, or until the meatballs are cooked through and the couscous is tender. Stir carefully by wiggling the smaller end of a wooden spoon in with the couscous to ensure it doesn't stick to the pan.

06. Serve with a sprinkling of extra herbs and the zested lemon cut into wedges for squeezing.

FEASTING ONES

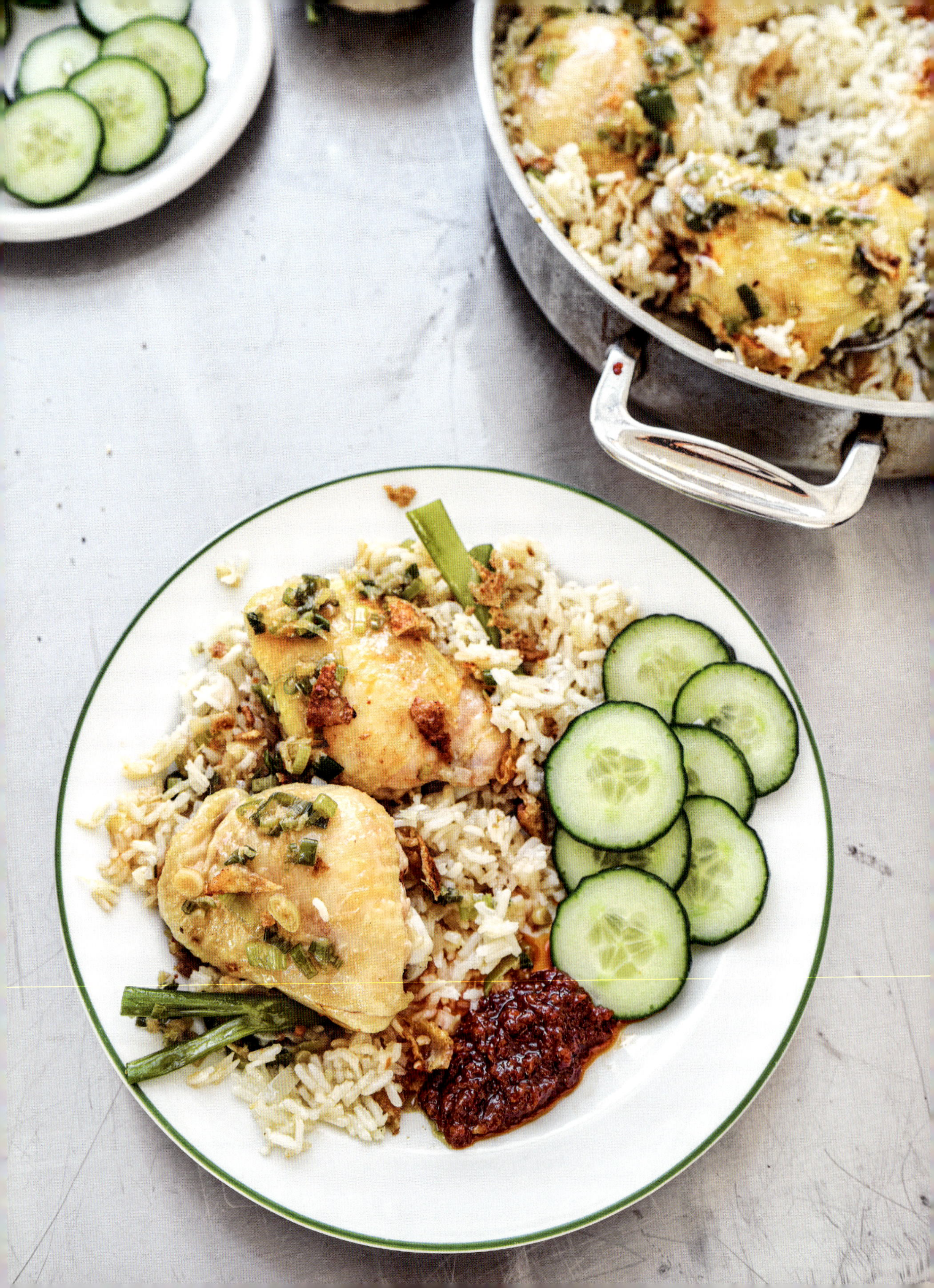

Chicken Rice with Sprunion Sauce

Serves 4
Takes 1 hour 20 minutes

Use a large ovenproof casserole dish with a lid

Gluten-free

8 skin-on, bone-in chicken thighs
8 garlic cloves
2 shallots
30g fresh ginger
3 spring onions
250g jasmine rice
500ml hot chicken stock (check the label if making this gluten-free)
½ cucumber, to serve
sambal oelek, sriracha or other hot sauce, to serve (check the label if making this gluten-free)
salt and black pepper

FOR THE SPRUNION SAUCE
1 bunch of spring onions
5 tbsp (75ml) vegetable oil
50g fresh ginger
2 garlic cloves
3 tbsp tamari (or soy sauce if not gluten-free)
2 tbsp rice vinegar

This is our one-pot take on Hainanese chicken rice. Traditionally, this chicken and rice dish is made by poaching a whole chicken and serving it with aromatic rice, the fragrant poaching liquor and dipping sauces. We've taken a few shortcuts to make this one, though, and loaded it with crispy chicken skin on top for a bit of crunch.

01. Trim the excess fat and skin from the chicken thighs, cutting each piece of skin into 4 pieces – anything overhanging that doesn't cover the meat gets cut off. Season the chicken thighs. Put the trimmed fat and skin into the casserole dish over a medium heat. Cook for 10–15 minutes, turning often, until the fat has rendered out and the skin is crisp and golden, then remove the skin from the pan and set aside.

02. Meanwhile, finely chop the garlic and shallots, then peel and finely chop the ginger. Slice the spring onions into 3cm lengths.

03. Add the garlic, ginger and shallots to the chicken fat left in the dish and fry for 2 minutes until fragrant.

04. Pop the jasmine rice into a sieve and rinse at least 3 times under cold running water until the water runs clear. Add the chicken thighs to the dish, stir well to coat in the aromatics and pour in the stock.

Continued overleaf

Continued from previous page

05. Bring to a boil, then reduce the heat to a simmer and pop the lid on. Simmer gently for 10 minutes, flipping the chicken halfway. Lift the chicken out, then stir through the washed rice and level out to make sure it is all just covered in the stock (add a splash more water if needed). Snuggle the chicken in, top with the spring onion strips, cover the pan tightly with the lid and simmer very gently for 25–30 minutes. Turn off the heat and leave to rest for 10 minutes without removing the lid, so the chicken and rice steam and cook to fluffy perfection.

06. While the dish is resting, finely slice the cucumber and grab your hot sauce to put in a little bowl.

07. To make the sauce, finely chop the spring onions, then put into a microwave-safe bowl or jug with the oil. Peel and finely grate the ginger in with the garlic. Cover and microwave on high for 2 minutes until sizzling, then season with the tamari and rice vinegar.

08. Serve the chicken rice with the sprunion sauce, slices of cucumber, the sambal oelek (or other chilli sauce) and the crunchy chicken skin crumbled on top.

Scan for more tasty recipes like this one

Brisket Lasagn-ish

Serves 6

Takes about 4 hours

Use a large ovenproof casserole dish with a lid

1 x 1–1.5kg beef brisket, unrolled
3 tbsp olive oil
150g smoked pancetta cubes
2 carrots
2 celery sticks
2 onions
6 garlic cloves
4 sprigs of thyme
4 sprigs of rosemary
350ml red wine
1 x 400g tin of finely chopped tomatoes or passata
500ml hot beef stock
250g fresh lasagne sheets
10g basil leaves, to garnish
salt and black pepper

FOR THE TOPPING
50g Parmesan
125g ricotta
125g mascarpone
2 tbsp Dijon mustard

A low-and-slow brisket ragù you can leave for hours to bubble away and do its thing. When it's ready to go, simply tear in fresh lasagne sheets, dot over a quick béchamel, and be mentally prepared to never want a normal lasagne ever again. If you can't find a whole brisket, use chuck, shin or any other bit of stewing beef you can get your hands on.

01. Set the casserole dish over a medium-high heat. Cut the brisket into large 5cm chunks and salt all over. Add the oil to the pan and enough beef to cover the base (you may need to fry it in batches). Sear in the hot dish on all sides until deeply golden and caramelised (about 4–6 minutes). Remove from the pan and set aside.

02. Throw in the pancetta, reduce the heat to medium and cook for about 5–8 minutes until the fat has rendered out and the cubes are crispy.

03. Meanwhile, finely dice the carrots, celery and onions (or you can chuck them all in a food processor to save time!). Finely chop or grate the garlic. Strip the leaves from the thyme and rosemary sprigs and finely chop.

Continued overleaf

FEASTING ONES

Continued from previous page

04. Once the pancetta is golden, increase the heat to medium-high, add the carrots, onions and celery and fry for 8 minutes until soft. Add the garlic and herbs and fry for another minute until fragrant. Pour in the wine and bubble away until the liquid has reduced by two-thirds.

05. Pour in the chopped tomatoes, then add a tinful of water. Add the stock, bring to the boil, then turn to a very low heat. Return the brisket to the dish and and cover with the lid, leaving a small gap for steam to escape. Simmer gently for about 3 hours until the brisket is very tender and easily shreds with a fork. If it's not tender, keep checking every 15 minutes.

06. When the ragù is ready, preheat your grill to its highest setting. To make the topping, grate the Parmesan into a bowl, then mix together with the ricotta, mascarpone and mustard. Season to taste.

07. Remove the lid from the dish and shred the brisket with 2 forks, then tear in the lasagne sheets and mix well to evenly distribute them. Dot over the ricotta topping. Whack under the grill for 10–15 minutes until golden and bubbling, by which point the lasagne will be perfectly al dente.

08. Garnish with basil leaves and tuck in.

Scan for more tasty recipes like this one

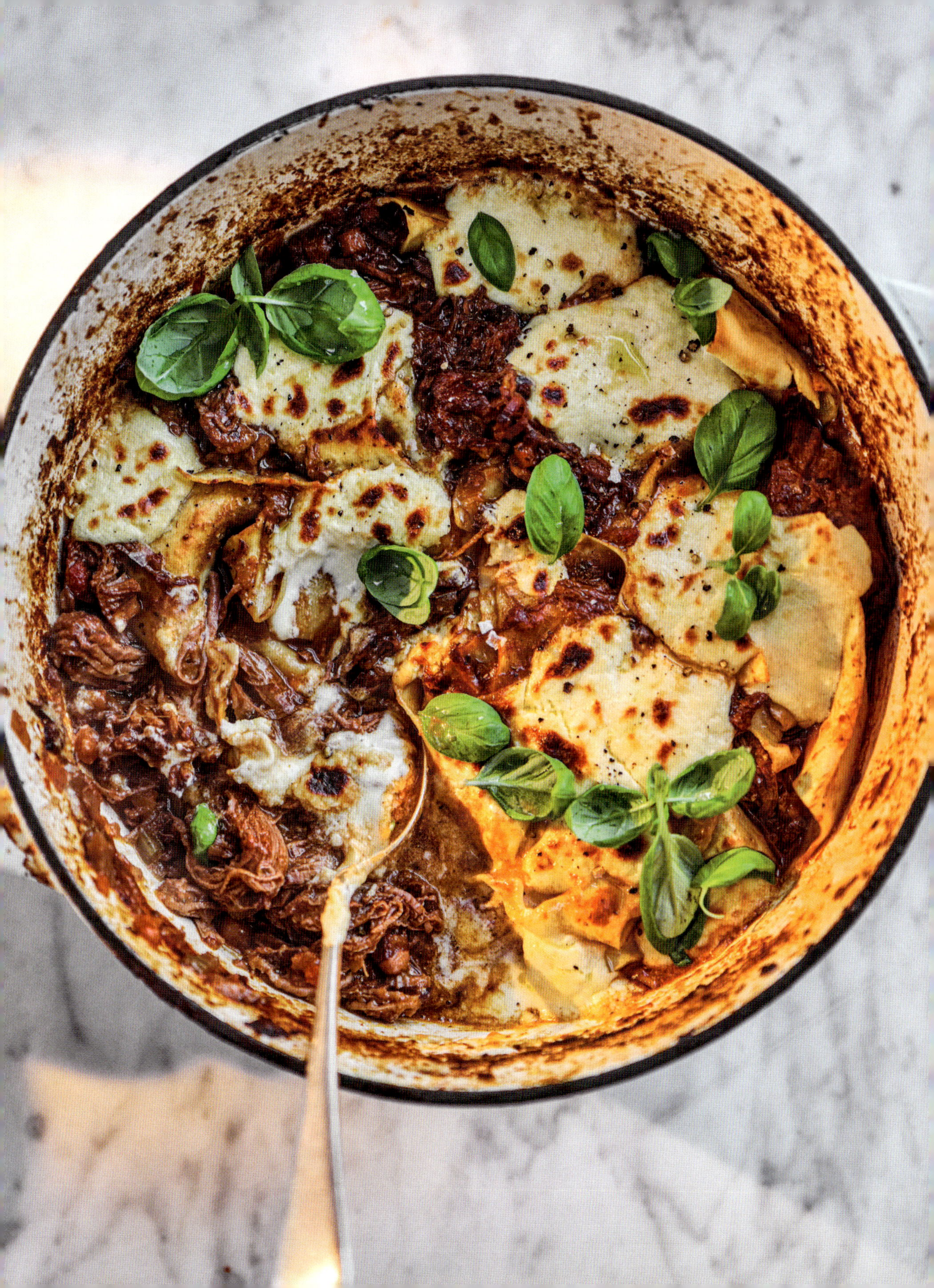

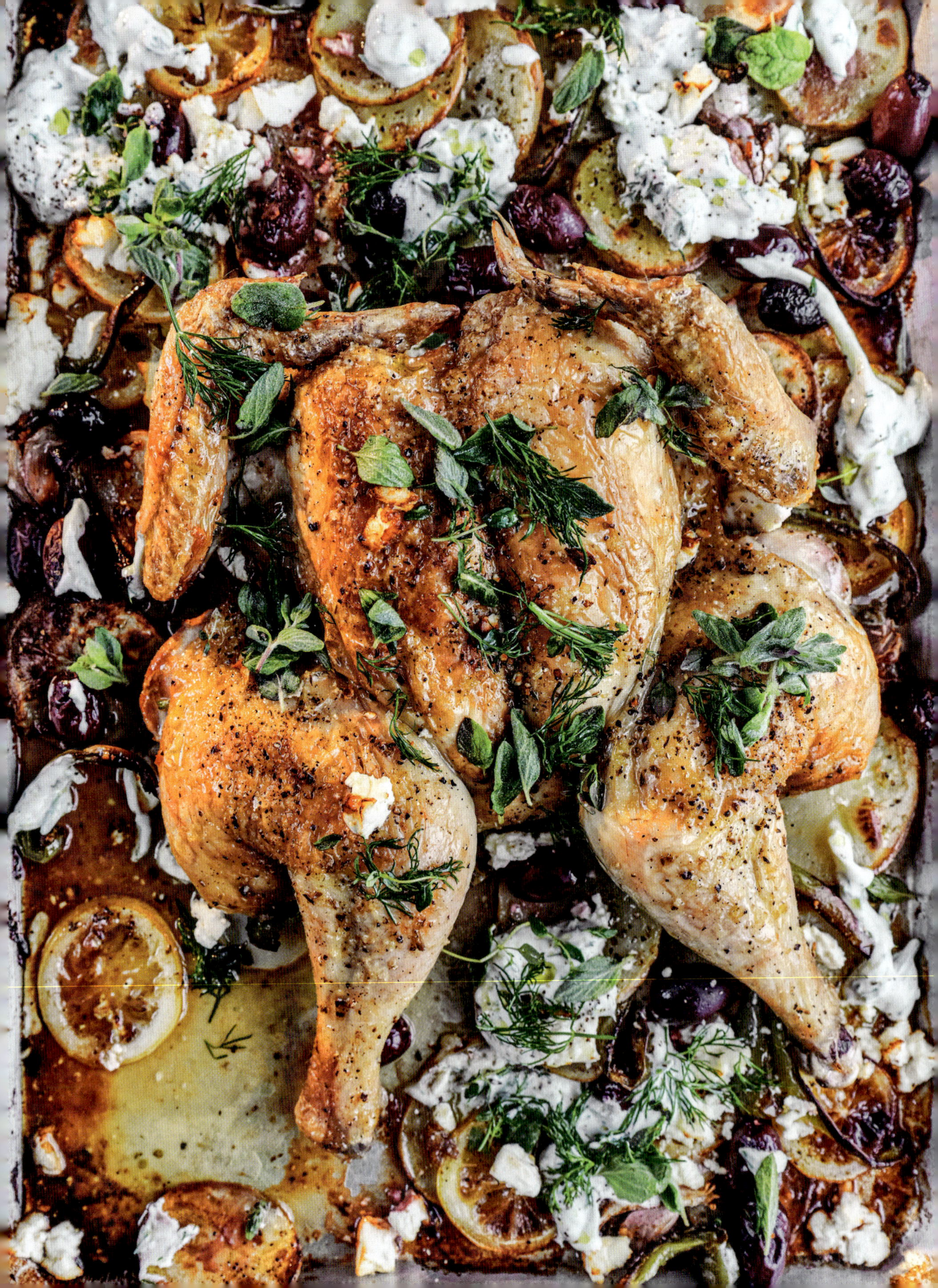

Feta + Olive Spatchcock Chicken

Serves 4
Takes 1 hour 30 minutes

Use a large roasting tin

Gluten-free

700g Maris Piper potatoes
2 lemons
1 green pepper
4 garlic cloves, skin on
4 tbsp extra virgin olive oil
2 tsp dried oregano
1 large chicken (about 1.5kg)
150g feta
150g pitted Kalamata olives
salt and black pepper

FOR THE TZATZIKI
250g Greek yoghurt
1 tbsp extra virgin olive oil
1 lemon
1 garlic clove
¼ cucumber
a small handful of dill leaves

TO GARNISH
6 sprigs of oregano
6 sprigs of lemon thyme
a small handful of dill

Scan for more tasty recipes like this one

Spatchcocking the chicken makes it cook faster, and means there's more surface area for crispy skin. That's science. This dish is inspired by flavours used in Greek cooking. We love how the lemons and green pepper get all sticky and jammy and sweet, and the potatoes soak up the chicken juices. If you're feeling extra lazy, pick up a tzatziki from the supermarket.

01. Preheat the oven to 220°C/200°C fan.

02. Slice the potatoes and lemons to about the thickness of a pound coin (discard any seeds). Deseed the green pepper and cut into 1–2cm strips. Add the potatoes, lemons and green pepper to the roasting tin. Bash the garlic cloves in their skins and add to the tin with 3 tablespoons of the olive oil and the dried oregano. Use your hands to coat everything well.

03. Using sharp kitchen scissors, cut the backbone out of the chicken using the cavity as a guide. Discard the backbone, then lay the chicken, breast-side up, on top of the potatoes and push down hard on the breast-bone until you hear a click. Arrange the thighs splaying outwards, to make sure as much of the chicken skin is exposed as possible. Season everything generously and drizzle the chicken with the remaining olive oil.

04. Roast for 50 minutes, or until the chicken is almost cooked through and the skin is lovely and golden. After 50 minutes, scatter over the feta and olives and return to the oven for a further 10 minutes, or until the juices run clear when the thickest part of the chicken is pierced with a sharp knife.

05. Meanwhile, make the tzatziki. Put the yoghurt and olive oil into a bowl. Finely grate in the lemon zest and the garlic, then squeeze in the lemon juice. Coarsely grate the cucumber and finely chop the dill, then add both to the bowl and mix to combine. Season to taste.

06. Remove the chicken from the oven. Strip the leaves from all the herb sprigs and scatter over, then serve with the tzatziki.

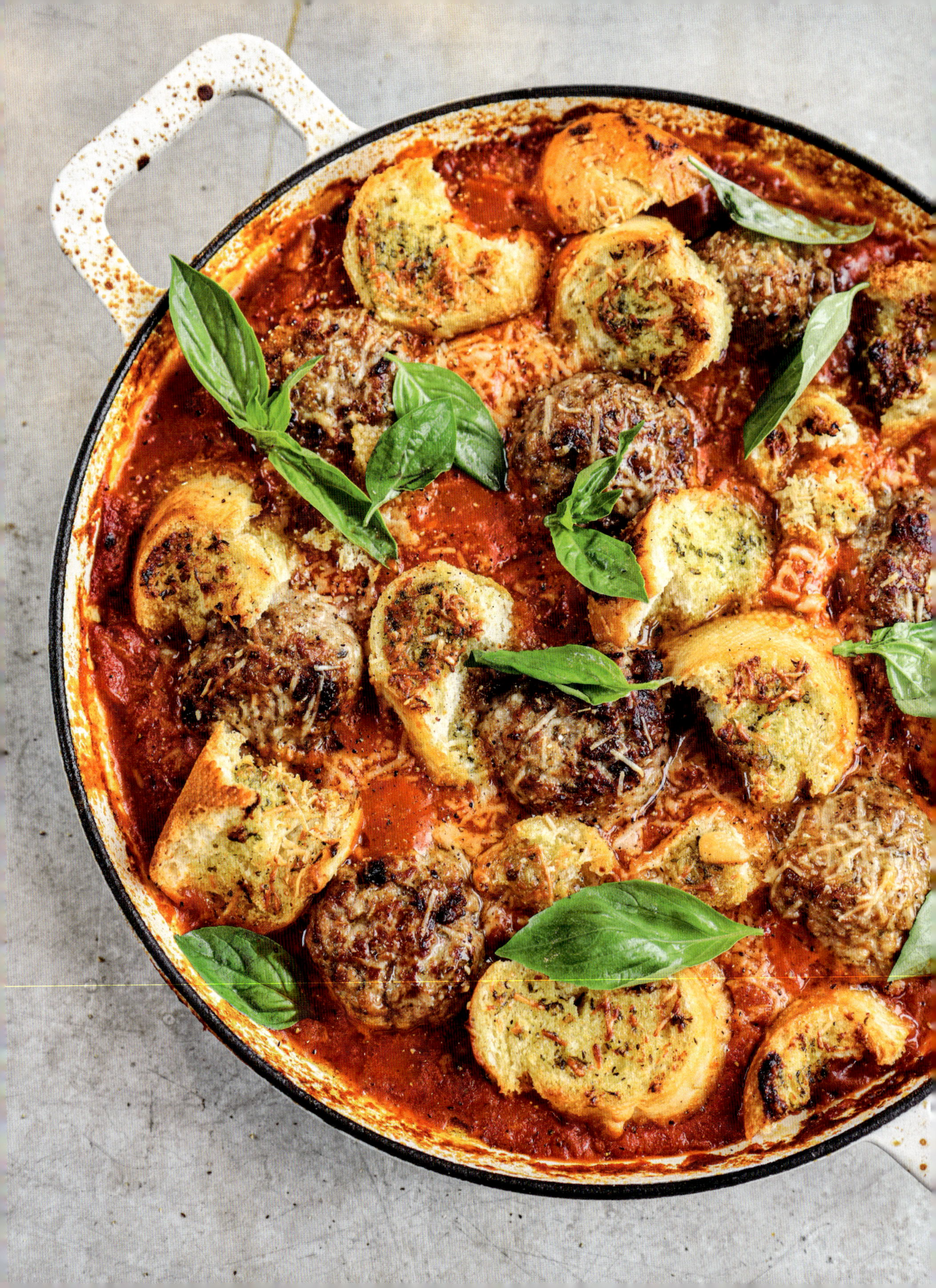

Baked Meatballs with Garlic Bread Topper

Serves 4
Takes 1 hour

Use a large non-stick ovenproof frying pan or shallow casserole pan

2 onions
75g Parmesan
250g beef mince
250g pork mince
1 tsp dried oregano
2 tbsp extra virgin olive oil, plus extra to drizzle
4 garlic cloves
½ tsp dried chilli flakes
2 tbsp tomato purée
2 x 400g tins of plum tomatoes
2 tsp Worcestershire sauce
2 shop-bought garlic baguettes
basil, to garnish
salad, to serve
salt and black pepper

Scan for more tasty recipes like this one

We're pretty thrilled with this one, to be honest. It's a dish that wouldn't look out of place on the menu at your favourite Italian red sauce joint. Soft and juicy meatballs in a rich tomato sauce with crispy crunchy garlic bread croutons? *Madone.*

01. Finely chop the onions and add half to a large bowl. Finely grate the Parmesan into a separate bowl, then tip two-thirds (50g) into the onion bowl, reserving the remaining cheese.

02. Add both the minces, the dried oregano and plenty of salt and pepper to the grated onion and use clean hands to mix together really well. Form into 8 large meatballs (about 75–80g).

03. Preheat the oven to 190°C/170°C fan.

04. Heat 1 tablespoon of the oil in the frying pan over a medium-high heat, add the meatballs and fry for 3–4 minutes on each side until caramelised. Scoop them out onto a clean plate.

05. Pour the remaining oil into the pan, reduce the heat to medium and add the remaining onions along with a pinch of salt. Cook for 5–6 minutes until soft. Meanwhile, finely slice the garlic, then scrape into the pan and cook gently for another minute. Scatter in the chilli flakes, spoon in the tomato purée and cook for 1 minute before tipping in the plum tomatoes. Break up with the back of your wooden spoon and bubble for 5 minutes.

06. Remove the pan from the heat and, using a potato masher, crush the sauce until smooth, then season with the Worcestershire sauce. Return the meatballs to the sauce, then tear 1 garlic bread into pieces over the top. Scatter with the reserved Parmesan and drizzle with more oil.

07. Transfer to the oven for 20 minutes until the topping is golden and crisp. Put the other garlic bread onto a baking tray and bake at the same time.

08. Garnish with basil and serve with a big salad and the extra garlic bread to mop up all that sauce. This is as great at room temperature as it is warm.

Crispy Potato Nacho Pizza

Scan for more tasty recipes like this one

Serves 4
Takes 1 hour

Use a large baking tray

Gluten-free

750g baby potatoes
4 tbsp extra virgin olive oil
4 pickled guindilla chilli peppers
a few sprigs of basil
150g ready-grated mozzarella
250g passata or pizza sauce
1 x small pack pepperoni slices (about 90–120g)
5 tbsp mascarpone
3 tbsp hot honey (or honey mixed with 1½ tsp chilli flakes)
salt and black pepper

TIP: Keep the leftover passata or pizza sauce in the fridge for a few days (or freeze in a small Tupperware) ready to use in your next batch of pasta sauce, soup or breakfast shakshuka.

Can't decide between pizza, chips and nachos? Introducing the Crispy Potato Nacho Pizza™. Roast the baby potatoes until they're tender, smash them down until crisp, then load 'em up with all of your favourite pizza toppings. This one has mozzarella, pepperoni, pickled chillies, mascarpone and hot honey for a spicy, creamy diavolo vibe. It's as good as it sounds.

01. Preheat the oven to 240°C/220°C fan.

02. Halve the baby potatoes if they're large and arrange on the baking tray. Drizzle with 2 tablespoons of the olive oil and season. Roast for 20–25 minutes until tender.

03. Remove the tray from the oven, then using the bottom of a heavy glass, smash down the potatoes (it can help to use a piece of baking paper on top, to prevent the potato sticking to the glass) until they're thin and the skins break – you want them to be just thicker than a pound coin. Once they're all smashed, drizzle with the remaining oil and pop back in the oven for 20 minutes until crisp.

04. Meanwhile, thinly slice the guindilla chillies. Pick the leaves from the basil sprigs and set aside.

05. Once the potatoes are crisp, scatter over the chillies and mozzarella. Pour over the passata and evenly dot with the pepperoni slices. Return to the oven for 8–10 minutes until bubbling and golden.

06. Dollop over the mascarpone, drizzle over the hot honey and scatter with the basil leaves.

FEASTING ONES

Sticky Tamarind Wings

Scan for more tasty recipes like this one

Serves 6
Takes 55 minutes

Use a roasting tin

Gluten-free

These addictive sticky wings are roasted until they're super crispy before being tossed in a sweet, spicy and sour glaze. Jazzed up with coriander, chilli and lime to add an extra bit of zip at the end, these wings are ideal for feeding a group.

1kg chicken wings
2 tbsp olive oil
3 tbsp tamarind paste
2 tbsp honey
1 tbsp sambal oelek or chilli garlic sauce (check the label if making this gluten-free)
2 tbsp ketchup (check the label if making this gluten-free)
salt and black pepper

TO SERVE
a small handful of coriander
1 red chilli
1 spring onion
1 tbsp toasted sesame seeds
1 lime

01. Preheat the oven to 210°C/190°C fan.

02. Pat the chicken wings dry, then place in the roasting tin and drizzle with the oil. Season generously with salt and pepper and toss together. Space them out in the tin and roast for 30–35 minutes.

03. Meanwhile, mix together the tamarind paste, honey, sambal oelek and ketchup in a small bowl.

04. Remove the wings from the oven and pour over the tamarind glaze, mixing to evenly coat. Return to the oven for 10 minutes, tossing halfway through, until cooked through and sticky.

05. Meanwhile, pick the coriander leaves, discarding the stalks, and finely slice the chilli. Slice the spring onion.

06. To serve, zest the lime over the chicken, then scatter over the coriander leaves, chilli and spring onion. Scatter with sesame seeds. Serve with the lime cut into wedges for squeezing over.

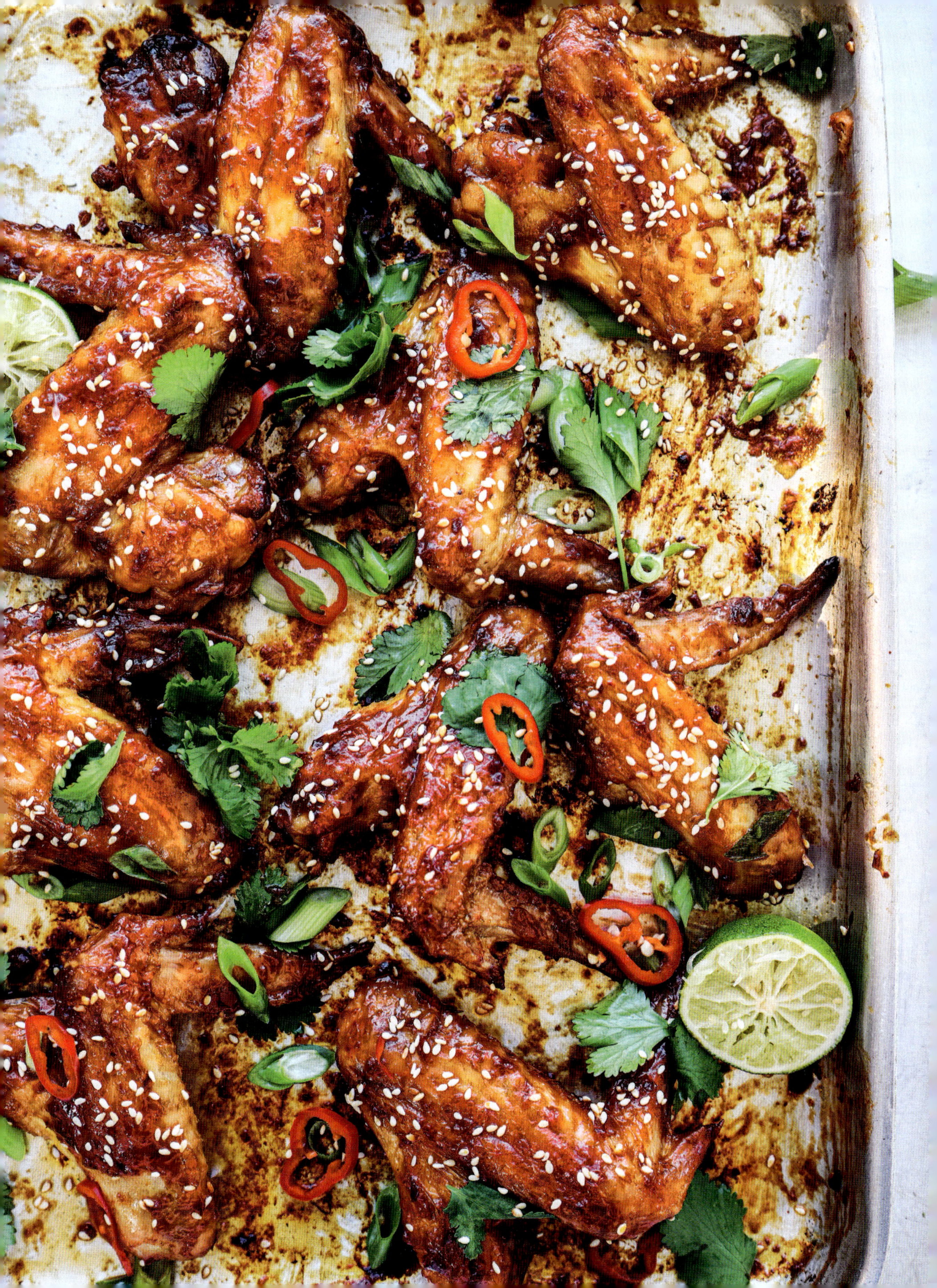

Red Curry Bouillabaisse

Scan for more tasty recipes like this one

Serves 4
Takes 40 minutes + curing (optional)

Use a large, deep saucepan or ovenproof casserole dish with a lid

800g skinless fish fillets (we use a mix of cod, haddock and salmon)
4 large tomatoes
2 tbsp olive oil
a thumb-sized chunk of fresh ginger
4 garlic cloves
3–4 tbsp Thai red curry paste, to taste
2 tbsp tomato purée
1 x 400ml tin of coconut milk
200ml hot fish stock
300g mussels
1 lime
200g large raw prawns
salt and black pepper

TO SERVE
coconut cream (optional)
a handful of coriander leaves
1 lime
1 baguette

This is a bit of a cross between a Thai red curry and a bouillabaisse. It's deceptively easy to make but looks (and tastes) so impressive that it's a great dish to whip out when you feel like showing off. Make sure to mop it up with a crunchy hunk of baguette.

01. Cut the fish into 3cm chunks. If you have time, put the fish into a bowl and add 2 tablespoons of salt. Toss well, then leave to cure in the fridge, uncovered, for up to 24 hours (even 45 minutes will make a difference to how flaky it'll be).

02. Roughly chop the tomatoes. Heat the oil in the saucepan or casserole dish over a medium-high heat. Peel the ginger, then grate with the garlic into the pan or dish and fry for 1 minute. Add the red curry paste and tomato purée and fry for a further 2–3 minutes.

03. Tip in the tomatoes and pour in the coconut milk and stock. Reduce the heat to medium and simmer for 15 minutes.

04. Meanwhile, rinse the mussels in cold water, removing the beards and discarding any that have broken shells or don't close when tapped.

05. Remove the sauce from the heat and, using a stick blender, blend until smooth. Juice the lime, then add to the sauce. Season well.

06. Add the fish chunks, mussels and prawns and cover with the lid. Cook over a medium heat for 4–5 minutes, until the fish is flaking apart, the prawns are cooked through and the mussels have opened. Discard any that remain shut.

07. Serve in the pan or dish, drizzled with a little coconut cream, if you like, and scattered with the coriander. Serve with the lime, cut into wedges, and chunky bread on the side.

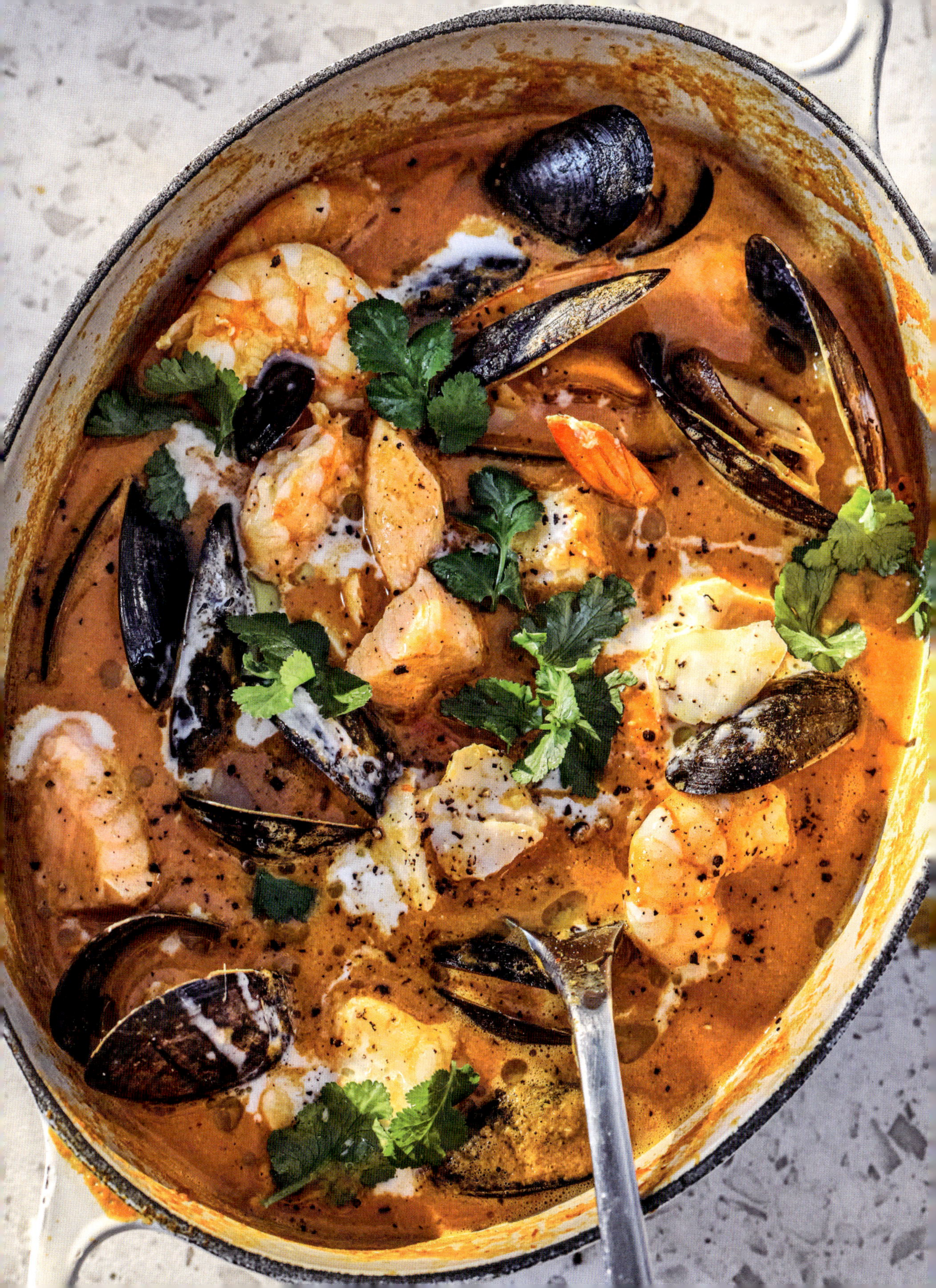

fancy

fancy ones fancy

Guinness Soda Bread + Cornichon Butter

Serves 4–6
Takes 45 minutes

Use a large baking tray

Veggie

300g plain flour
200g wholemeal bread flour, plus extra for sprinkling
2 tsp bicarbonate of soda
1 tsp fine sea salt
250ml Guinness
200ml buttermilk
2 tbsp black treacle

FOR THE CORNICHON BUTTER
150g unsalted butter, softened
50g extra mature Cheddar cheese
a handful of chives
10 cornichons, plus liquid from the jar if needed
salt and black pepper

Scan for more tasty recipes like this one

Soda bread is probably the easiest bread to make. We've added in Guinness and black treacle to give it a deep, dark, malty finish. You'll likely end up making a bit more cornichon butter than you need but that's the exact opposite of a bad thing. Slather it on slabs of your bread before building some big bolshy sandwiches.

01. Preheat the oven to 200°C/180°C fan and line the baking tray with baking paper.

02. Tip the flours into a large bowl and add the bicarb and salt. Mix briefly. Pour the Guinness into a measuring jug and leave it to settle for a bit to make sure you have 250ml. Add the buttermilk, then whisk in the black treacle.

03. Make a well in the flour, then pour the liquid into the middle. Use a spoon to mix into an even dough with no streaks of flour left, but be careful not to overmix.

04. Shape into a rough round, then place on the lined tray. Sprinkle the dough with a little flour, then use a knife to mark a cross into the dough. Bake for 30–35 minutes until risen, caramelised and the bread sounds hollow when tapped on the base. Leave to cool on the tray.

05. Meanwhile, make the cornichon butter. Tip the butter into a bowl and beat with a wooden spoon until really soft, then grate in the Cheddar. Finely chop the chives and cornichons, then mix into the butter. Add a little splash of the liquid from the jar of cornichons if the butter is a little thick, then season.

06. Slice the bread while it's still warm and slather with the butter.

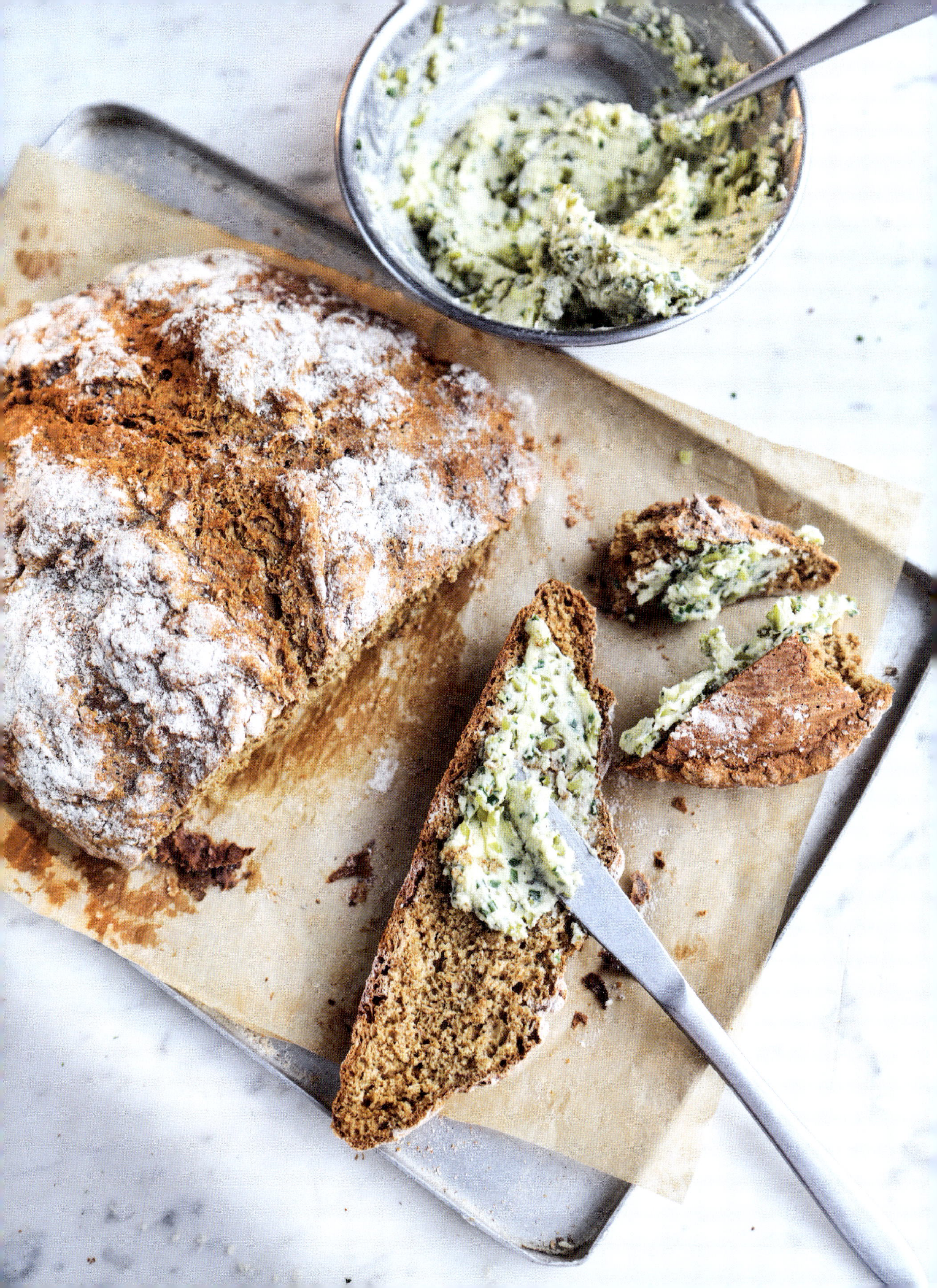

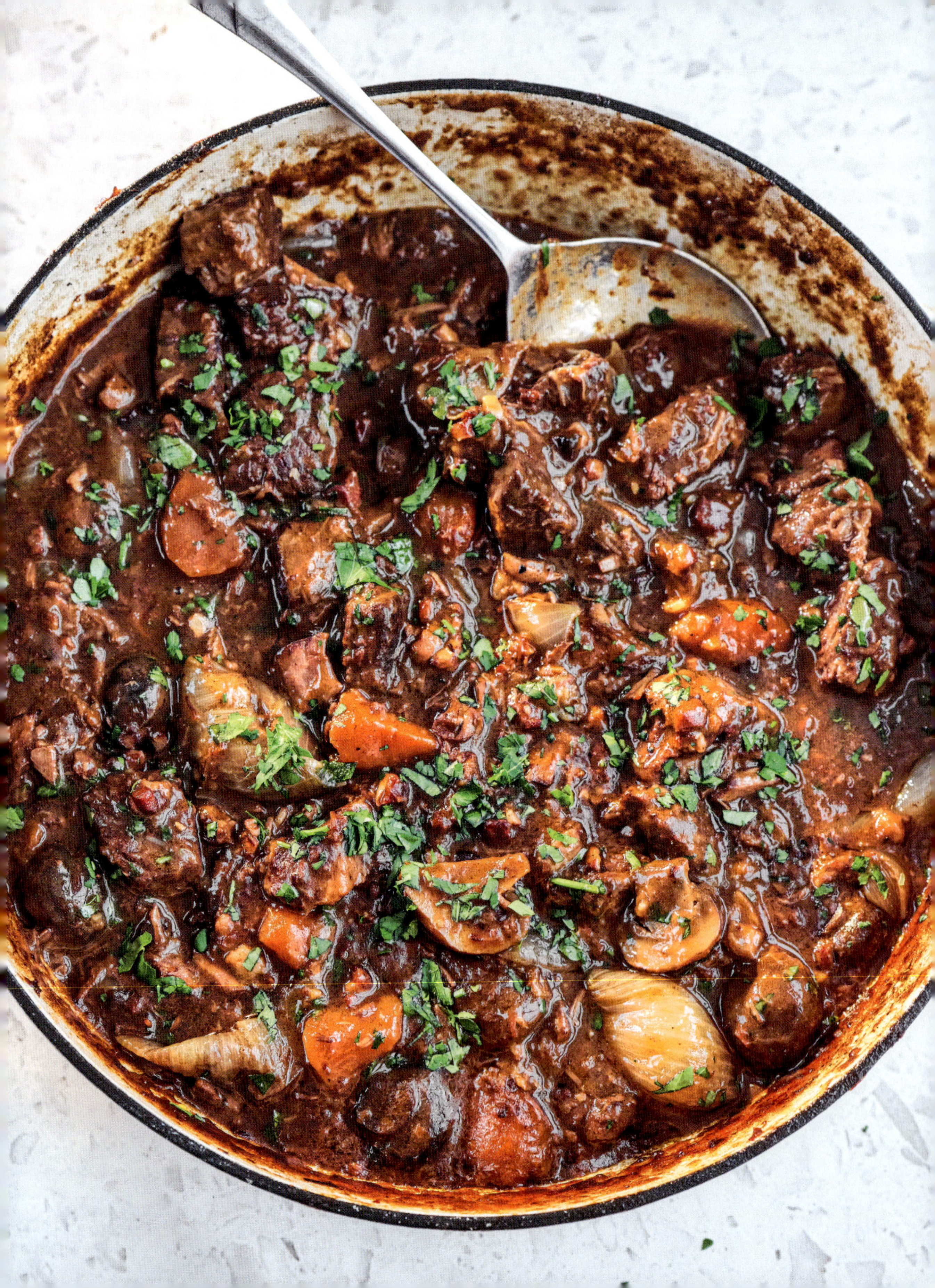

Beef Buckfastignon

Serves 4–6
Takes 3 hours 30 minutes

Use an ovenproof casserole with a lid

1 onion
2 carrots
1kg beef brisket or boneless shin of beef
250g smoked bacon lardons
3 tbsp plain flour
2 tbsp tomato purée
750ml Buckfast Tonic Wine
250ml hot beef or chicken stock
a handful of thyme sprigs
250g baby shallots
250g chestnut mushrooms
2 tbsp apple cider vinegar
salt and black pepper

TO SERVE
75g strong mature Cheddar
a handful of flat leaf parsley

Now Buckfast has a bit of a ropey reputation in the UK, but it's perfectly suited for this recipe. It's fruity, sweet and packs a punch. Mingle Bucky's unique flavour profile with slow-cooked beef and you've got a stew going. We'd recommend buying two bottles for the occasion – cook with one and serve it with the other. Just don't blame us when you wake up stark naked on Tower Bridge with a full stomach.

01. Roughly chop the onion, then roughly chop the carrots and set aside.

02. Cut the beef into 5cm pieces and season generously.

03. Put the smoked bacon lardons into the casserole dish and set over a medium-high heat. Cook for 3–4 minutes, stirring, until caramelised. Using a slotted spoon, scoop out onto a small plate. Add the brisket pieces to the pan, in batches, and cook until really caramelised on both sides, transferring each batch to a plate.

04. Tip the onion and carrots into the pan and fry for 3–4 minutes until starting to brown. Reduce the heat to medium and stir in the flour and tomato purée. Cook for 2 minutes, stirring. Pour in the Buckfast and stock, and scatter in the thyme leaves from the sprigs, then add the beef back to the pan along with any resting juices.

05. Bring to a simmer, then reduce the heat to low, cover with the lid and cook gently for 2 hours.

Continued overleaf

Continued from previous page

SWAP: This is a phenomenal beef bourguignon recipe, if you use red wine instead of buckfast.

Scan for more tasty recipes like this one

06. Halve any large baby shallots and mushrooms. Remove the lid and scatter the lardons, shallots and mushrooms into the pan, then cook for another hour, uncovered, until the meat is meltingly tender and the sauce reduced. Season and stir through the apple cider vinegar.

07. Just before serving, coarsely grate the Cheddar and roughly chop the leaves of the parsley.

08. Spoon the stew into shallow bowls, then top with loads of grated cheese and the parsley leaves.

Coffee-Roasted Pork Belly + Oregano Salsa

Serves 4
Takes 3 hours + overnight salting + resting

Use a large roasting tin

Gluten-free

1 x 1kg pork belly (unrolled)
1 tbsp instant coffee granules
1 tbsp paprika
1 tbsp brown sugar
1kg baby potatoes
6 shallots
1 garlic bulb
500ml hot chicken stock (check the label if making this gluten-free)
200ml dry white wine
½ x 25g pack fresh oregano
1 red chilli
1 tbsp red wine vinegar
salt and black pepper

The spiced coffee rub we've coated this pork belly in is what gives it a robust, rich and smoky flavour. Nestled in the tin with a boatload of Hasselback baby potatoes, this little piggy is a real showstopper.

01. Trim any sinew from the meaty side of the pork belly, then score the skin. Rub with salt all over and leave on a rack in the fridge overnight.

02. The next day, preheat the oven to 180°C/160°C fan.

03. Mix together the instant coffee, paprika and brown sugar in a small bowl. Remove the pork from the fridge and rub the flesh side with the spice mix (leave the skin plain).

04. Using a sharp knife, cut slits into each baby potato from top to bottom, without cutting all the way through, to make Hasselback potatoes (pop a wooden spoon either side to make this easier if you like). Cut the shallots and the garlic bulb in half.

05. Grab the roasting tin and tip in the shallots and potatoes, then sit the garlic in the corner of the tin, cut-sides down. Whack the pork on top, skin-side up, and pour around the stock and wine, taking care not to pour any on the pork. Place in the oven for 1½ hours, then crank up the oven to its highest setting and roast the pork at the top of the oven for a further 30–45 minutes until the skin is super crispy; add a splash of water if the tray starts to dry out too much.

Continued overleaf

Continued from previous page

06. Remove the pork to a plate and leave to rest for 15 minutes or so. Turn the oven off, but keep the potatoes and shallots warm in there.

07. Just before serving, strip the leaves from the oregano sprigs and thinly slice the chilli. Pour the pork fat, stock and wine from the roasting tin into a bowl and mix through the chilli, oregano leaves and vinegar. Season and squeeze in the roasted garlic. Mix together to a make a delicious dressing, loosening with a splash of water if needed

08. Cut the pork into thick slices and serve family-style with the Hasselback baby potatoes, roasted shallots and oregano and chilli dressing.

Scan for more tasty recipes like this one

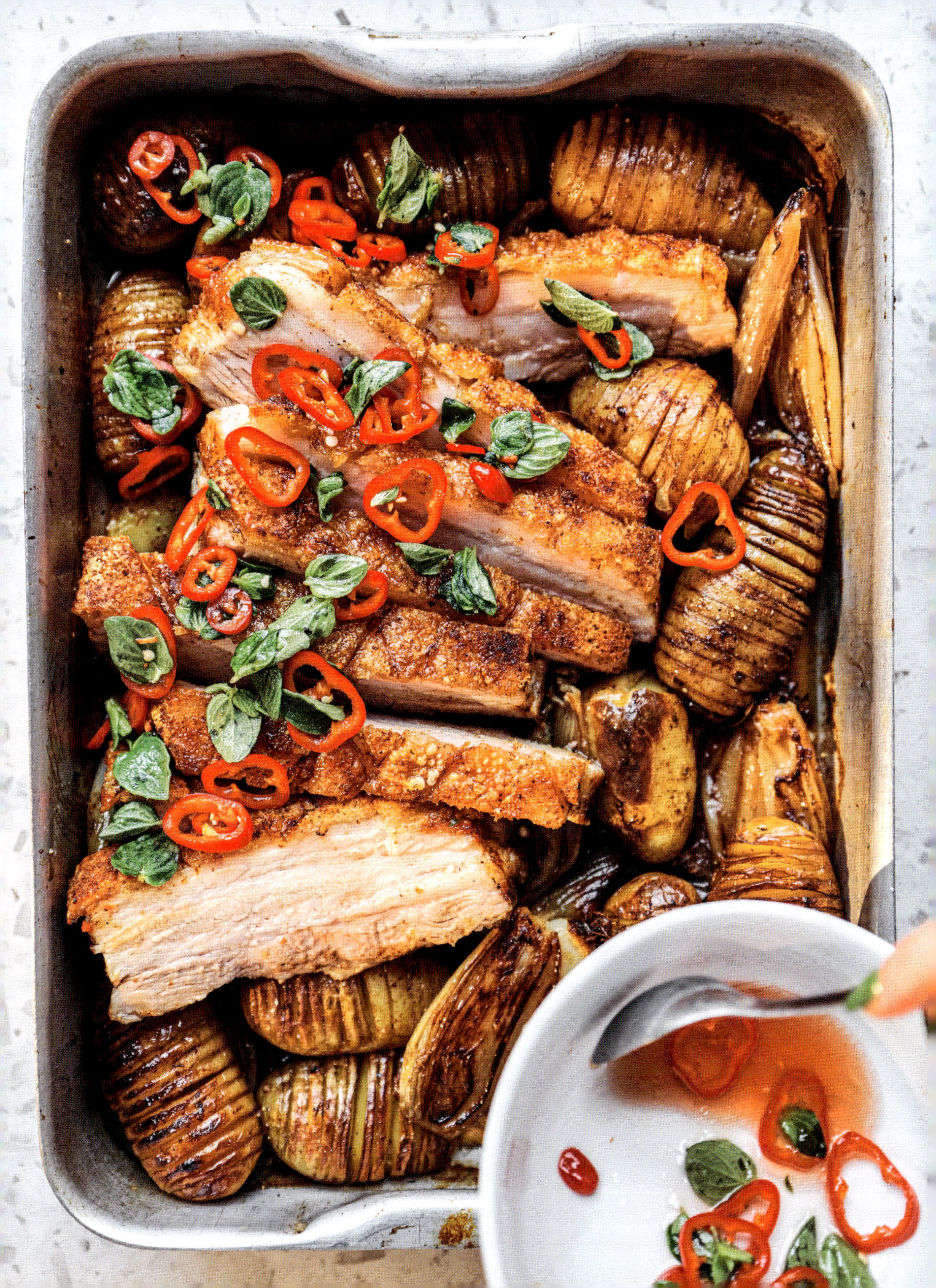

Date-Night Chimichurri Ribeye

Serves 2
Takes 40 minutes + salting + resting

Use a large ovenproof non-stick frying pan

Gluten-free

750-800g bone-in ribeye steak
500g Maris Piper potatoes
2 tsp vegetable oil
200g green beans
25g butter
1 garlic clove
1 tbsp pink peppercorns
100g feta (optional)
salt and black pepper

FOR THE CORIANDER CHIMICHURRI
1 small shallot
1 red chilli
a small bunch of coriander
2 tbsp extra virgin olive oil
2 tbsp red wine vinegar
1 tsp dried oregano

Scan for more tasty recipes like this one

A one-pan, date-night banger. Need we say more?

01. Remove the steak from the fridge 1 hour before you want to cook it, so that it comes up to room temperature. Season generously with salt.

02. Peel the potatoes and cut into 1cm-thick strips.

03. Preheat the oven to 200°C/180°C fan. Heat the frying pan over a high heat. Once hot, drizzle in 1 teaspoon of the oil and lay the potato strips in a single layer. Fry for 5 minutes until browned; turn the heat down a touch if they start to catch too much. Push to the side of the pan, stacking them up if you need to, to make room for your giant steak.

04. Rub the steak with the remaining oil, then add to the pan and sear for 2–3 minutes on each side. Flip the steak again, then arrange the potatoes around the steak and scatter around the green beans. Top the steak with the butter, garlic clove (don't worry about peeling) and peppercorns.

05. Transfer to the oven and cook for 8–16 minutes (depending on the thickness of the steak) until the internal temperature of the steak reads 50°C on a digital thermometer. Remove the steak to a plate and leave to rest for 5–10 minutes. Test the potatoes; if still a little firm, return the pan to the oven for 5 minutes further, or until cooked through.

06. Meanwhile, make the chimichurri. Finely chop the shallot and chilli, then the coriander. Scrape into a bowl and add the oil, vinegar and oregano, season and mix well.

07. Remove the steak from the bone and slice. Pour any resting juices into the pan, then arrange the steak in the pan. Smush the garlic clove (discard the skin) and stir through the veg.

08. Spoon over the chimichurri, crumble over the feta (if using) and serve.

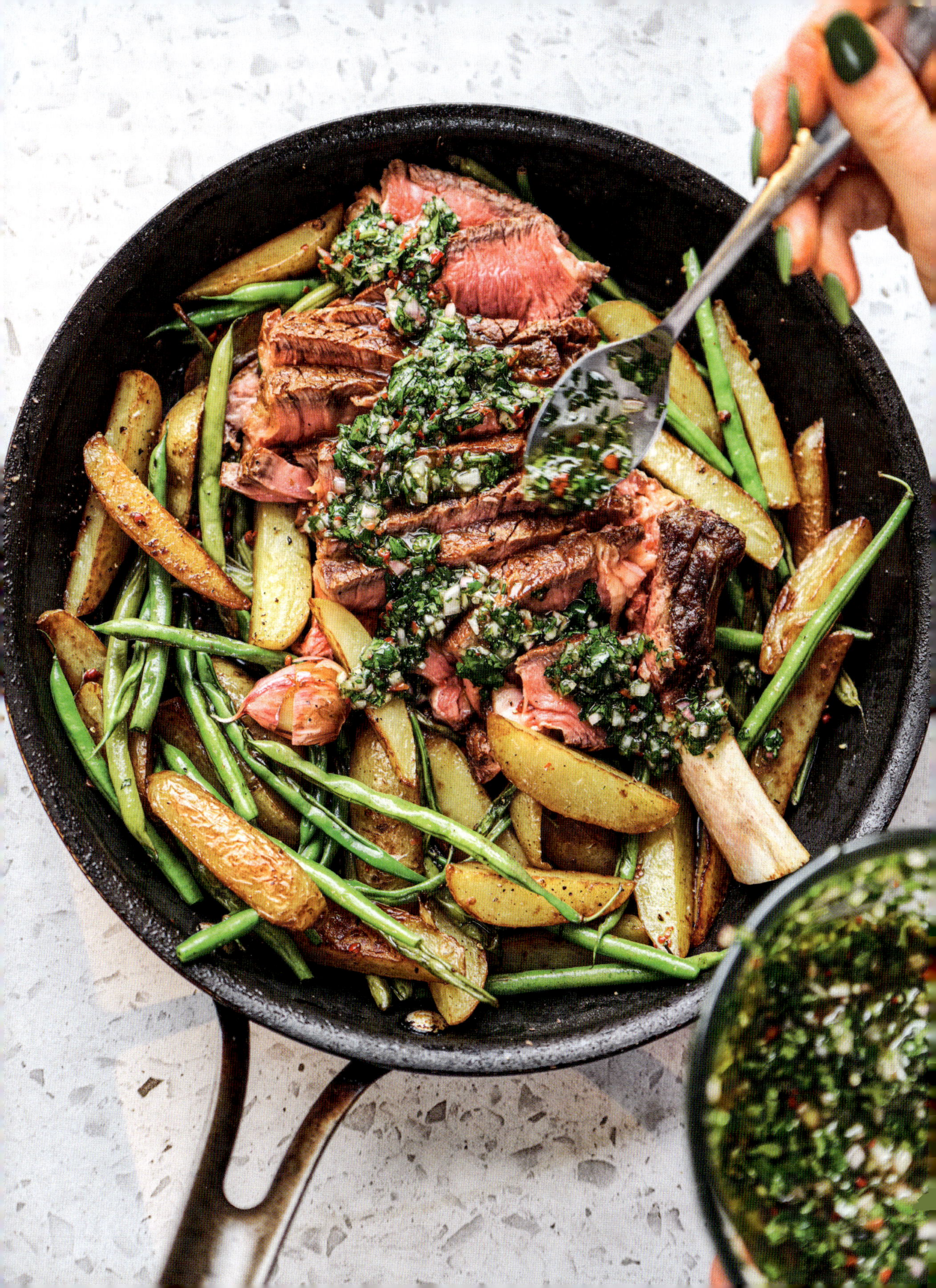

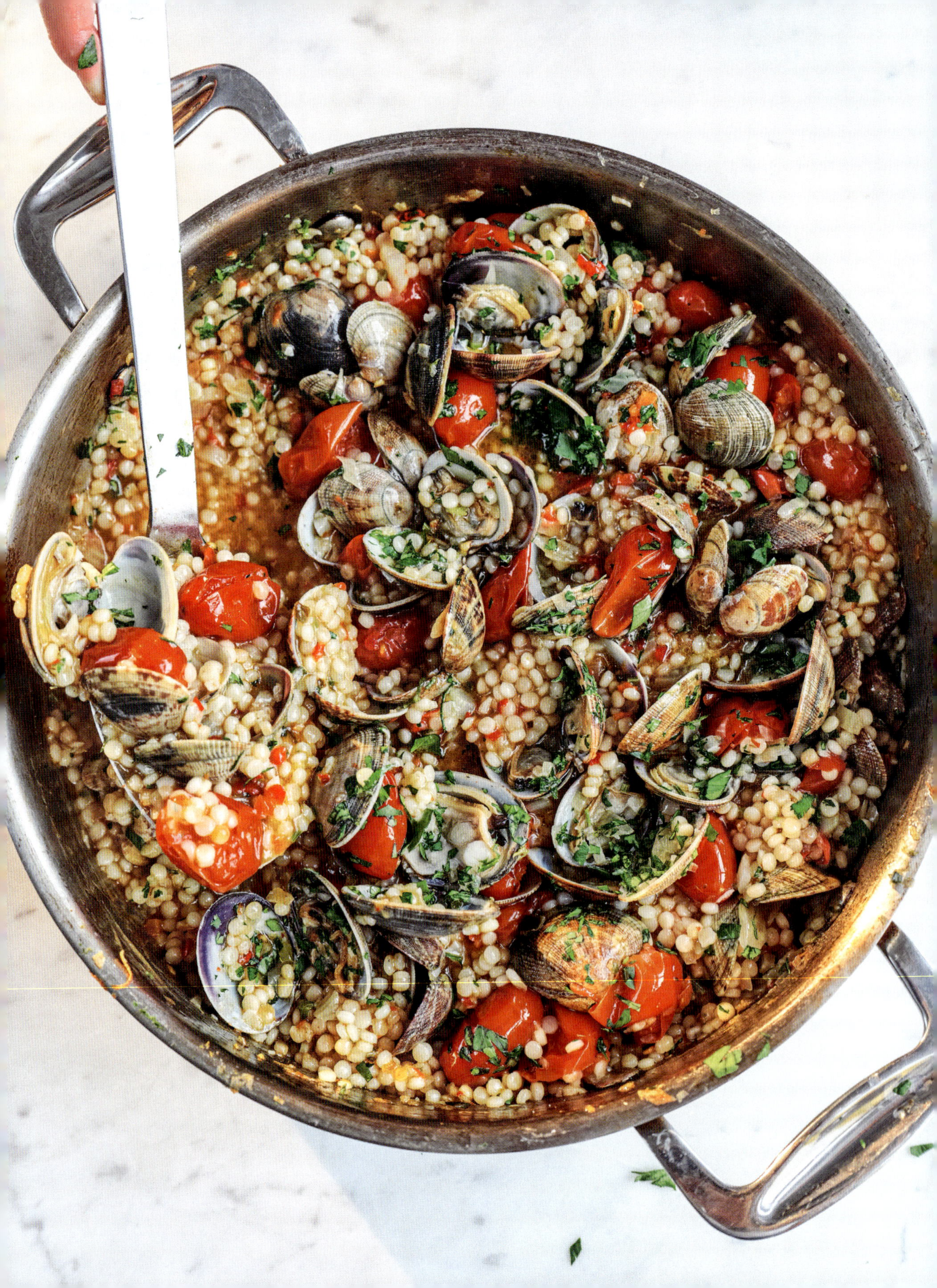

Calabrian Chilli Clams + Burst Tomatoes

Serves 4
Takes 35 minutes

Use a saucepan with a lid

500g clams
1 fennel bulb
1 shallot
4 garlic cloves
25g flat leaf parsley
4 tbsp olive oil
100ml dry white wine
200g fregola or giant couscous
400g Datterini tomatoes
2 tsp Calabrian chilli paste
150ml hot vegetable stock
1 lemon
salt and black pepper

SWAP: If you can't find Calabrian chilli paste, you can use harissa or an alternative chilli paste.

Scan for more tasty recipes like this one

This is a great dish for hosting. Spicy, umami and unbelievably fresh, these clams and fregola come bobbing in a hot Calabrian chilli and tomato broth that'll brighten up any mealtime.

01. Discard any clams that have a broken shell or that don't close when tapped. Give them a rinse under cold water until the shells are clean, then leave in a bowl of cold water to purge for 20 minutes to 1 hour to make sure they're not sandy or gritty. Set aside.

02. Next, finely dice the fennel and shallot, then finely slice the garlic. Pick the parsley leaves and finely slice the stalks.

03. Drain the clams and set aside.

04. Heat the oil in the saucepan over a medium heat, add the parsley stalks, fennel, shallot and garlic and cook everything for 5–7 minutes until softened. Pour in the wine and add the clams, cover with the lid and cook for 5–7 minutes until the clams have opened.

05. Remove the clams from the pan and discard any that remain shut. If you prefer, you can remove the clam meat and discard the shells.

06. Add the fregola, tomatoes, chilli paste and half of the stock to the pan and cook for about 10 minutes until the fregola is al dente, adding more stock if needed.

07. Meanwhile, finely mince the parsley leaves and juice the lemon. Once cooked, stir the parsley and clams through the fregola, then season with the lemon juice and salt and pepper.

FANCY ONES

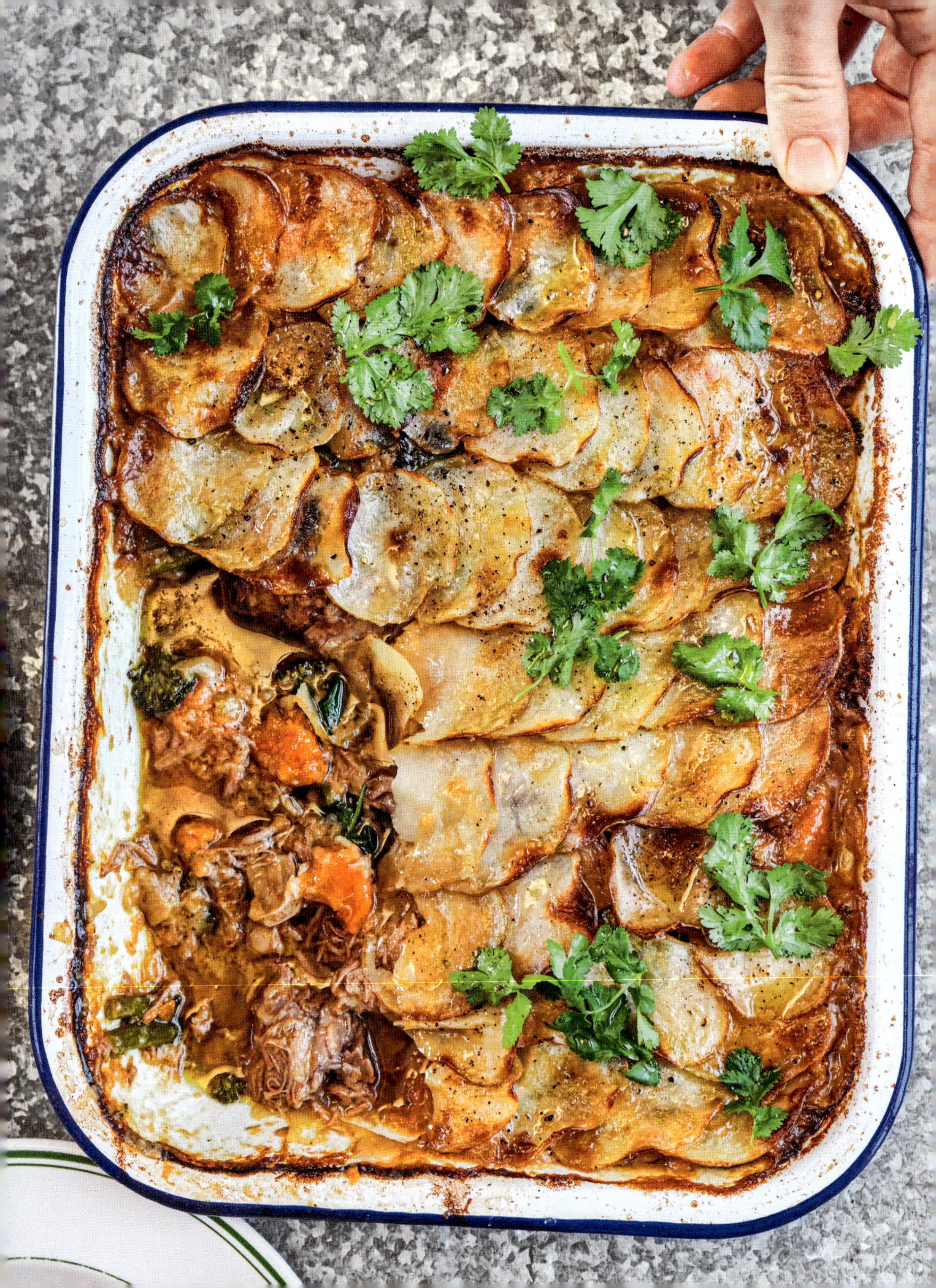

Massaman-Spiced Lamb Pie

Serves 4–6
Takes about 4 hours

Use a large deep roasting tin

Gluten-free

1.5–1.8kg shoulder of lamb
4 tbsp vegetable oil
10 small shallots
3 carrots
1 Thai chilli
3 tbsp massaman curry paste (check the label if making this gluten-free)
500ml hot chicken stock (check the label if making this gluten-free)
1 x 400ml tin of coconut milk
600g Maris Piper potatoes
1 tbsp fish sauce (check the label if making this gluten-free)
2 tbsp smooth peanut butter
250g Tenderstem broccoli
a large handful of coriander leaves, to garnish
salt and black pepper

Scan for more tasty recipes like this one

This massaman-spiced lamb pie is hot and rich, just like we all aspire to be. Half curry, half hotpot, half pie (yes, we know that's three halves, but whatever), this is the perfect Sunday dinner party number.

01. Preheat the oven to 170°C/150°C fan.

02. Set the roasting tin over a medium-high heat. Rub the lamb with salt, then add to the hot tin with 1 tablespoon of oil. Cook until browned, turning halfway through until dark golden on each side, around 8–10 minutes.

03. Meanwhile, peel the shallots, but leave them whole. Peel and cut the carrots into chunks similar in size to the shallots, then split the chilli down the middle.

04. Remove the lamb from the tin and set aside. Pop the veg into the roasting tin with another 1 tablespoon of oil and sauté for 5–6 minutes. Add the massaman paste and cook for a further 2–3 minutes. Pour in the stock and coconut milk, then bring the whole lot to the boil.

05. Nestle the lamb in the tin, wrap tightly with foil and put in the oven for 2½–3 hours, until meltingly tender.

06. Just before the lamb is ready, thinly slice the potatoes (use a mandoline if you have one).

07. Whip the tin out of the oven and use a spoon to skim off any excess fat. Discard the bone which should be easy to slide out and pull the lamb into generous chunks. Add the fish sauce and peanut butter and stir through. If it seems very watery, you may want to reduce it for 10–15 minutes until glossy. Chunk up the broccoli and stir through the lamb.

08. Increase the oven temperature to 220°C/200°C fan. Arrange the potato slices over the top of the pulled lamb and veggies in an overlapping layer, then drizzle with the remaining 2 tablespoons of oil. Return to the oven for 30–35 minutes until bubbling and crispy.

09. Tear the coriander leaves over the top of the pie and serve.

FANCY ONES

'Nduja Chicken with Creamy Rigatoni

Serves 4
Takes 55 minutes

Use a large non-stick ovenproof frying pan

125g ball mozzarella
4 boneless, skinless chicken breasts
4 tbsp 'nduja paste (about 50g)
glug of olive oil
4 shallots
3 garlic cloves
2 tsp tomato purée
400ml chicken stock
350g fresh rigatoni (or other short pasta, such as penne or fusilli)
25g basil
2 tbsp mascarpone
40g Parmesan
salt and black pepper

Some people are anti-chicken and anti-pasta. We are not those people. This recipe has got all the Mob buzzwords we could ever ask for so, as you can predict, it's an absolute corker.

01. Preheat the oven to 230°C/210°C fan.

02. Cut your mozzarella into small chunks. Using a sharp knife, cut a little pocket in each chicken breast, then stuff each cavity with 1 tablespoon of the 'nduja paste and a quarter of the mozzarella.

03. Heat the frying pan over a high heat and once hot, add a good glug of oil. Fry the chicken for 2–3 minutes until golden brown.

04. Meanwhile, finely dice the shallots and thinly slice the garlic.

05. Remove the chicken from the pan and set aside. Add the veg with a pinch of salt and sizzle away over a medium-high heat for 5 minutes, then add the tomato purée and cook for a further 5–6 minutes, stirring, until nicely caramelised.

06. Pour in the stock and deglaze, scraping the bits up from the bottom of the pan with a wooden spoon, then bring to a boil. Add the pasta and stir through. Pop the chicken on top, skin-side up, then transfer to the oven and roast for 20 minutes. Check the chicken is cooked through; if not, pop it back in for a further 5 minutes and check again.

07. Meanwhile, tear the basil leaves, discarding the stalks, and set aside.

08. Remove the chicken breasts from the pan, then stir the mascarpone through the pasta and grate in the Parmesan. Stir until super glossy. Sit the chicken back on top of the pasta, scatter with the basil leaves and finish with a grind of black pepper.

Scan for more tasty recipes like this one

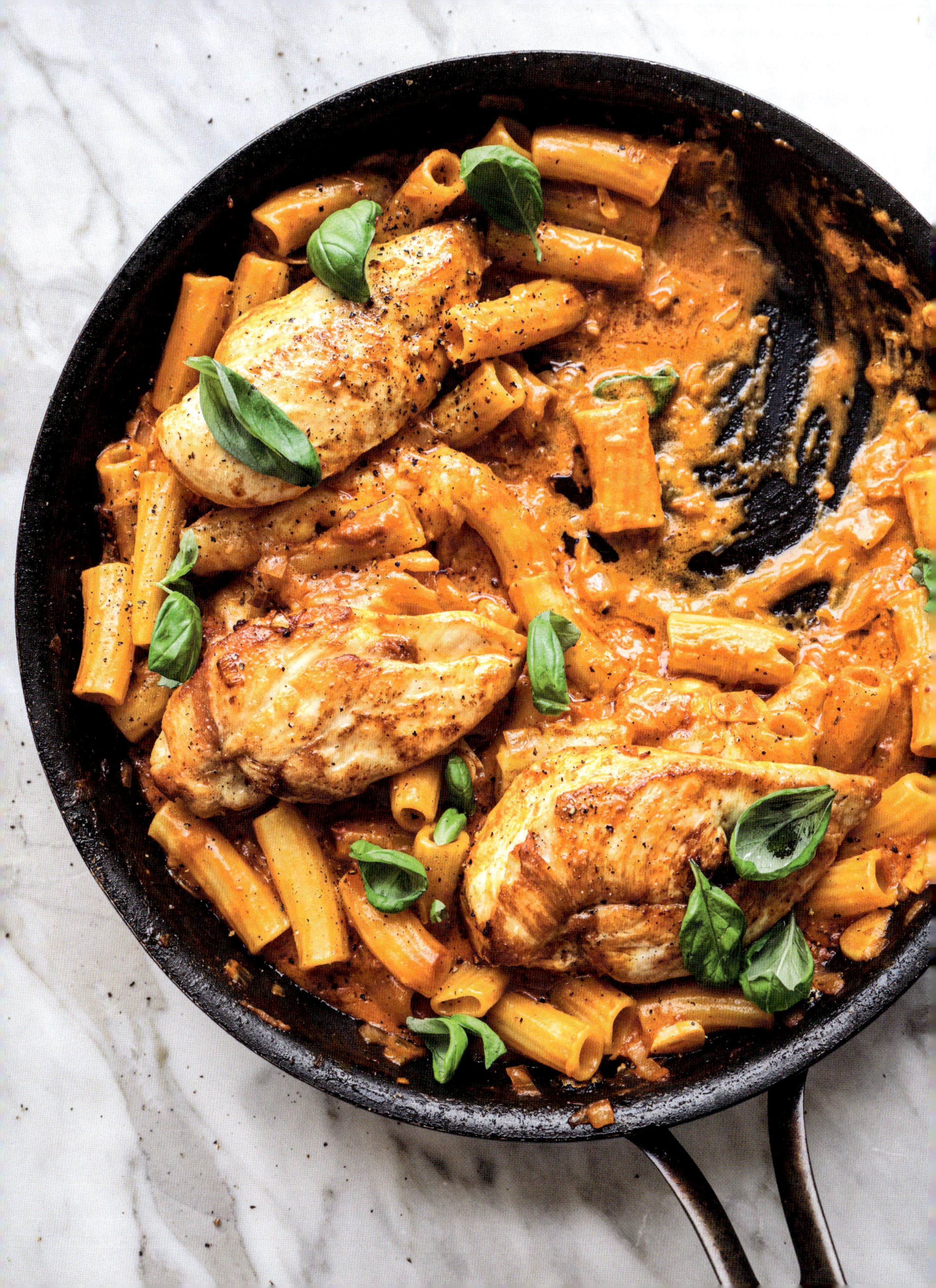

Salmon, Crushed Potatoes + Olive Salsa

Scan for more tasty recipes like this one

Serves 4
Takes 50 minutes

Use a roasting tin

Gluten-free

750g new potatoes
4 tbsp extra virgin olive oil
2 tsp dried oregano
1 side of salmon (about 850g)
2 tsp honey
200g green beans
salt and black pepper

FOR THE OLIVE SALSA
120g pitted Gordal olives
1 banana shallot
a large handful of dill leaves
a large handful of flat leaf parsley leaves
2 tbsp capers
5 cornichons
1 lemon
2 tbsp sherry vinegar
1 tbsp extra virgin olive oil

Briny, salty goodness. The olive salsa has got huge tartare energy and it's what really makes this dish sing. Definitely go for Gordal olives if you can – they're meaty and juicy and make all the difference.

01. Preheat the oven to 220°C/200°C fan. Halve the new potatoes, then pop into a bowl and toss with 2 tablespoons of the olive oil and the dried oregano. Season generously with salt and pepper. Tip into the roasting tin and roast for 25 minutes until almost tender.

02. Remove from the oven. Using the bottom of a heavy glass, press down the potatoes (it can help to use a piece of baking paper on top, to prevent potato sticking to the glass) until they burst and crush. Return to the oven for 10 minutes until golden and crisp.

03. Nestle the salmon in the tin and spread the honey on top. Trim the green beans, then scatter around. Drizzle all the ingredients with the remaining olive oil and season generously. Return to the oven and roast for 12 minutes until the salmon is pink and opaque.

04. While the salmon is cooking, make your salsa. Smash the Gordal olives with the back of your knife and roughly chop. Finely chop the shallot, dill, parsley, capers and cornichons, then put into a small bowl. Zest the lemon into the bowl, then squeeze in the juice. Stir in the vinegar and olive oil.

05. When the salmon is cooked through, spoon over the salsa and enjoy.

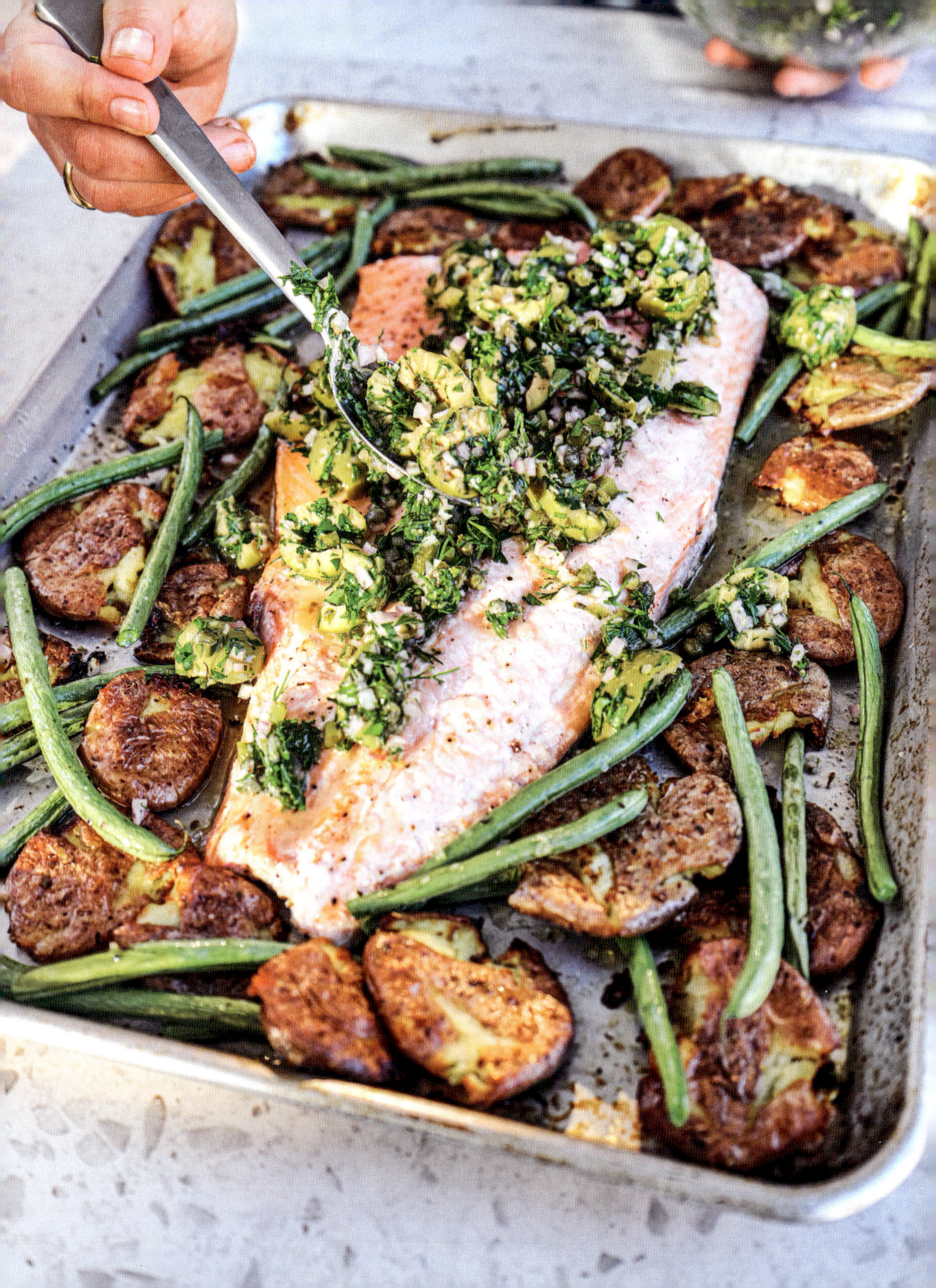

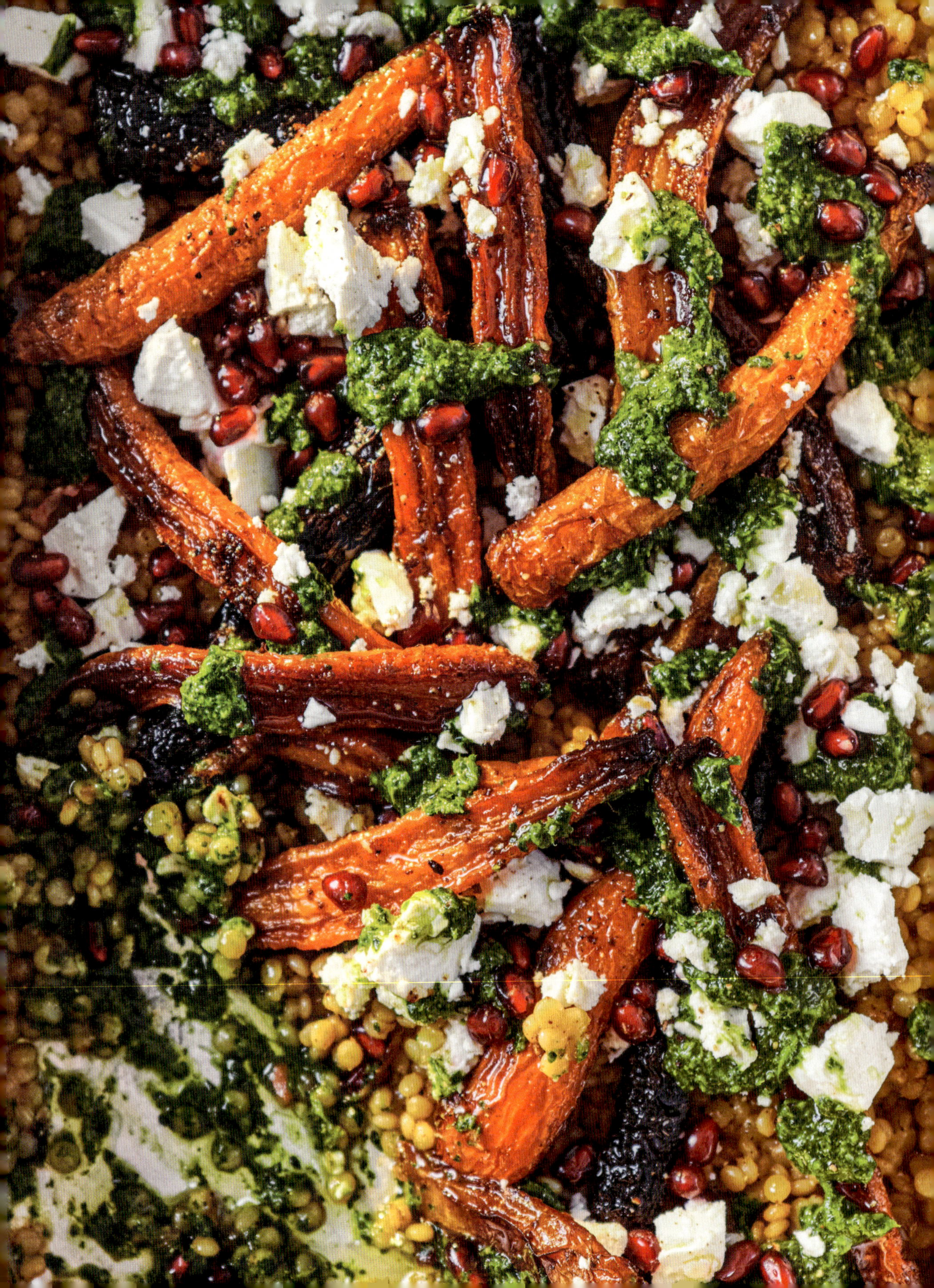

Caramelised Carrots With Feta + Zhoug

Scan for more tasty recipes like this one

Serves 4
Takes 50 minutes

Use a roasting tin

Veggie

500g carrots
3 tbsp butter, softened
2 tbsp brown sugar
2 tsp ground cumin
200g giant couscous
500ml hot vegetable stock
60g feta
20g pomegranate seeds
salt and black pepper

FOR THE ZHOUG
1 garlic clove
1 lemon
100ml extra virgin olive oil
a bunch of coriander
½ bunch of flat leaf parsley
1–3 green chillies, to taste
½ tsp ground cumin
½ tsp ground cardamom
1 tsp sea salt

SWAP: You coud try this with butternut squash chunks instead of carrots. It would also be lovely with crushed walnuts or pistachios on top.

Zhoug is a spicy Middle Eastern sauce that has an unbeatable freshness which cuts through the sweet carrots and tangy feta in this like a hot knife through butter. Go easy on the green chillies when you're starting off the zhoug, you can always add more later but you can't take any away.

01. Preheat the oven to 220°C/200°C fan.

02. Halve the carrots lengthways, then place in the roasting tin and toss with the butter, sugar and cumin. Arrange the coated carrots, cut-sides down, in the tin and season generously. Roast for 30–35 minutes until the cut sides are deeply caramelised.

03. Meanwhile, make the zhoug. Finely grate the garlic into a food processor, then zest in the lemon and squeeze in the juice. Add the olive oil, coriander, parsley, chillies and spices and blitz to combine. Alternatively, chop everything as finely as you can by hand. Season with the sea salt and set aside.

04. Remove the carrots from the roasting tin and set aside. Add the giant couscous to the tin and pour over the stock. Cover with foil and return to the oven for 8 minutes until tender.

05. Remove the foil from the tin, then scatter the carrots over the couscous and return to the oven for 2 minutes to warm.

06. Serve with a drizzle of zhoug, crumble over the feta and scatter over the pomegranate seeds

FANCY ONES

Whole Roast Cauliflower Curry

Serves 4
Takes 1 hour 45 minutes

Use a large, deep ovenproof frying pan or shallow casserole pan

Veggie

150g unsalted butter, softened
2 tbsp black mustard seeds
2 tsp Kashmiri or other mild chilli powder
1 tbsp ground cumin
1 tbsp ground coriander
1 tbsp garam masala
1 large cauliflower (about 800–900g)
vegetable oil, to drizzle
1 onion
6 garlic cloves
a thumb-sized chunk of fresh ginger
1 x 400g tin of chopped tomatoes
150ml double cream, plus extra to serve (optional)
100g baby spinach
½ lemon
salt and black pepper

TO SERVE
4 naan
handful of coriander leaves

Scan for more tasty recipes like this one

This is a proper veggie showstopper. Expect to hear a chorus of 'oohs' and 'aahs' when you bring it to the table. The cauliflower and sauce get a gnarly roasted and smoky flavour after being cooked in the oven.

01. Preheat the oven to 190°C/170°C fan.

02. Tip the butter into a large deep bowl and beat until completely smooth and soft. Add the mustard seeds and all the ground spices along with loads of salt and pepper and beat together.

03. Trim the base of the cauliflower and get rid of any thicker outer leaves, then put it whole into the middle of the frying pan. Smear two-thirds of the butter all over the surface of the cauliflower and drizzle with oil. Place the frying pan in the oven and roast the cauliflower for 40 minutes.

04. Transfer the remaining butter to a small bowl and set aside. Keep the big bowl out (there's no need to wash it).

05. Meanwhile, make the sauce. Roughly chop the onion and garlic and pop into the big bowl. Peel and roughly chop the ginger, then add to the bowl. Pour in the chopped tomatoes, then add a tinful of water and the cream. Using a stick blender, whizz until completely smooth, then season.

06. Remove the frying pan from the oven and pour in the sauce, mixing it around and spooning it over the cauliflower. Return to the oven for 30–40 minutes, then stir the spinach through the sauce around the sides of the cauliflower. Return to the oven for a final 10 minutes until the spinach is wilted, the sauce has thickened and the cauliflower is cooked through.

07. When you add the spinach, put the naan directly on to the oven tray. Put into the oven for the final 10 minutes to crisp up a bit. Remove and slather with the remaining butter.

08. Remove the cauli pan from the oven and squeeze in the lemon juice. Scatter over coriander leaves and serve with the spiced butter naan. Drizzle over a little more cream, if you like.

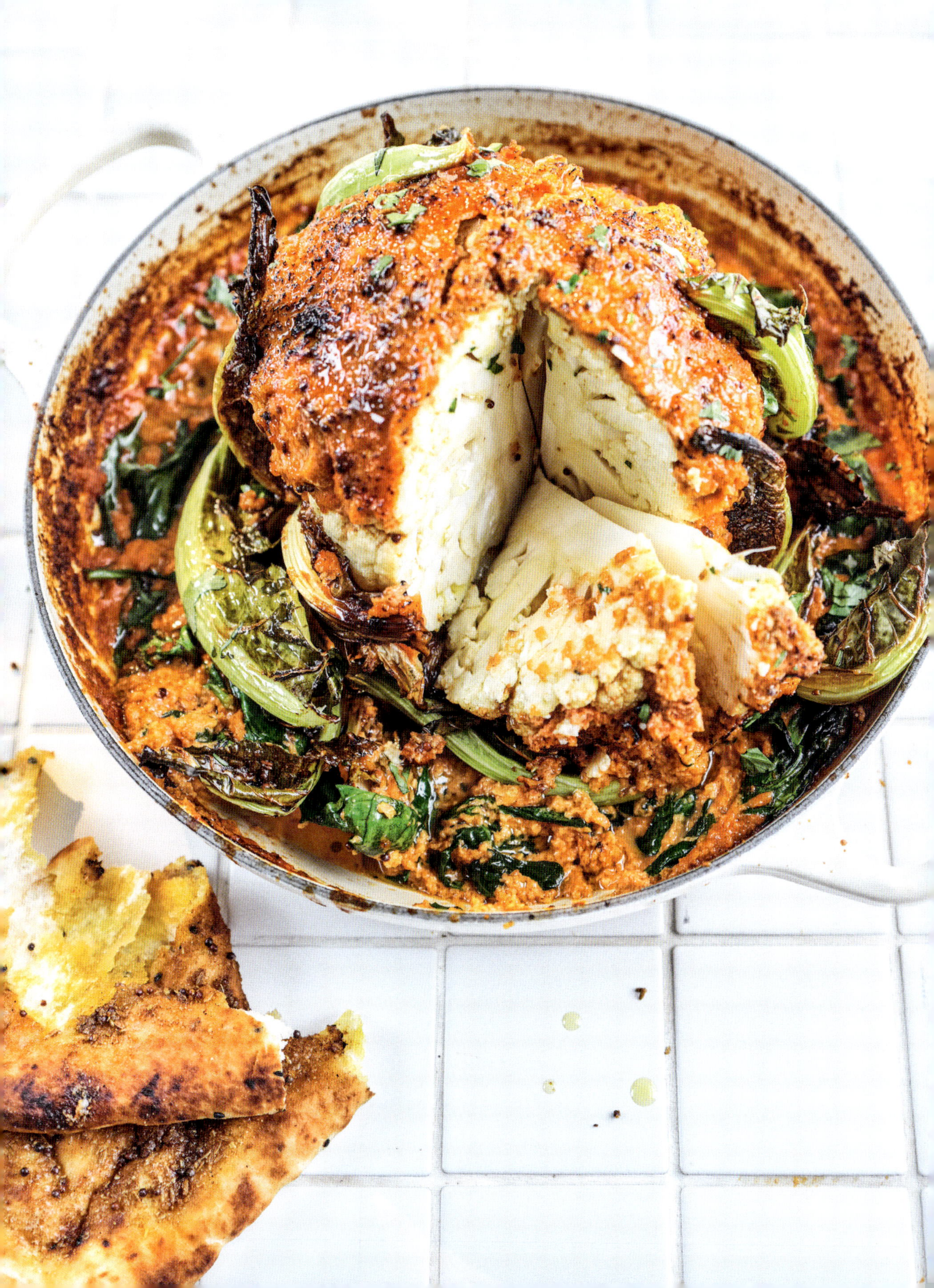

Coconut + Lime Leaf Duck Leg Curry

Scan for more tasty recipes like this one

Serves 4
Takes 1 hour 25 minutes

Use a roasting tin

Gluten-free

4 duck legs
4 shallots
500g baby potatoes
4 tbsp rendang curry paste (check the label if making this gluten-free)
1 x 400ml tin of coconut milk
4 makrut lime leaves
salt and black pepper

FOR THE MANGO SALAD
1 mango
2 makrut lime leaves
1 red chilli
1 lime
20g mint leaves
100g beansprouts

TIP: If you don't want to throw away the excess duck fat, pop it into a small saucepan and slowly render over a low heat. Pour into a sterilized jar and leave to cool, then seal. It will keep in the fridge for up to 1 month.

This aromatic duck leg curry is packed with the flavour of rendang curry paste, creamy coconut milk and lots of fragrant lime leaves. Once it's out of the oven, serve it with a tangy mango and beansprout salad on the side. It's virtually impossible not to be drooling by the time you smell this dish wafting from the oven.

01. Preheat the oven to 240°C/220°C fan.

02. Trim off the excess fat and skin from the duck legs and discard. Halve the shallots lengthways. Halve the baby potatoes (quarter any large ones) and set aside.

03. Arrange the duck legs, skin-side down, in the roasting tin and season well, then nestle in the shallots and potatoes. Roast for 20 minutes, then reduce the oven temperature to 200°C/180°C fan and remove the tin from the oven. Flip the duck legs over and add the curry paste, coconut milk and lime leaves.

04. Cover the tin with foil and return to the oven for 15 minutes, then remove the foil, stir well and cook for 30 minutes until the sauce is bubbling, the potatoes are tender and the duck is golden brown.

05. Meanwhile, make the salad. Peel the mango and dice the flesh. Finely shred the lime leaves and thinly slice the chilli. Zest the lime into a bowl, then squeeze in the juice. Add all the prepped ingredients to the bowl, tear in the mint leaves, add the beansprouts and mix together. Season generously.

06. Serve the curry with the mango salad and enjoy.

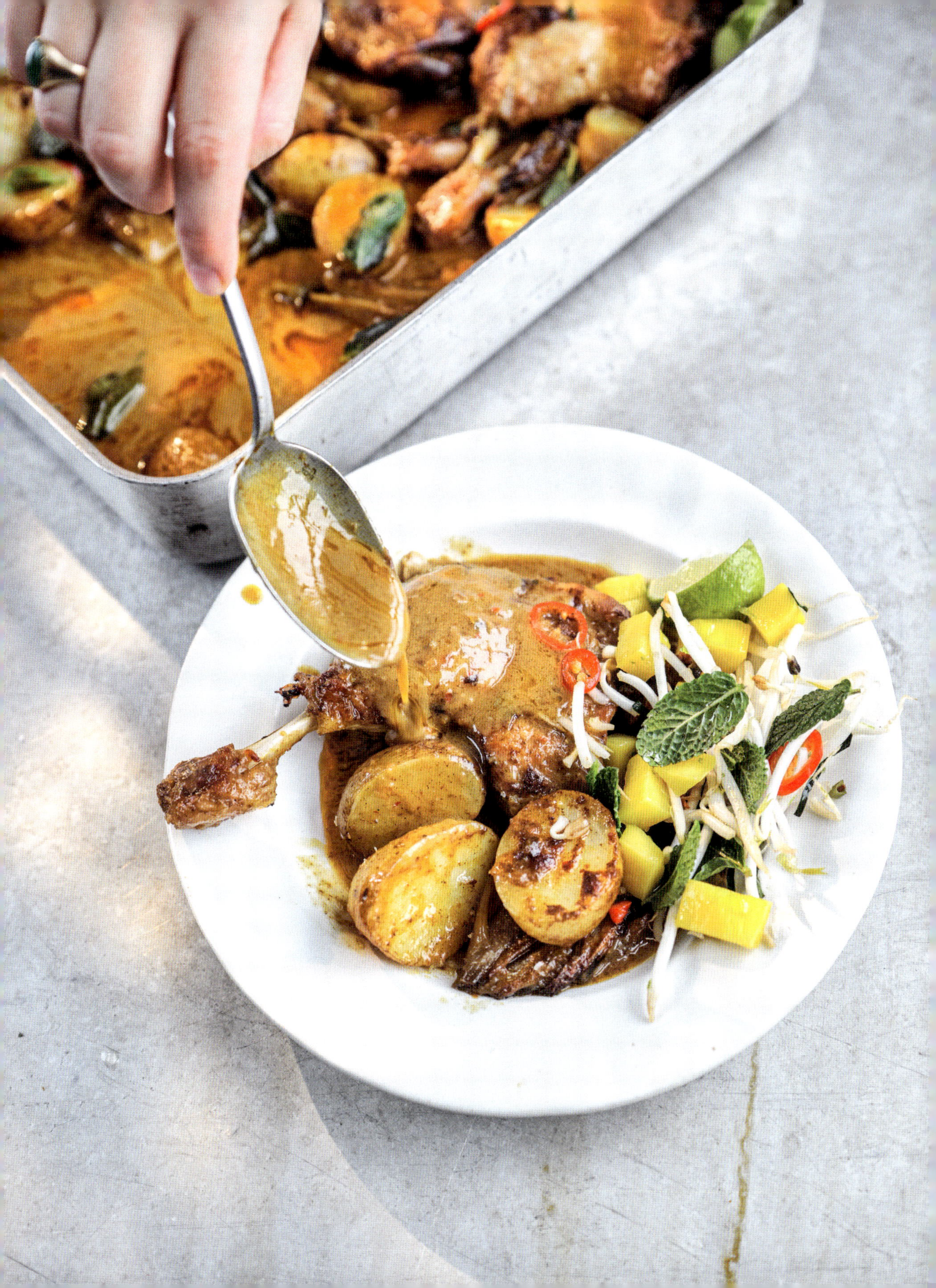

Spinach + Paneer Filo Pie

Serves 4
Takes 1 hour 10 minutes

Use a non-stick ovenproof frying pan or shallow casserole pan

Veggie

450g paneer
1 onion
1 green chilli
20g fresh ginger (a chunk of about 2.5cm)
4 garlic cloves
3 tbsp ghee
1 tbsp cumin seeds
1½ tbsp garam masala
1 tsp ground coriander
1 tsp chilli powder
500g spinach
25g bunch of coriander
150ml double cream
1 tsp sugar
1 lemon
1 x 250g pack of filo pastry
1 tbsp nigella seeds
mango chutney, to serve
salt

Scan for more tasty recipes like this one

Inspired by an Indian favourite, saag paneer, but rolled into a crispy filo pie. No need to faff around with a pie bottom, the scrunched-up filo pastry topper is the easiest hack for a crowd-pleasing pie that looks as impressive as it tastes. Mango chutney to serve is non-negotiable!

01. Preheat the oven to 200°C/180°C fan. Cut the paneer into 2.5cm cubes. Finely chop the onion and chilli, and mince the ginger and garlic. Melt 1 tablespoon of the ghee in the pan over a medium-high heat. Add the paneer and fry for around 1–2 minutes on each side, until golden. Remove from the pan and set aside.

02. Add another tablespoon of ghee and fry the onion with a good pinch of salt for 6–8 minutes, until golden. Add the spices, fresh chilli, ginger and garlic and fry for 2 minutes.

03. Add a splash of water to the pan, then add the spinach – you will need to do this in 3–4 batches – and cook until wilted.

04. Add 350ml water and roughly blitz the mixture with a stick blender (alternatively, tip the contents into a blender, blitz and then return to the pan). Simmer for 5 minutes, stirring often, until thickened a little. Roughly chop the coriander and add to the pan, along with the cream, sugar, the juice of the lemon and the fried paneer. Season to taste with salt.

05. Melt the final tablespoon of ghee, covered, in the microwave.

06. Working with one sheet of filo at a time, scrunch up the sheets and place on top of the filling. Drizzle over the melted ghee, scatter over the nigella seeds and bake for 20–25 minutes, rotating halfway, until golden. Serve with mango chutney.

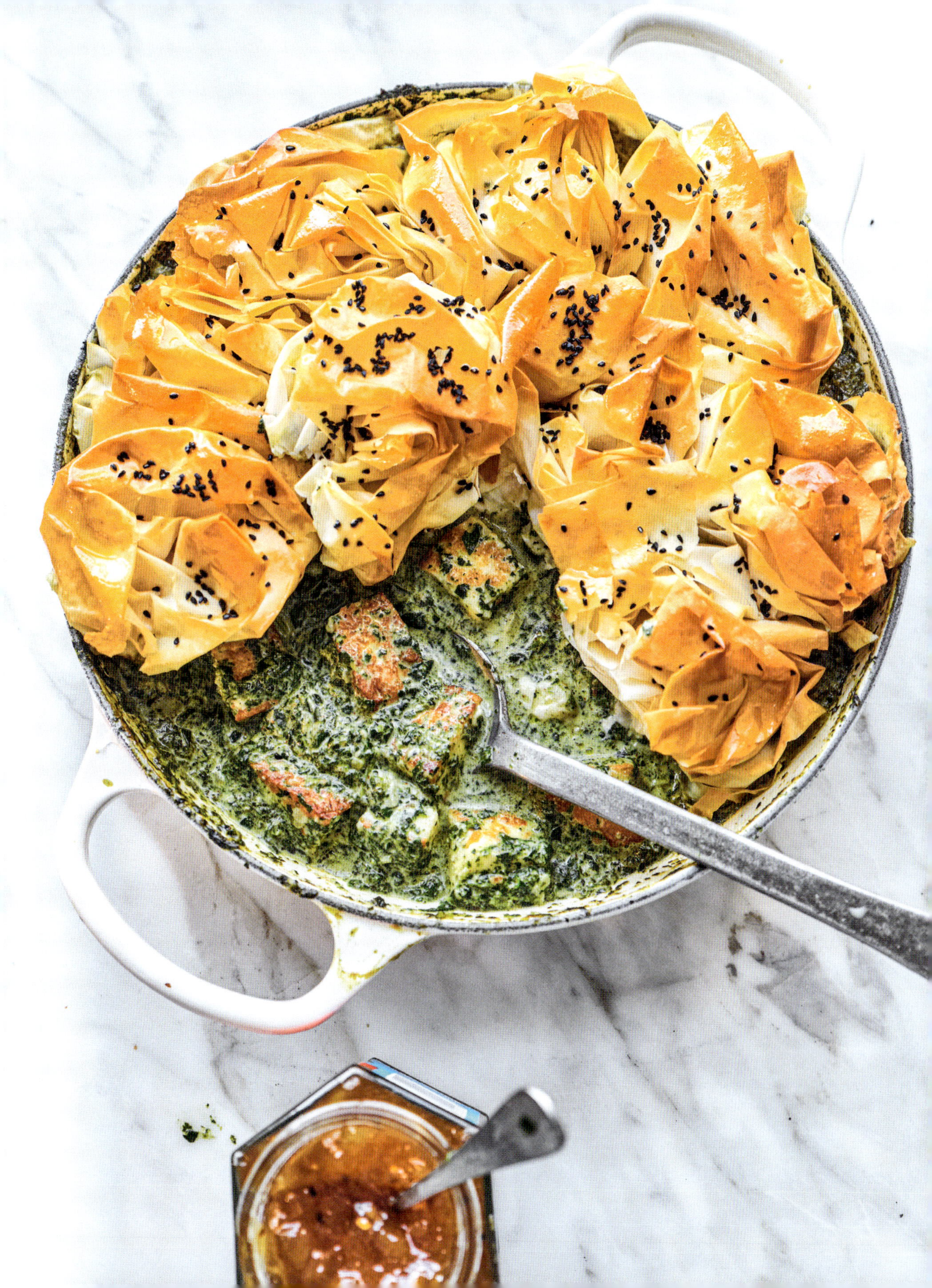

Sesame Hispi Bake

Scan for more tasty recipes like this one

Serves 4
Takes 45 minutes

Use a roasting tin

Vegan

1 hispi cabbage (also known as sweetheart or pointed cabbage)
2 tbsp vegetable oil
2 tsp miso paste
3 tbsp tahini
1 tbsp mirin
2 tbsp rice vinegar
200g frozen or fresh edamame beans
salt and black pepper

TO SERVE
5 radishes
1 lime
a handful of coriander sprigs
2 x 250g microwaveable pouches of brown rice
3 tbsp crispy onions
2 tbsp sesame seeds

This absolute beauty of a traybake is cooked in the same miso tahini dressing (which gets the cabbage all caramelised and gorgeous) that you drizzle on top at the end (for a cooling saucy touch). Clever.

01. Preheat the oven to 220°C/200°C fan.

02. Cut the hispi into 4 wedges, leaving them attached at the root. Place them in the roasting tin, drizzle with the oil and season generously. Roast for 20 minutes.

03. Meanwhile, mix together the miso, tahini, mirin and rice vinegar with 2 tablespoons of water in a small bowl.

04. Brush half of the mixture onto the hispi wedges, then return to the oven for a further 15 minutes until tender and charred. Remove from the oven and scatter in the edamame beans. Return to the oven for 5 minutes until warmed through.

05. Just before serving, thinly slice the radishes, cut the lime into wedges and pick the coriander leaves, discarding the stalks. Heat the rice according to the packet instructions.

06. To serve, drizzle the remaining dressing over the cabbage and garnish with the radish slices, coriander leaves, crispy onions and sesame seeds. Enjoy with the rice and the lime wedges for squeezing over.

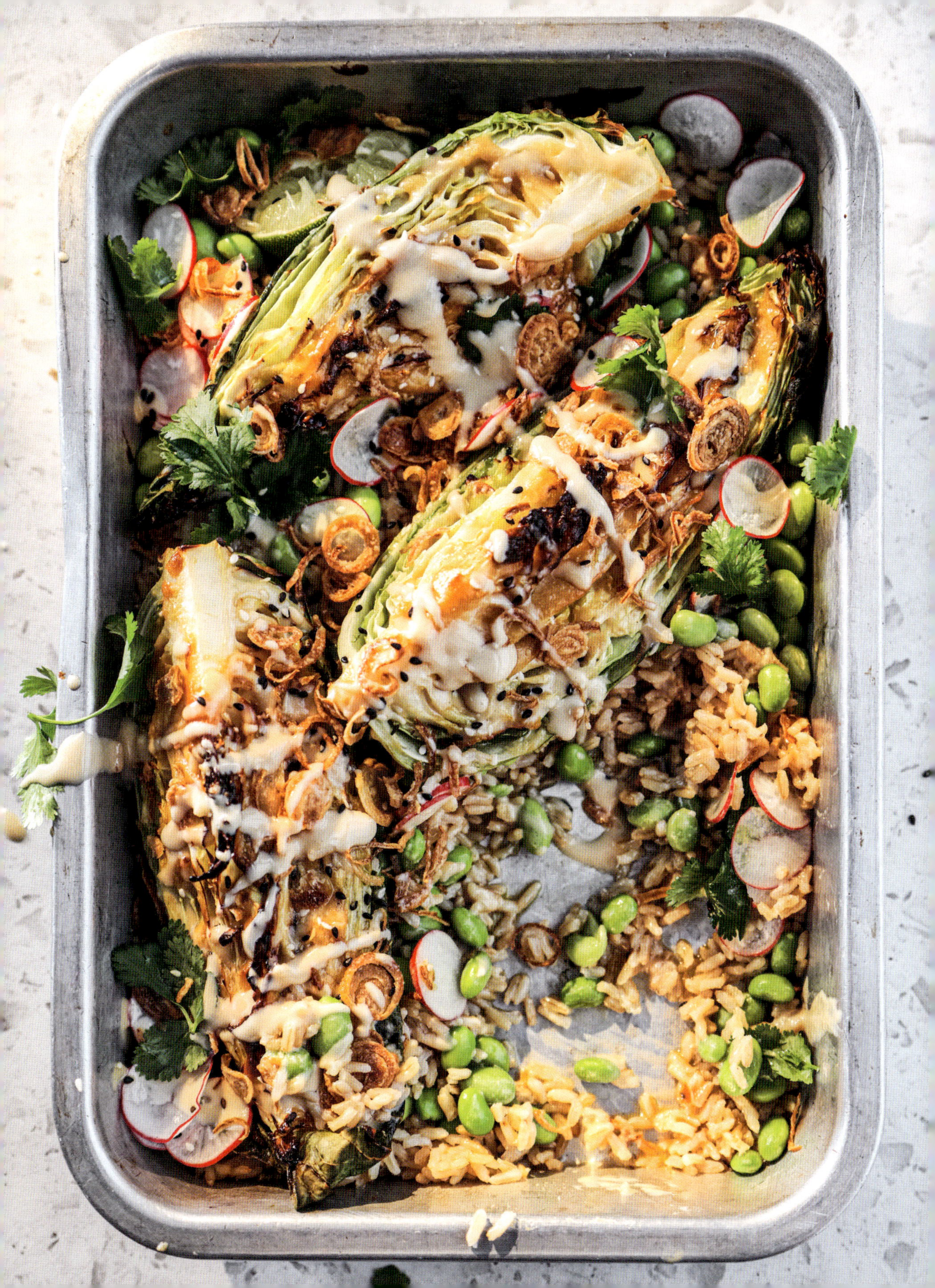

Mushroom + Pickled Onion Stew

Serves 4
Takes 1 hour 25 minutes

Use a large casserole dish

Vegan, Gluten-free

25g dried porcini mushrooms
250g baby shallots or baby onions
4 garlic cloves
400g chestnut mushrooms
400g baby button mushrooms
5 tbsp olive oil
½ tsp ground allspice
2 tbsp tomato purée
200ml red wine
1 x 400g tin of chopped tomatoes
1 bay leaf
1 cinnamon stick
1 tsp dried oregano
150g pickled onions, plus 1 tbsp of pickling liquid
pinch of sugar
25g flat leaf parsley
creamy mashed potatoes or boiled rice, to serve
salt and black pepper

Scan for more tasty recipes like this one

Inspired by the classic Greek stifado, this mushroom dish hits all the same spots and makes the ideal veggie alternative. It's basically a big hug in a bowl, with the pickled onions adding a little something something to cut through the richness.

01. Soak the porcini in 500ml just-boiled water and set aside. Remove the skins from baby shallots and cut in half. Finely chop the garlic. Clean the mushrooms and slice the chestnut mushrooms. Halve any large button mushrooms.

02. Place the casserole dish over a high heat. Heat 1 tablespoon of olive oil and add the baby shallots, flat-side down, with a good pinch of salt. Cook for 5 minutes until golden brown and a little charred, then remove from pan.

03. Add the mushrooms to the pan, along with the remaining 4 tablespoons of olive oil and a large pinch of salt. Fry for 6–8 minutes until any liquid has evaporated and they're deeply browned in places. Add the garlic and allspice and fry for 2 minutes further.

04. Add the tomato purée and stir to coat the mushrooms. Cook for a minute, then add the red wine and allow to bubble away for 2–3 minutes until almost completely reduced. Drain the porcini, reserving the liquid, and roughly chop.

05. Add the chopped porcini and their liquid to the pan, along with the chopped tomatoes, bay leaf, cinnamon, dried oregano, fried baby shallots, 100g of the pickled onions and 1 tablespoon of their liquid, the sugar and a good pinch of salt. Bring to the boil, then pop the lid on to simmer for 30–40 minutes until the shallots are tender. Remove the lid and reduce for 10 minutes until glossy and thick.

06. Chop the remaining 50g of pickled onions in half.

07. Serve with a crack of black pepper, a scattering of the pickled onions and parsley leaves. Serve with creamy mash or rice.

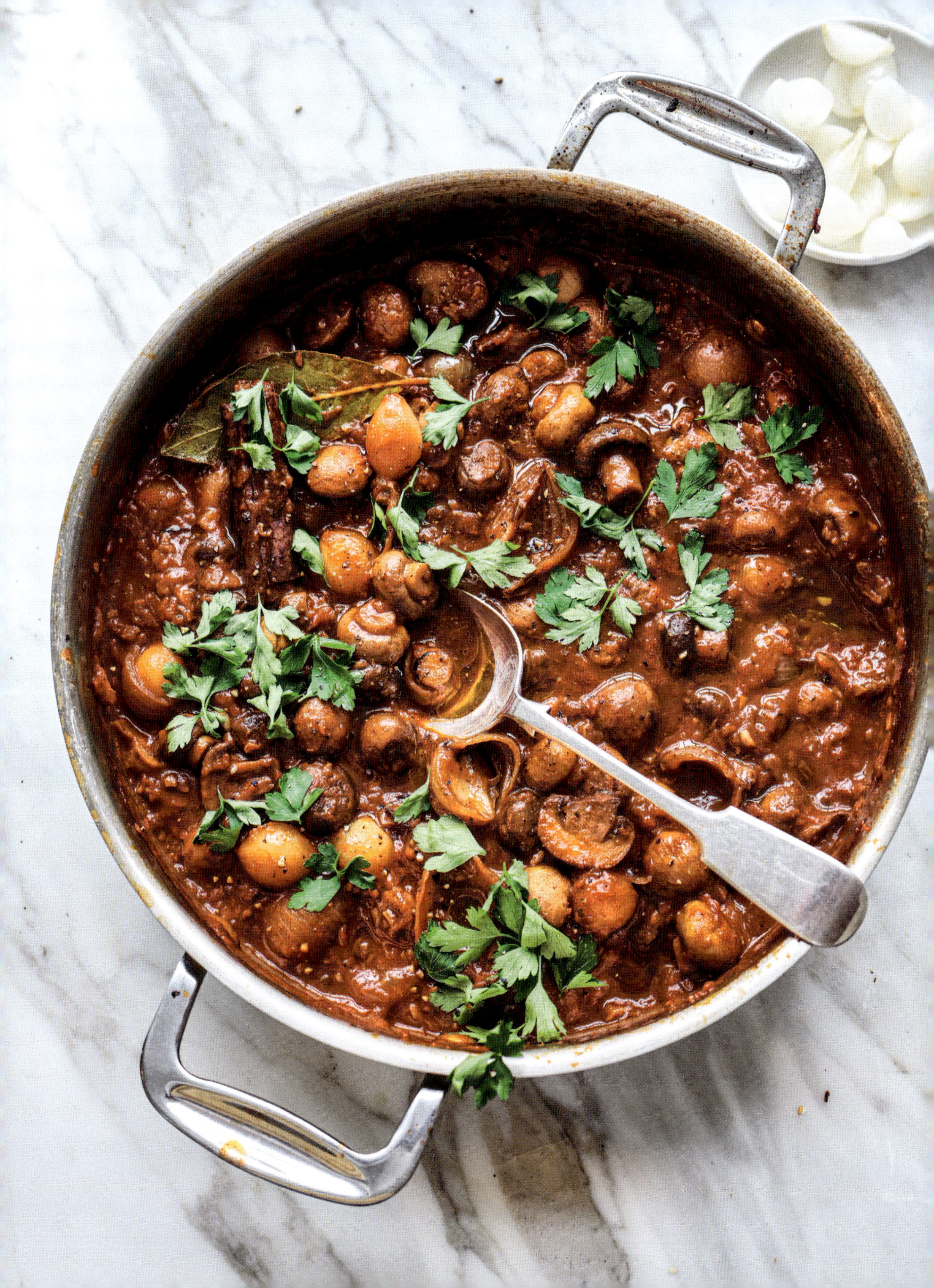

"fresh fresh

Ones

fresh

Ones

Big Bad Deli Chopped Salad

Scan for more tasty recipes like this one

Serves 4
Takes 15 minutes

Use a large salad bowl

1 medium red onion
2 x 400g tins of chickpeas, drained and rinsed
100g pitted green olives
200g cherry tomatoes
100g sun-dried tomatoes
150g Gruyère
2 Little Gem lettuce
25g flat leaf parsley
60g salami (optional)

FOR THE DRESSING
1 lemon
1 tsp honey
1 tsp Dijon mustard
4 tbsp olive oil
salt and black pepper

We've always been a bit obsessed with those big American chopped salads where you chop up loads of the ingredients on one big chopping board and then whack them into a bowl. This is exactly that, but with the addition of chickpeas. It's all the best things from a deli mashed together.

01. Start with the dressing. Squeeze the juice of the lemon into your bowl, add the remaining ingredients and whisk together, season well.

02. Finely dice the red onion and add to the dressing, tossing it to let it marinate, then add the chickpeas.

03. Put the olives, cherry tomatoes, sun-dried tomatoes and cheese onto a large chopping board.

04. Tear the lettuce leaves onto the board and add the parsley leaves (discard the stalks) and salami, if using.

05. Run a knife through everything until all the ingredients are similar sizes.

06. Tip into the salad bowl and toss everything together, then serve immediately.

FRESH ONES 193

Charred Pineapple + Peanut Salad

Serves 2
Takes 30 minutes

Use a non-stick frying pan

Vegan, Gluten-free

2 banana shallots
1 red chilli
2 limes
½ medium pineapple (about 1kg)
200g sugar snap peas
3 tsp vegetable oil
2 Little Gem lettuce
a small bunch of coriander
a handful of salted peanuts
a thumb-sized chunk of fresh ginger
2 garlic cloves
2 tbsp crunchy peanut butter
2 tbsp coconut cream
2 tablespoons tamari
salt and black pepper

Scan for more tasty recipes like this one

This salad is everything we love about Southeast Asian flavours: it's umami, it's sweet, it's sour, it's spicy – it's a proper party for your taste buds.

01. Thinly slice the shallots into rings. Deseed the chilli and thinly slice into rings. Add both to a non-reactive bowl, then squeeze in the juice of the limes. Season and set aside.

02. Slice off the pineapple skin, then cut into quarters lengthways. Remove the core from each piece, then cut into chunky wedges.

03. Set the dry frying pan over a high heat. Tip the pineapple pieces and sugar snaps into a bowl and drizzle in 1 teaspoon of the oil and season. Toss together very gently. Once the pan is smoking, lay in the pineapple wedges and scatter around the sugar snaps. Cook for 1–2 minutes until charred, then flip over and char on the other side. Arrange the charred pieces on a platter. Remove the pan from the heat and leave to cool.

04. Meanwhile, cut the lettuce into wedges. Nestle these in and around the charred pineapple and sugar snaps.

05. Pick the coriander leaves, discarding the stalks, and chop the peanuts. Set aside.

06. Peel the ginger, then finely chop with the garlic. Heat the remaining 2 teaspoons of oil in the pan over a medium heat, add the garlic and ginger and fry for 2 minutes until smelling amazing. Remove the pan from the heat and spoon in the peanut butter, coconut cream and tamari, then pour in the lime juice from the shallot and chilli bowl. Whisk together to make a warm dressing, adding a splash of just-boiled water if it's a little thick or splits.

07. Tear the coriander leaves, then scatter over the platter. Spoon over the warm satay dressing, then top with the pickled shallot rings, chilli and the chopped peanuts.

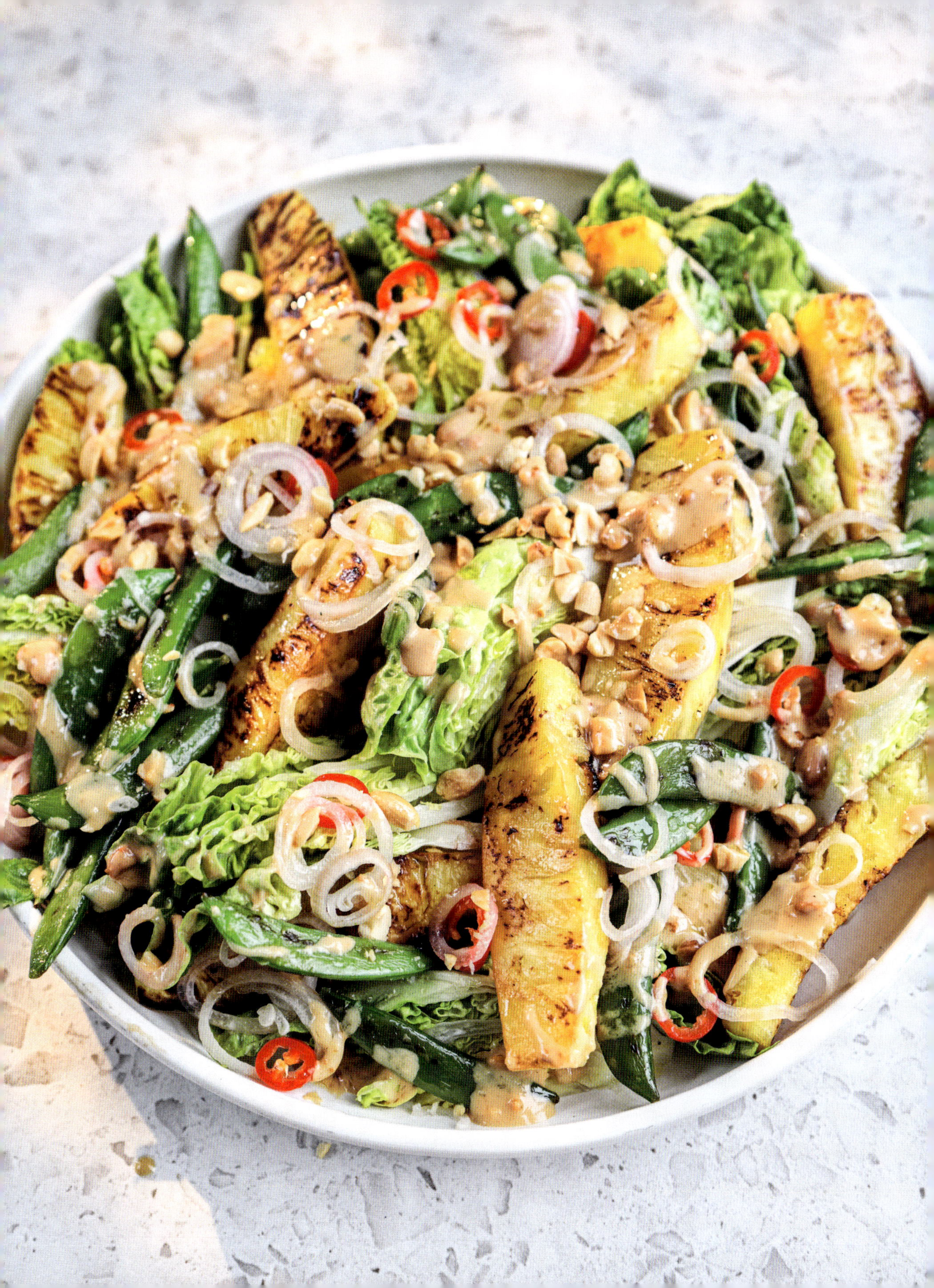

Broccoli, Burst Tomatoes + Hot Honey

Scan for more tasty recipes like this one

Serves 2
Takes 20 minutes

Use a large non-stick frying pan

Veggie, Gluten-free

a handful of walnuts
200g Tenderstem broccoli
1 tbsp olive oil
250g cherry tomatoes
2 tbsp cider vinegar
2 tbsp hot honey (or honey mixed with 1 tsp chilli flakes)
2 red chicory
a small bunch of flat leaf parsley
75g Comté, Manchego or mature Cheddar cheese (use Cheddar if making vegetarian)
salt and black pepper

The sticky sweet heat of hot honey and burst tomatoes join forces here for a lush dressing that'll have you cleaning the plate. Who knew broccoli could be this exciting?

01. Toast the walnuts in the dry frying pan over a medium-high heat for 3–4 minutes, tossing regularly, until smelling really toasty. Tip onto a chopping board and roughly chop. Set aside.

02. Trim the ends of the broccoli and halve any thick pieces lengthways. Heat the oil in the pan over a high heat. Once hot, add the broccoli and fry for 1–2 minutes until beginning to char. Add the cherry tomatoes and cook for a further 4–6 minutes until the broccoli is cooked through and the tomatoes have begun to burst.

03. Remove from the heat and leave to cool for a minute, then pour in the vinegar and hot honey. Toss to coat and season.

04. Trim the ends off the chicory, then snap into cups and arrange on a platter or 2 plates. Pick the leaves from the parsley, discarding the stalks. Set aside.

05. Spoon the broccoli, burst tomatoes and all of the sticky dressing over the chicory cups. Using a peeler, shave lots of cheese over the top, then scatter with the parsley leaves and the toasted walnuts.

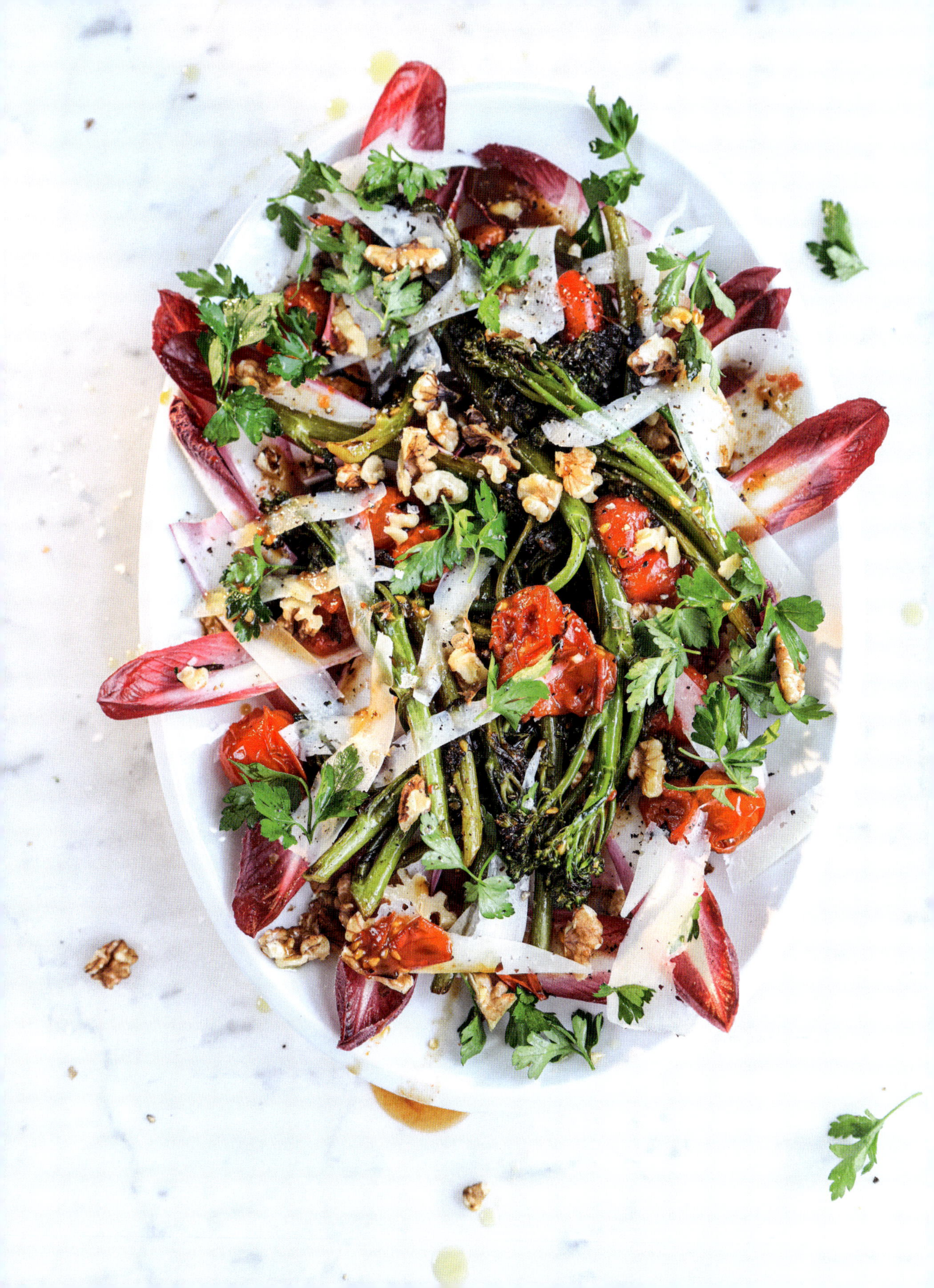

Fish Sauce Carrots + Rice Noodles

Serves 2
Takes 30 minutes

Use a small-medium roasting tin

Gluten-free

---

3 medium carrots (about 300g)
3 garlic cloves
a thumb-sized chunk of fresh ginger
2 tsp vegetable oil
1 bird's eye chilli
3 tbsp fish sauce (check the label if making this gluten-free)
2 limes
2 tbsp soft light brown sugar
100g vermicelli rice noodles
a handful of salted peanuts
a small handful each of mint, Thai basil and coriander leaves
salt and black pepper

Scan for more tasty recipes like this one

This is an autumnal take on a zingy summer favourite. Roasting and pickling the carrots using the same dressing doubles down on the tang factor. Make sure you toss the noodles in the tin so they soak up all those lovely caramelised bits. It's free flavour! Literally!

01. Preheat the oven to 220°C/200°C fan.

02. Peel all the carrots, then using the peeler, slice 1 of them lengthways into ribbons and set aside.

03. Cut the remaining carrots into 2–3cm chunky pieces, then tip into the roasting tin. Smash 2 of the garlic cloves, don't worry about peeling, then peel and slice the ginger. Chuck these into the tin with the carrots. Season, pour over the oil and toss well. Roast for 20 minutes until charred and cooked through.

04. Meanwhile, finely chop the remaining garlic clove and the chilli. Tip into a non-reactive bowl, then pour in the fish sauce, squeeze in the juice of both limes, add the sugar and mix well. Add the carrot ribbons and leave to pickle in the dressing.

05. Put the vermicelli noodles into a heatproof bowl and soak in boiling water according to the packet instructions, refresh in cold water until completely cold, then drain again.

06. Chop the peanuts and set aside.

07. When the carrots are roasted, spoon over 3 tablespoons of the pickle dressing so that they become a bit sticky and glazed (discard the garlic skins). Add the noodles and gently toss together.

08. Scatter over all of the herbs and the carrot ribbons, then top with the chopped peanuts and any remaining dressing.

FRESH ONES

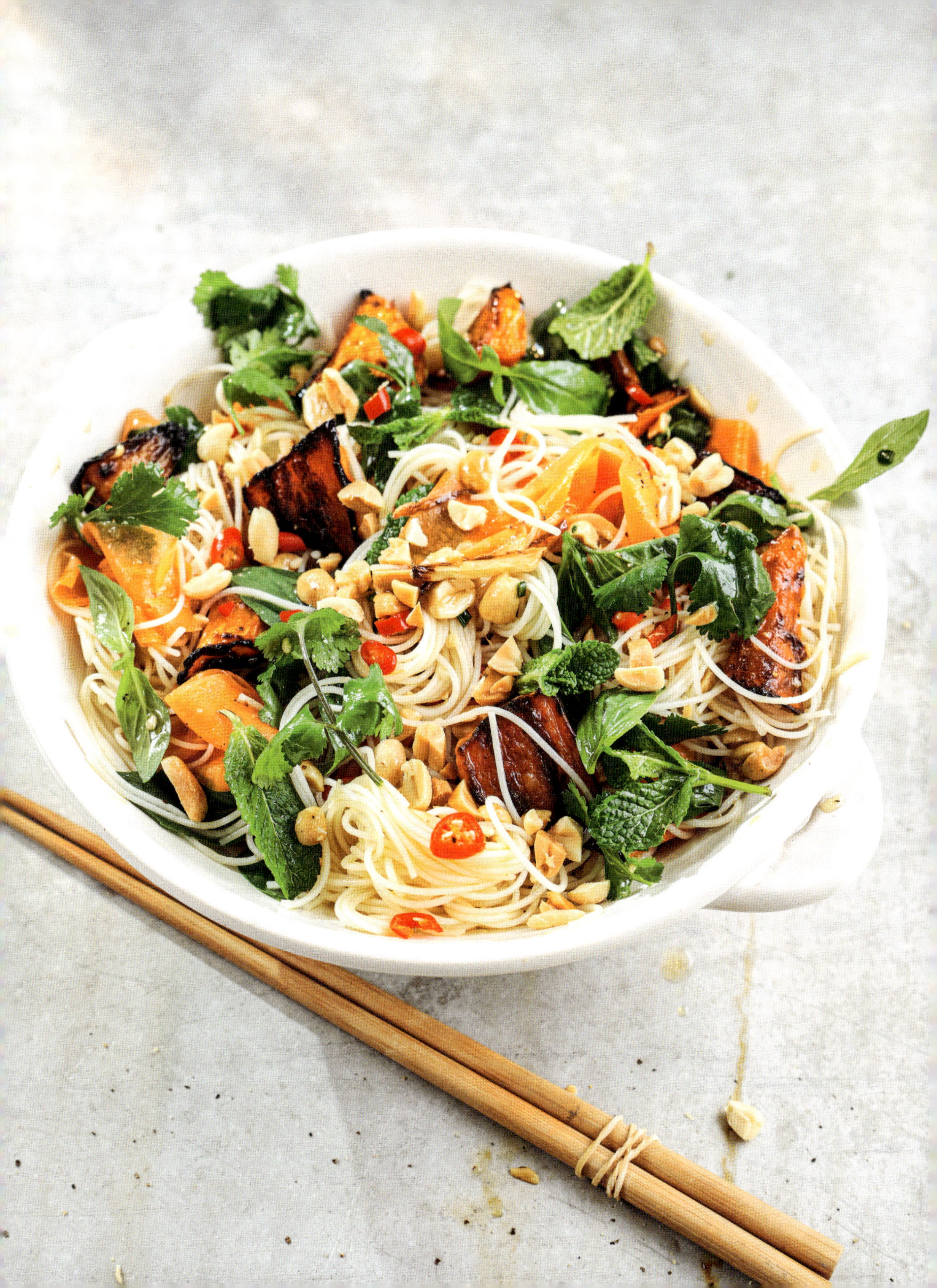

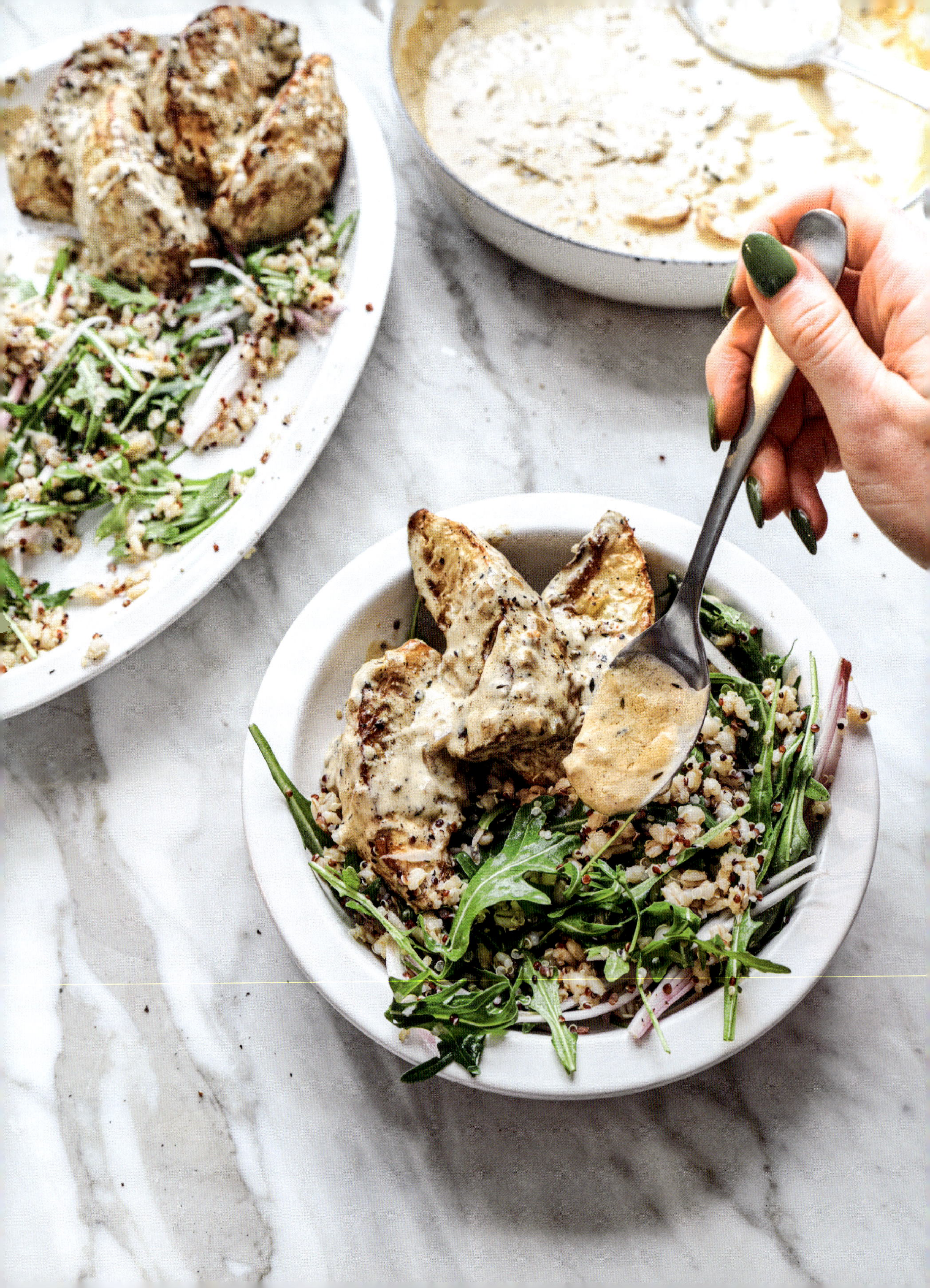

Celeriac au Poivre

Serves 4
Takes 1 hour

Use a large ovenproof non-stick frying pan

Veggie

1 medium celeriac (about 850g)
1 tbsp black peppercorns
2 tbsp olive oil
75g unsalted butter
a handful of thyme sprigs
2 garlic cloves
2 banana shallots
100ml brandy, whisky or dark rum
250ml hot vegetable stock
150ml double cream
1 tbsp red wine vinegar, plus more to taste
2 x 250g microwaveable pouches of mixed grains
60g wild rocket
salt and black pepper

Salads don't have to be relegated to the summer. We've taken celeriac here and treated it a bit like steak by basting it with butter and roasting it until it's all caramelised on the outside and fudgy in the middle. We've then paired it with a piquant 'au poivre' dressing. This is our kind of salad.

01. Preheat the oven to 200°C/180°C fan.

02. Peel the celeriac, then cut it in half and then again into 8 chunky wedges.

03. Toast the peppercorns in the dry frying pan over a medium-high heat for 1 minute until smelling amazing, then tip into a pestle and mortar.

04. Drizzle the oil into the pan, then arrange the celeriac pieces so they fit snugly and season. Brown for 3–4 minutes on each of the 2 biggest sides until caramelised. Add the butter, thyme and garlic cloves (in their skins) and baste everything for a further 2 minutes until golden and smelling wonderful. Transfer to the oven for 20 minutes until the celeriac is cooked through and roasted.

Continued overleaf

Continued from previous page

05. Meanwhile, coarsely crush the peppercorns and set aside. Finely chop 1 of the shallots and thinly slice the other.

06. Remove the pan from the oven, then move the celeriac pieces to a plate and cover with foil.

07. Keeping an oven glove over the handle (as it will be raging), set the pan with the garlic and thyme over a medium heat. Scrape in the finely chopped shallot and a pinch of salt. Cook for 5 minutes until softened, then add the brandy (carefully, as it might flame!) and simmer for 2 minutes. Pour in the stock and simmer for a further 2 minutes.

08. Pour in the cream and add the crushed pepper, then bubble away for 8–10 minutes, smooshing the now soft garlic from its skin (discard the skin), until the sauce coats the back of your spoon. Pour in the vinegar and adjust the seasoning to taste.

09. Add the celeriac back into the pan and toss to coat, bubbling for a few minutes more if needed, until nicely coated and warmed through.

10. Meanwhile, heat the grains according to the packet instructions, then tip onto a serving platter or into a large salad bowl. Mix through the rocket and thinly sliced shallot.

11. Arrange the celeriac pieces over the platter (discard the thyme sprigs), then spoon over the warm dressing to finish.

Scan for more tasty recipes like this one

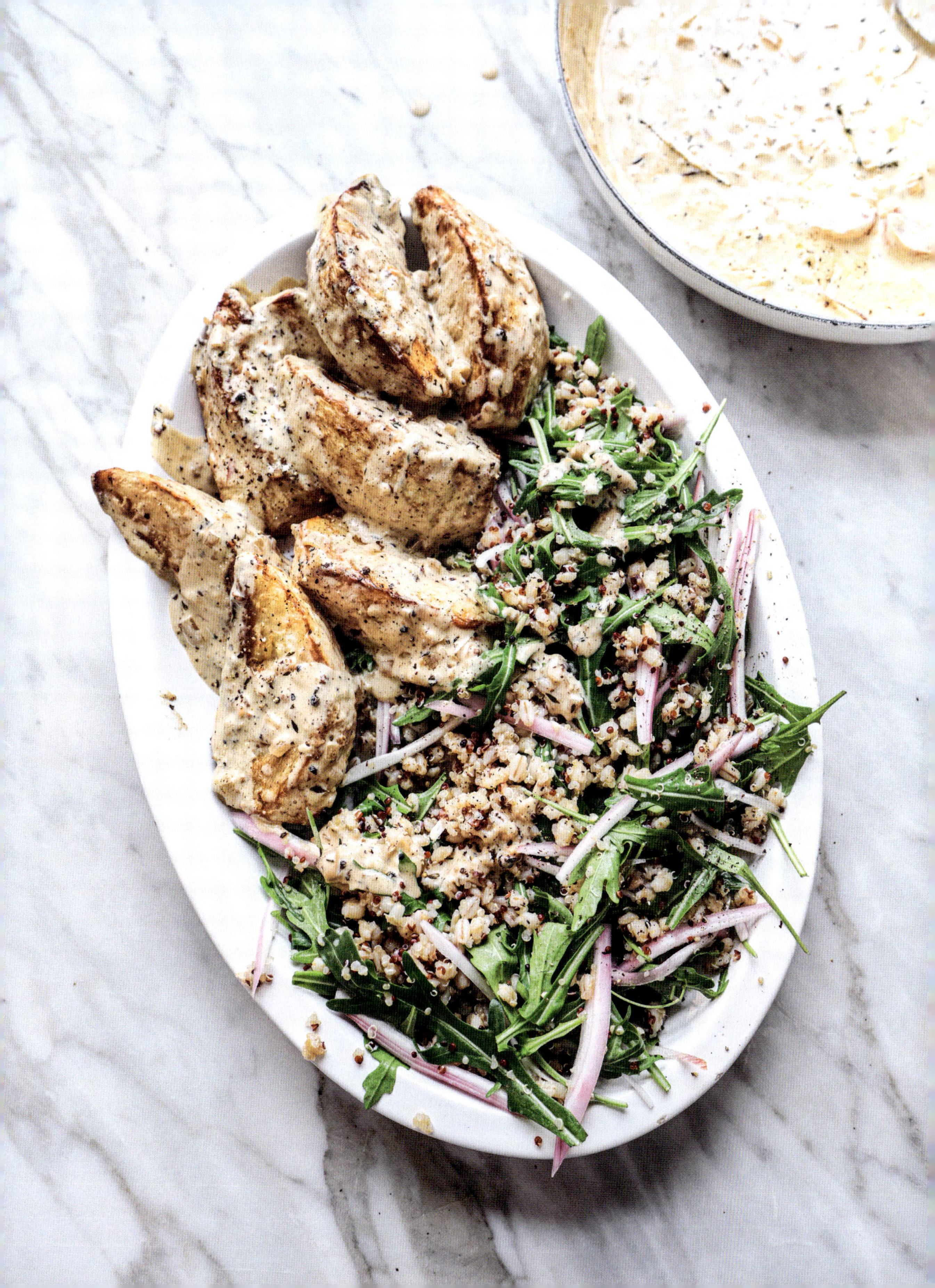

Mango Chutney Glazed Paneer Salad

Serves 4
Takes 35 minutes

Use a large non-stick frying pan

Veggie

---

1 small red onion
200g mange tout or sugar snap peas
½ cucumber
a small bunch of coriander
1 x 250g pack of fresh mango chuncks
3 x 225g packs of paneer
2 naan (about 260g)
2 tbsp vegetable oil
2 tsp nigella seeds (optional)
5 tbsp mango and chilli chutney (we use Geeta's)
a thumb-sized chunk of fresh ginger
2 limes
100g salted cashews

Scan for more tasty recipes like this one

You know those people who say they don't like salad? They've never tried this one.

01. Start by getting all of your salad ingredients prepped and into a big salad bowl. Thinly slice the red onion and mange tout, then tip into the bowl. Using a peeler, slice the cucumber lengthways into ribbons (discard or snack on the core – chef's treat!) and tear the coriander leaves, discarding the stalks, straight into the bowl. Slice the mango thinly and then tip into the bowl.

02. Cut the paneer into 3cm cubes and set aside. Tear the naan into bite-sized croutons.

03. Heat 1 tablespoon of the oil in the frying pan over a medium-high heat. Scatter in the naan croutons and fry for 3–5 minutes, tossing regularly, until golden and crunchy. Scoop out of the pan into the salad bowl.

04. Heat the remaining oil in the pan, add the paneer and fry for 1–2 minutes on each side until golden and crisp and all the sides are caramelised.

05. Sprinkle in the nigella seeds, if using, then remove the pan from the heat and leave to cool for a minute.

06. Add 3 tablespoons of the mango chutney, then toss with the paneer until it is completely glazed. Fish out the paneer and pop onto a plate.

07. Spoon in the remaining 2 tablespoons of the mango chutney. Peel the ginger, then grate into the pan. Squeeze in the lime juice, then whisk together to create a warm dressing.

08. Spoon three-quarters of the dressing over the salad ingredients, tossing to coat. Divide between 4 bowls, then top with the glazed paneer pieces. Roughly chop the cashews and scatter over, then spoon over the remaining dressing.

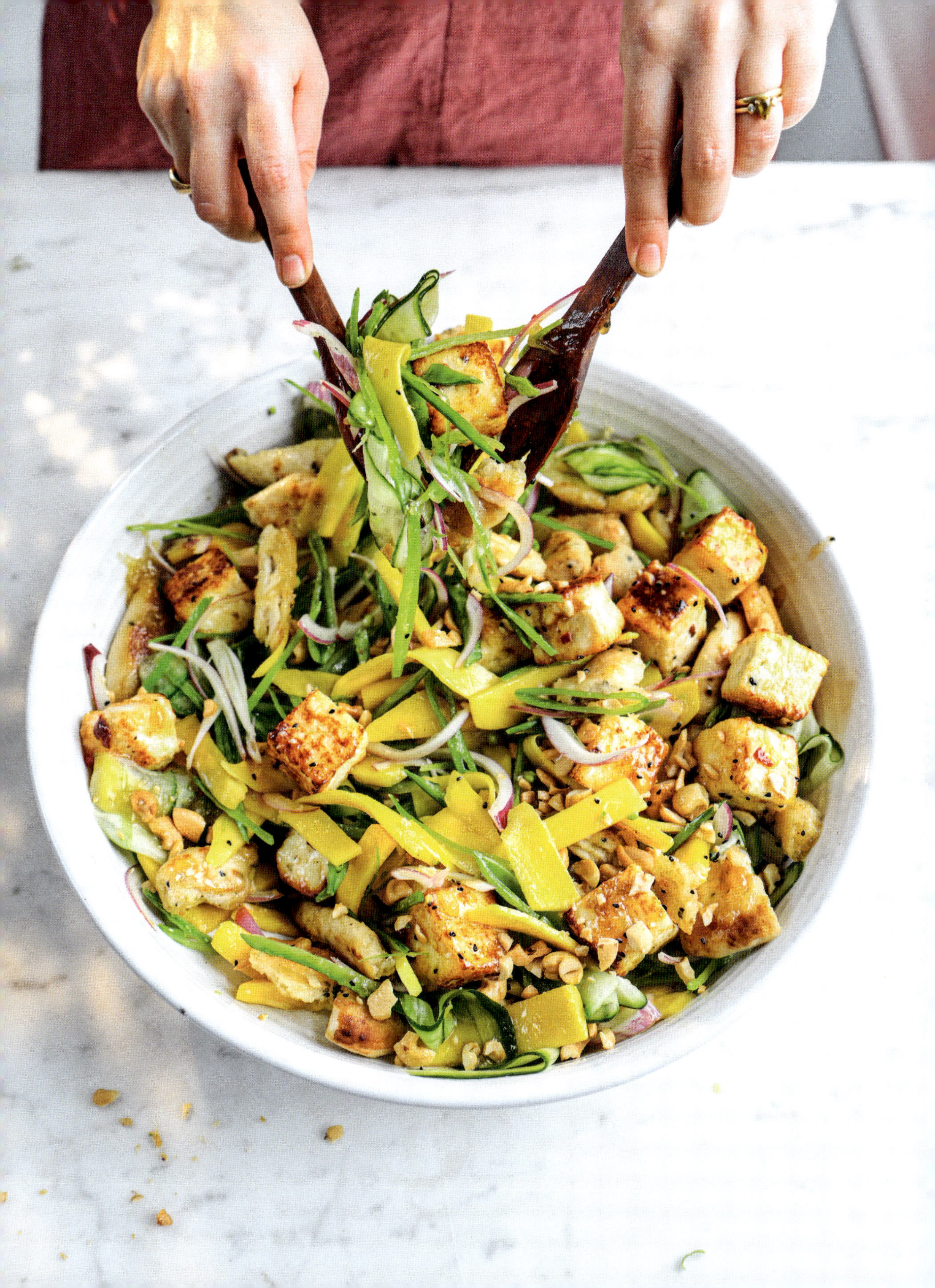

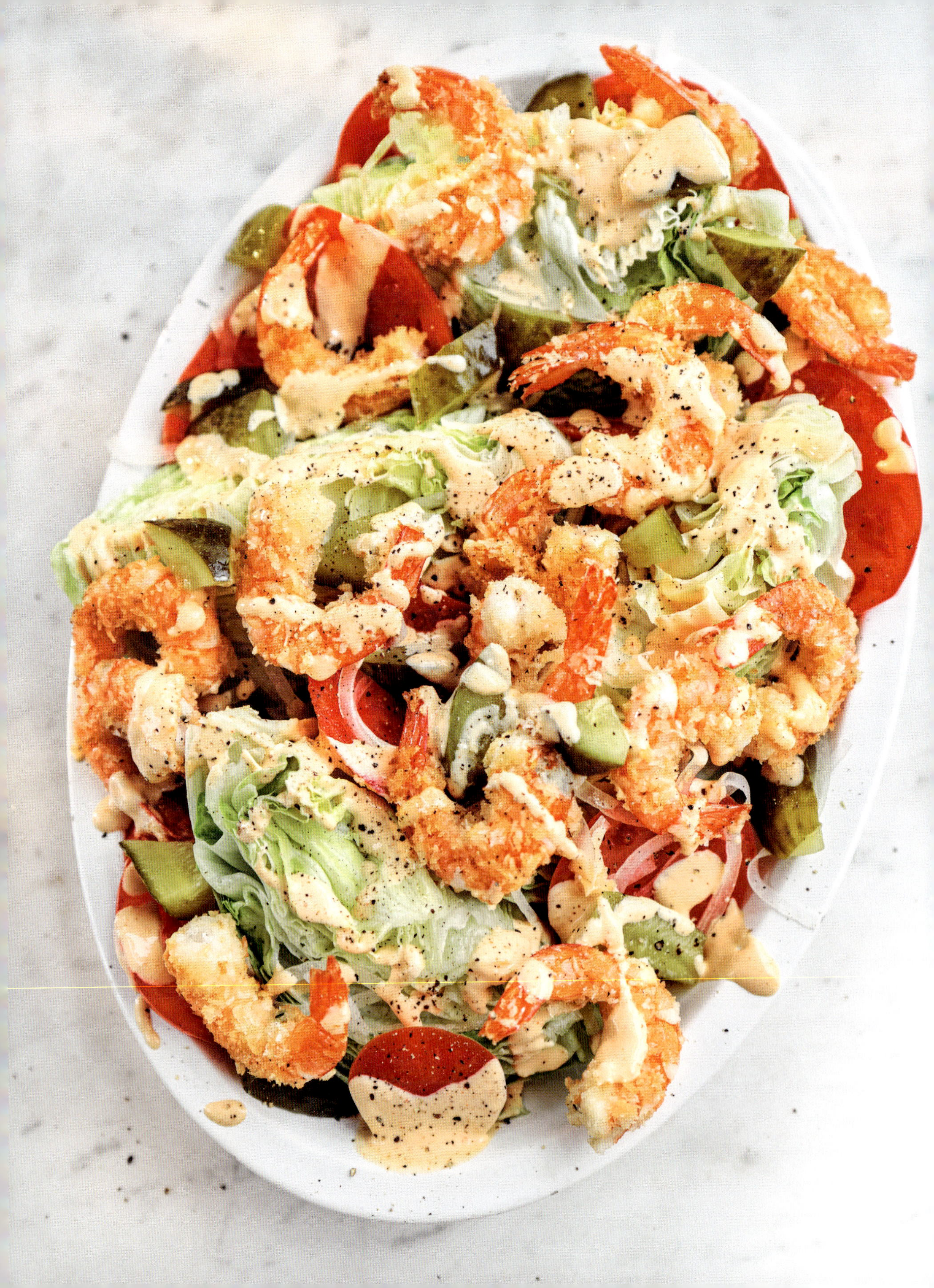

Coconut Shrimp Salad

Scan for more tasty recipes like this one

Serves 4
Takes 45 minutes

Use a large frying pan

1 iceberg lettuce
1 small onion
3 large ripe tomatoes (about 500g total)
6 jarred dill spear gherkins, plus (optional) liquid from the jar
9 tbsp mayonnaise
2 tbsp hot sauce
1 tsp garlic granules
1 tsp American, Dijon or English mustard
½ lemon
50g desiccated coconut
50g panko breadcrumbs
2 x 180g packs of raw king prawns
4 tbsp olive oil, plus a little extra if needed
salt and black pepper

TIP: Use the 'wet hand, dry hand' cooking hack: when breadcrumbing the prawns, keep one hand for the mayo and one hand for the breadcrumbs to keep from breadcrumbing your hands!

This one's all about the crispy prawns. It is inspired by a Louisiana po' boy, with the addition of desiccated coconut in the breadcrumbs which brings out the sweetness of the prawns and supercharges their, er, prawniness. Slather it in a homemade hot sauce dressing and the job's a good 'un.

01. Find a nice, big, oval platter. Cut the lettuce in half lengthways, then each half into 4 wedges. Arrange these on your platter. Very thinly slice the onion and scatter over the lettuce. Cut the tomatoes into rounds and the gherkins into chunky pieces, then add to the salad and season.

02. Whisk together 4 tablespoons of the mayo, the hot sauce, garlic granules and mustard in a bowl, then squeeze in the lemon juice. Season to taste and add a splash of the dill pickle liquid, if you like. Spoon half the dressing over the salad, then set aside the rest.

03. Put the remaining mayonnaise into a wide shallow bowl, then put the coconut and panko breadcrumbs into a second bowl and mix together.

04. Pat the prawns dry on kitchen paper and season well. Dip each prawn first into the mayonnaise and then into the breadcrumbs, before transferring to a plate.

05. Heat half of the oil in the frying pan over a medium-high heat, then add half of the prawns (you may need to do 3 batches using a little extra oil, depending on the size of your pan) and cook for 3–4 minutes, turning over halfway through, until golden brown and cooked through. Arrange on the salad. Repeat with the remaining oil and coated prawns.

06. Spoon the reserved dressing over the salad and sprinkle with any crispy coconut breadcrumbs left in the pan.

Sprouts, Orange + Radicchio

Scan for more tasty recipes like this one

Serves 4
Takes 35 minutes

Use a frying pan with a lid

Vegan

400g Brussels sprouts
1 head of radicchio (about 250g)
2 tbsp extra virgin olive oil
2 oranges
6 radishes
1 x 250g pouch of mixed grains
100g baby spinach
50g pomegranate seeds
2 tsp sumac
3 tbsp tahini
salt and black pepper

FOR THE DRESSING
1 shallot
1 orange
1 small garlic clove
2 lemons
1 tsp sumac
2 tbsp pomegranate molasses
6 tbsp extra virgin olive oil

This salad makes perfect use of stunning winter veg. We're talking bruise-coloured bitter leaves, juicy citrus, pomegranate and the nation's most contentious vegetable: Brussels sprouts.

01. Start by making the dressing. Finely chop the shallot and add to a large bowl. Finely grate in the orange zest, then squeeze in the juice. Finely grate in the garlic. Add the juice of the lemons, the sumac, pomegranate molasses and olive oil and mix well to combine; season well.

02. Cut half of the Brussels sprouts in half and set aside. Finely shred the rest and place in the bowl with the dressing. Shred the radicchio and add to the bowl. Scrunch with your hands to evenly distribute and set aside.

03. Heat the olive oil in the frying pan over a high heat, add the halved sprouts, and cook for 2–3 minutes until deeply golden and charred. Toss, then pour in 4 tablespoons of water and pop the lid on. Cook for a further 1–2 minutes until they're cooked through and all the water has evaporated.

04. Meanwhile, peel the oranges, then slice into rounds. Slice the radishes thinly.

05. Cook the grains according to the packet instructions and add with the spinach and pomegranate seeds to the bowl of shredded veg. Season generously, then toss well to combine.

06. Arrange the salad on a serving platter, scatter over the orange and radish slices, charred sprouts and sprinkle with the sumac. Drizzle over the tahini and enjoy.

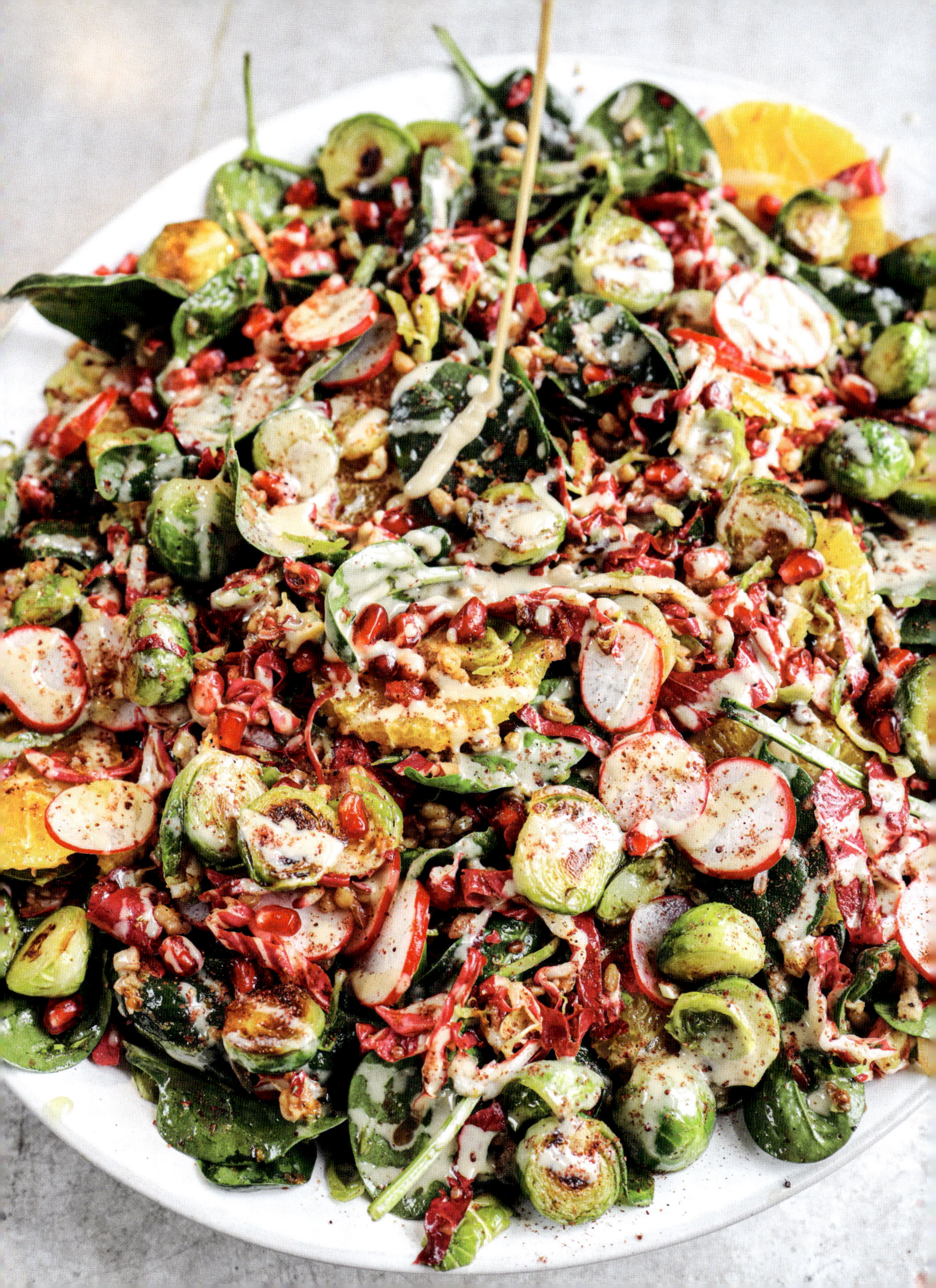

Tortilla Chip Salad

Scan for more tasty recipes like this one

Serves 4
Takes 20 minutes

Use a large bowl

Veggie

2 x 200g tins of sweetcorn, drained
300g cherry tomatoes
3 jarred roasted red peppers, drained
2 x 400g tins of black beans, drained and rinsed
25g coriander
a bunch of spring onions
200g feta
2 avocados
2 tbsp pickled jalapeño slices
1 lime
100ml soured cream
½ x 180g bag of spicy tortilla chips (we use Doritos Chilli Heatwave), plus extra to serve if liked

FOR THE DRESSING
1 lime
2 tbsp pickled jalapeño liquid from the jar
1 tsp honey
1 tsp English mustard
4 tbsp olive oil
salt and black pepper

Replacing croutons with tortilla chips in a salad is one of our favourite moves. It's dead important to use spicy-flavoured tortilla chips as the spiciness works so well with everything else.

01. Whisk together all the ingredients for the dressing in your bowl, then season and tip in the sweetcorn.

02. Halve or quarter the cherry tomatoes and add to the bowl. Roughly chop the roasted peppers and add them as well, then tip in the black beans.

03. Pick the coriander leaves, discarding the stalks, and add most of the leaves to the bowl (save a few for the garnish). Finely slice the spring onions and chuck them in, then crumble in the feta.

04. Halve the avocados, remove the stones and dice the flesh. Add to the bowl along with the pickled jalapeños. Toss the salad together, then tip onto a platter or into 4 bowls.

05. Halve the lime and squeeze the juice into your mixing bowl. Add the soured cream, then whisk together and season well.

06. Drizzle the salad with the soured cream dressing and scatter with tortilla chips. Garnish with the reserved coriander leaves.

FRESH ONES

Five Spice Chicken Salad

Scan for more tasty recipes like this one

Serves 4
Takes 35 minutes

Use a large frying pan

---

4 boneless, skinless chicken breasts
1 tbsp olive oil
4 tbsp soy sauce
1½ tbsp five spice
2 tbsp honey
3 tbsp sesame seeds

FOR THE SALAD
400g cabbage (use a mix of red and sweetheart)
100g sugar snap peas
½ cucumber
4 small spring onions
1 large carrot
20g coriander leaves
10g mint leaves
2 oranges
a handful of toasted flaked almonds

FOR THE DRESSING
1 lemon
1 orange
6 tbsp tahini (about 90g)
3 tbsp extra virgin olive oil
3 tbsp soy sauce
2 garlic cloves
a large chunk of fresh ginger (about 30g)

Yes, the ingredients list is a little on the long side but it's really just a shredded salad situ with some sticky chicken chunks and a zesty dressing. Look past the list. Make the salad. Trust the process.

01. Start with the dressing. Juice the lemon and orange, then pour into a large salad bowl. Stir in the tahini, olive oil and soy sauce. Grate in the garlic, then peel and grate in the ginger. Mix well to combine.

02. Next, prep the salad veg. Shred the cabbage, then slice the sugar snaps, cucumber and spring onions. Add to the bowl on top of the dressing, but don't mix it yet. Peel the carrot, then grate it into the bowl. Roughly chop the coriander and mint leaves, and peel and slice the oranges, then set these aside for later.

03. Cut the chicken into 2cm chunks. Heat the oil in the frying pan over a high heat and add the chicken. Cook for 3–4 minutes until sealed all over, then add the soy sauce, five spice, honey and sesame seeds. It will bubble up and coat the chicken. Cook for 2–3 minutes, or until it is nice and fragrant and sticky, and the chicken is cooked through. Turn off the heat.

04. Toss everything in the salad bowl, then top with the orange slices, chopped herbs, flaked almonds and sticky chicken.

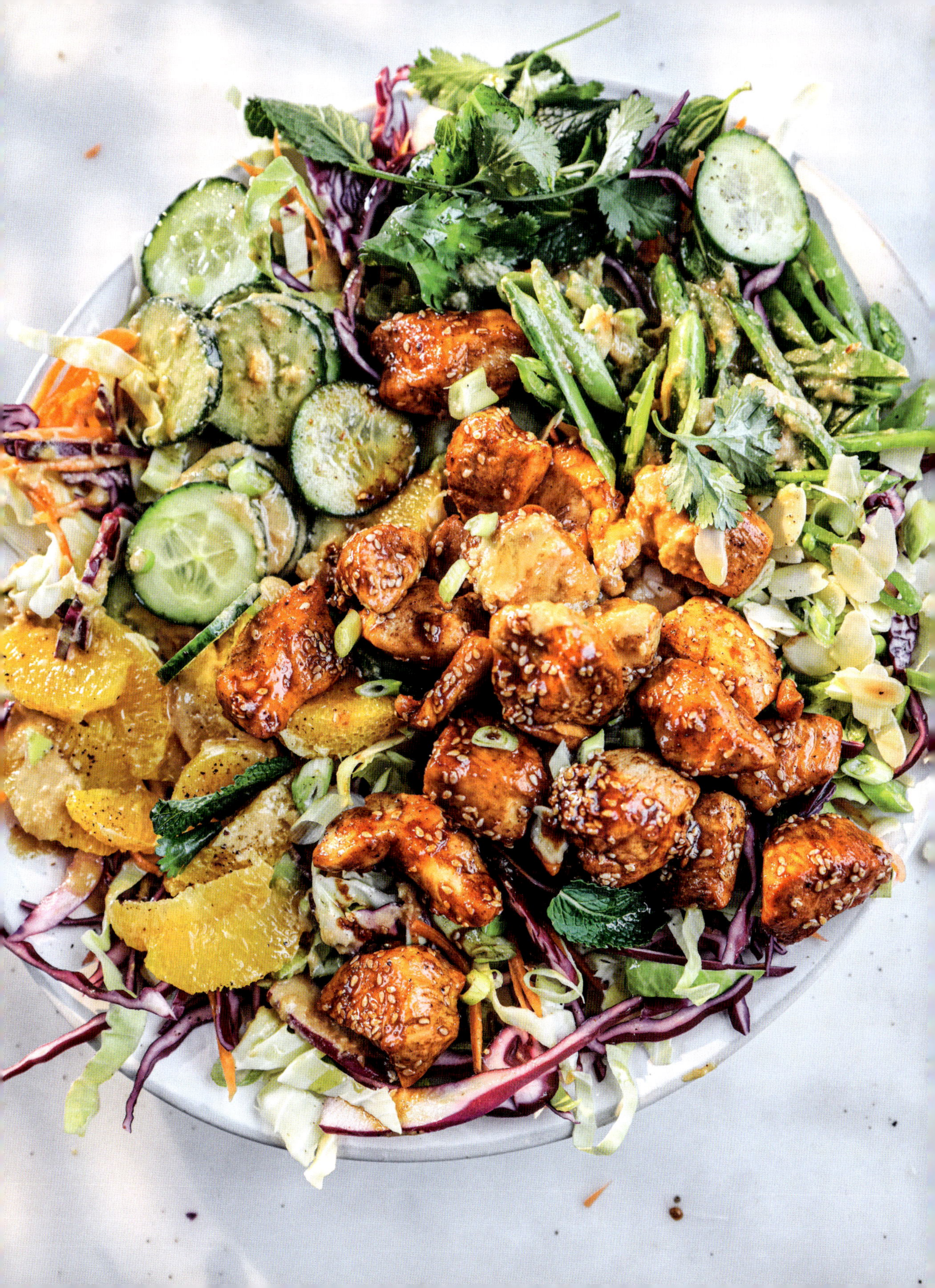

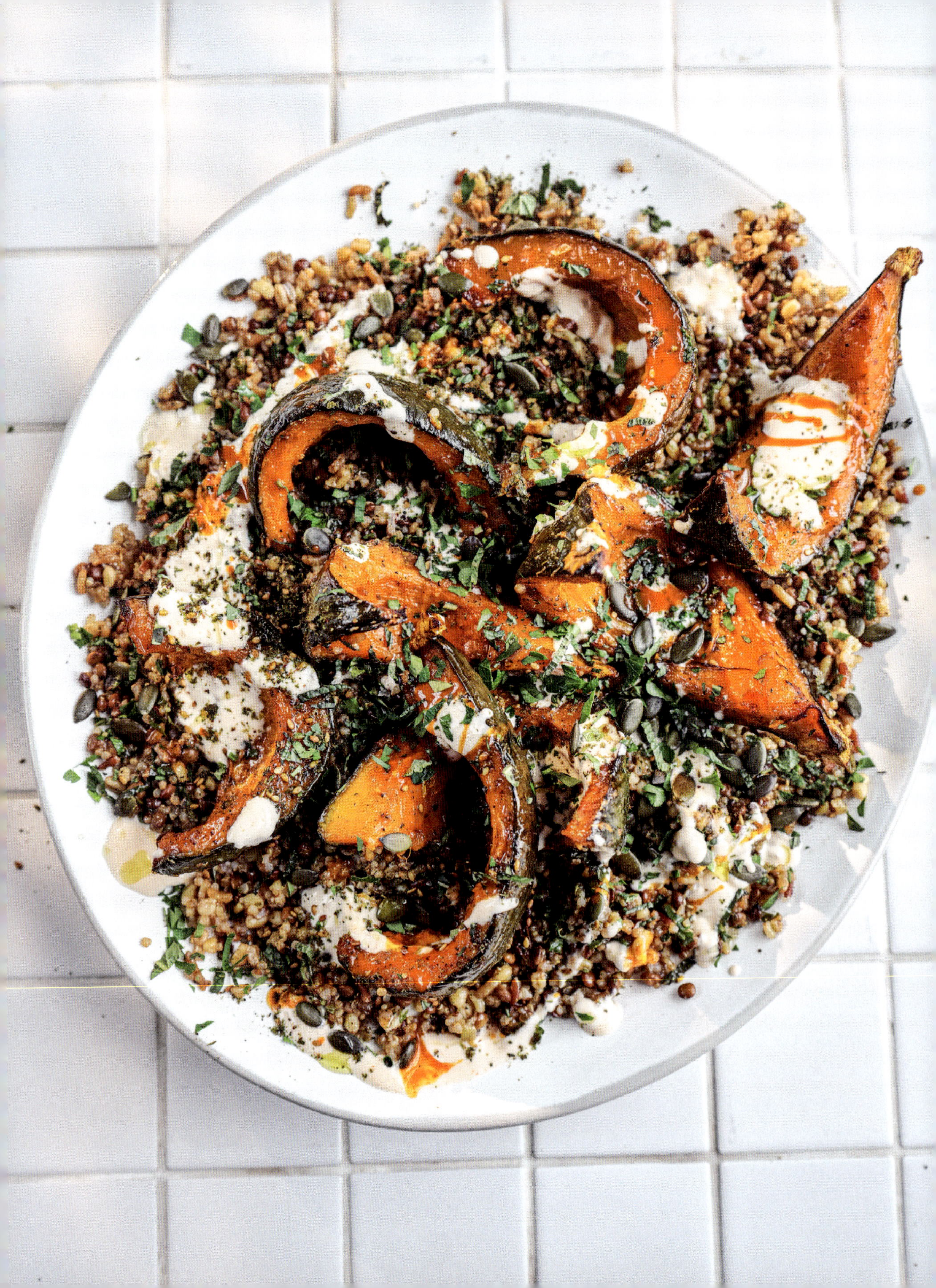

Winter Grains + Pumpkin Bowl

Scan for more tasty recipes like this one

Serves 4
Takes 1 hour

Use a roasting tin

Vegan

When it's pumpkin season, you need to run and get yourself a beautiful Delica – they caramelise as they roast and, piled on top of these herby, lemon-y grains, make for a healthy but delicious meal we could eat on repeat for the whole of autumn.

1 medium-large pumpkin (we like Delica) or butternut squash (about 1kg)
3 tbsp olive oil, plus extra to drizzle
1 garlic bulb
25g flat leaf parsley
25g mint
½ lemon
3 x 250g microwaveable pouches of mixed grains
salt and black pepper

FOR THE HOT SAUCE YOGHURT
200g natural yoghurt (use dairy-free if vegan)
1 tbsp hot sauce
½ lemon

TO SERVE
za'atar
handful of toasted pumpkin seeds

01. Preheat the oven to 220°C/200°C fan. Deseed and cut the pumpkin into 8 wedges (discard the seeds) and place, skin-side down, in the roasting tin. Drizzle with olive oil and season, then snuggle the garlic bulb in on the side. Slide into the oven and cook for 30–40 minutes until the veg is totally soft. Remove the pumpkin wedges to a plate and set the garlic bulb aside. Leave the oven on.

02. Pick the leaves from the herbs, discarding the stalks, then roughly chop. Juice the lemon. Tip the mixed grains into the tin and add a big splash of water. Add most of the chopped herbs (save some for the garnish) and the lemon juice, then squeeze in the soft garlic cloves from the bulb. Season well and stir together, then snuggle the pumpkin wedges back into the tin. Return to the oven for a further 10 minutes.

03. Meanwhile, make the hot sauce yoghurt. Put the yoghurt and hot sauce into a bowl, then squeeze in the lemon juice. Mix together and season well.

04. Remove the tin from the oven and leave to cool for a few minutes. Divide between 4 bowls, then top with the hot sauce yoghurt and reserved herbs. Sprinkle with za'atar and toasted pumpkin seeds. Finish with a drizzle of olive oil and serve.

Kale Waldorf with Roasted Grapes

Serves 4
Takes 30 minutes

Use a large non-stick frying pan

Veggie, Gluten-free

180ml natural yoghurt
½ large lemon
a small bunch of dill
1 garlic clove
75g blue cheese
4 celery sticks
500g red grapes, on the vine
1 x 200g bag of ready-chopped kale
100g walnuts or pecans
1 tbsp olive oil, plus extra to drizzle
1 tbsp honey
salt and black pepper

Scan for more tasty recipes like this one

This one's all about clever combos. Kale, raw grapes, roasted grapes and blue cheese might sound like a bit of an odd combination but all of those ingredients are able to put their differences aside and work together for the ultimate winter salad.

01. Put the yoghurt into a bowl. Zest the lemon into the bowl, then squeeze in the juice. Pick the dill leaves, and finely chop most of them, saving a few to serve. Add to the yoghurt bowl. Finely grate the garlic into the dressing, then crumble in the cheese. Use a fork to whisk together, pressing the cheese against the side of the bowl to crush it further. Season with salt and loads of black pepper, then mash into a creamy dressing. Tip into a large salad bowl.

02. Thinly slice the celery sticks into slices and halve a third of the grapes, then tip into the bowl with the kale (discard any large bits of stalk). Use your clean hands to really massage the dressing into the leaves to soften.

03. Toast the walnuts in the dry frying pan over a medium-high heat for 2–3 minutes until smelling amazing, then tip onto a chopping board and roughly chop. Season. Mix half of the nuts through the salad, reserving the rest.

04. Heat 1 tablespoon of the oil in the pan over a high heat, add the remaining grapes and cook for 2–3 minutes, turning occasionally, until beginning to blacken and burst. Drizzle with honey, then remove from the heat

05. Drape the grapes on top of the salad, spooning over any pan juices, then scatter over the reserved walnuts and dill. Serve with a final drizzle of olive oil.

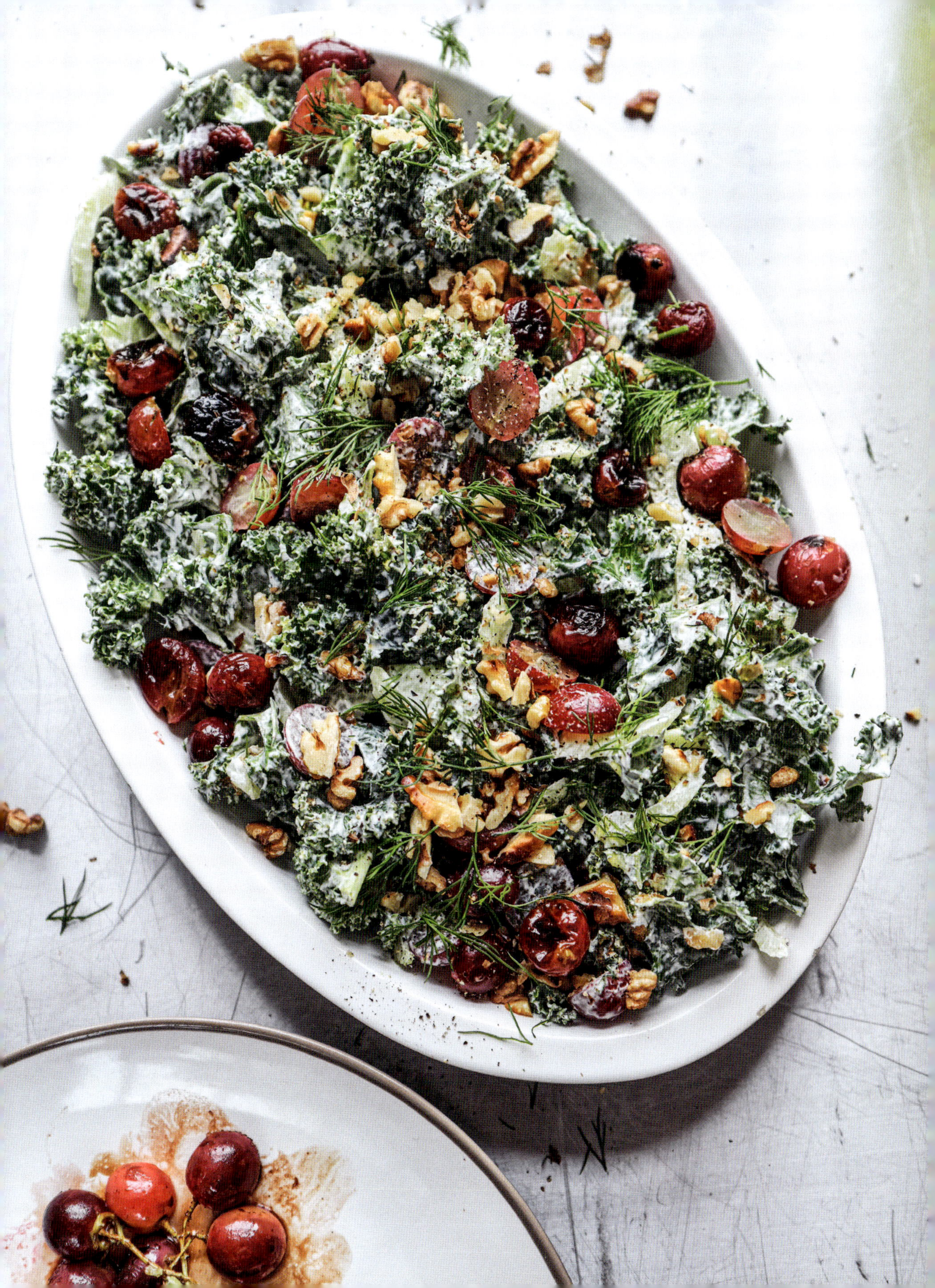

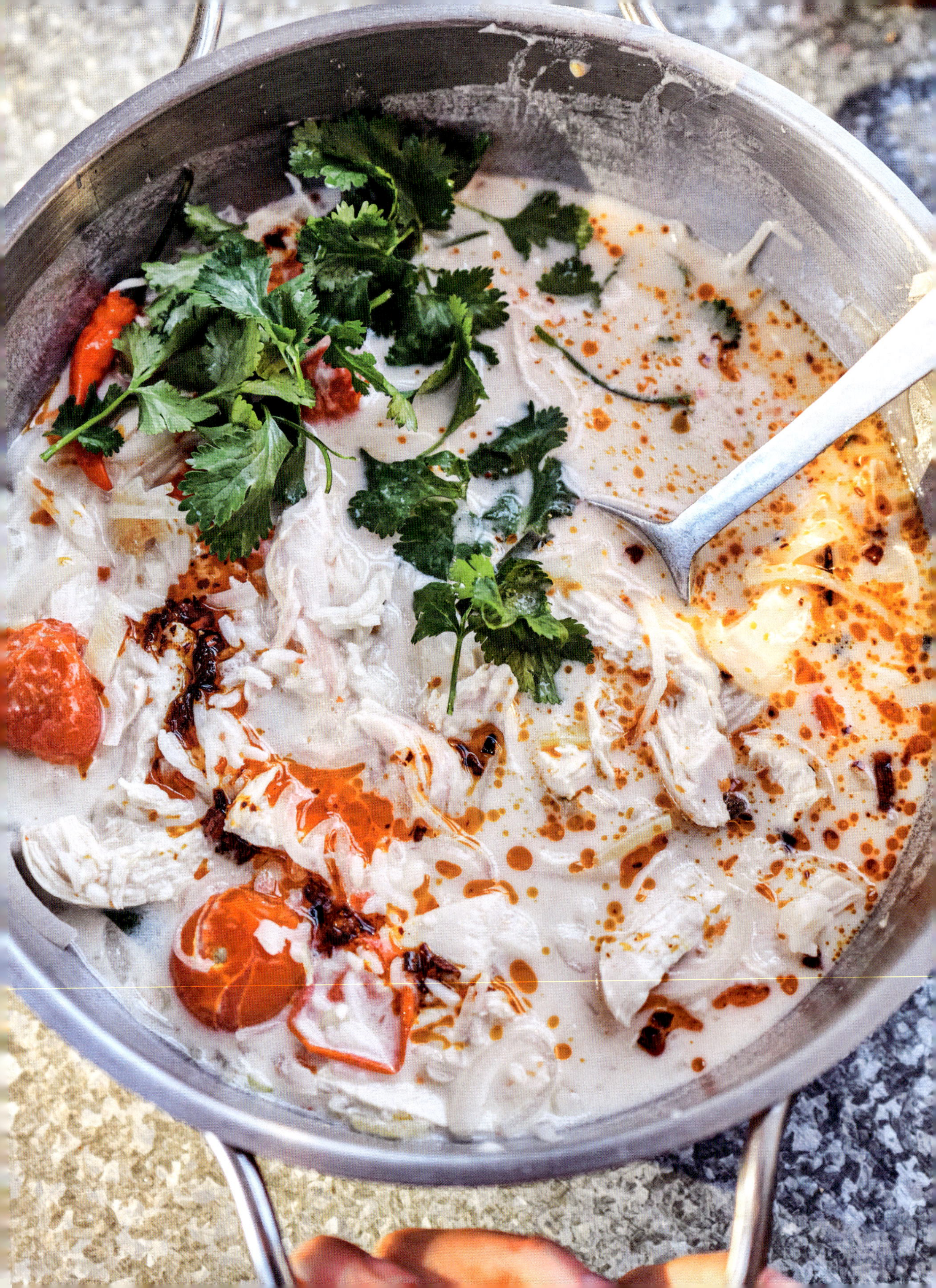

Coconut Chicken Soup

Serves 2
Takes 30 minutes

Use a medium-sized saucepan with a lid

Gluten-free

---

1 lemongrass stalk
a thumb-sized chunk of fresh ginger
2 banana shallots
30g bunch of coriander
1 x 400ml tin of coconut milk
1 tbsp honey
2 boneless, skinless chicken breasts
150g cherry tomatoes
2–3 bird's eye chillies
2 fresh makrut lime leaves
2 limes
2½ tbsp fish sauce (check the label if making this gluten-free)
1 x 250g microwaveable pouch of jasmine rice
1 tablespoon crispy chilli oil, to garnish

SWAP: If you can't find lime leaves, use the zest of 2 limes instead.

Scan for more tasty recipes like this one

This comforting, creamy coconut chicken soup is inspired by tom kha kai. This feel-good recipe involves poaching chicken, which might be slightly alarming for newbies, but once you realise how juicy and delicious poached chicken can be, you might never cook it any other way again. Which is highly unlikely. But still. It's that good.

01. Start with the prep. Trim the lemongrass, remove the outer leaves and slice very finely. Peel and slice the ginger, then slice the shallots and finely chop the coriander stalks (reserve the leaves to serve).

02. Put a big spoonful of the thick part of the coconut milk at the top of the tin into your saucepan, add a spoonful of water and all the prepped aromatics and cook over a medium-high heat for 2 minutes, or until fragrant. Pour in the remaining coconut milk, then add a tinful of water. Add the honey and bring to the boil.

03. Add the chicken, cherry tomatoes and whole chillies and bring to the boil, then immediately reduce to a very gentle simmer. Cover with the lid and simmer for 5 minutes, taking care that the liquid is not boiling. Turn off the heat and leave with the lid on for 10 minutes until the chicken is cooked through.

04. Remove the chicken to a chopping board and leave to rest.

05. Meanwhile, thinly shred the lime leaves (discard the innner stalk), then add to the soup with the juice of 1 ½ limes and fish sauce, and simmer for 2 minutes.

06. Shred the chicken and return to the soup with the jasmine rice to heat through for 2–3 minutes.

07. Garnish with the coriander leaves and crispy chilli oil. Slice the final lime half into wedges to serve and enjoy.

FRESH ONES

SEGW

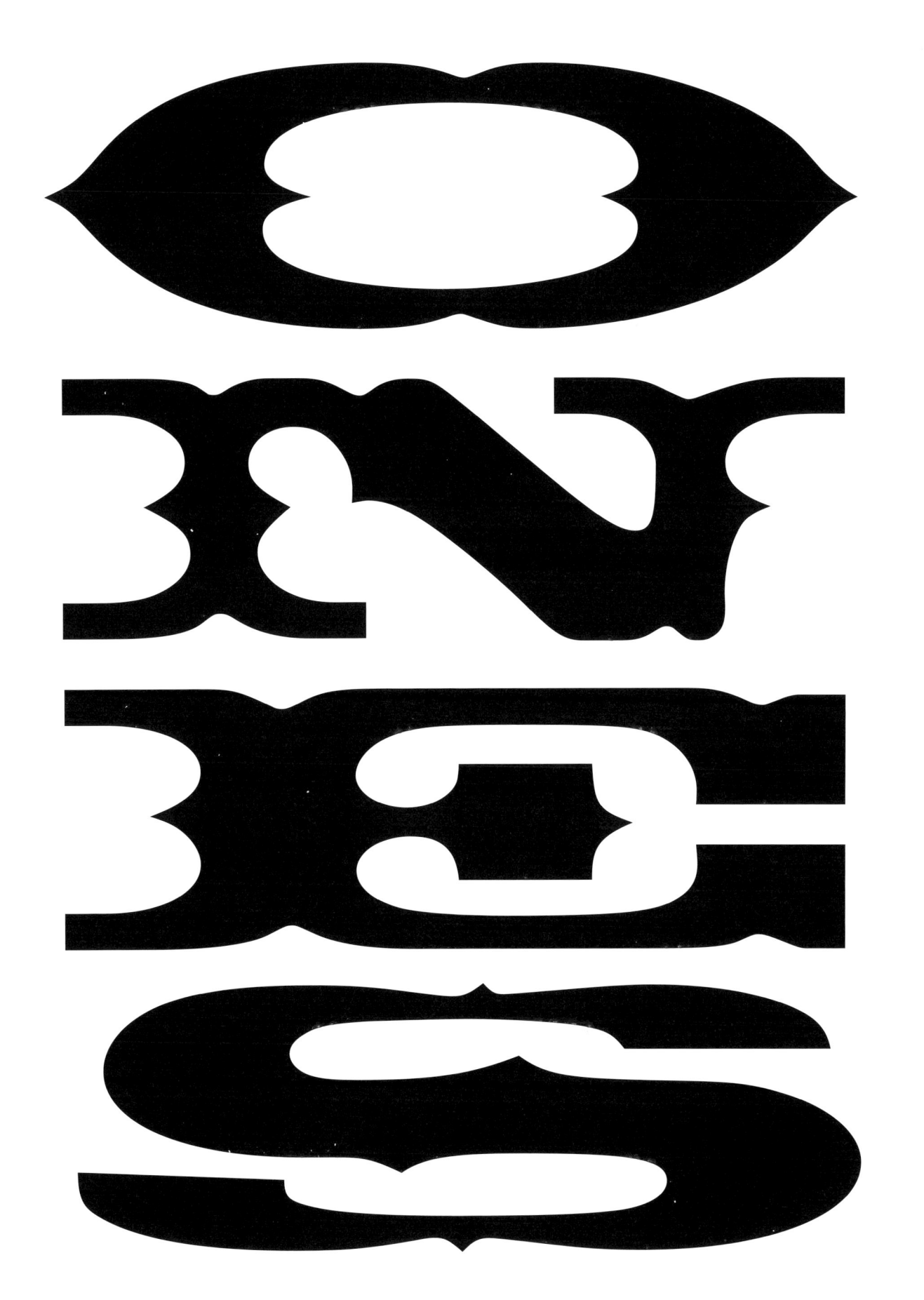

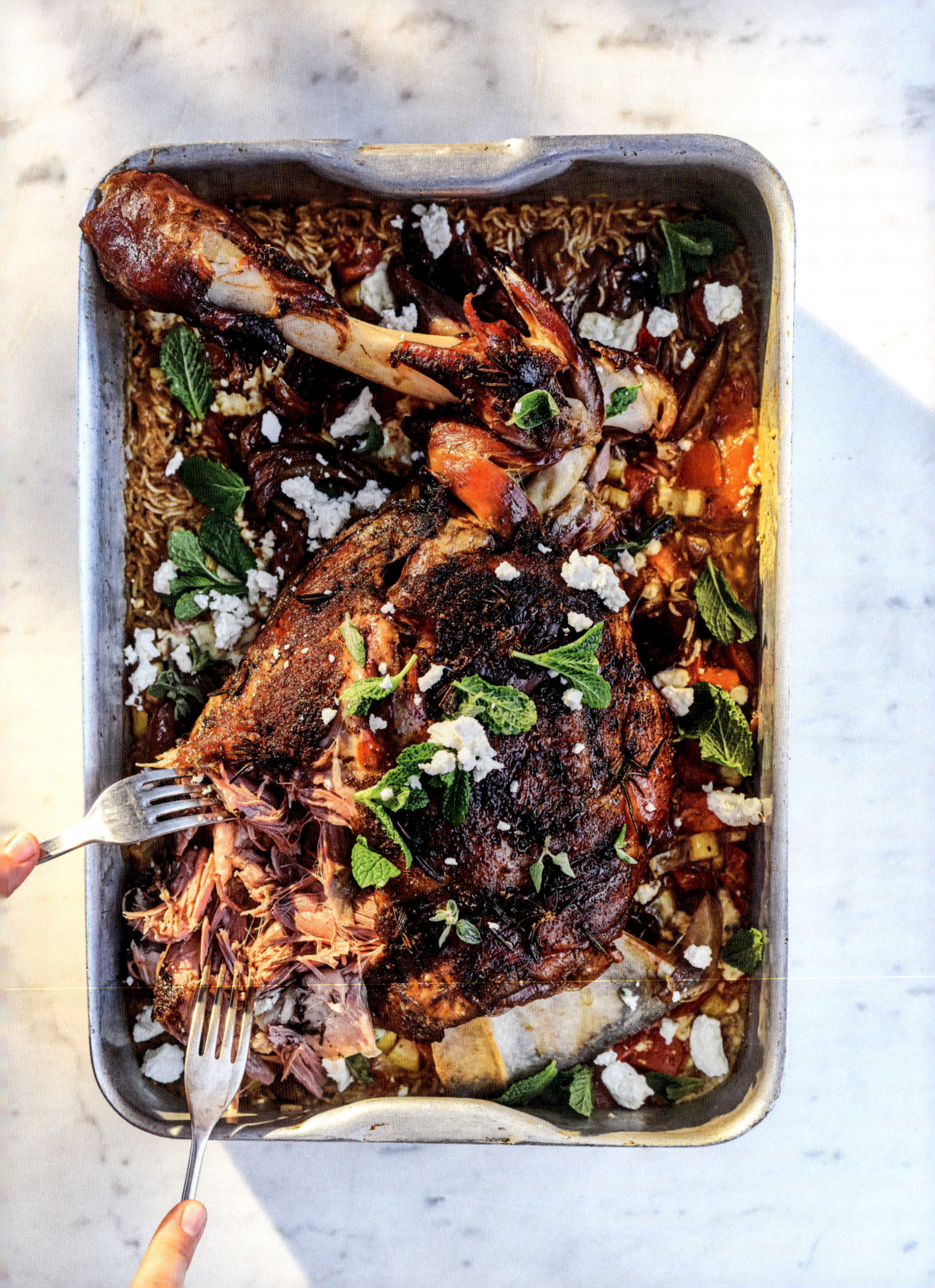

Lemon + Feta Lamb

Serves 6
Takes 3¾–4¾ hours

Use a large roasting tin

Gluten-free

- 1.5kg bone-in shoulder of lamb
- 3 garlic cloves
- 3 sprigs of rosemary
- 1 tbsp dried oregano
- 1 tbsp sumac
- 3 onions
- 2 lemons
- 2 large beef tomatoes
- 250g basmati rice
- 200g feta
- 500ml hot chicken stock (check the label if making this gluten-free)
- a handful of mint leaves
- a handful of oregano leaves
- salt and black pepper

Scan for more tasty recipes like this one

This stunning shoulder of lamb is roasted low and slow before being paired up with a baked tomato and lemon rice to soak up all of those lovely lamb juices. Dicing the rind of the lemon into little pieces gives you rice that's studded with a bitter, zesty intensity you're going to love.

01. Preheat the oven to 240°C/220°C fan.

02. Using a sharp knife, pierce the lamb all over. Thinly slice the garlic cloves and pick the leaves from the rosemary sprigs. Nestle the garlic slices and rosemary in the cuts you've made, then season the lamb generously with salt, pepper and the dried oregano and sumac.

03. Cut the onions into wedges, then arrange them in the bottom of the roasting tin and lay the lamb on top.

04. Roast for 20 minutes, then remove the tin from the oven and pour 750ml of water around the lamb. Cover with foil. Reduce the oven temperature to 180°C/160°C fan and return to the oven for 3–4 hours, depending on the size of your lamb shoulder. The meat should visibly come away from the bone and feel very tender when poked with a fork.

05. Meanwhile, finely chop 1 of the lemons, discarding any seeds but including the peel. Dice the tomatoes. Set aside.

06. Remove the lamb to a chopping board and leave to rest. Scoop out half of the roasting juices into a jug and set aside to drizzle over later.

07. Rinse the basmati rice in a sieve until the water runs clear, then tip into the tin. Sprinkle in the chopped lemon and tomato and crumble in half of the feta. Pour over the stock, re-cover with foil, then return to the oven for 10 minutes. After 10 minutes, remove the foil and cook for a final 5 minutes until the rice is tender.

08. Remove the tin from the oven, pop the lamb back in and sprinkle with the remaining feta and the herbs. Drizzle over the reserved lamb juices and serve with the remaining lemon, cut into wedges. Enjoy!

Braised Green Beans with Olives + Feta

Serves 4
Takes 1 hour 10 minutes + cooling

Use a heavy saucepan or casserole pan

Veggie, Gluten-free

1 onion
4 garlic cloves
100ml extra virgin olive oil
3 tomatoes (about 300g)
3 large waxy potatoes (we like Cyprus) (about 750g)
500g green beans
1 x 400g tin of chopped tomatoes
1 tsp dried oregano
80g pitted Kalamata olives
15g flat leaf parsley
15g mint
100g feta
1 lemon
bread, to serve (optional)
salt

Scan for more tasty recipes like this one

This Greek-ish banger, inspired by fasolakia yiahni, tastes like summer in Greece. It sits in a category of cooking called *lathera*, which basically means 'cooked in olive oil'. Don't be scared of the amount of olive oil used here – it might seem like a lot but the Greeks have been doing it for centuries and their food is some of the best on the planet. Enjoy!

01. Finely chop the onion and finely slice the garlic. Heat the olive oil in the saucepan over a low heat, then add the onion and garlic with a nice big pinch of salt. You need to cook them really gently until softened without taking on any colour, about 10 minutes.

02. Meanwhile, halve the tomatoes widthways and then grate, cut-side, into a bowl. Peel and halve the potatoes, then cut into wedges. Trim the green beans.

03. Add the tinned and grated tomatoes, the potatoes and beans to the pan, then stir in 100ml of water. Add the oregano and bring to the boil, then reduce the heat to medium-low and simmer for about 40–50 minutes until the sauce has reduced and is clinging onto the very tender beans.

04. Remove from the heat and stir through the olives, parsley and most of the mint, reserving some leaves for garnish, then leave to cool until it's just a bit warmer than room temperature.

05. To serve, crumble the feta over the top, scatter with the reserved mint leaves, squeeze over the lemon juice and enjoy with bread, if you like.

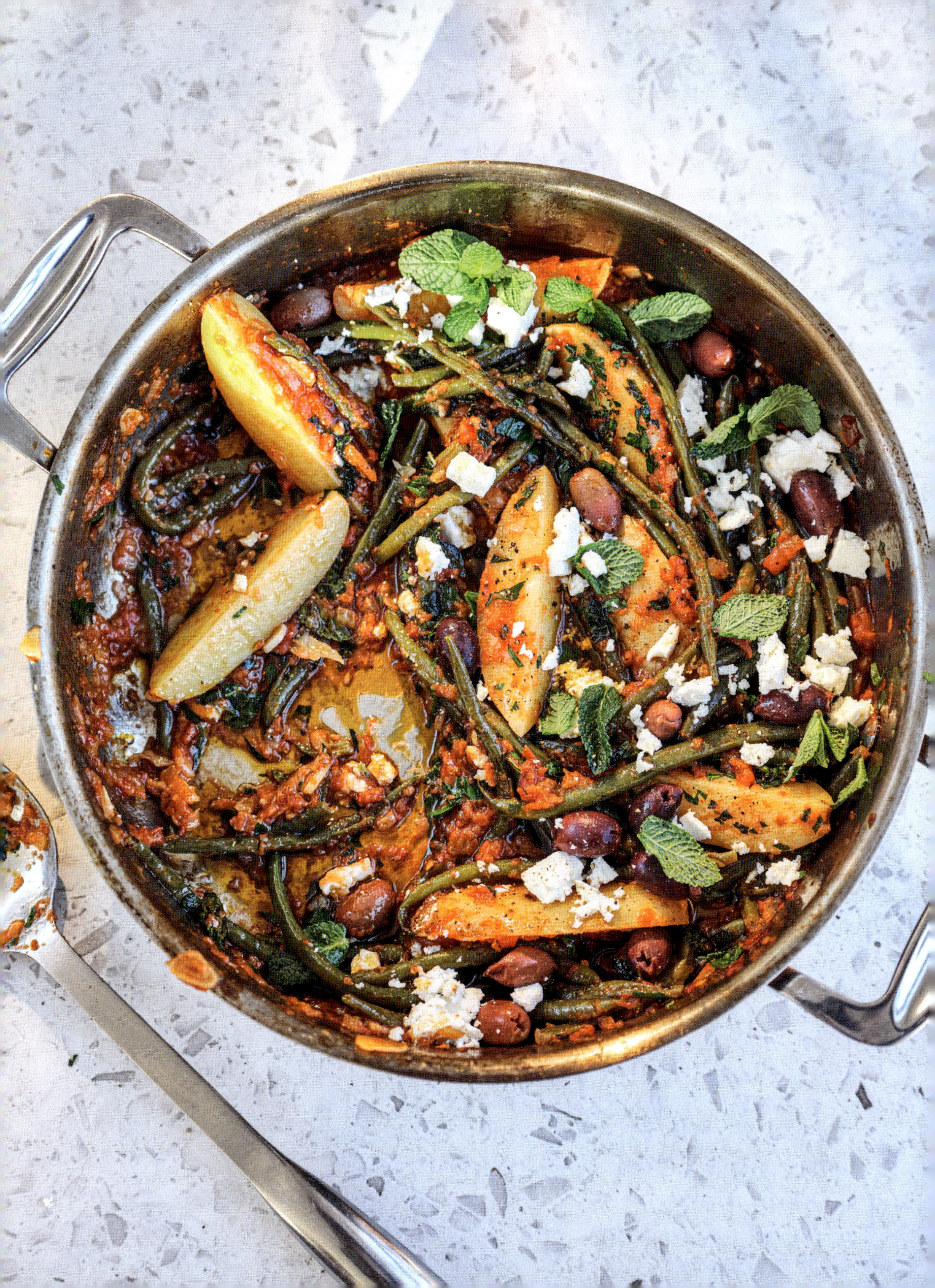

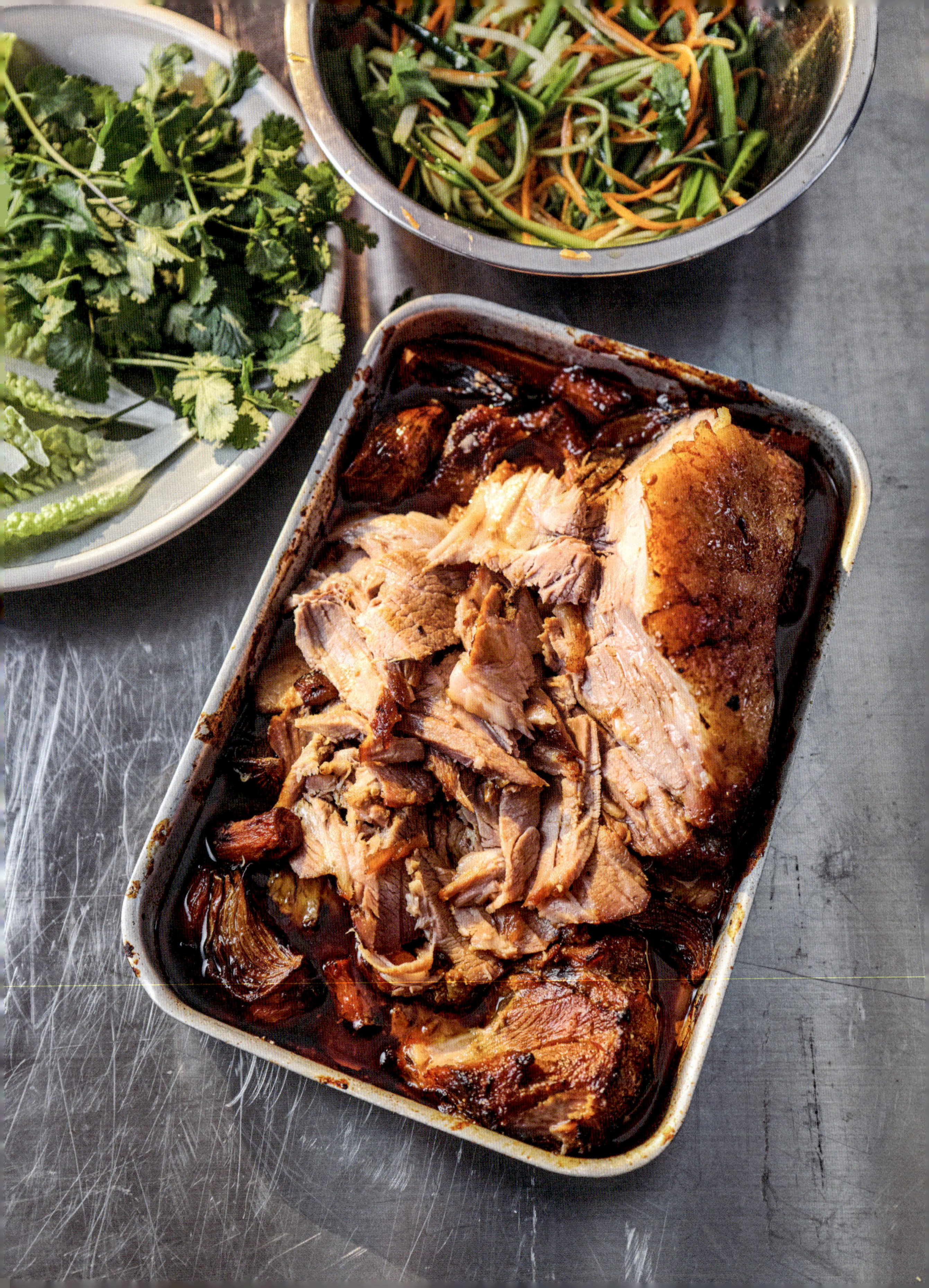

Pork Shoulder Lettuce Cups

Serves 8
Takes about 5 hours

Use a large roasting tin

1 x 2kg boneless, skinless pork shoulder (see Tip overleaf)
30g fresh ginger
5 garlic cloves
3 tbsp gochujang
3 tbsp soy sauce
2 tbsp mirin
2 tbsp rice vinegar
2 carrots
2 onions
salt

FOR THE SLAW
1 kohlrabi (about 450g)
200g sugar snaps
2 carrots
1 cucumber
15g coriander
2 tbsp soy sauce
1 tbsp sesame oil
1 tbsp mirin
2 tbsp rice vinegar

TO SERVE
3 x 250g microwaveable pouches of basmati rice
Baby gem lettuce
Sriracha or other chilli sauce (optional)

Slow-roasted with garlic, ginger, gochujang and mirin, this Korean-inspired pork shoulder is the kind of dish that's perfect for a weekend dinner party. Everyone will be impressed, and you'll get to feel incredibly smug because – aside from chucking it in the oven – you hardly did any work at all.

01. Pop your pork shoulder into the roasting tin and remove any string that may be tying it up. Salt it generously. Preheat the oven to 160°C/140°C fan.

02. Peel the ginger, then finely grate with the garlic into a small bowl. Add the gochujang, soy sauce, mirin and rice vinegar and mix together.

03. Peel the carrots, then cut them into big chunks. Cut the onions into wedges.

04. Lift up the pork from the tin and chuck the onions and carrots in the bottom, then smother the pork in the sauce.

Continued overleaf

Continued from previous page

TIP: If your pork shoulder comes with its skin on, remove it with a sharp knife. Alternatively, you can use pork belly and score the skin at 1cm intervals, being careful not to cut all the way through to the meat. Don't cover the tin with foil, and avoid getting the sauce on the skin so you don't end up with burnt crackling.

Scan for more tasty recipes like this one

05. Cover the tin with foil and roast for 3–3½ hours. Remove the foil and roast for a further 1–1½ hours, basting regularly, until the meat is very tender and the sauce is sticky and reduced.

06. About 20 minutes before your pork is ready, make the slaw. Peel the kohlrabi and cut into matchsticks, then cut the sugar snaps into thin long strips. Slice the carrots and the cucumber lengthways into nice thin strips. Place all the veg in a bowl, pick the coriander leaves (discard the stalks) and add most to the bowl, reserving a few to serve. Add the soy sauce, sesame oil, mirin and rice vinegar and mix it all together. Set aside.

07. When the pork is cooked, shred it with 2 forks and coat it in the pan juices.

08. Heat the rice in the microwave according to the packet instructions, then serve the pork loaded into lettuce cups with slaw, and chilli sauce and the reserved coriander leaves.

Scotch Bonnet Lamb + Pineapple Salsa

Serves 4–6
Takes 3¾–4¾ hours
+ marinating

Use a large roasting tin

1 x 2kg shoulder of lamb, bone-in
300ml hot chicken stock
3 x 250g microwaveable pouches of coconut rice, to serve

FOR THE MARINADE
a bunch of spring onions
6 garlic cloves
1½ scotch bonnet chillies
a thumb-sized chunk of fresh ginger
2 tbsp hot curry powder
1 tbsp ground allspice
2 tsp ground cloves
2 tsp ground ginger
a handful of thyme sprigs
1 tbsp Maggi seasoning
3 tbsp white wine vinegar
2 tbsp honey
salt and black pepper

FOR THE SALSA
250g cherry tomatoes
½ ripe pineapple
a handful of coriander
2 limes

Inspired by some of our favourite Caribbean flavours, this curry unites fall-apart lamb with spicy, fruity scotch bonnet in a lovely hot gravy. The whole thing is livened up with a punchy pineapple salsa. The flavour of this is as deep and layered as a classic Russian novel.

01. Start by whizzing together your marinade. Put 2 spring onions to one side for later, then roughly chop the rest, along with the garlic and 1 of the scotch bonnets. Peel and roughly chop the ginger. Put the prepped veg into a high-powered blender or food processor with the spices. Strip the leaves from the thyme sprigs and pop these in too. Pour in the Maggi seasoning, vinegar and honey and season well. Whizz until completely smooth, adding a splash of water if it needs it to come together.

02. Make some shallow slashes in the lamb shoulder with a sharp knife, then put it into the roasting tin and pour over the marinade, rubbing it in really well. At this point, you can cover it loosely with cling film and leave to marinate in the fridge for up to 12 hours.

Continued overleaf

Continued from previous page

03. When ready to cook, preheat the oven to 220°C/200°C fan.

04. Pour the stock over the lamb, mixing well to amalgamate everything together. Cover tightly with foil, then roast for 30 minutes. Reduce the oven temperature to 170°C/150°C fan and cook for a further 3–4 hours until the lamb is meltingly tender.

05. When the lamb is nearly ready, make the salsa. Quarter the cherry tomatoes and tip into a bowl. Slice off the pineapple skin, then cut the flesh into small dice. Very thinly slice the reserved spring onions and finely chop the remaining scotch bonnet. Roughly chop the coriander, stalks and all. Add all the prepped ingredients to the bowl and season lightly, then juice the limes and stir in.

06. Just before serving, ping the coconut rice in the microwave according to the packet instructions. Using a large spoon, skim the glossy fat from the top of the sauce around the lamb.

07. Pull the lamb into big chunks in the sauce, discard the bone, then serve with the rice and salsa.

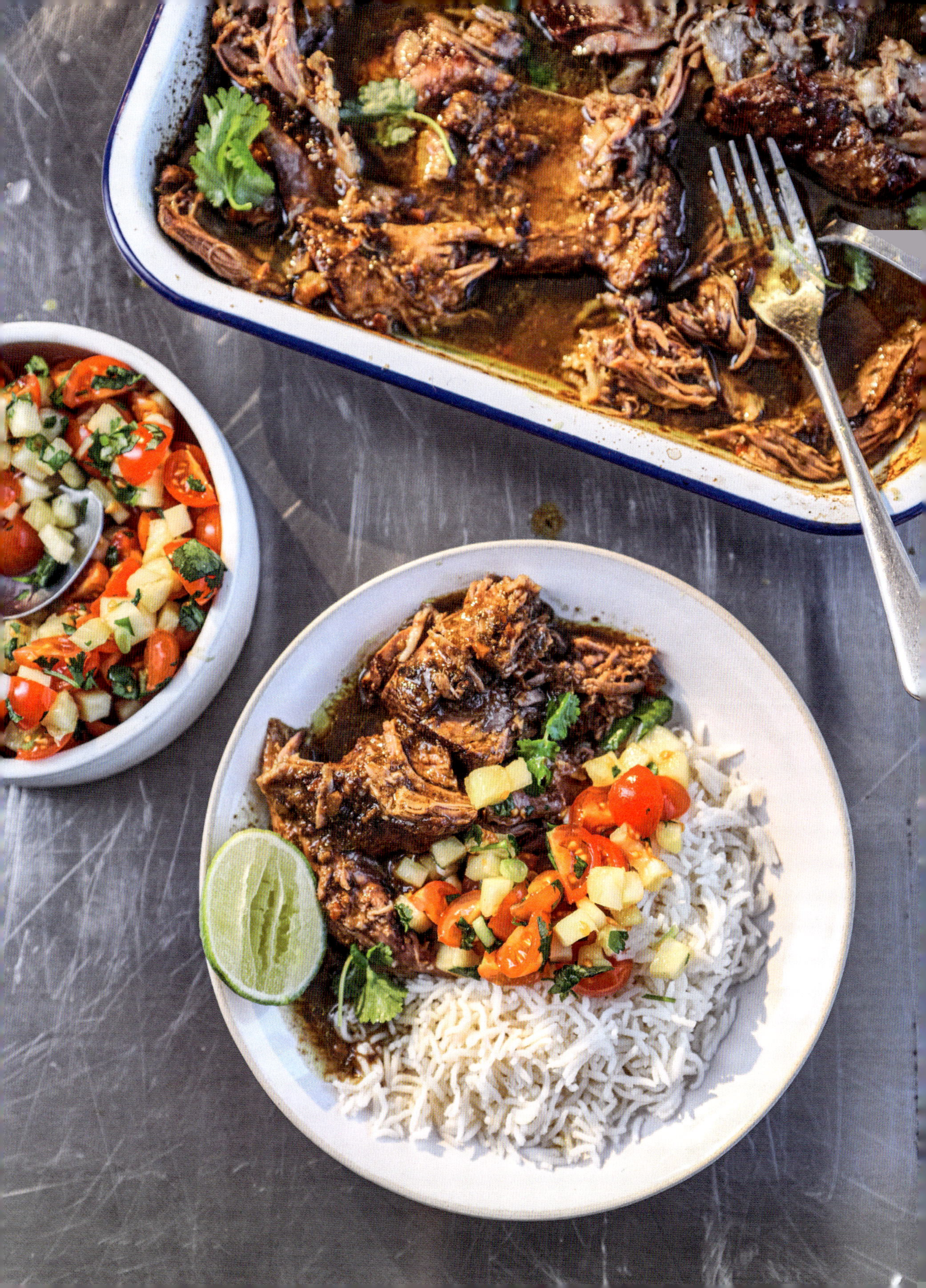

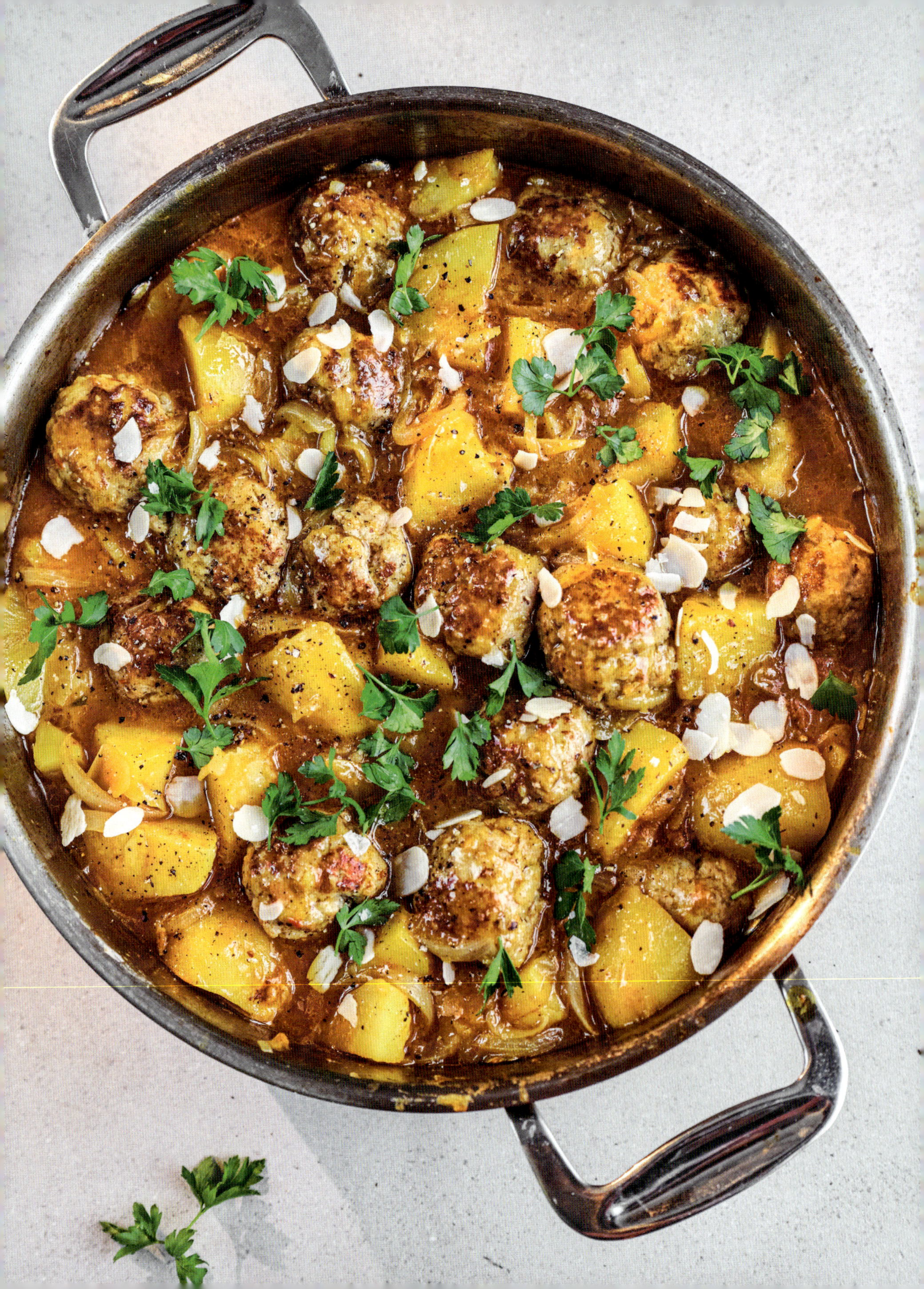

Saffron Albondigas

Serves 6
Takes 1 hour

Use a large ovenproof casserole dish

---

2 slices of stale white bread
1 garlic clove
1 egg
500g pork mince
1 tbsp ground cumin
2 tbsp extra virgin olive oil
3 onions
500g Maris Piper potatoes
2 tbsp plain flour
200ml sherry or dry white wine
a big pinch of saffron
2 tsp sweet paprika
a good grating of nutmeg
700ml hot chicken stock
2 tbsp sherry vinegar
salt and black pepper

TO GARNISH
a large handful of flat leaf parsley leaves
a large handful of flaked almonds

These Spanish meatballs are a secret family recipe of Saskia Sidey's. They are subtle, aromatic and almost unbelievably unctuous. You won't find a more appropriate autumn supper.

---

01. Start by making the meatballs. Crumble the stale bread into a bowl to make breadcrumbs, then finely grate in the garlic. Add the egg, pork mince and cumin with a generous amount of salt and pepper and combine. Alternatively, you can blitz the ingredients together in a food processor. Roll the mixture into golf-ball-sized meatballs.

02. Heat the olive oil in the casserole dish over a medium heat, add the meatballs and fry on all sides for about 2 minutes until golden. Remove from the dish and set aside.

03. Slice the onions. Peel and cube the potatoes into 3cm chunks.

04. Add the onions to the dish and cook over a medium heat for 5–6 minutes until softened, then stir in the flour and cook for 2 minutes. Pour in the sherry and add the saffron, paprika and nutmeg, then bubble away until the liquid has reduced by two-thirds.

05. Pour in the stock and add the potatoes, then bring to the boil. Reduce the heat and simmer for about 25 minutes until the potatoes are tender and the sauce has thickened.

06. Return the meatballs to the pan, season with the sherry vinegar, salt and pepper and simmer for 10 minutes, or until they are cooked through.

07. Sprinkle over the parsley leaves and almonds and serve.

Cauliflower Mac 'n' Cheese

Serves 4
Takes 40 minutes

Use a large, deep ovenproof frying pan

Veggie

- 1 large cauliflower (about 800–900g)
- 100g stale sourdough or any crusty bread (about 2 large slices)
- 300g macaroni
- 300g garlic and herb soft cheese (we use Boursin)
- 1 x 250g packet of ready-grated mixed Cheddar cheese and mozzarella
- 1 tbsp Dijon mustard
- 1–3 tsp crispy chilli oil (we like Lao Gan Ma), plus extra (optional) to serve
- a large handful of crispy onions, to serve
- salt and black pepper

The sauce for this mac and cheese is one of the greatest cheat codes ever. Using a garlic and herb cheese gives you the creamiest, super garlicky sauce and you don't have to faff about making a béchamel! Topped with crispy onions, crispy chilli oil and crispy croutons? Yes, please.

01. Preheat the oven to 220°C/200°C fan.

02. Trim off the cauliflower stalk, then cut into 1cm pieces. Cut the head into bite-sized florets, saving and setting aside any nice small leaves. Cut the sourdough into 2.5cm cubes and pop into a bowl.

03. Pour 1.5 litres of boiling water into the frying pan over a high heat, lightly season and bring to the boil. Tip in the macaroni and boil for 6 minutes, stirring regularly so that the macaroni doesn't stick to the bottom of the pan. Stir in the cauliflower florets and stalk pieces and cook for a further 5 minutes.

04. Take off the heat, add the soft cheese, 200g of the grated cheese and the mustard and season with salt and loads of black pepper. Mix together really well.

05. Scatter over the sourdough cubes and cauliflower leaves, drizzle over the crispy chilli oil and sprinkle over the remaining grated cheese.

06. Bake for 10 minutes until the cheese has melted and the bread is browned and crisp. Serve scattered with the crispy onions and a little more chilli oil, if you like.

Scan for more tasty recipes like this one

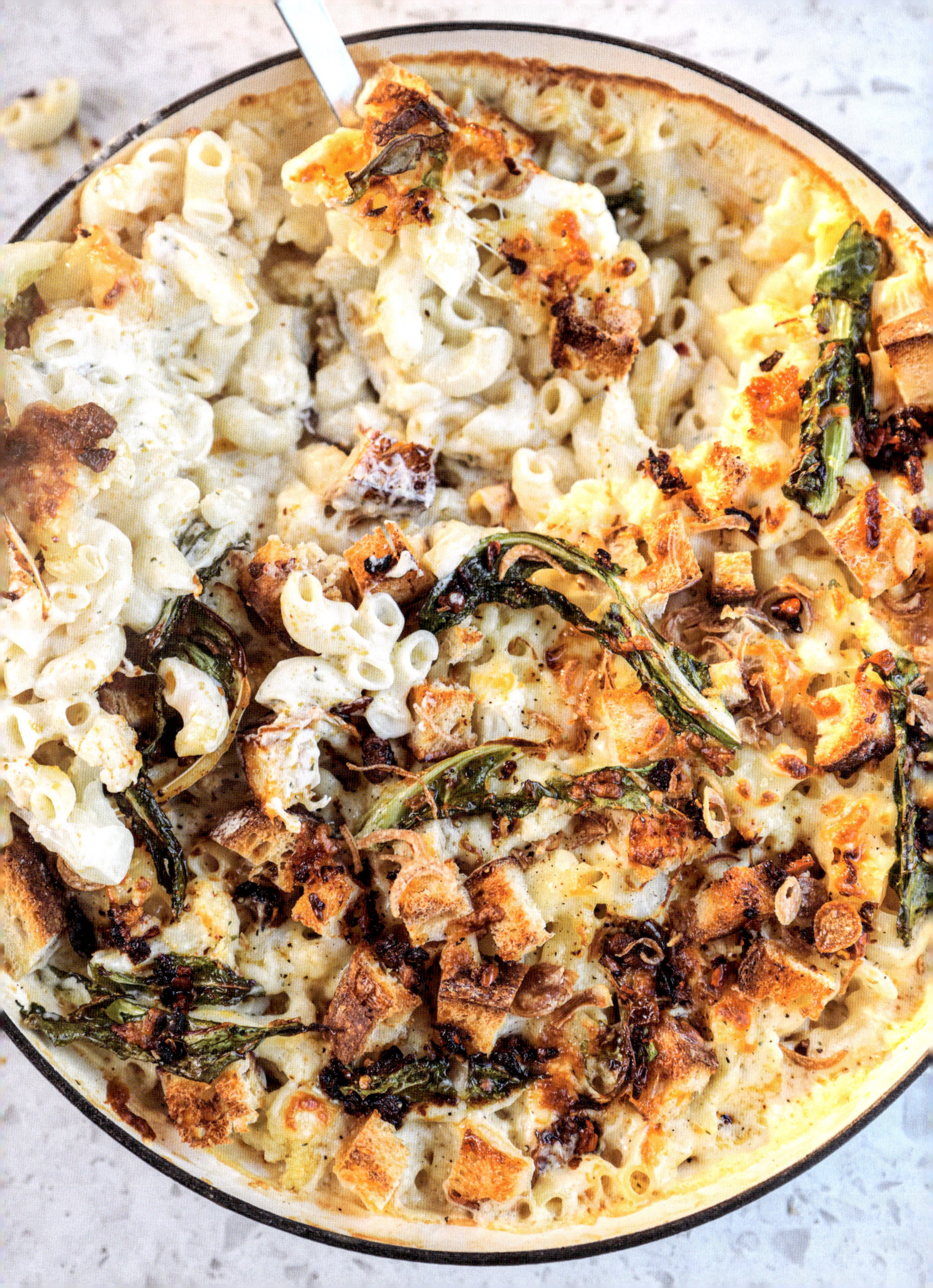

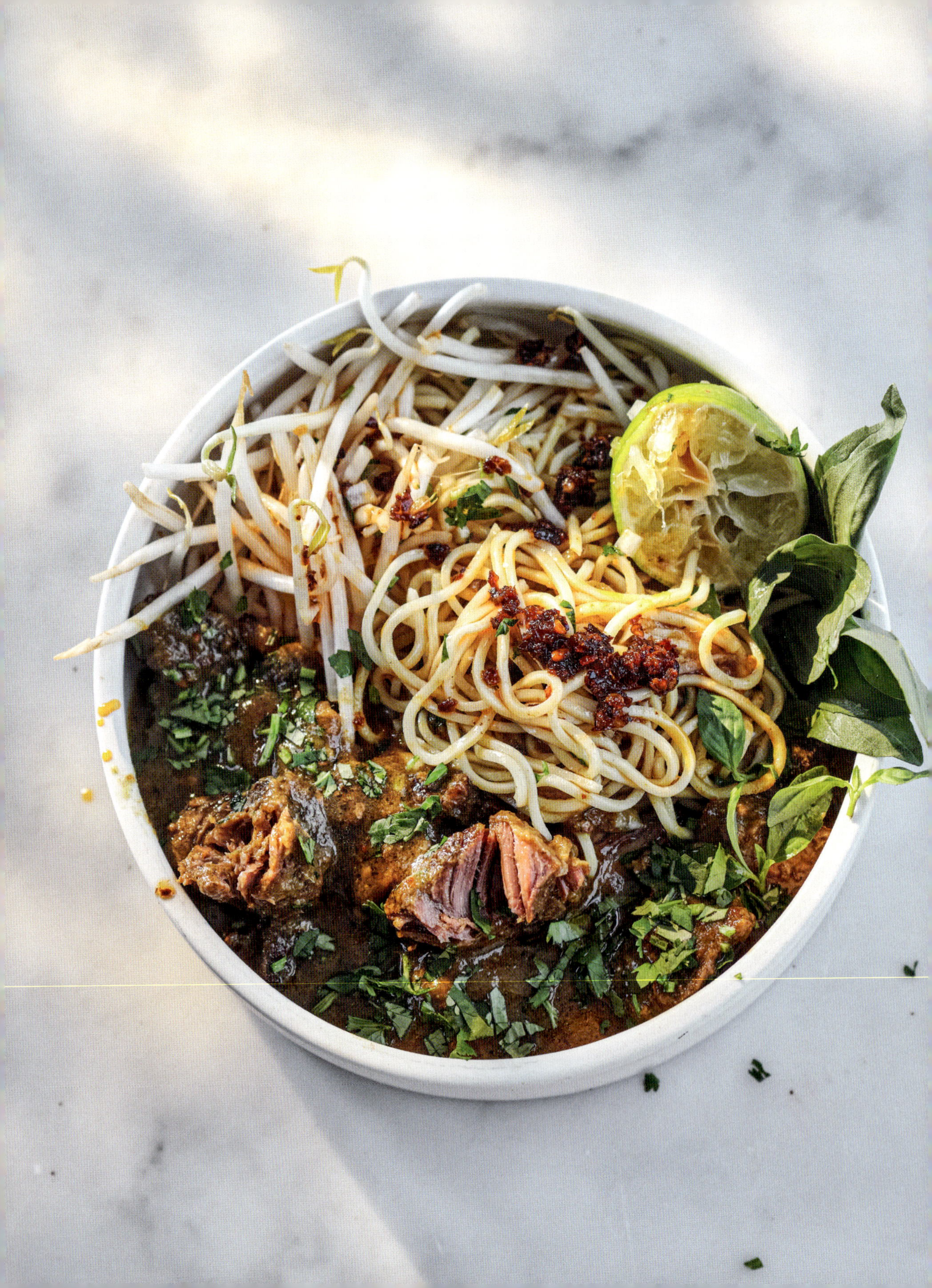

Beef Shin Noodle Curry

Serves 4
Takes 3 hours 45 minutes

Use a large, deep roasting tin

1kg boneless shin of beef
vegetable oil, to drizzle
600ml hot chicken stock
1 x 400ml tin of coconut milk
1 banana shallot
3 limes
1 x 400g pack of microwaveable fresh egg noodles
3 tbsp fish sauce
2 tbsp soft light brown sugar
100g beansprouts
2 tbsp crispy chilli oil (we like Lao Gan Ma)
a small handful of Thai basil leaves
a small bunch of coriander
salt and black pepper

FOR THE SPICE PASTE
4–6 small dried chillies (depending on how spicy you like it)
3 banana shallots
10 garlic cloves
2 thumb-sized chunks of fresh ginger
2 lemongrass stalks
1 tbsp ground turmeric
1 tbsp ground coriander
1 tbsp hot curry powder
1 tbsp shrimp paste

This one is loosely inspired by a northern Thai noodle soup known as khao soi. It's rich, spicy, aromatic and has plenty of zing to boot. In Thailand, the curried soup is typically served with a crispy nest of noodles on top but we've taken that step out to keep it one-pan. You'll likely have to go to the butcher to get the beef shin but it's more than worth the extra effort.

01. Preheat the oven to 220°C/200°C fan. Cut the beef into 5cm pieces, then tip into the roasting tin. Season generously, then drizzle all over with vegetable oil. Roast for 30 minutes until browned.

02. Meanwhile, make the spice paste. Put the dried chillies into a small heatproof bowl and pour over 100ml of boiling water. Leave to stand while you prep all the other bits. Roughly slice the shallots, then roughly chop the garlic. Peel and roughly chop the ginger. Trim the lemongrass, remove the outer leaves and finely slice. Put the prepped ingredients into a food processor or high-powered blender. Add the chillies and their soaking liquid, the ground spices and shrimp paste and whizz to a paste.

03. Remove the beef from the oven. Spoon over the spice paste, mix well and return to the oven for a further 5 minutes.

04. Reduce the oven temperature to 170°C/150°C fan. Remove the tin from the oven, pour in the stock and coconut milk and mix well. Cover with foil, return to the oven and roast for 2 hours. Carefully remove the foil (you'll put it back on in a minute) and give everything a good stir, then re-cover and roast for a further 1 hour until the meat is meltingly tender and the gravy reduced.

Continued overleaf

Continued from previous page

Scan for more
tasty recipes
like this one

05. Just before serving, chop the shallot and juice the limes. Heat the noodles in the microwave according to the packet instructions.

06. Remove the beef from the oven and stir in the fish sauce, sugar and lime juice. Add more water if needed to make the gravy a thick sauce consistency. Depending on the surface area of your tin you'll need up to 350ml.

07. Divide the noodles and beef between 4 bowls, then scatter over the chopped shallot and beansprouts. Drizzle with the crispy chilli oil and scatter with the Thai basil and coriander leaves to serve.

Anchovy + Tomato Sfincione

Serves 6–8
Takes 1 hour + resting and proving

Use a 25 x 35cm roasting tin

1 x 7g sachet of fast-action dried yeast
500g strong white bread flour
3 tbsp extra virgin olive oil, plus extra for oiling and to serve
1 tbsp fine sea salt
1 x 400g tin of finely chopped tomatoes
1 fat garlic clove
1 x 50g tin of anchovy fillets in oil, drained
50g capers
100g pecorino
a small bunch of basil, to garnish
salt and black pepper

Sfincione is a Sicilian pizza which is a bit like a light and airy loaded focaccia. The base crisps up nicely while the top remains soft and squidgy in some places yet crunchy in others. Every bite is a delight.

01. Pour 350ml of warm water into a measuring jug, then tip in the dried yeast. Give it a really good mix, then leave to fully rehydrate and activate for 2 minutes.

02. Put the flour into a large bowl, then make a well in the middle. Give the yeasted water another really good mix, then pour into the centre and add the olive oil. Mix together until it forms a shaggy dough with no lumps of flour remaining. Leave to rest in the bowl for 15 minutes.

03. Add 3 more tablespoons of warm water and the salt to the dough, then mix until completely incorporated. Cover with a clean tea towel and leave to rest for a further 15 minutes.

04. Using wet hands, lift a corner of the dough and stretch it up, then fold it over on itself. Turn the bowl 90 degrees, then repeat 3 more times. Leave to rest for 15 minutes, then repeat the process again. Cover and leave to prove for 2 hours or until doubled in size.

05. Line your roasting tin with baking paper and lightly oil. Tip the dough straight into it and leave to rest for 15 minutes. Once it's relaxed, use lightly oiled hands to tease the dough into all the corners of the tin, pressing it down into an even layer. Leave to prove for 30 minutes until puffy and risen.

Continued overleaf

Continued from previous page

06. Meanwhile, preheat the oven to 220°C/200°C fan. Set a metal sieve over your sink and pour in the chopped tomatoes. Leave to drain for 15 minutes, then tip into a small bowl. Season with salt and pepper, crush in the garlic and mix really well.

07. Spoon the tomato mixture evenly over the top of the dough. Lay the anchovy fillets on top and scatter the capers all over. Finely grate the pecorino on top and bake for 30–35 minutes until risen and bubbling, but golden on the bottom.

08. Pick the basil leaves, discarding the stalks. Drizzle the sfincione with more olive oil and scatter over the basil leaves.

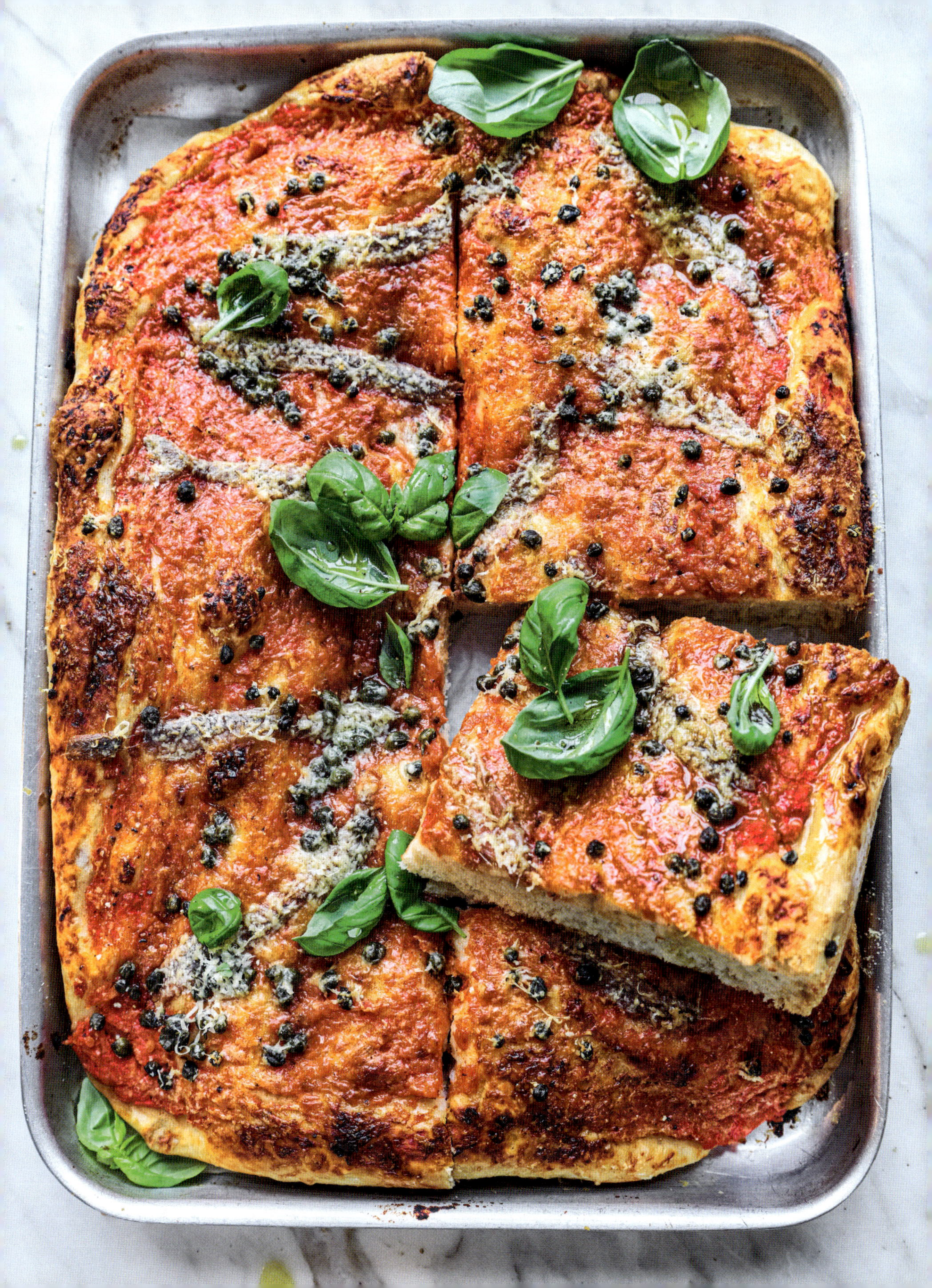

Slow-Roast Short Ribs with Chickpeas

Serves 4
Takes 4 hours 40 minutes

Use a roasting tin

Gluten-free

4 bone-in beef short ribs
1 tbsp pink peppercorns
2 star anise
1 tbsp sumac
1 tbsp ground cumin
3 shallots
8 pickled chillies (pepperoncini, guindilla, frenk etc.)
a bunch of flat leaf parsley
1 x 450g jar of roasted red peppers, drained
1 x 570g jar of queen chickpeas
3 tbsp sherry vinegar
salt and black pepper

Scan for more tasty recipes like this one

These short ribs are slow-roasted with an aromatic medley of pink peppercorns, star anise, sumac and cumin. The ribs get incredibly tender, but retain a lovely crisp texture on the outside due to the long cooking time. The tangy, sweet and sour combo of roasted red peppers, chickpeas, pickled chillies and sherry vinegar makes a worthy partner for the ribs.

01. Preheat the oven to 180°C/160°C fan.

02. Pop the short ribs into the roasting tin. Bash the peppercorns and star anise in a pestle and mortar, then stir through the sumac and cumin. Rub this spice mixture into all of the short ribs and season well with salt and pepper. Pour 200ml of water around the ribs and cover the tin tightly with foil.

03. Roast for 3 hours, then remove the foil and cook for a further 1–1½ hours until the meat is extremely tender, deeply golden and pulls away from the bone easily.

04. Just before the ribs are ready, thinly slice the shallots into rounds, thinly slice the pickled chillies and roughly chop the parsley. Cut the roasted peppers into strips.

05. Remove the ribs from the tin and skim off half of the fat. Vigorously toss the sauce together with a whisk to make a thickened gravy – adding a splash of hot water to help loosen the flavour deposits on the tin. Then throw in the shallots, chillies, parsley, red peppers and chickpeas (including the liquid from the jar). Add the sherry vinegar and toss well to combine – the vinegar and chickpea liquid will mix with the roasting juices and fat to make a great sauce and the heat from the tin will warm everything through nicely.

06. Serve the short ribs with the tangy pepper chickpeas.

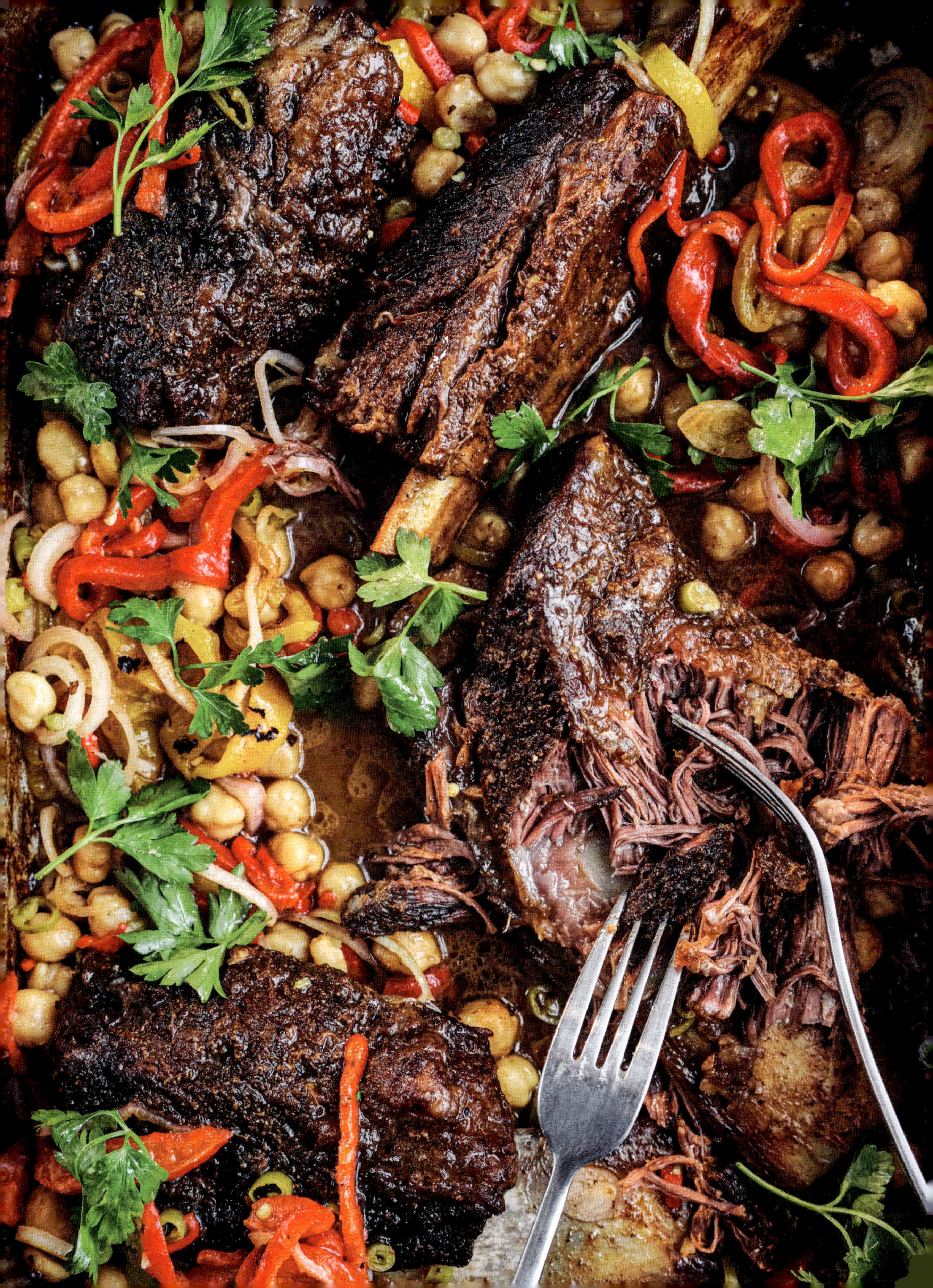

Lamb + Sweet Potato Hotpot

Serves 4
Takes 1 hour 45 minutes

Use a deep, non-stick ovenproof frying pan

2 aubergines
1 onion
4 garlic cloves
4 sprigs of thyme
4 tbsp extra virgin olive oil, plus extra to drizzle
500g lamb mince (about 20% fat)
2 tsp ground cinnamon
½ tsp ground cumin
2 tsp dried oregano, plus extra for sprinkling
1 x 400g tin of chopped tomatoes
2 large sweet potatoes (about 650–700g in total)
350g shop-bought cheese sauce
50g Cheddar cheese
salt and black pepper

TIP: Serve with a crispy green salad.

Scan for more tasty recipes like this one

We love a traditional moussaka, but it can be a real labour of love. Thankfully for you, this recipe takes all the familiar flavours of moussaka and rams them into a single pan. Big on flavour but little on effort.

01. Cut the aubergines into bite-sized chunks and finely chop the onion and garlic. Strip the leaves from the thyme sprigs.

02. Heat the frying pan over a high heat. Once smoking, add 3 tablespoons of the olive oil and carefully add the aubergines. Fry for 4–6 minutes until charred all over and softening, then scoop out into a bowl with a slotted spoon.

03. Drizzle a little more oil into the pan, then add the mince. Cook for a few minutes until it starts to really brown, then stir, breaking up the meat with a wooden spoon. Cook for another few minutes until browned. Scoop out into the bowl.

04. Reduce the heat to medium and drizzle in 1 tablespoon of oil. Tip in the onion and add a pinch of salt. Cook gently for 8 minutes until the onion is soft, then add the garlic, spices, dried oregano and half the thyme leaves. Cook for a further 2 minutes.

05. Tip in the chopped tomatoes and add half a tinful of water, then return the mince and aubergines to the pan. Season, then simmer for 30 minutes until the sauce has thickened.

06. Meanwhile, peel the sweet potatoes, then cut into roughly 5mm-thick slices. Preheat the oven to 190°C/170°C fan.

07. Remove the pan from the heat. Arrange half the sweet potato slices in a layer over the top to completely cover the sauce, then pour over the cheese sauce. Arrange the remaining sweet potatoes over the top, then sprinkle with a little dried oregano and the remaining thyme leaves. Grate the Cheddar over the top.

08. Drizzle lightly with oil, then bake for 45 minutes, or until golden, bubbling and the sweet potatoes are cooked through.

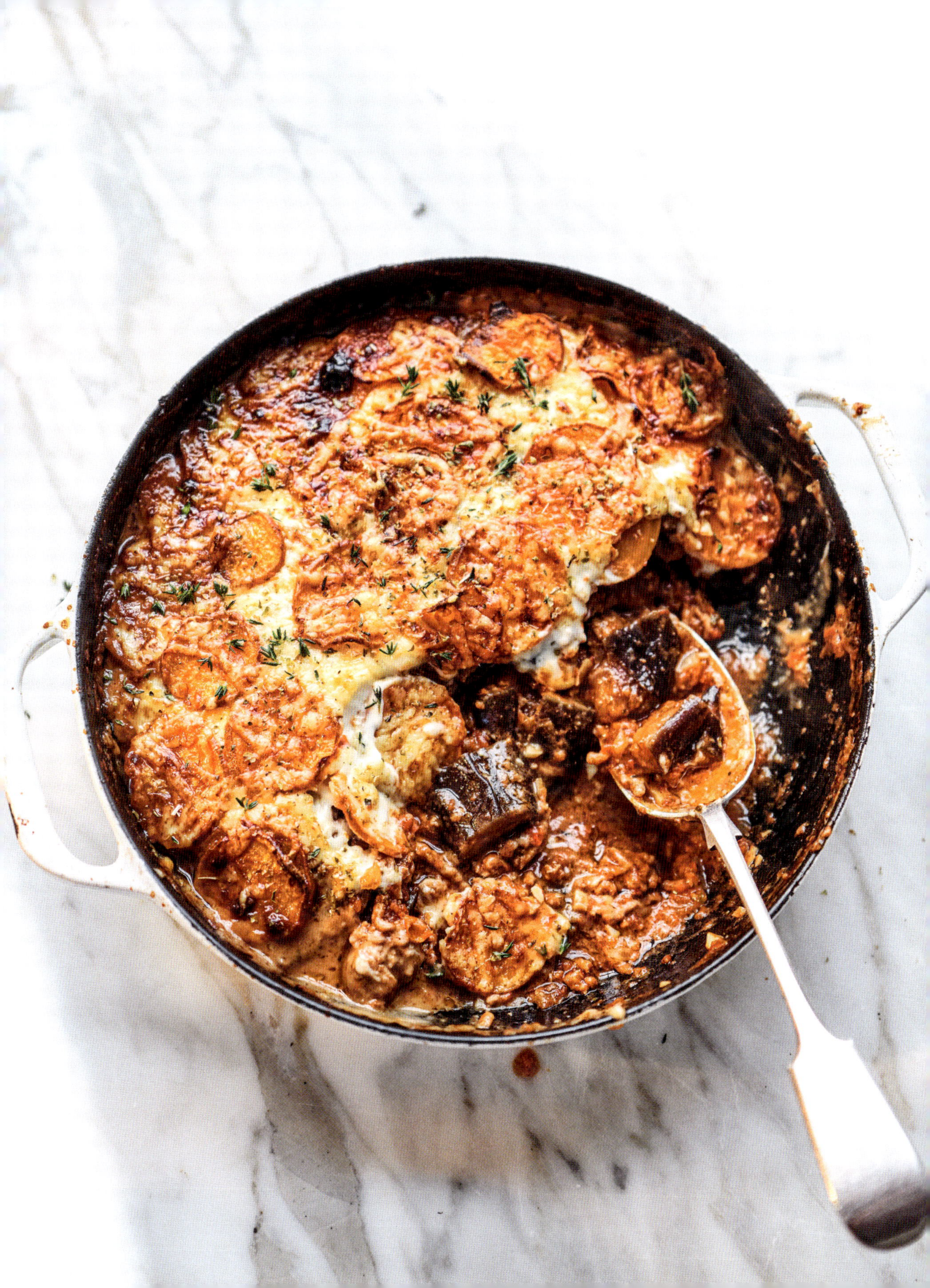

Tweet Ones

Sweet Ones

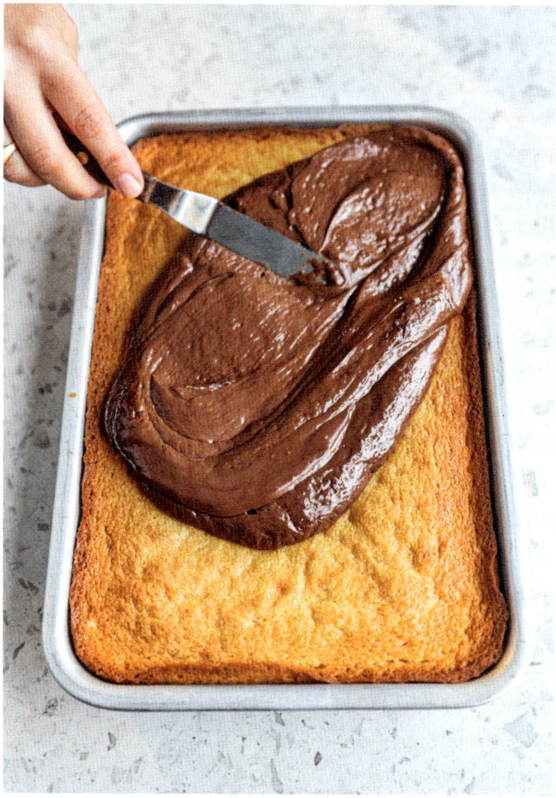
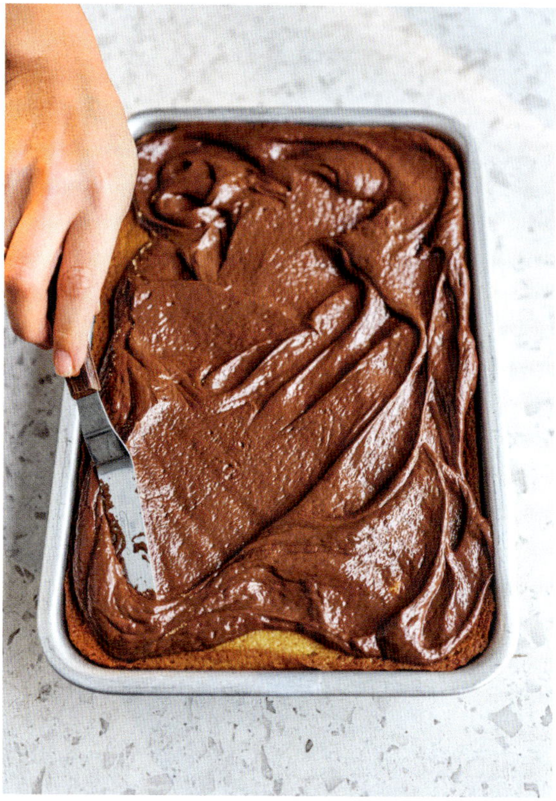
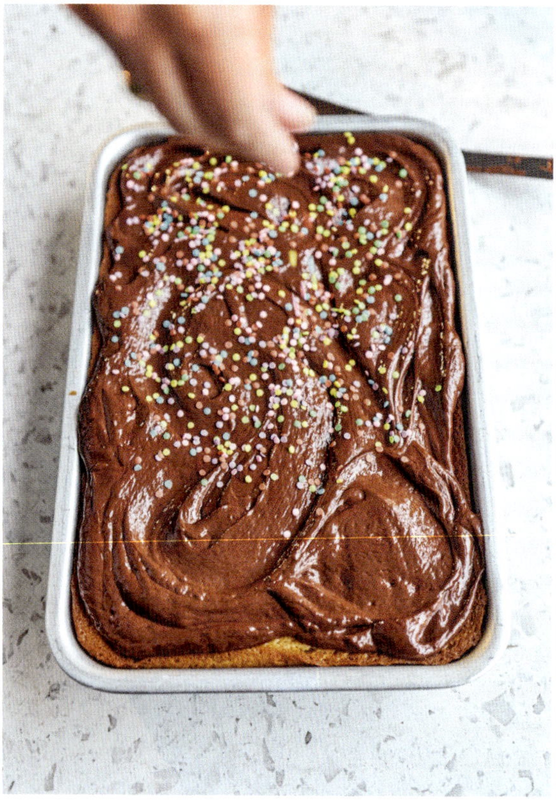
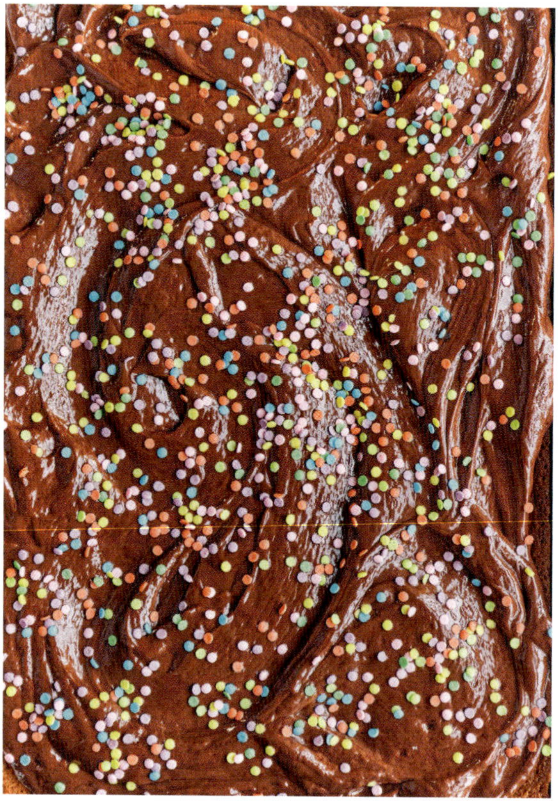

Ultimate Birthday Cake

Serves 12
Takes 45 minutes + cooling

Use a 23 x 33cm baking tin

Veggie

200g unsalted butter, plus extra (optional) for greasing
375g caster sugar
200ml natural yoghurt
3 eggs
2 tsp vanilla bean paste
2 tbsp vegetable oil
½ tsp salt
350g self-raising flour
sprinkles, to decorate

FOR THE ICING
50g unsalted butter
90g dark chocolate
90g milk chocolate
180g cream cheese
100ml double cream
75g icing sugar

Scan for more tasty recipes like this one

This is the perfect birthday cake, with tangy yoghurt-spiked vanilla sponge cake and a decadent chocolate cream cheese icing. No elaborate whisking. Impossible for you to mess up. Easy to slice for mates. Can't beat it. The only thing you need here is a microwave for a bit of help with the melting.

01. Preheat the oven to 200°C/180°C fan. Line the baking tin with baking paper or grease with extra butter.

02. Chop the butter into small cubes, then put into a large microwave-safe bowl. Microwave in 15-second bursts, stirring after each interval, until melted (it should take about 45 seconds).

03. Add the sugar and whisk to combine. Pour in the yoghurt, crack in the eggs and add the vanilla, oil and salt. Whisk to combine. Add the self-raising flour and mix by hand until no visible bits of dry flour remain.

04. Pour the batter into the prepared baking tin and smooth out to all the corners. Bake for 20–30 minutes or until golden, risen and when a skewer is inserted in the centre, it comes out clean. Leave to cool completely.

05. Once cool, crack on with the icing. Put the butter and broken-up chocolate into a microwave-safe bowl and microwave in 15-second bursts, stirring after each interval, until melted together (it should take about 45–60 seconds).

06. Using a spatula, beat in the cream cheese, cream and icing sugar until you have a smooth luscious icing.

07. Spread the icing all over the cake and decorate with the sprinkles. Cut into squares and serve.

SWEET ONES

Preserved Lemon Cheesecake

Serves 8
Takes 20 minutes + chilling

Use a 24cm springform tin

Veggie

250g ginger nut biscuits
100g butter
180g white chocolate
400g cream cheese
250g thick Greek yoghurt (we use Fage 5%)
2 preserved lemons
a few sprigs of thyme
1 tbsp ready-chopped stem ginger, plus syrup from the jar

SWAP: If you can't find stem ginger, leave it out and drizzle the cheesecake with honey instead.

The intensity that preserved lemons deliver is unbeatable. They add a real punch to this cheesecake which is made using a decadent mixture of Greek yoghurt, cream cheese and white chocolate. Lemon and ginger are a match made in heaven, so we've gone for a ginger nut biscuit base plus a scattering of stem ginger on top to really drive the point home.

01. Whizz the gingernut biscuits in a food processor, or alternatively use a rolling pin to bash the biscuits while they're still in the packet (or pop in a sealable food bag) until they resemble breadcrumbs. Put the butter into a medium microwave-safe bowl. Microwave in 15-second bursts, stirring after each interval, until melted (it should take 30–45 seconds). Pour in the biscuit crumbs and mix well to combine. Tip the mixture into the springform tin and press down with the back of a spoon to create the base. Set aside.

02. Crumble the white chocolate into the same microwave-safe bowl (wipe with a cloth) and microwave in 15-second bursts, stirring after each interval, until melted (this should take 45–60 seconds). Add to the food processor with the cream cheese and yoghurt and blitz until smooth. Alternatively, beat in by hand, stirring well to ensure no lumps. Halve the preserved lemons and scoop out and discard the flesh. Finely chop the peel. Add two-thirds of the peel to the cream cheese mixture, then spread the mix over the biscuit base.

03. Strip the leaves from the thyme sprigs. Sprinkle the remaining preserved lemon rind and chopped stem ginger over the cheesecake and decorate with the thyme leaves.

04. Refrigerate for at least 1 hour. When you're ready to serve, drizzle with the stem ginger syrup and enjoy.

Scan for more tasty recipes like this one

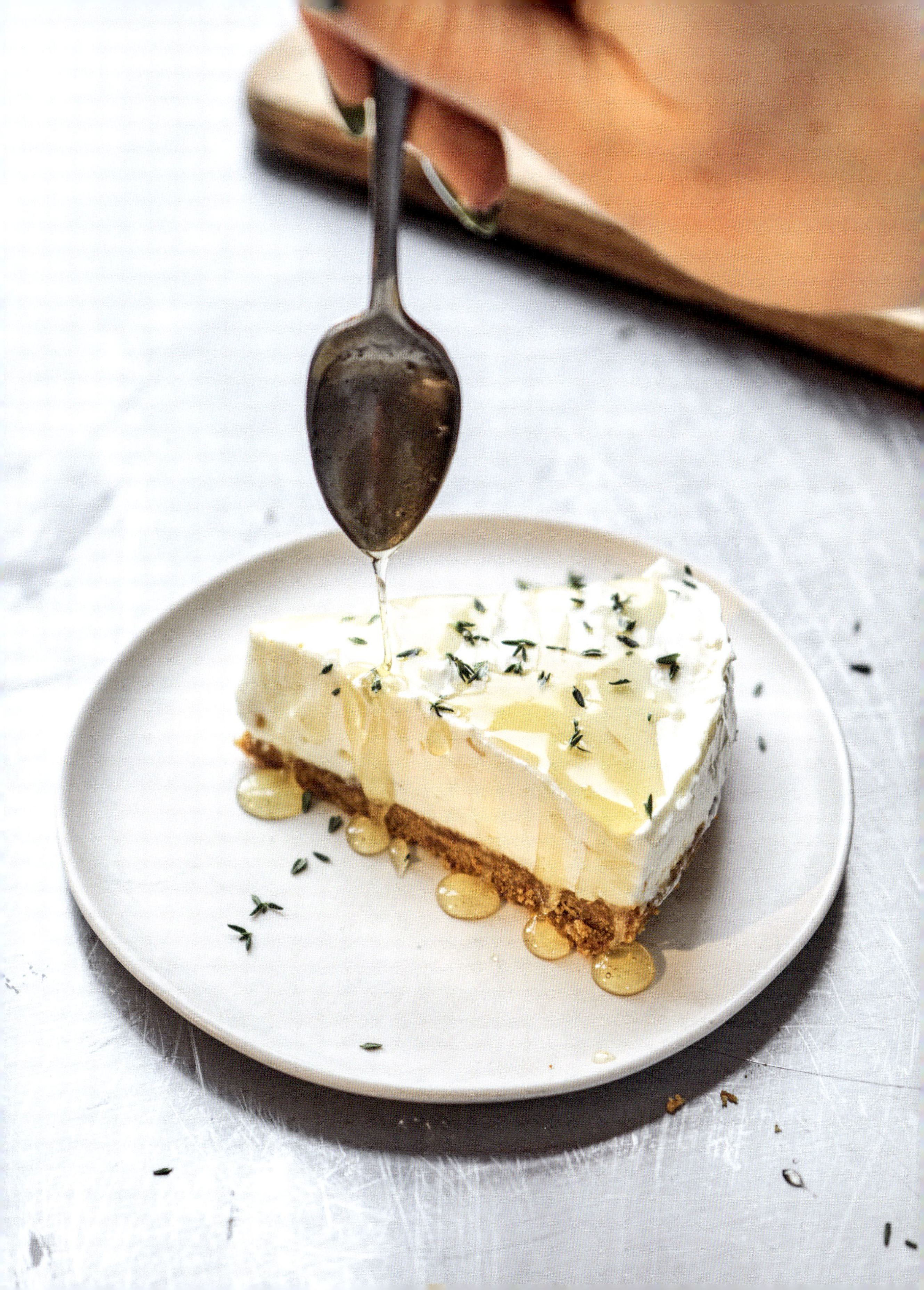

Banana Bread Skillet Cookie

Serves 4
Takes 30 minutes

Use a small (about 25cm) ovenproof non-stick frying pan

Veggie

50g pecans
1 ripe banana
120ml vegetable oil
170g light soft brown sugar
1 egg yolk
150g plain flour
½ tsp baking powder
1 tsp vanilla extract
1 tsp ground cinnamon
100g dark chocolate chips
ice cream, to serve
salt

Scan for more tasty recipes like this one

Like banana bread? Like cookies? Like the sound of eating a *giant* banana bread cookie that's warm from the oven? This one is a no-brainer, then.

01. Preheat the oven to 180°C/160°C fan. Grease the frying pan and set aside.

02. Toast the pecans in the dry frying pan over a medium heat until smelling amazing. Tip onto a chopping board and roughly chop. Set aside the pan to cool.

03. Using a fork, roughly mash the banana in a bowl. Add the oil and sugar and beat together, then add the egg yolk, flour, baking powder, a big pinch of salt, the vanilla and cinnamon and beat together to form a loose cookie dough. Stir in the toasted pecans and chocolate chips.

04. Dollop the cookie dough into the cooled pan and smooth into an even layer using a spoon.

05. Bake on the centre shelf of the oven for 16–18 minutes until the outside is set and the centre is still a little soft. Wait for a few minutes until it cools slightly before tucking in.

06. We like to serve this with big spoonfuls of salted caramel, vanilla or even praline and cream ice cream in the centre of the cookie for people to help themselves.

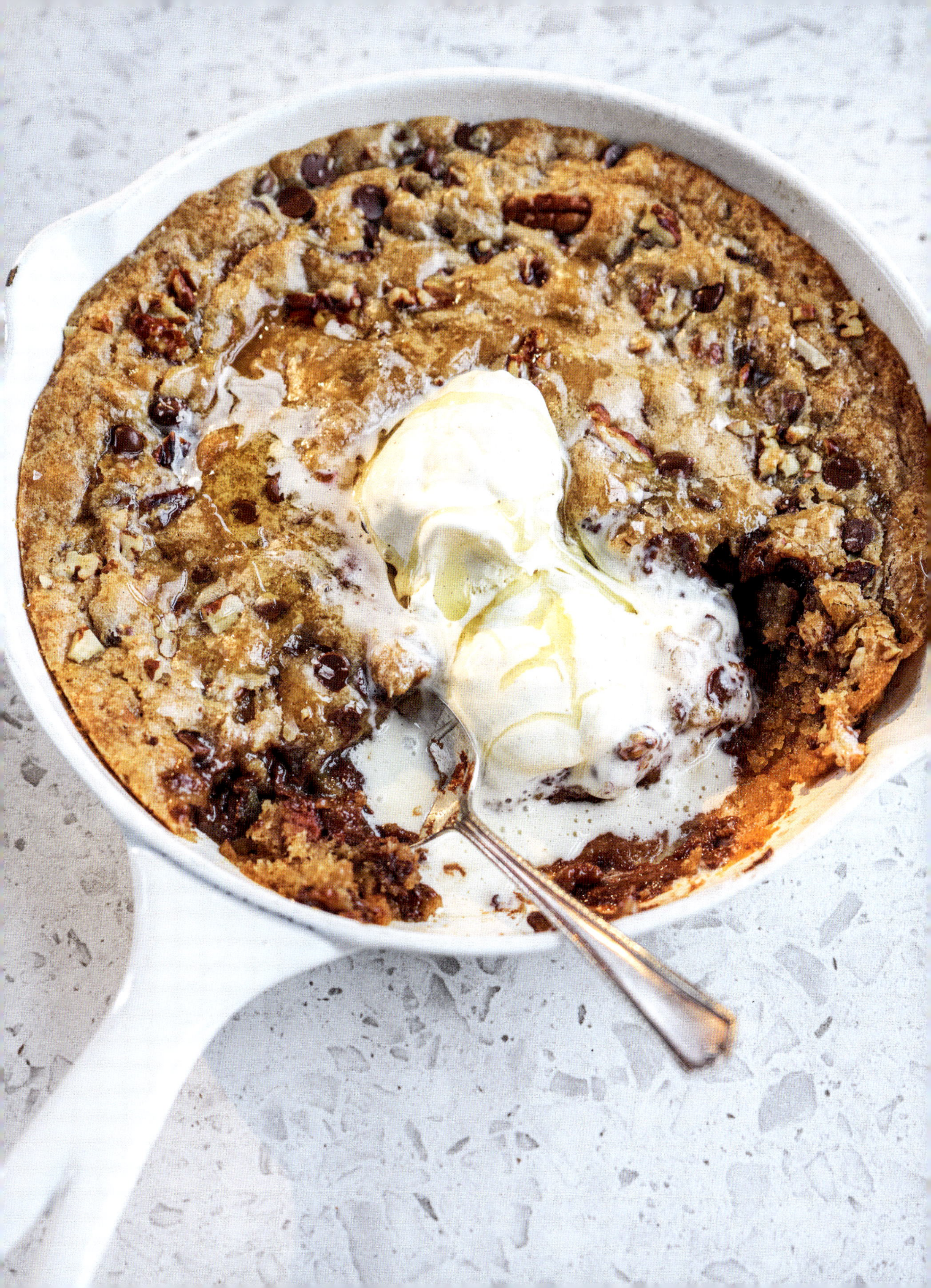

Chocolate Tahini Fudge

Makes 24 pieces
Takes 10 minutes + chilling

Use a 20 x 20cm brownie tin

Veggie, Gluten-free

500g dark chocolate chips
1 x 397g tin of condensed milk
30g butter
100g smooth peanut butter
2 tbsp tahini
2 tbsp mixed sesame seeds
flaky sea salt

TIP: You can swap the chocolate chips for regular chocolate – it just eliminates needing to chop anything!

Next time you have a group of people at yours, this is what you're going to make them. You only need a tiny square to be satisfied with this sweet treat. Keep it in the fridge until you're ready to serve and let it come to room temperature for 10–15 minutes before enjoying.

01. Line the brownie tin with cling film or baking paper.

02. Pop the chocolate chips, condensed milk and butter into a microwave-safe bowl. Microwave in 30-second bursts, stirring after each interval, until melted (it should take about 1½ minutes).

03. Stir through the peanut butter until everything is combined, then pour into the tin and smooth out, working quickly as it sets quite fast.

04. Drizzle the tahini all over the top, then sprinkle with the sesame seeds and flaky sea salt.

05. Leave to set in the fridge for at least 30 minutes before cutting into small pieces. It will keep in the fridge for up to 1 week.

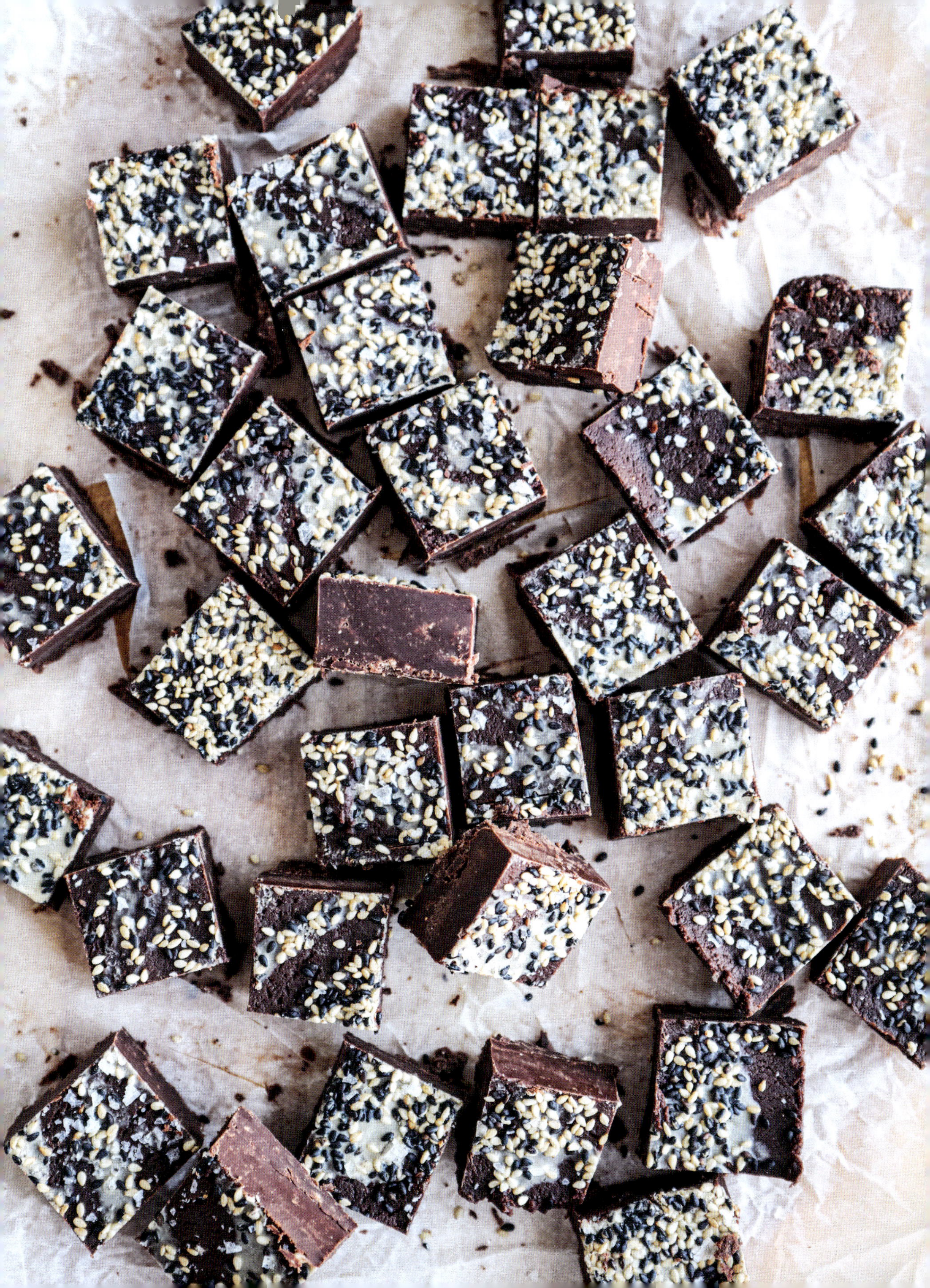

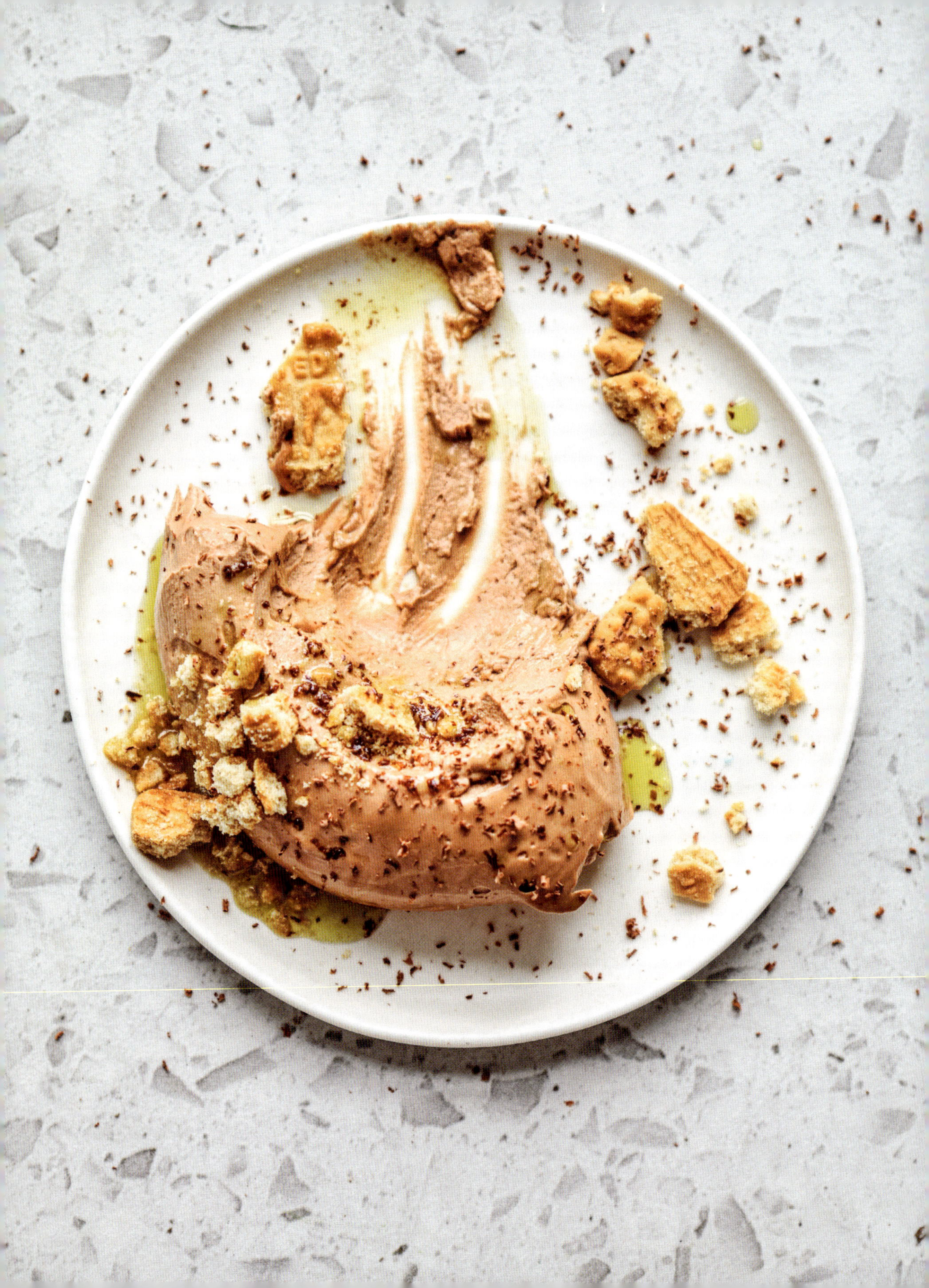

Malted Chocolate Mousse

Serves 4
Takes 15 minutes + chilling

Use a saucepan

Veggie

100g milk chocolate
100g dark chocolate, plus extra to grate over the top
400ml double cream
80g malt powder (we use Horlicks)
olive oil, to serve
malted milk bisuits, to serve

Scan for more tasty recipes like this one

This nostalgic banger is the dessert equivalent of a Girls Aloud track. The malted Horlicks-y chocolate mousse is topped with shaved chocolate and a biscuity crunch, so light and moreish, and it tastes like all the best bits of a Malteser combined.

01. Finely chop all the chocolate and add to a large bowl.

02. Tip the double cream into a saucepan over a medium heat, warm through for a few minutes, then gradually whisk in the malt powder, making sure to whisk out any lumps. Pour over the chocolate in the bowl, allow to sit for a few minutes then whisk until smooth.

03. Cover with cling film, making sure it's touching the chocolatey mixture so it doesn't get a skin. Place the bowl in the fridge for 3–4 hours, until cold and firmed up.

04. Use a handheld or electric whisk to whisk until light and fluffy. Spoon onto plates, then drizzle with a little olive oil. Finely grate a little dark chocolate over the top, then crunch the malted milk biscuits over the top.

Chuck-In Cherry Cobbler

Scan for more tasty recipes like this one

Serves 4
Takes 1 hour

Use an ovenproof frying pan

Veggie

2 peaches
400g cherries
1 tsp ground cardamom
175g demerara sugar
175g plain flour
125g unsalted butter
5 tbsp mascarpone
1 tsp vanilla bean paste
1 lemon
a few basil or mint leaves

TIP: Pit the cherries by pushing a reusable straw from top to bottom through each one – the stones should just pop out.

This is a riff on an American 'dump' cake, which is basically a cheat's crumble or cobbler. Call it what you want: it'll still be just as delicious. Swap out the fruit and herbs for whatever's in season.

01. Preheat the oven to 220°C/200°C fan.

02. Cut the peaches into wedges, discarding the stones, and pit the cherries (see Tip).

03. Toss the cherries, peaches and ground cardamom together in your pan.

04. In a small bowl, mix together the sugar and flour, then sprinkle this over the fruit in an even layer. Cut the butter into thin pats, then evenly distribute them all over the top of the flour mixture.

05. Bake for 45 minutes until golden, crisp and bubbling.

06. Meanwhile, mix together the mascarpone with the vanilla bean paste in a bowl.

07. Once the cobbler is ready, dollop over the vanilla mascarpone, zest the lemon over the top and garnish with the herb leaves.

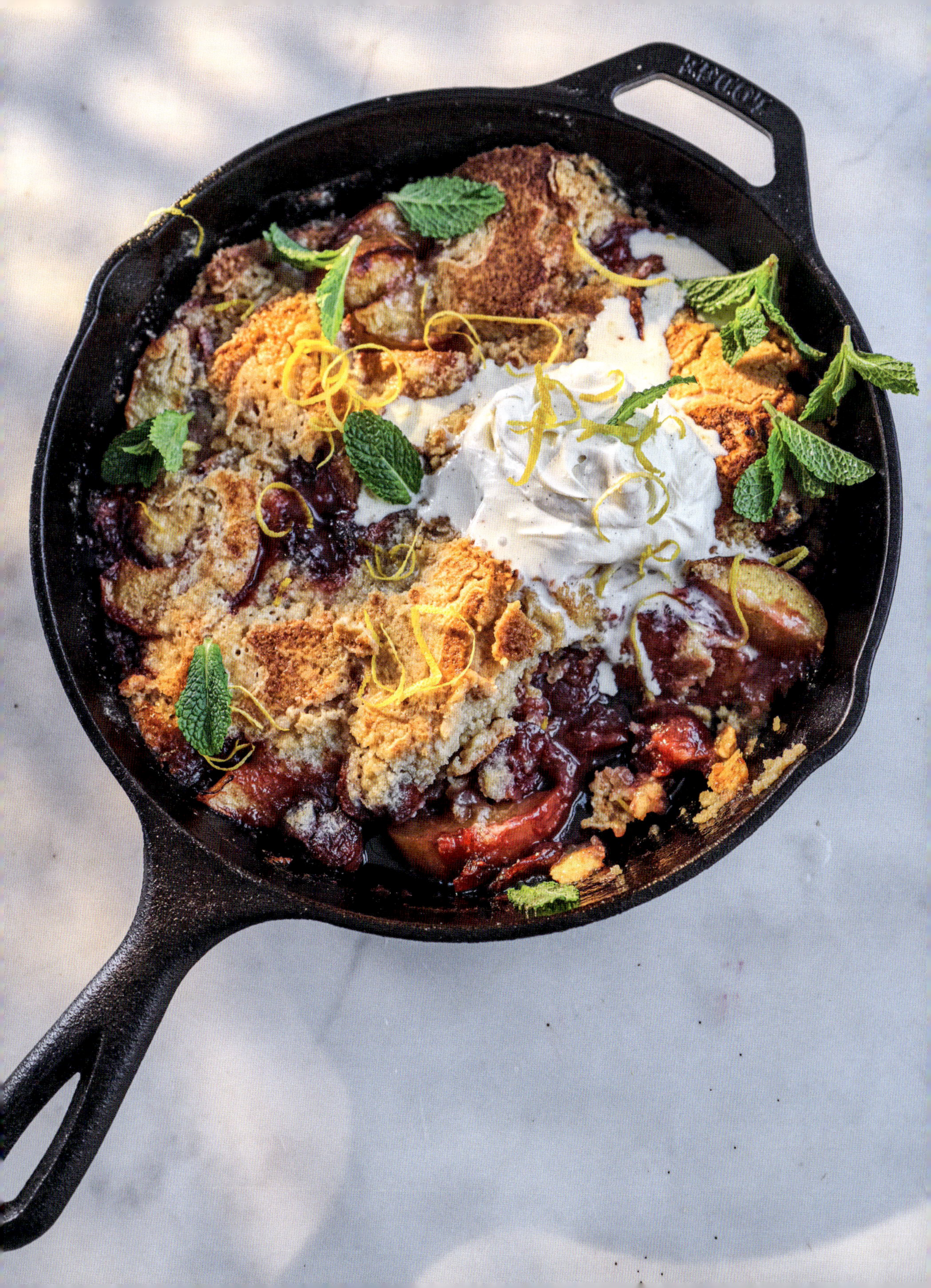

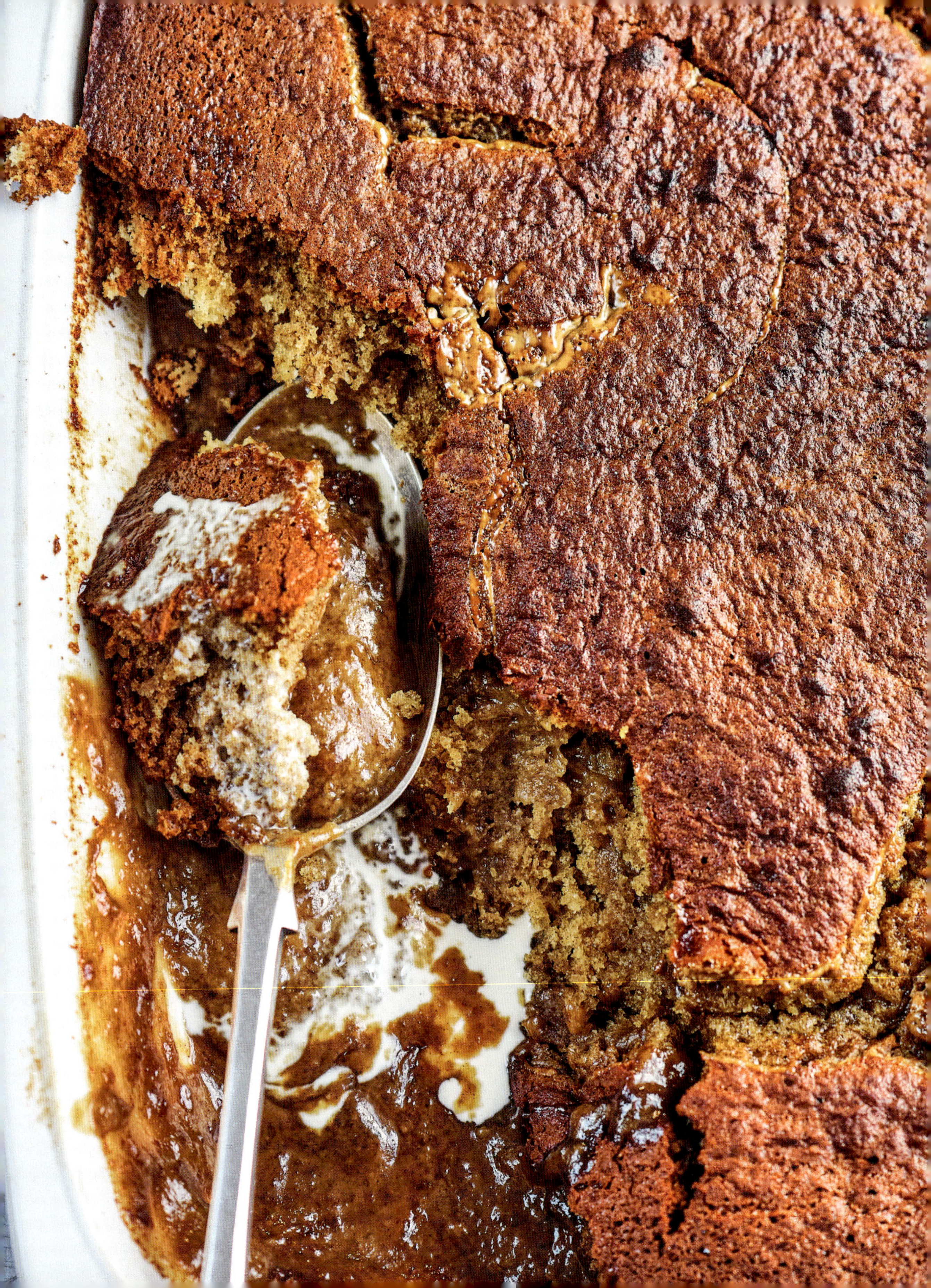

Self-Saucing Sticky Toffee Pudding

Serves 6
Takes 1 hour

Use a 20 x 30cm deep baking tin

Veggie

80g unsalted butter, at room temperature, plus extra for greasing
125g light soft brown sugar
2 tbsp black treacle
2 eggs
200g self-raising flour
220g medjool dates
1 tsp vanilla extract
2 tsp bicarbonate of soda
cream or ice cream, to serve
salt

FOR THE TOFFEE SAUCE
150g dark soft brown sugar
1 tbsp treacle
300ml double cream

Scan for more tasty recipes like this one

The beauty of this dish is scooping out the sponge to find the well of sticky toffee sauce lurking at the bottom. Serve it with massive scoops of caramel ice cream for the ultimate winter comfort dessert. It's not quite as 'all in one' as some of the other desserts, but it's perfect for those Sunday lunches where you want to show off a bit!

01. Preheat the oven to 180°C/160°C fan. Grease the baking tin with butter.

02. Start with the toffee sauce. Cover the dark brown sugar and treacle with 200ml boiling water in a jug, allow to sit for a minute, then stir until the sugar has dissolved. Add the cream and set side.

03. Using an electric whisk, beat the butter and light brown sugar together in a bowl until light and fluffy, then add the treacle. Add the eggs, one at a time, beating well with each addition. Fold in the flour along with a pinch of salt until the mixture has the consistency of a thick paste.

04. Tip the dates into a blender with 250ml of boiling water, add the vanilla and blitz into a paste. Remove the lid and whisk in the bicarbonate of soda (it'll froth up a little), then tip into the sponge batter and mix well.

05. Spoon the batter into the greased tin. Pour over the toffee sauce (it'll sink to the bottom while the rest bakes). Bake for 40–45 minutes until firm to the touch. Leave to cool in the tin.

06. Scoop out and serve with cream or ice cream.

Pistachio Custard Pots

Serves 4
Takes 35 minutes + infusing and chilling

Use a saucepan

Veggie, Gluten-free

600ml double cream
1 vanilla pod
250g egg yolks (about 12)
60g caster sugar
4 tbsp chopped pistachios
50g dark chocolate
30g raspberries
salt

TIP: If you'd like to make this into a showstopping dessert that everyone can dig a spoon into, set the custard in one large bowl, and add all your toppings.

Scan for more tasty recipes like this one

Everyone knows pistachio gelato is the best ice cream out there, and these rich little pots are like a cousin to our favourite cold treat. With flecks of dark chocolate and tangy raspberries to cut through the sweetness – these are pretty epic.

01. Pour the cream into the saucepan. Split the vanilla pod, then add to the pan with its seeds. Set over a medium heat and bring to just below a simmer. Leave to infuse for 20 minutes.

02. Combine the egg yolks with the sugar and a pinch of salt in a bowl and whisk until light and fluffy (about 1 minute of vigorous whisking should do it!).

03. Tip about a third of the infused cream into the yolk mixture and whisk together until homogenous. Tip the mixture back into the pan and whisk through.

04. Cook over a low heat for 10–15 minutes, stirring constantly, until the mixture thickens. Once it starts to thicken, start whisking vigorously and cook it until it wobbles like jelly when you shake it (if you have a thermometer, it needs to be 81°C). Pour through a sieve back into the bowl, you can either set it in the bowl and serve it sharing style or pour into whatever serving vessels you like.

05. Leave to set, uncovered, in the fridge for at least 4 hours.

06. When you are ready to serve, chop together the pistachios and chocolate and mix with a pinch of salt. Smoosh the raspberries with a fork, then spread over the custard pots. Scatter with the chocolate and pistachios and get stuck in.

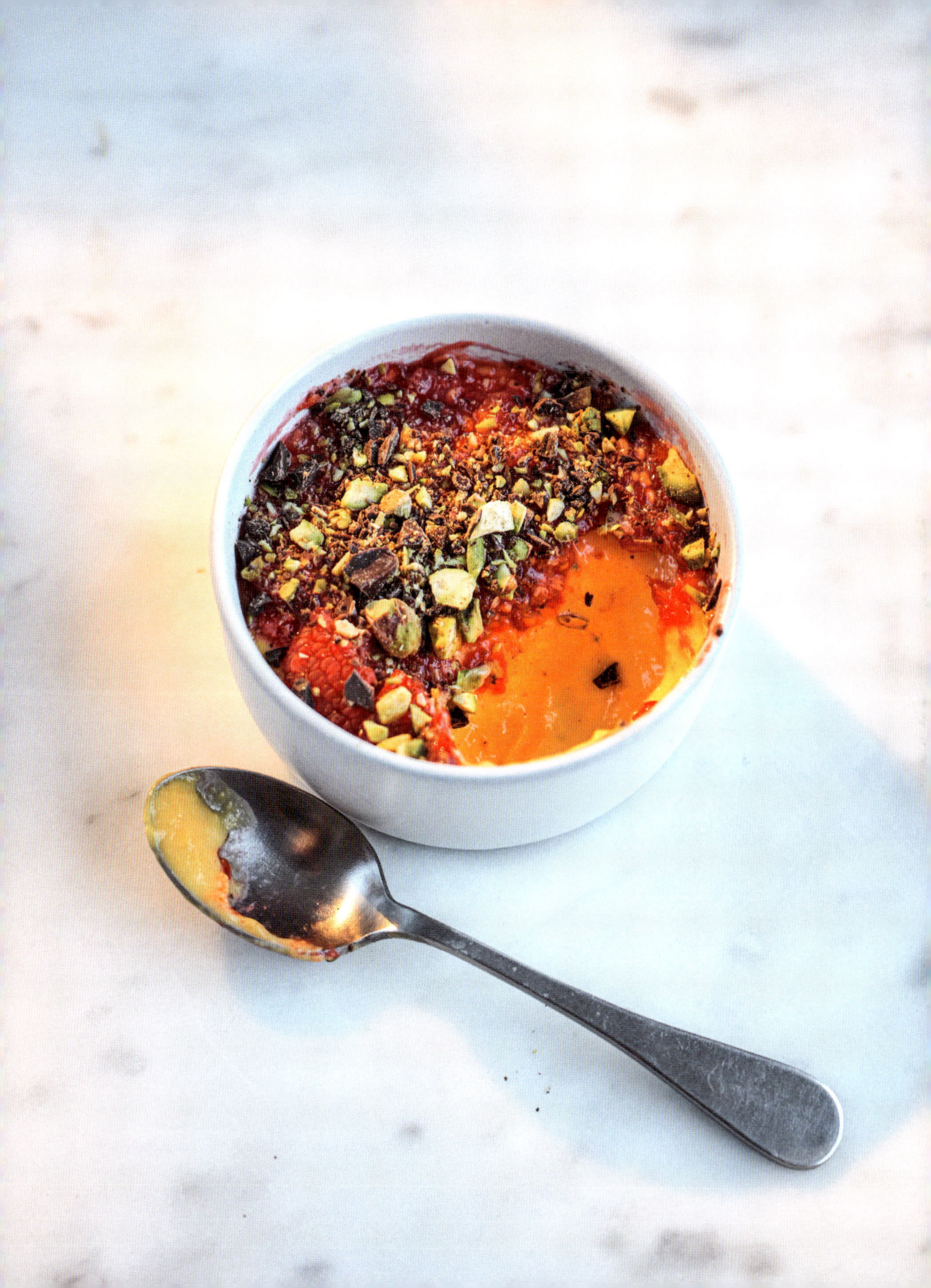

Patchwork Blueberry Pie

Serves 4–6
Takes 1 hour

Use a 24 x 24cm lipped pie or baking dish

Veggie

900g blueberries
100g light soft brown sugar
1 lemon
2 tsp ground cinnamon
4 tbsp cornflour
2 tbsp demerara sugar
1 x 320g sheet of ready-rolled puff pastry
1 egg
double cream or vanilla ice cream, to serve
salt

Scan for more tasty recipes like this one

Not only does tiling the pastry like this make for a beautiful pie, it also gives you the occasional super crunchy, super cinnamon-y pocket of flavour among the sharp blueberries and crisp pastry. Winner.

01. Preheat the oven to 200°C/180°C fan.

02. Tip the blueberries into a bowl with the soft brown sugar, then zest in the lemon and squeeze in the juice. Spoon in 1 teaspoon of the cinnamon and the cornflour. Mix really well and add a pinch of salt. Tip into the dish.

03. Mix together the demerara sugar and remaining cinnamon in a small bowl.

04. Unroll the pastry sheet and use a sharp knife to cut it into 3cm squares.

05. Crack the egg into a bowl and whisk it really well. Brush all the squares with the beaten egg, then dust them with the sugar and cinnamon mix.

06. Brush the lip of the dish with egg, then starting from the edge, lay the squares around the pie to make a rustic tile pattern.

07. Bake for 35–45 minutes until the pastry is cooked through and golden. Leave to cool for 10 minutes, then serve with double cream or ice cream.

SWEET ONES

Raspberry Croissant + Butter Pudding

Serves 4
Takes 1 hour 5 minutes

Use a deep baking dish (round, oval or square works well)

Veggie

300ml double cream, plus extra to serve
300ml whole milk
1 tsp vanilla extract (buy the best you can)
3 eggs
1 tbsp custard powder (we like Bird's)
75g caster sugar
4 large croissants
50g salted butter, softened
100g raspberry jam
100g raspberries
2 tbsp demerara sugar

Scan for more tasty recipes like this one

The idea for this dessert came to us when one of our recipe developers woke up in a cold sweat at night and, scrawling in their bedside notebook, replaced the word 'bread' in bread and butter pudding with 'croissant'. The rest, as they say, is history. Sandwiching those croissants with fresh raspberries and raspberry jam was another stroke of genius.

01. Put the cream, milk and vanilla into a large microwave-safe jug and cover with cling film. Microwave in 20-second bursts, stirring after each interval, until just steaming.

02. Crack the eggs into a heatproof bowl, then add the custard powder and caster sugar and whisk together to combine.

03. Pour a third of the steaming milk mixture over the eggs, whisking all the time. Pour over the next third, whisking again, then whisk in the remaining milk until incorporated. Set aside.

04. Preheat the oven to 160°C/140°C fan. Cut the croissants in half horizontally, then spread butter on one side of each. Spread the other sides with a thick layer of raspberry jam, then put the lids on the bases. Arrange the croissants so they fit snugly in the baking dish.

05. Pour the warm custard mix all around the croissants, pressing them down to soak up some of the liquid. Scatter over the raspberries, then finally scatter with the demerara sugar (this will give a super crunchy top).

06. Bake for 55 minutes, or until the custard is just set. We like to serve this with a splash of extra cream, and it's as good cold as it is hot.

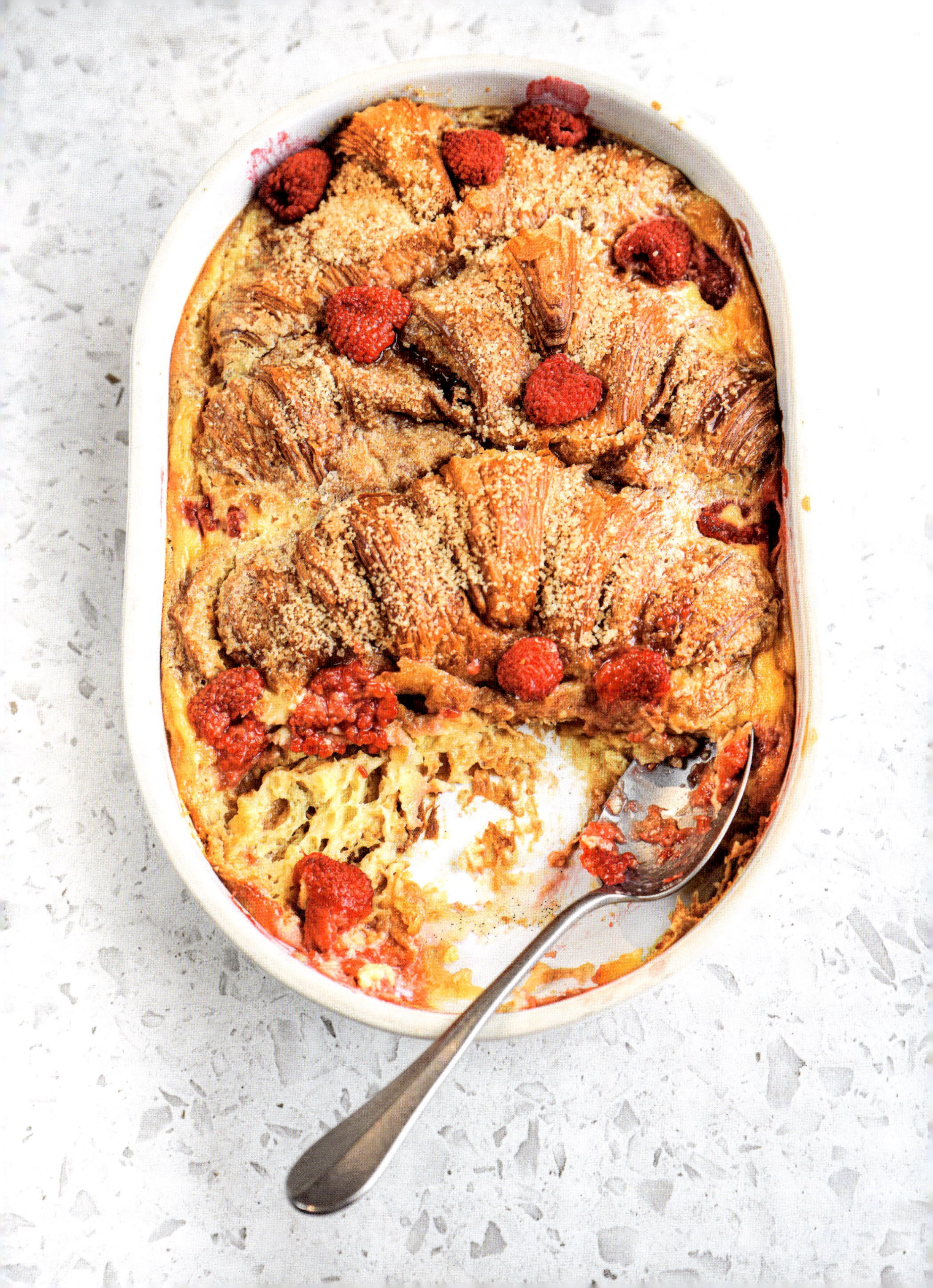

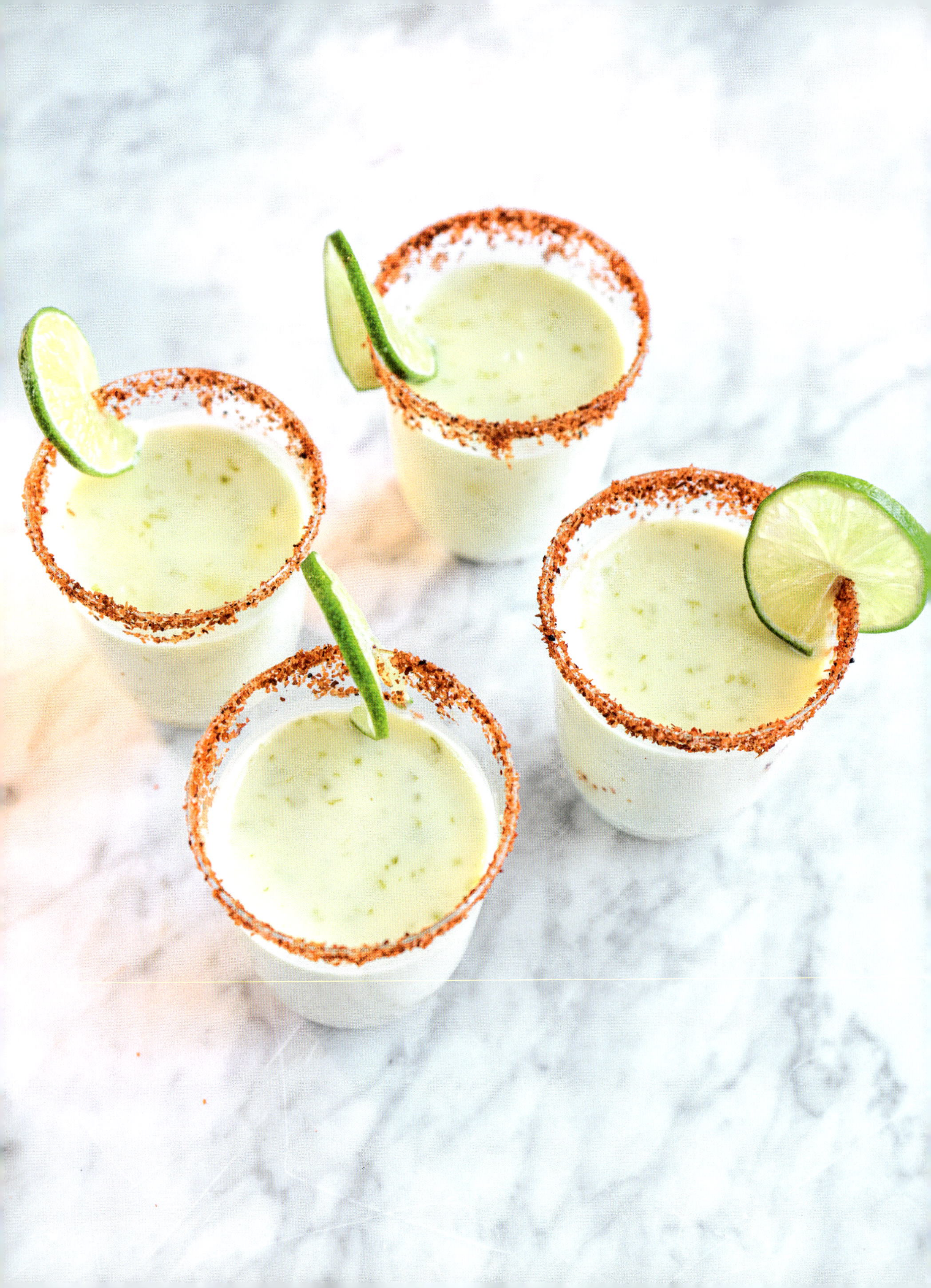

Margarita Possets

Scan for more tasty recipes like this one

Serves 4
Takes 20 minutes + chilling

Use a saucepan

Veggie

---

4 tsp Tajín seasoning (see Swap)
5 limes
500ml double cream
150g caster sugar
75ml tequila
8 ginger biscuits, to serve
4 slices of lime, to decorate

SWAP: If you can't get hold of Tajín, then a mix of 1 teaspoon fine sea salt, 1 teaspoon hot chilli powder and the zest of 1 lime will work well in its place.

This is the easiest dessert ever. All you have to do is heat together cream and sugar and bung in some lime zest and juice for the badness. We've turned up the volume a couple of notches by adding tequila and Tajín – which is basically a Mexican seasoning made with citric acid, chilli powder and salt. You'll be putting it on everything.

---

01. Put 2 teaspoons of the Tajín onto a small plate. Cut 1 of the limes in half. Rub the rims of 4 tumblers or wine glasses with a lime half, then push each one into the seasoning to create a chilli rim. Set aside.

02. Pour the cream into the saucepan and add the sugar. Heat gently until simmering, then simmer for 2 minutes. Meanwhile, zest 2 of the limes and squeeze the juice of 4.

03. Remove the pan from the heat and stir in the tequila, lime zest and lime juice.

04. Pour the mixture into a jug, then carefully divide between the 4 glasses. Chill for at least 3 hours until fully set.

05. When ready to serve, sprinkle with the remaining Tajín and serve with the ginger biscuits for scooping and crunching. Decorate with slices of lime, if you like.

Chocolate Caramel Fondant

Serves 6
Takes 40 minutes

Use a 20 x 30cm deep baking tin

Veggie

320g butter, plus extra for greasing
300g dark chocolate
80g cocoa powder, plus extra for dusting
1 tsp vanilla extract
200g shop-bought dulce de leche or caramel
6 eggs
2 egg yolks
285g caster sugar
100g plain flour
ice cream, to serve
sea salt

Scan for more tasty recipes like this one

We used to make chocolate fondants in individual moulds, then we worked out this method of making it all in one big tray instead. It's so much easier. A word of advice: you want your fondant to be set on the sides with a little jiggle in the middle so it's still nice and gooey. It will continue cooking a little as it rests, so take that into consideration.

---

01. Preheat the oven to 180°C/160°C fan.

02. Chop the butter into small cubes, then put it into a large microwave-safe bowl. Finely chop the chocolate and add to the bowl. Microwave in 10-second bursts, stirring between each interval, until totally melted. Stir in the cocoa powder, vanilla and a pinch of salt. Set aside.

03. Grease the baking tin with butter, then sprinkle over 1 tablespoon of cocoa powder. Shake the tin so the cocoa dusts the surface, then tip out any excess. Pour the dulce de leche into the tin.

04. Put the eggs, egg yolks and sugar into a bowl and whisk with an electric whisk until the mixture is light and fluffy. Fold in the chocolate mixture, using a spatula to gently mix the ingredients together – try not to knock out too much of the air you've whisked into the eggs!

05. Sift the flour over the top of the mixture, then fold it through, making sure there are no white streaks of flour and the mixture is homogenous.

06. Spoon into the prepared tin and give it a wiggle to level out the mixture. Bake for 25–30 minutes until set around the edges but still with a decent wobble in the middle.

07. Dust with cocoa powder and sprinkle with a pinch of sea salt. Serve immediately with ice cream.

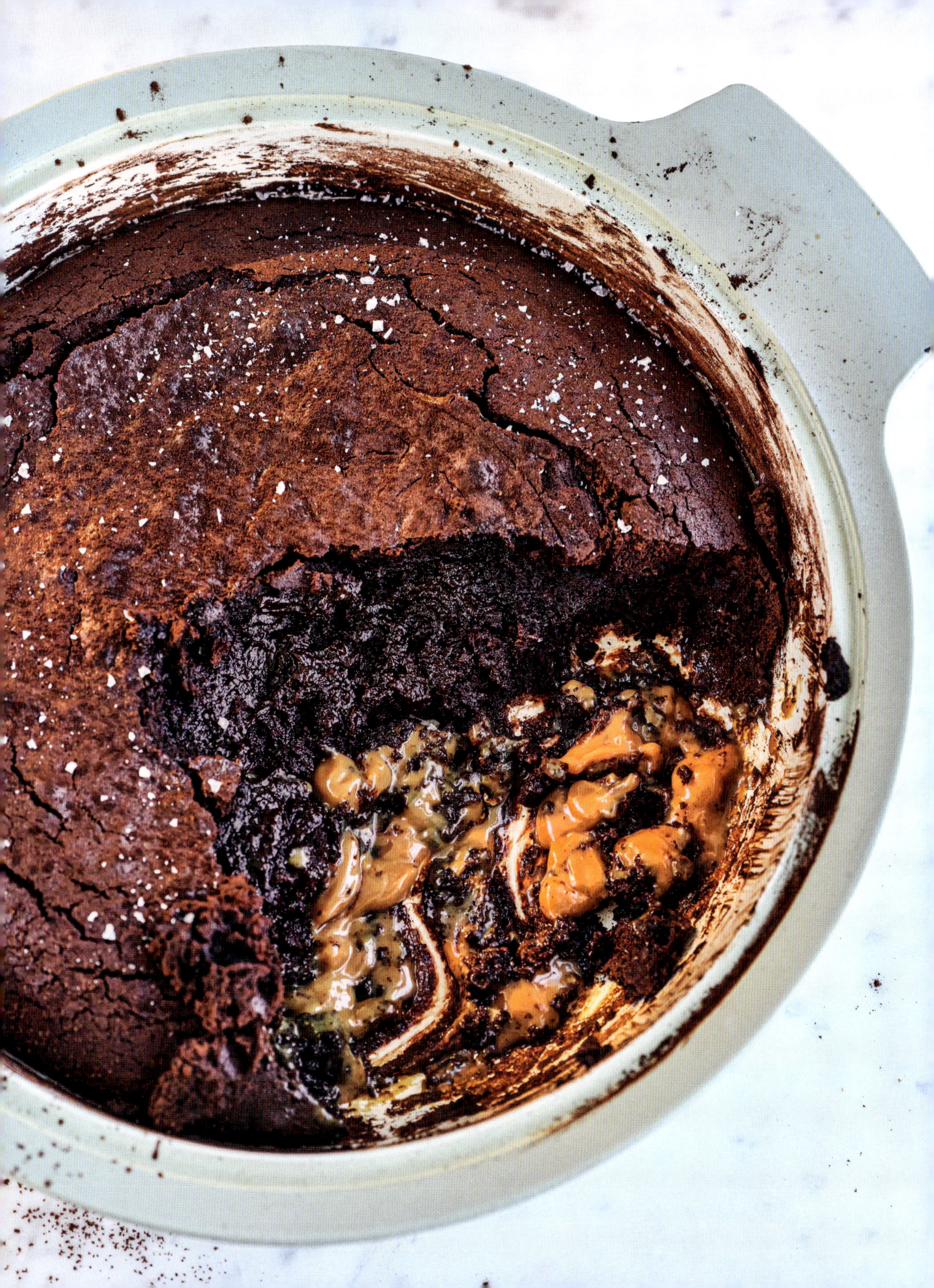

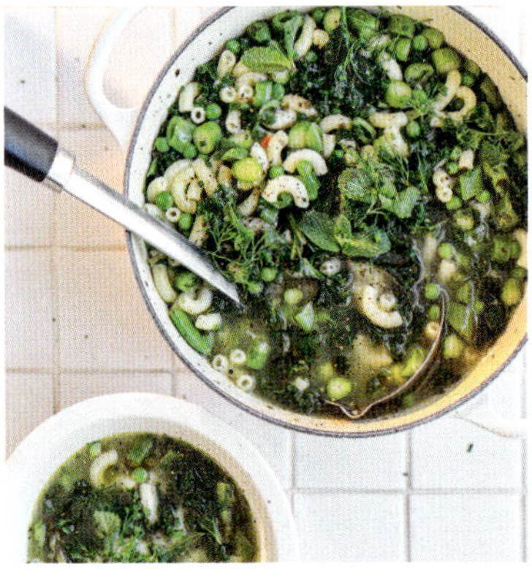
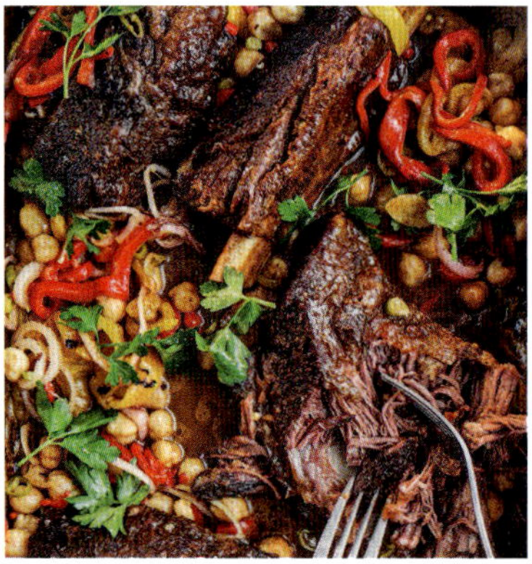
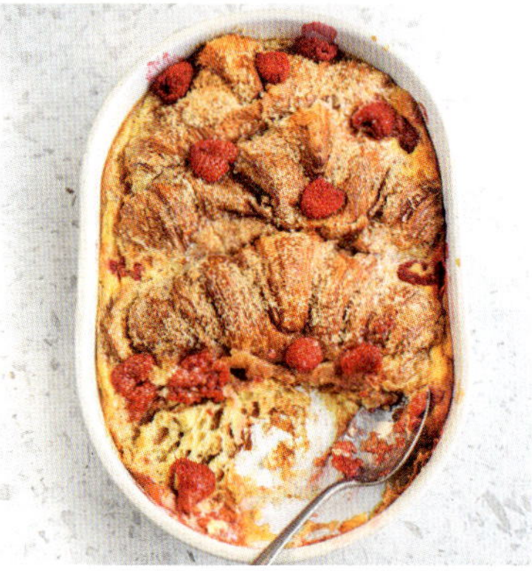
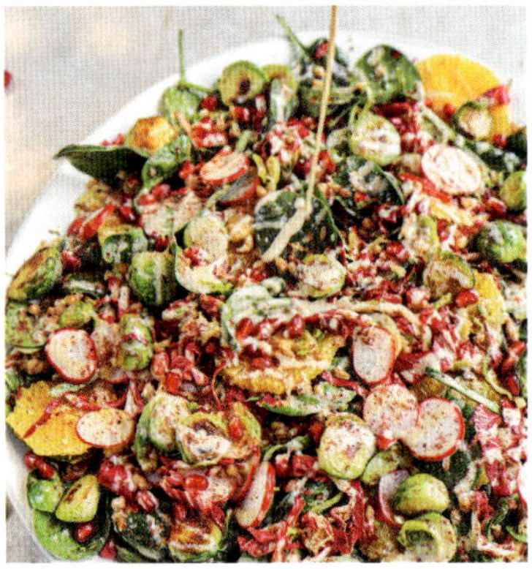
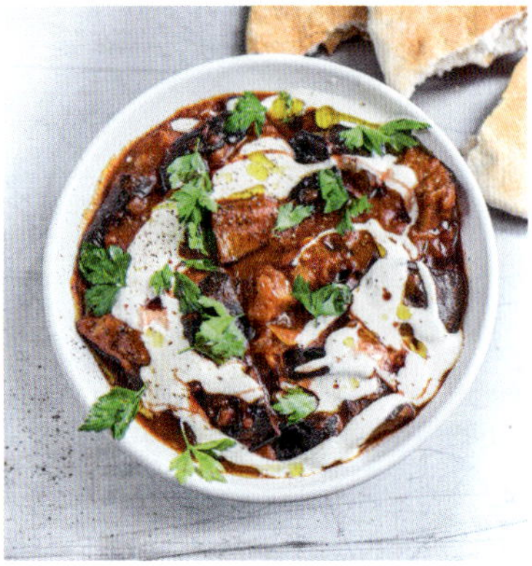
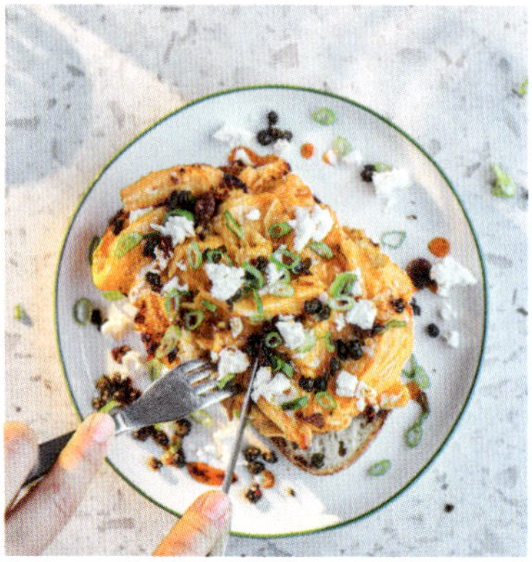
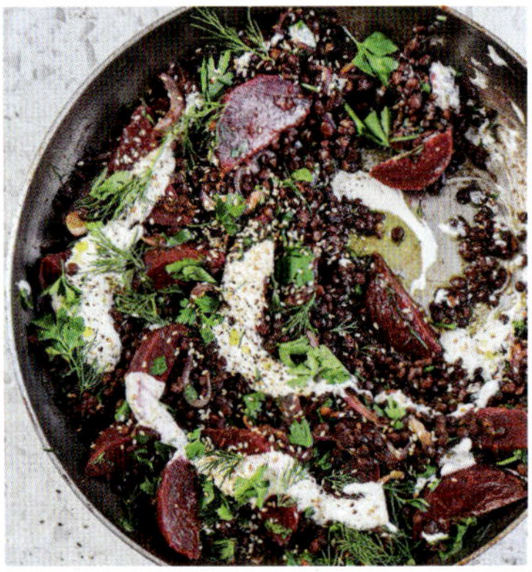
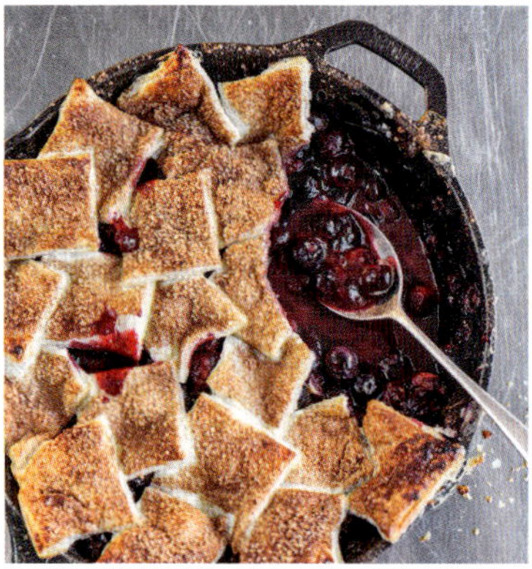
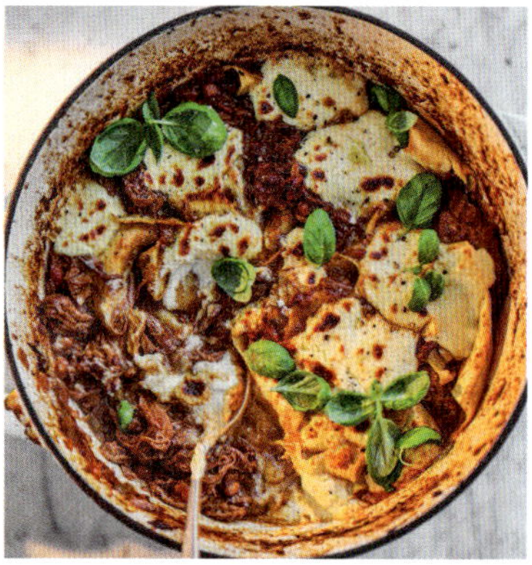
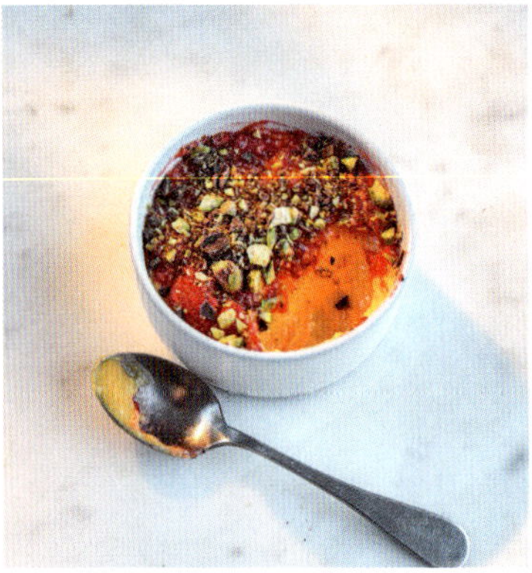
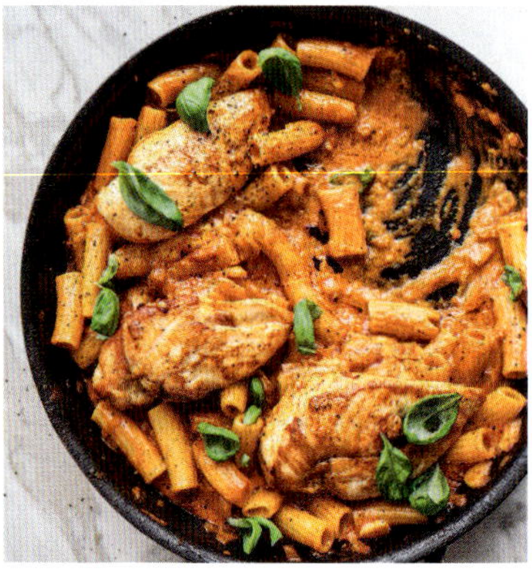
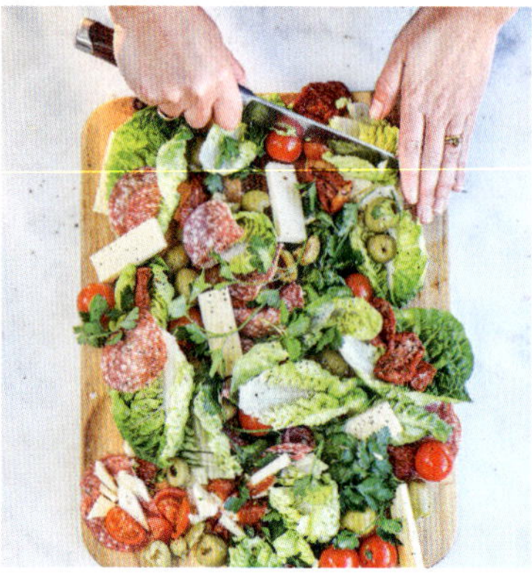

273

Conversion Tables

All of these recipes have been tested using metric measurements, and using imperial conversions may yield different results. Follow one set of measurements only – do not mix metric and imperial.

VOLUME

METRIC	IMPERIAL
25ml	1 fl oz
50ml	2 fl oz
85ml	3 fl oz
150ml	5 fl oz (¼ pint)
300ml	10 fl oz (½ pint)
450ml	15 fl oz (¾ pint)
600ml	1 pint
700ml	1¼ pints
900ml	1½ pints
1 litre	1¾ pints
1.2 litres	2 pints
1.25 litres	2¼ pints
1.5 litres	2½ pints
1.6 litres	2¾ pints
1.75 litres	3 pints
1.8 litres	3¼ pints
2 litres	3½ pints
2.1 litres	3¾ pints
2.25 litres	4 pints
2.75 litres	5 pints
3.4 litres	6 pints
3.9 litres	7 pints
5 litres	8 pints (1 gal)

WEIGHTS

METRIC	IMPERIAL
15g	½ oz
25g	1 oz
40g	1½ oz
50g	2 oz
75g	3 oz
100g	4 oz
150g	5 oz
175g	6 oz
200g	7 oz
225g	8 oz
250g	9 oz
275g	10 oz

METRIC	IMPERIAL
350g	12 oz
375g	13 oz
400g	14 oz
425g	15 oz
450g	1 lb
550g	1¼ lb
675g	1½ lb
900g	2 lb
1.5kg	3 lb
1.75kg	4 lb
2.25kg	5 lb

MEASUREMENTS

METRIC	IMPERIAL
0.5cm	¼ inch
1cm	½ inch
2.5cm	1 inch
5cm	2 inches
7.5cm	3 inches
10cm	4 inches

METRIC	IMPERIAL
15cm	6 inches
18cm	7 inches
20cm	8 inches
23cm	9 inches
25cm	10 inches
30cm	12 inches

OVEN TEMPERATURES

°C	FAN °C	°F	GAS MARK
140°C	120°C	275°F	Gas Mark 1
150°C	130°C	300°F	Gas Mark 2
160°C	140°C	325°F	Gas Mark 3
180°C	160°C	350°F	Gas Mark 4
190°C	170°C	375°F	Gas Mark 5
200°C	180°C	400°F	Gas Mark 6
220°C	200°C	425°F	Gas Mark 7
230°C	210°C	450°F	Gas Mark 8
240°C	220°C	475°F	Gas Mark 9

CONVERSION TABLES

Index

A
anchovy + tomato sfincione 239–40
asparagus
  mint-estrone 105
'au poivre' dressing
  celeriac au poivre 201–2
aubergines
  aubergine dal traybake 55
  aubergine + halloumi spiced rice 132
  aubergine + tomato stew with tahini swirl 68
  lamb + sweet potato hotpot 244
avocados
  burnt lime steak fajitas 78
  smoky cod traybake tacos 72
  tortilla chip salad 210

B
bacon
  bacon + egg yaki udon 109–10
  bacon + hot honey sheet pancakes 24
  beef Buckfastignon 163–4
  gochujang chilli con carne 136
  kimchi okonomiyaki 113
bagels
  kimchi omelette bagel 14

baked beans
  sausage, baked beans + runny eggs 36
baked meatballs with garlic bread topper 151
baked white fish + garlic croutons 42
banana bread skillet cookie 252
beans
  chipotle chicken + bean tacos 106
  gochujang chilli con carne 136
beans marinara 89
beansprouts
  beef shin noodle curry 237–8
  green curry noodles 100
beef
  baked meatballs with garlic bread topper 151
  beef Buckfastignon 163–4
  beef shin noodle curry 237–8
  brisket lasagn-ish 145–6
  gochujang chilli con carne 136
  pickle-y chopped cheese 121–2
  slow-roast short ribs with chickpeas 242
beetroot + lentils with tahini yoghurt 93

big bad deli chopped salad 192
black beans
  sweet potato + black bean traybake 84
  tomatillo + chilli hash 32
  tortilla chip salad 210
blue cheese
  kale Waldorf with roasted grapes 216
blueberries
  patchwork blueberry pie 264
Boursin
  cauliflower mac 'n' cheese 234
braised green beans with olives + feta 224
bread
  Guinness soda bread + cornichon butter 160
  herby, cheesy breakfast flatbread 20
brisket lasagn-ish 145–6
broccoli
  broccoli, burst tomatoes + hot honey 196
  fish curry with onion bhaji topper 48
  herby fried rice 102
  massaman-spiced lamb pie 173
  mint + peanut pesto noodles 60
  sausage, beans + greens 81

Brussels sprouts
  sprouts, orange + radicchio 208
buffalo sauce spaghetti 116
burrata
  beans marinara 89
butter beans
  beans marinara 89
  fondue-ish butter beans + cornichons 97
  leeky butter bean baked eggs 27
  sausage, beans + greens 81
butternut squash
  whole miso-roasted butternut squash 138
  winter grains + pumpkin bowl 215

C

cabbage
  bacon + egg yaki udon 109–10
  five spice chicken salad 212
  kimchi okonomiyaki 113
  sesame hispi bake 186
cakes
  ultimate birthday cake 249
Calabrian chilli clams + burst tomatoes 171
capers
  silky scramble with popped capers + feta 35
caramel
  chocolate caramel fondant 270
caramelised carrots with feta + zhoug 179
carrots
  caramelised carrots with feta + zhoug 179
  fish sauce carrots + rice noodles 198
  pork shoulder lettuce cups 227–8
  tikka roast chicken 130
cauliflower
  cauliflower mac 'n' cheese 234

whole roast cauliflower curry 180
cavolo nero
  fondue-ish butter beans + cornichons 97
  sausage, beans + greens 81
  veggie pasta e ceci 114
celeriac au poivre 201–2
charred pineapple + peanut salad 194
Cheddar
  broccoli, burst tomatoes + hot honey 196
  cauliflower mac 'n' cheese 234
  chipotle chicken + bean tacos 106
  herby, cheesy breakfast flatbread 20
  kimchi omelette bagel 14
  lamb + sweet potato hotpot 244
  pickle-y chopped cheese 121–2
  tomatillo + chilli hash 32
  tuna kewpie sando 82
cheesecake
  preserved lemon cheesecake 250
cherries
  chuck-in cherry cobbler 258
  herby sizzled feta 118
chicken
  chicken, chorizo + chickpeas 66
  chicken, lemon + olive stew 76
  chicken, peaches + goat's cheese 57
  chicken pesto meatballs 75
  chicken rice with sprunion sauce 143–4
  chipotle chicken + bean tacos 106
  coconut chicken soup 219
  feta + olive spatchcock chicken 149
  five spice chicken salad 212

'nduja chicken with creamy rigatoni 174
  sticky tamarind wings 154
  tikka roast chicken 130
  yoghurt chicken curry 126
chickpeas
  big bad deli chopped salad 192
  chicken, chorizo + chickpeas 66
  slow-roast short ribs with chickpeas 242
  spicy chickpea pie 45
  veggie pasta e ceci 114
chicory
  broccoli, burst tomatoes + hot honey 196
chillies
  beef shin noodle curry 237–8
  'nduja + pickled pepper pasta 90
  Scotch bonnet lamb + pineapple salsa 229–30
chimichurri
  date-night chimichurri ribeye 168
chipotle chicken + bean tacos 106
chocolate
  banana bread skillet cookie 252
  chocolate caramel fondant 270
  chocolate tahini fudge 254
  malted chocolate mousse 257
  pistachio custard pots 262
  ultimate birthday cake 249
chorizo
  chicken, chorizo + chickpeas 66
  'nduja + pickled pepper pasta 90
  sweet potato + black bean traybake 84
chuck-in cherry cobbler 258
clams
  Calabrian chilli clams + burst tomatoes 171
coconut chicken soup 219

INDEX

coconut + lime leaf duck
  leg curry 182
coconut shrimp salad 207
cod
  smoky cod traybake tacos
    72
coffee-roasted pork belly
  + oregano salsa 165–6
coriander yoghurt
  yoghurt chicken curry
    126
cornichons
  fondue-ish butter beans
    + cornichons 97
  Guinness soda bread
    + cornichon butter
    160
couscous
  Calabrian chilli clams +
    burst tomatoes 171
  caramelised carrots
    with feta + zhoug 179
  chicken, lemon + olive stew
    76
  Moroccan-spiced lamb
    meatballs 141
cream
  malted chocolate mousse
    257
  margarita possets 269
  pistachio custard pots
    262
cream cheese
  preserved lemon
    cheesecake 250
  ultimate birthday cake
    249
crispy mushroom gnocchi
  125
crispy potato nacho pizza
  152
crispy rosti + smoked
  salmon 31
croissants
  raspberry croissant +
    butter pudding 266
croutons
  baked white fish + garlic
    croutons 42
cucumber
  feta + olive spatchcock
    chicken 149

five spice chicken salad
  212
mango chutney glazed
  paneer salad 204
pork shoulder lettuce
  cups 227–8
whole miso-roasted
  butternut squash
  138
custard
  pistachio custard pots
    262

D

date-night chimichurri
  ribeye 168
dates
  self-saucing sticky toffee
    pudding 261
desserts
  banana bread skillet
    cookie 252
  chocolate caramel
    fondant 270
  chuck-in cherry
    cobbler 258
  malted chocolate
    mousse 257
  margarita possets
    269
  patchwork blueberry
    pie 264
  pistachio custard
    pots 262
  preserved lemon
    cheesecake 250
  raspberry croissant +
    butter pudding 266
  self-saucing sticky
    toffee pudding 261
dipping sauce
  spiced sweetcorn
    fritters 46
duck
  coconut + lime leaf
    duck leg curry 182

E

edamame beans
  sesame hispi bake 186

eggs
  bacon + egg yaki udon
    109–10
  chocolate caramel fondant
    270
  harissa soufflé omelette
    28
  hash brown tortilla + herby
    salad 18
  herby, cheesy breakfast
    flatbread 20
  herby fried rice 102
  kimchi omelette bagel 14
  leeky butter bean baked
    eggs 27
  pistachio custard pots
    262
  raspberry croissant +
    butter pudding 266
  salsa roja eggs 16
  sausage, baked beans +
    runny eggs 36
  silky scramble with
    popped capers + feta
    35

F

feta
  braised green beans
    with olives + feta 224
  burnt lime steak fajitas
    78
  caramelised carrots
    with feta + zhoug 179
  date-night chimichurri
    ribeye 168
  feta + olive spatchcock
    chicken 149
  herby sizzled feta 118
  leeky butter bean baked
    eggs 27
  lemon + feta lamb 223
  salsa roja eggs 16
  silky scramble with popped
    capers + feta 35
  tortilla chip salad 210
fish
  baked white fish + garlic
    croutons 42
  crispy rosti + smoked
    salmon 31

fish curry with onion
  bhaji topper 48
red curry bouillabaisse
  156
salmon, crushed potatoes
  + olive salsa 176
smoky cod traybake
  tacos 72
tuna kewpie sando 82
fish sauce carrots + rice
  noodles 198
five spice chicken salad
  212
flatbread
  herby, cheesy breakfast
    flatbread 20
fondue-ish butter beans
  + cornichons 97
French onion orzo 134
fritters
  spiced sweetcorn
    fritters 46
fudge
  chocolate tahini fudge
    254
full English tart 39

G

gnocchi
  crispy mushroom
    gnocchi 125
goat's cheese
  chicken, peaches +
    goat's cheese 57
gochujang chilli con
  carne 136
grains, mixed
  celeriac au poivre
    201–2
  sprouts, orange +
    radicchio 208
grapes
  kale Waldorf with
    roasted grapes 216
green beans
  braised green beans
    with olives + feta 224
  date-night chimichurri
    ribeye 168
  green curry noodles
    100

green curry noodles
  100
Gruyère
  big bad deli chopped
    salad 192
  Guinness soda bread +
    cornichon butter 160

H

hake
  fish curry with onion
    bhaji topper 48
halloumi
  aubergine + halloumi
    spiced rice 132
  full English tart 39
  harissa soufflé omelette
    28
  hash brown tortilla +
    herby salad 18
  herby, cheesy breakfast
    flatbread 20
  herby fried rice 102
  herby sizzled feta 118
honey
  bacon + hot honey
    sheet pancakes 24

K

kale
  kale Waldorf with
    roasted grapes 216
  mint-estrone 105
kimchi
  kimchi okonomiyaki 113
  kimchi omelette bagel
    14
  rabokki 94
kohlrabi
  pork shoulder lettuce
    cups 227–8

L

laksa paste
  sweet potato laksa-spiced
    soup 52
lamb
  lamb + sweet potato
    hotpot 244

lemon + feta lamb 223
  massaman-spiced lamb
    pie 173
  Moroccan-spiced lamb
    meatballs 141
  Scotch bonnet lamb +
    pineapple salsa 229–30
lasagne
  brisket lasagn-ish 145–6
leeks
  leeky butter bean baked
    eggs 27
lemons
  chicken, lemon + olive stew
    76
  lemon + feta lamb 223
  preserved lemon
    cheesecake 250
  triple lemon risotto 58
lentils
  aubergine dal traybake
    55
  beetroot + lentils with
    tahini yoghurt 93
lettuce
  pork shoulder lettuce
    cups 227–8
limes
  margarita possets
    269

M

macaroni
  cauliflower mac 'n'
    cheese 234
malted chocolate
  mousse 257
Manchego
  chicken, chorizo +
    chickpeas 66
mange tout
  mango chutney glazed
    paneer salad 204
mango
  coconut + lime leaf
    duck leg curry 182
  mango chutney glazed
    paneer salad 204
margarita possets 269
masala hash breakfast
  skillet 23

mascarpone
  chuck-in cherry cobbler 258
  crispy potato nacho pizza 152
  fondue-ish butter beans + cornichons 97
  'nduja chicken with creamy rigatoni 174
  spinach orecchiette + green pangritata 70
massaman-spiced lamb pie 173
meatballs
  baked meatballs with garlic bread topper 151
  chicken pesto meatballs 75
  Moroccan-spiced lamb meatballs 141
  saffron albondigas 233
milk
  raspberry croissant + butter pudding 266
mint-estrone 105
mint + peanut pesto noodles 60
mint sauce
  mint-estrone 105
miso glaze
  whole miso-roasted butternut squash 138
Moroccan-spiced lamb meatballs 141
mousse
  malted chocolate mousse 257
mozzarella
  cauliflower mac 'n' cheese 234
  chicken pesto meatballs 75
  chipotle chicken + bean tacos 106
  crispy potato nacho pizza 152
  herby, cheesy breakfast flatbread 20
  'nduja chicken with creamy rigatoni 174
  'nduja + pickled pepper pasta 90

roasted Portobello caprese 65
mushrooms
  bacon + egg yaki udon 109–10
  beef Buckfastignon 163–4
  crispy mushroom gnocchi 125
  full English tart 39
  mushroom + pickled onion stew 188
  rabokki 94
  roasted Portobello caprese 65
mussels
  red curry bouillabaisse 156

N
'nduja chicken with creamy rigatoni 174
'nduja + pickled pepper pasta 90
noodles
  beef shin noodle curry 237–8
  fish sauce carrots + rice noodles 198
  green curry noodles 100
  mint + peanut pesto noodles 60
  rabokki 94
nori
  kimchi okonomiyaki 113

O
olives
  baked white fish + garlic croutons 42
  braised green beans with olives + feta 224
  chicken, lemon + olive stew 76
  feta + olive spatchcock chicken 149
  salmon, crushed potatoes + olive salsa 176
omelettes
  harissa soufflé omelette 28

  kimchi omelette bagel 14
onion bhajis
  fish curry with onion bhaji topper 48
onions
  crispy rosti + smoked salmon 31
  French onion orzo 134
  mushroom + pickled onion stew 188
oranges
  five spice chicken salad 212
  sprouts, orange + radicchio 208
orecchiette
  spinach orecchiette + green pangritata 70
oregano
  coffee-roasted pork belly + oregano salsa 165–6
orzo
  French onion orzo 134
  vodka orzotto 63

P
pancakes
  bacon + hot honey sheet pancakes 24
pancetta
  brisket lasagn-ish 145–6
paneer
  mango chutney glazed paneer salad 204
  spinach + paneer filo pie 184
pangritata
  spinach orecchiette + green pangritata 70
Parmesan
  buffalo sauce spaghetti 116
  crispy mushroom gnocchi 125
  fondue-ish butter beans + cornichons 97
  'nduja + pickled pepper pasta 90
  spinach orecchiette + green pangritata 70

triple lemon risotto 58
vodka orzotto 63
walnut + za'atar spaghetti 98
parsnips
  tikka roast chicken 130
pasta
  brisket lasagn-ish 145–6
  buffalo sauce spaghetti 116
  cauliflower mac 'n' cheese 234
  French onion orzo 134
  mint-estrone 105
  'nduja chicken with creamy rigatoni 174
  'nduja + pickled pepper pasta 90
  spinach orecchiette + green pangritata 70
  veggie pasta e ceci 114
  vodka orzotto 63
  walnut + za'atar spaghetti 98
patchwork blueberry pie 264
peaches
  chicken, peaches + goat's cheese 57
  chuck-in cherry cobbler 258
peanut butter
  charred pineapple + peanut salad 194
  chocolate tahini fudge 254
  mint + peanut pesto noodles 60
peas
  mint-estrone 105
pecans
  banana bread skillet cookie 252
pecorino
  anchovy + tomato sfincione 239–40
pepperoni
  crispy potato nacho pizza 152
peppers
  baked white fish + garlic croutons 42

burnt lime steak fajitas 78
hash brown tortilla + herby salad 18
pork chops in smoked paprika sauce 51
slow-roast short ribs with chickpeas 242
tortilla chip salad 210
pesto
  mint + peanut pesto noodles 60
pickle-y chopped cheese 121–2
pies & tarts
  full English tart 39
  patchwork blueberry pie 264
  spicy chickpea pie 45
  spinach + paneer filo pie 184
pineapple
  charred pineapple + peanut salad 194
  Scotch bonnet lamb + pineapple salsa 229–30
pistachio custard pots 262
pizzas
  anchovy + tomato sfincione 239–40
  crispy potato nacho pizza 152
pork
  baked meatballs with garlic bread topper 151
  coffee-roasted pork belly + oregano salsa 165–6
  pork chops in smoked paprika sauce 51
  pork shoulder lettuce cups 227–8
  saffron albondigas 233
potatoes
  braised green beans with olives + feta 224
  coconut + lime leaf duck leg curry 182
  coffee-roasted pork belly + oregano salsa 165–6
  crispy potato nacho pizza 152

crispy rosti + smoked salmon 31
date-night chimichurri ribeye 168
feta + olive spatchcock chicken 149
masala hash breakfast skillet 23
massaman-spiced lamb pie 173
saffron albondigas 233
salmon, crushed potatoes + olive salsa 176
tikka roast chicken 130
tomatillo + chilli hash 32
prawns
  coconut shrimp salad 207
  green curry noodles 100
  red curry bouillabaisse 156
preserved lemon cheesecake 250
puddings
  raspberry croissant + butter pudding 266
  self-saucing sticky toffee pudding 261

R

rabokki 94
radicchio
  sprouts, orange + radicchio 208
radish salsa
  smoky cod traybake tacos 72
raspberries
  pistachio custard pots 262
  raspberry croissant + butter pudding 266
red curry bouillabaisse 156
Red Leicester
  harissa soufflé omelette 28
rice
  aubergine + halloumi spiced rice 132

chicken pesto meatballs 75
chicken rice with sprunion sauce 143–4
coconut chicken soup 219
herby fried rice 102
lemon + feta lamb 223
pork shoulder lettuce cups 227–8
Scotch bonnet lamb + pineapple salsa 229–30
sesame hispi bake 186
triple lemon risotto 58
whole miso-roasted butternut squash 138
rice cakes
  rabokki 94
rigatoni
  'nduja chicken with creamy rigatoni 174
risottos
  triple lemon risotto 58
roasted Portobello caprese 65
rocket
  celeriac au poivre 201–2
  roasted Portobello caprese 65

S

saffron albondigas 233
salads
  big bad deli chopped salad 192
  charred pineapple + peanut salad 194
  coconut shrimp salad 207
  hash brown tortilla + herby salad 18
  mango chutney glazed paneer salad 204
  sprouts, orange + radicchio 208
  tortilla chip salad 210
salami
  big bad deli chopped salad 192
salmon
  crispy rosti + smoked salmon 31

salmon, crushed potatoes + olive salsa 176
salsa
  masala hash breakfast skillet 23
  salsa roja eggs 16
  Scotch bonnet lamb + pineapple salsa 229–30
sandwiches
  tuna kewpie sando 82
sausages
  sausage, baked beans + runny eggs 36
  sausage, beans + greens 81
Scotch bonnet lamb + pineapple salsa 229–30
sea bass
  baked white fish + garlic croutons 42
self-saucing sticky toffee pudding 261
sesame hispi bake 186
silky scramble with popped capers + feta 35
slaw
  pork shoulder lettuce cups 227–8
soup
  coconut chicken soup 219
  mint-estrone 105
  sweet potato laksa-spiced soup 52
sour cream
  crispy rosti + smoked salmon 31
spaghetti
  buffalo sauce spaghetti 116
  walnut + za'atar spaghetti 98
spice paste
  beef shin noodle curry 237–8
spiced sweetcorn fritters 46
spicy chickpea pie 45
spinach
  chicken pesto meatballs 75

spinach orecchiette + green pangritata 70
spinach + paneer filo pie 184
sprouts, orange + radicchio 208
whole roast cauliflower curry 180
spring onions
  chicken rice with sprunion sauce 143–4
sprouts, orange + radicchio 208
steak
  burnt lime steak fajitas 78
  date-night chimichurri ribeye 168
sticky tamarind wings 154
sugar snap peas
  charred pineapple + peanut salad 194
  fish curry with onion bhaji topper 48
  five spice chicken salad 212
  mint-estrone 105
  pork shoulder lettuce cups 227–8
sweet potatoes
  lamb + sweet potato hotpot 244
  sweet potato + black bean traybake 84
  sweet potato laksa-spiced soup 52
sweetcorn
  masala hash breakfast skillet 23
  spiced sweetcorn fritters 46
  tortilla chip salad 210

T

tahini
  aubergine + tomato stew with tahini swirl 68
  beetroot + lentils with tahini yoghurt 93

chocolate tahini fudge 254
Taleggio
  fondue-ish butter beans + cornichons 97
  roasted Portobello caprese 65
tamarind paste
  sticky tamarind wings 154
tequila
  margarita possets 269
tikka roast chicken 130
toffee sauce
  self-saucing sticky toffee pudding 261
tofu
  mint + peanut pesto noodles 60
tomatillo + chilli hash 32
tomatoes
  anchovy + tomato sfincione 239–40
  aubergine + tomato stew with tahini swirl 68
  baked white fish + garlic croutons 42
  beans marinara 89
  big bad deli chopped salad 192
  braised green beans with olives + feta 224
  brisket lasagn-ish 145–6
  broccoli, burst tomatoes + hot honey 196
  Calabrian chilli clams + burst tomatoes 171
  chicken pesto meatballs 75
  full English tart 39
  gochujang chilli con carne 136
  harissa soufflé omelette 28
  lamb + sweet potato hotpot 244
  masala hash breakfast skillet 23
  Moroccan-spiced lamb meatballs 141
  mushroom + pickled onion stew 188

'nduja + pickled pepper pasta 90
pork chops in smoked paprika sauce 51
roasted Portobello caprese 65
Scotch bonnet lamb + pineapple salsa 229–30
spicy chickpea pie 45
tomatillo + chilli hash 32
tortilla chip salad 210
whole roast cauliflower curry 180
yoghurt chicken curry 126
tortilla chips
  salsa roja eggs 16
tortillas
  burnt lime steak fajitas 78
  chipotle chicken + bean tacos 106
  hash brown tortilla + herby salad 18
  smoky cod traybake tacos 72
  tortilla chip salad 210
tuna kewpie sando 82
tzatziki
  feta + olive spatchcock chicken 149

V

vegetables
  tikka roast chicken 130
  veggie pasta e ceci 114
veggie pasta e ceci 114
vodka orzotto 63

W

walnuts
  kale Waldorf with roasted grapes 216
  walnut + za'atar spaghetti 98
whole miso-roasted butternut squash 138
whole roast cauliflower curry 180

winter grains + pumpkin bowl 215

Y

yakisoba sauce
  bacon + egg yaki udon 109–10
yoghurt
  beetroot + lentils with tahini yoghurt 93
  winter grains + pumpkin bowl 215
  yoghurt chicken curry 126

Z

za'atar
  walnut + za'atar spaghetti 98
zhoug
  caramelised carrots with feta + zhoug 179

Acknowledgements

So, that was *Mob One*. It's a cookbook we've wanted to write for a long time but were always a little hesitant about pulling the trigger on. One of the things holding us back from writing a cookbook dedicated to one-pan and one-pot dishes was a fear that the recipes might end up feeling a bit repetitive. Too samey. We were also worried that we might not be bringing anything new to the table. I'm pleased to say that all of those fears turned out to be completely unfounded. This cookbook is one of our most useful to date, packed with over a hundred simple recipes you can make with minimal equipment and just a handful of simple ingredients. We didn't realise the limitless potential of what you could cook with a single pan or pot until we started writing this book. But we're very glad we did.

This cookbook wouldn't exist without the recipes inside of it (if it did, it wouldn't be much of a cookbook at all!) so I'd like to take this opportunity to thank everyone who helped bring it to life. Saskia Sidey was integral in coming up with a great deal of the dishes you'll find in these pages and I can't thank her enough for her diligence, wisdom and endless creativity. I'd also like to give kudos to all of the other talented cooks and recipe developers who contributed to this book. Special thanks goes out to Elena Silcock, Adam Bush, Ben Lippett, Jodie Nixon, Chloe René, Romany Henry and Sophie Mann – you've all made *Mob One* an absolute joy to work on. Massive thanks to Myles Williamson who tested every recipe within this book so we could be 100% certain that they were all perfect.

Not only do they taste great but every single dish in this cookbook looks beyond stunning and for that the credit goes to our hugely talented team of food stylists. Saskia and Elena led the charge with their years of experience and knowledge and were assisted in the styling department by Susanna Unsworth, Alice Katie Hughes, Caitlin Macdonald and Immy Mucklow. All of the prop styling wizardry was courtesy of the wonderful Charlie Phillips.

As always, I'm forever indebted to David Loftus. David has been the photographer for most of our cookbooks and it's always a complete and utter pleasure to work with one of the best (and most beloved) food photographers in the industry. You and Ange have been an endless source of support and inspiration and I can't thank you enough for the hard work you've put into this book. The thrill we get from seeing the finished photos of the recipes is one of the main reasons we keep writing cookbooks. It's addictive.

The designs for *Mob One* were done by the consistently brilliant Studio Nari. Thank you for turning this book from a jumble of images and recipes into a cohesive, beautiful object. I don't think I'm over-egging it when I say this might be the best-looking cookbook we've made to date. Credit also goes out to our in-house Art Lead, Joe Jarvis, who worked with the Nari team to make sure not a single hair (or letter) was out of place.

Thanks to everyone on the Ebury team who have helped me so much along the way. Special thanks to Emily Brickell, our ever-patient Editor – you've been a real rock and your steady hand and calming presence helped make the process as painless as possible. Another big thank you to Stephanie Milner, Ebury's Publishing Director, for being unbelievably brilliant at her job. I've learned so much from the both of you and the rest of the Ebury team including Lucy Harrison and Alice King.

Now, I couldn't get this far without giving a shout-out to the rest of the Mob team. There's so much work that goes into these books beyond just the writing of them and I'm grateful for the time and effort of everyone at Mob who has helped to make it happen. We wouldn't be where we are today without all of your hard work.

Last, but not least, I'd like to thank my family and friends for their tireless support. I know it hasn't always been easy but I'm forever grateful that you've stuck by my side throughout all the stressful days and sleepless nights. I owe it all to you. Always.

Ben x

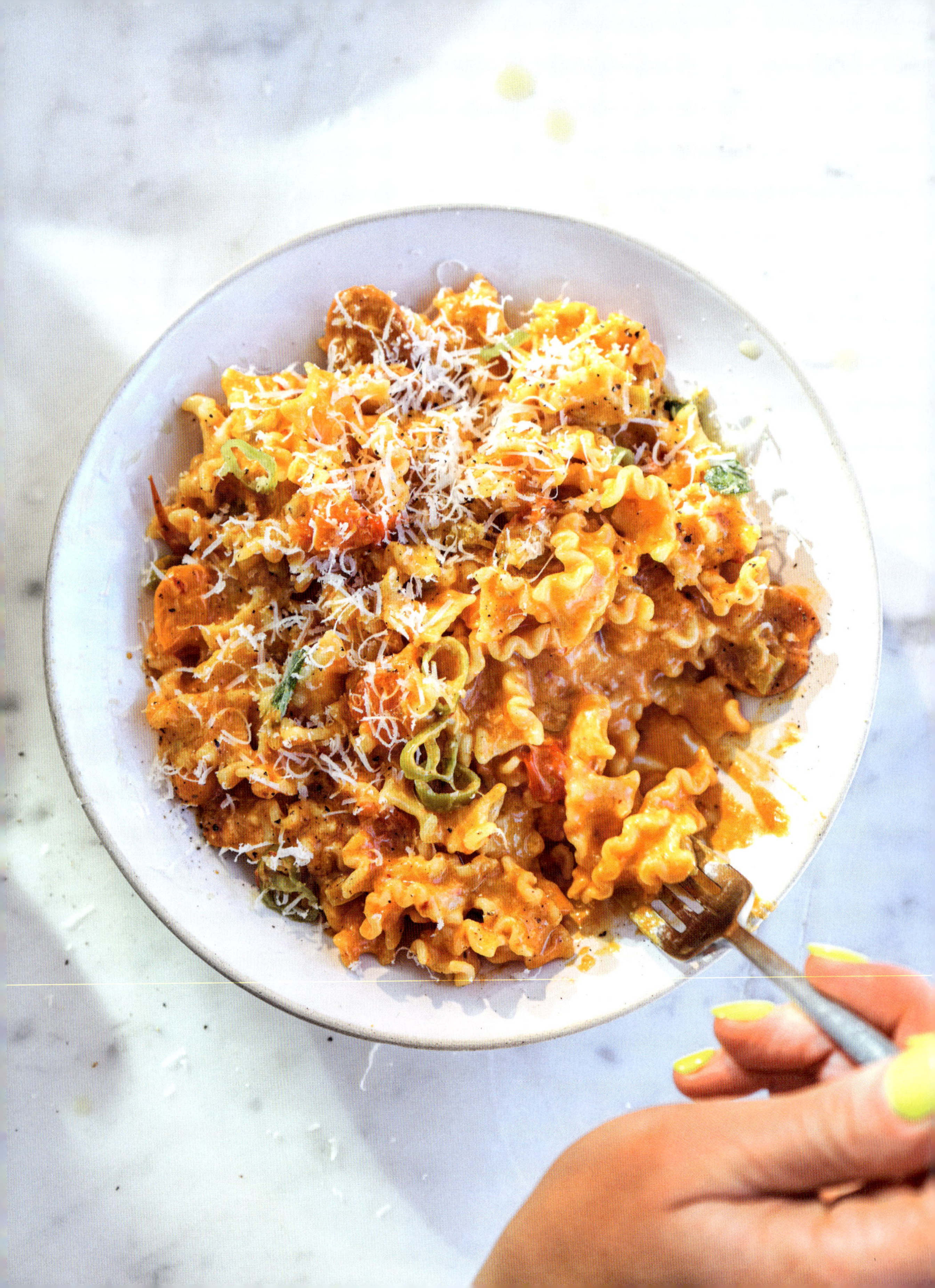

About Mob

Mob is built around one key principle: food you'll actually cook. Mob started out as an idea – as most things do – when the founder, Ben, realised that barely any of his friends at university were able to cook. Armed with nothing but a kitchen, a camera and a handful of recipes, Ben started posting videos online of simple and delicious dishes that people could easily recreate at home. Mob has only gone from strength to strength since, earning a loyal, ever-growing following.

With seven bestselling cookbooks already in the bag, Mob is always on the lookout for new and exciting ways to provide ambitious home cooks with the freshest recipes possible. It doesn't matter whether that's through cookbooks like this or on social media platforms such as Instagram, Facebook and TikTok – the Mob mission is always the same. To inspire, educate and engage with as many people as possible, connecting with them through what we love and know the most. Which is food.

Give Mob a follow to keep up-to-date with our latest recipes and visit the Mob website to get access to an unlimited selection of the hottest dishes around.

mob.co.uk
@mob

1

Ebury Press, an imprint of Ebury Publishing.
Penguin Random House UK One Embassy Gardens,
8 Viaduct Gardens, London SW11 7BW

Ebury Press is part of the Penguin Random House group of companies whose addresses can be found at global.penguinrandomhouse.com

Penguin Random House UK

Copyright © Mouth Group Limited 2024
Photography © David Loftus 2024

Mouth Group Limited has asserted its right to be identified as the author of this Work in accordance with the Copyright, Designs and Patents Act 1988

First published by Ebury Press in 2024

www.penguin.co.uk

A CIP catalogue record for this book is available from the British Library

Design by Studio Nari
Artworking by maru studio G.K.
Photography by David Loftus
Food styling by Saskia Sidey and Elena Silcock
Prop styling by Charlie Phillips

ISBN 9781529902297

Colour origination by Altaimage Ltd
Printed and bound in Germany by Mohn Media

Penguin Random House values and supports copyright. Copyright fuels creativity, encourages diverse voices, promotes freedom of expression and supports a vibrant culture. Thank you for purchasing an authorized edition of this book and for respecting intellectual property laws by not reproducing, scanning or distributing any part of it by any means without permission. You are supporting authors and enabling Penguin Random House to continue to publish books for everyone. No part of this book may be used or reproduced in any manner for the purpose of training artificial intelligence technologies or systems. In accordance with Article 4(3) of the DSM Directive 2019/790, Penguin Random House expressly reserves this work from the text and data mining exception.

The authorised representative in the EEA is Penguin Random House Ireland, Morrison Chambers, 32 Nassau Street, Dublin D02 YH68.

FSC MIX Paper | Supporting responsible forestry FSC® C018179

Penguin Random House is committed to a sustainable future for our business, our readers and our planet. This book is made from Forest Stewardship Council® certified paper.